# SHARAWADGI
## The Romantic Return to Nature

Ciaran Murray

International Scholars Publications
San Francisco - London - Bethesda
1999

*Library of Congress Cataloging-in-Publication Data*

Murray, Ciaran, 1945-
Sharawadgi : the romantic return to nature / Ciaran Murray.
p. cm.
Includes bibliographical references and index.
ISBN 1-57309-329-7 (hardcover : alk. paper)
1. English literature--Japanese influences. 2. English literature--18th century--History and criticism. 3. Romanticism--Great Britain--History--18th century. 4. Great Britain--Intellectual life--18th century. 5. Temple, William, Sir, 1628-1699--Aesthetics. 6. England--Civilization--Japanese influences. 7. Addison, Joseph, 1672-1719--Aesthetics. 8. Pope, Alexander, 1688-1744--Aesthetics. 9. Gardens, English--History--18th century. 10. Gardens, Japanese--Japan--History. 11. Gardens in literature. 12. Nature in literature. I. Title.
PR129.J3M87 1998
820.9'145--dc21 98-24897
CIP



*Editorial Inquiries:*
International Scholars Publications
7831 Woodmont Avenue, #345
Bethesda, MD 20814

*To order: (800) 55-PUBLISH*

# CONTENTS

# SHARAWADGI

## A Western View

by

**SEAMUS DEANE**

Keough Professor of Irish Studies

University of Notre Dame

WHEN Ciaran Murray proposed to explore the Japanese influence on romanticism, he already had a distinguished academic record. I therefore persuaded the National University of Ireland to waive the normal coursework in Dublin, while he continued his research in Tokyo, London and a plethora of places between. The results were endlessly fascinating, as he established a new axis for the intellectual history of the eighteenth century, and dismantled conventional notions of its favourite literary characters in favour of altogether more irregular personalities. The asymmetry of his subject was counterpointed by the symmetry of his structure. Here everything was serenely in order, the writing lucid and masterful. It was submitted to the most searching examination, and emerged unchallenged. I advised Ciaran then to make his findings available to a wider audience, and am gratified that he has done so. This is an important book.

# SHARAWADGI

## An Eastern View

by

**MINE OKACHI**

Head of English Department

Chuo University

AS a specialist in English romanticism, I was asked to read Dr. Murray's work as a prelude to offering him a professorship at our university. I was greatly impressed by the meticulous detail with which he traced English landscape design to the decentralised gardens of Japan. I was no less impressed by the psychological subtlety with which he unravelled the personalities involved. And I was impressed, finally, by the comprehensive sweep with which he carried his story from beginning to end of the eighteenth century.

Professor Murray has broadened our understanding of romanticism by opening up an original perspective on the relations of Asia and Europe. His book will be indispensable to all students of comparative culture.

# PREFACE

SOME years ago, on a winter evening, as I watched the light fade on Mount Leinster from Oak Park, near Carlow, it was borne in upon me that the darkening lake in the middle distance, with its woods and its island, was as deliberate a creation as the Roman archway through which I had entered. I had lately come from Entsuji, in Kyoto, where the dark trunks of the cryptomeria frame the pale slopes of Mount Hiei in a geometrical arrangement; and for a moment I saw one in terms of the other. Each appeared to function on the principle of *shakkei*, or borrowed landscape, being built around the view of a distant mountain.

I spoke of this to Robert J. Smith, of Cornell, who sent me to the rare book cage of the Olin Library, and to Sirén's *China and the Gardens of Europe of the Eighteenth Century*, where I learned of the Asian antecedents of the English landscape garden; and, as I read on into the subject, this came to seem a fundamental notation for the eighteenth century. I have attempted, therefore, to record the phenomenon, from its discovery and domestication at the beginning of
the century to its strange disappearance, or transformation, at the end.

So large a canvas made imperative that impressionism which, Butterfield has observed, is the inevitable effect of ellipsis:

> the selection of facts for the purpose of maintaining the impression -- maintaining, in spite of omissions, the inner relations of the whole.[1]

I believe, indeed, with certain writers of the past, that it is desirable to make of a scientific inquiry a tale, *histoire*. 'The perfect historian', declared Macaulay,

> is he in whose work the...spirit of an age is exhibited in miniature. He relates no fact, he attributes no expression to his characters, which is not authenticated by sufficient testimony. But, by judicious selection, rejection, and arrangement, he gives to truth those attractions which have been usurped by fiction.[2]

Trevelyan went still further, asserting that imagination in history is no matter of ornament, but part of the very structure of the truth:

> The man who is himself devoid of emotion or enthusiasm can seldom credit, and can never understand, the emotions of others, which have none the less played a principal part in cause and effect.[3]

'Emotion or enthusiasm', indeed, might serve as a definition of romanticism: which, as I hope to demonstrate, was shaped by certain unusual individuals as they apprehended, or were possessed by, the spirit of their age. If I have formulated this on a broader scale than is customary, it is because, throughout, I see a single theme as continuous. That theme is *sharawadgi*, the mysterious formula under which the gardens of the east were to reshape those of the west.

My gratitude goes to all who have helped me. Liam Bergin and Terence de Vere White provided early encouragement and opportunity. Christopher Murray made a perceptive suggestion on subject; Augustine Martin directed my studies with his customary humanity; Denis Donoghue insisted on insight over information; and Seamus Deane combined intellectual openness with the art of the illuminating question. Howard Erskine–Hill approved an earlier version of 'The Tree of Life'; Peter Hayden gave me the benefit of his erudition in garden history, and Stephen Prickett the benefit of his in romanticism. None of these, however, is responsible for the result: all final decisions have been my own. Edward Talbot, meanwhile, has been untiring in the offices of friendship; and Cay van Ash was kind enough to look over my manuscript: a privilege that readers of his novels will appreciate.

Takeo Doi and Teruhisa Horio opened doors for me in Japan; Tsutomu Fujiwara, Kuniyoshi Munakata, Kazuyoshi Yamanouchi, Tatsuo Kimura, Seiichi

Yamaguchi, Seamus McElwain and Kenichi Matsumura helped create the successive spaces in which I have worked. My colleagues at Chuo University have been constant in their encouragement. I could not have begun this project without the well-chosen book collection formerly maintained in Tokyo by the British Council, nor finished it without the resources of the British Library. To the staff of both I record my thanks: as to the people who formed my community where I lived, or reached out to me on my travels.

Robert West has been an ideal editor, enthusiastic yet unobtrusive; while Ginger McNally has overseen the technical aspects of production with the same quiet efficiency.

For Fumiko, my gratitude is beyond words. She set me on the path when she brought me to Entsuji, accompanied me on it to Oak Park, where I learned to 'know the place for the first time';[4] and, with Genevieve, has kept me steady in this as in everything else.

# INTRODUCTION

THE English landscape garden, declared Arthur Lovejoy, was the earliest manifestation of romanticism; in and through it all the others came into being; and its story would form part of 'any truly philosophical history of modern thought'.[1]

If the philosophic history has yet to be written, it is perhaps because the facts have appeared so bizarre. The English garden, Lovejoy held, originated in Asia.[2]

The sequence is coherent and irrefutable.[3] The Restoration diplomat William Temple wrote a spellbound account of the gardens of the 'Chineses'.[4] The Queen Anne essayist Joseph Addison held these up as a pattern for England.[5] The Georgian poet Alexander Pope put Addison's programme into practice.[6] But to state this is only to pose further questions. Temple does not merely supply exotic information; he confers prestige upon it. This would seem to imply a certain originality of perception. Addison does not rest content with paraphrase; he urges adoption of the alien schema. This would seem to indicate a certain boldness of thought. Pope does not simply concur; he builds, we are told, a 'setting that expressed him' out of the creation of a man that he hated.[7] This would seem to involve a certain paradox.

Here is the tale of three men and an idea; and none of these three, as conventionally understood, can have done what he did.

PART ONE

# THE TREE OF LIFE

## Origins of Romanticism

*Light takes the Tree; but who can tell us how?*

ROETHKE

## CHAPTER ONE

# THE CASE OF THE FASTIDIOUS ENVOY

THE horseman swept along the river–meadows of Richmond, shortly before four on a June morning, and still hardly light. He turned into a maze of villas, their gardens stretching down to the water, which had been assembled from the ruined palace of Sheen. He brought the man he woke back with him to London, and into the presence of the secretary of state.[1]

It was a most imposing presence. A black patch ran in a thin crescent over Arlington's nose, concealing -- or did it exaggerate? -- a battlescar received on the royalist side during the Civil War. From a Commonwealth exile in Spain, he had brought back an air of stately decorum; and the sense of ceremony was enhanced by the gracious stare of the pale, bulbous eyes and the arabesques of the flabby hands.[2]

He had been perplexed, he told the man he had summoned: he had been perplexed as to whom he should send; he had been perplexed for several days. Then he had thought of the man in front of him, and had spoken to his majesty, and his majesty had agreed. But he must accept the mission without knowing what it was; and must leave immediately, telling nobody where he was bound.[3]

The newcomer hesitated. In his portrait, the obstinate squareness of the jaw is almost disguised by the long chestnut hair, curled and spilling over the shoulders, by the dandyism of the pencilled moustache, and by that Restoration look of a faintly anguished sensuality. 'So fantasticall is our composure', he had written, 'that the expectation of pleasure is a trouble as well as the apprehension of pain'. He had turned down an embassy to Sweden: he did not think he would care for the climate.

But here, he was told, was the entrance to his majesty's service, and the way to something he might like better.[4]

When his visitor had departed, the secretary may well have permitted himself a smile. Neither the dawn summons nor the injunction to silence had strictly been necessary. But Arlington had a distinct flair for theatre. He sat on a committee to take a maidenhead for the king; and it was at his house, in a burlesque wedding, that Charles bedded down the Frenchwoman who would outshine his queen in splendour, and his other mistresses in staying–power, until the moment in which she procured for him the last rites of the Church of Rome.[5]

The envoy struggled over mountain roads, shadowed by forest and broken by streams. He avoided highways and travelled incognito: he was in hostile territory. The barn where he slept on straw was entered by one of a troop of enemy horse. They had heard an English envoy was on the way. Yes, said his guide: he was a day or two behind.

As he approached the city, he was met by four thousand cavalry, a fast coach bowling along in front. The coach halted; the Prince–Bishop of Münster stepped out.

It was suspect, exaggerated. England, at war with the Dutch, had subsidised the bishop to attack them from the rear. Had he in fact made peace with them? The bishop prevaricated, and offered a 'mighty feast': the Englishman was violently sick. It was Ash Wednesday. When the bishop was finally pinned down, he admitted that the peace had been signed. He could, however, recommend a safe route home. The envoy, who knew that this was a detour, and that an instalment of the subsidy was expected, 'seemed to accept all'; but was on horseback at four the next morning, rode all day, took lodgings and left by the back door, and, in a neutral uniform, and, sustained by a flask of 'juniper water', reached friendly territory in time to cancel the payment.

He had meanwhile been created baronet, and was now Sir William Temple.[6]

## i

'TEMPLE', proclaimed Macaulay,

> is not a man to our taste. A temper not naturally good, but under strict command; a constant regard to decorum; a rare caution in playing that mixed game of skill and hazard, human life; a disposition to be content with small and certain winnings rather than to go on doubling the stake; these seem to us to be the most remarkable features of his character.

It is a failure of nerve:

> Temple, we fear, had not sufficient warmth and elevation of sentiment to deserve the name of a virtuous man. He did not betray or oppress his country; nay, he rendered considerable services to her; but he risked nothing for her. No temptation which either the King or the Opposition could hold out ever induced him to come forward as the supporter either of arbitrary or of factious measures. But he was most careful not to give offence by strenuously opposing such measures.

It is a retreat from life:

> He avoided the great offices of State with a caution almost pusillanimous, and confined himself to quiet and secluded departments of public business, in which he could enjoy moderate but certain advantages without incurring envy. If the circumstances of the country became such that it was impossible to take any part in politics without some danger, he retired to his library and his orchard, and, while the nation groaned under oppression, or resounded with tumult and with the din of civil arms, amused himself by writing memoirs and tying up apricots.

It is a refusal to spend and be spent:

> He loved fame, but not with the love of an exalted and generous mind. He loved it as an end, not at all as a means; as a personal luxury, not at all as an

instrument of advantage to others. He scraped it together and treasured it up with a timid and niggardly thrift; and never employed the hoard in any enterprise, however virtuous and useful, in which there was hazard of losing one particle. No wonder if such a person did little or nothing which deserves positive blame. But much more than this may justly be demanded of a man possessed of such abilities, and placed in such a situation.

It is a very sickness of the soul:

Had Temple been brought before Dante's infernal tribunal, he would not have been condemned to the deeper recesses of the abyss. He would not have been boiled with Dundee in the crimson pool of Bulicame, or hurled with Danby into the seething pitch of Malebolge, or congealed with Churchill in the eternal ice of Giudecca; but he would perhaps have been placed in the dark vestibule next to the shade of that inglorious pontiff

*Che fece per viltate il gran rifiuto.*[7]

## ii

THE opening of Temple's career, certainly, found him in a 'quiet and secluded' way of life. His house stood on a wooded hill in Ireland, with a view over the river–valley in which the town of Carlow stands. His woods have vanished; his house is marked only by the outline of its walls; and all that is left is his vista, over the hulk of the Plantagenet castle, and across to the western hills.[8]

Here, Macaulay tells us, he employed his time in 'farming, gardening, county business, and studies rather entertaining than profound'.[9] Entertaining, certainly; but none the less significant for that. Some lines that he translated here from Vergil have survived in a unique volume, privately printed and with corrections in his hand, that is preserved in the British Library. In these he makes the Roman poet say, of a life in harmony with the woodland deities:

Him move not Princes frowns, nor Peoples heats,
Nor faithless civil jars, nor foreign threats;
Not *Rome*'s affairs, nor transitory Crowns,
The fall of Princes, or the rise of Clowns,
All's one to him; nor grieves he at the sad

Events he hears, nor envies at the glad.[10]

Exactitude was not Temple's object: 'Translated, or rather, Imitated' is his own description; and a glance at the original will serve to bear him out:

*illum non populi fasces, non purpura regum*
*flexit et infidos agitans discordia fratres,*
*aut coniurato descendens Dacus ab Histro,*
*non res Romanae perituraque regna; neque ille*
*aut doluit miserans inopem aut invidit habenti.*[11]

While Temple has in the main followed the sense of the Latin, he has made the 'foreign threats' general rather than specific; and the rendering of *peritura regna* as 'transitory Crowns' has enabled him to add a gloss of his own. Henry Cromwell, son of the Lord Protector, who then ruled Ireland in his father's name, had at one time taken an interest in the young woman who had since become Temple's wife;[12] and the fact that Temple had thought of him as a threat will not have lessened the delight with which he now implied detachment from the fall of the Stuart princes and the subsequent 'rise of Clowns'.

Temple, then, was a man lacking neither in subtlety nor in spirit: a fact confirmed by all that followed. The county business took on a quickened pace when it was determined to recall the king: Temple represented Carlow in the Irish parliament, and secured the reversion of a lucrative office in Dublin.[13] The Temple of Macaulay, assured of his 'small and certain winnings', would at this point have retired from the game. But instead, in the quest for a public career, he had left his first garden for good.

## iii

THE war with Holland ended when the Dutch sailed up the Thames, and, while the king was engaged in hunting a moth, towed his flagship back to Holland, where its standard still fills a wall of the Rijksmuseum.[14] Temple visited the country with a deceptive casualness, and in the same spirit secured an interview with Jan de Witt, its effective head of state. 'I told him', says Temple, 'my only business was, to see the things most considerable in the country, and I thought I should lose my credit, if I left it without seeing him'. The Dutch leader took the compliment gracefully, and the talk turned to diplomacy.

De Witt was in a dilemma. France had been the ally of the Dutch since their war of independence from Spain; but the incursions of Louis XIV, in the name of his Spanish queen, into a still–Spanish Belgium threatened to turn a powerful friend into an overpowering neighbour. It was a nightmare at Amsterdam to see Antwerp reanimated as a port of France; London had reason to share the sensation; and de Witt, accordingly, proposed an alliance. But when Temple returned with instructions to conclude one, he hesitated: it meant irrevocable hostility with France. Temple argued that there was no middle way: either they stopped the French or were swallowed up by them. De Witt, however, doubted English intentions, and insisted on having Sweden as a third party. Temple peremptorily walked in on the Swedish ambassador, 'going straight into his chamber, taking a chair, and sitting down by him before he could rise out of his', remarking that 'ceremonies were intended to facilitate business, and not to hinder it'. This eccentric view of protocol perhaps startled the ambassador into candour. Was Temple aware that the alliance would need the separate approval of each of the Dutch provinces and towns?

*Eh bien*, shrugged the French ambassador when he heard of the project, they would speak of this in six weeks. It was finished in five days. Temple had convinced de Witt to 'sign the treaty immediately, and trust to the approbation of their several Provinces and towns after it was done'. To de Witt's protest that 'no such thing had ever been done since the first institution of their commonwealth', that 'they should venture their heads in signing it', he retorted that they would venture them with reason if the alliance should founder over 'too great caution...in point of form'. Afterwards, de Witt congratulated Temple for having persuaded his associates into an unprecedented 'resolution and conclusion'. Now that it was done, he said, 'it looked like a miracle'. So, indeed, it appeared. Louis retreated, giving encouragement to all later combinations against him; salvoes of artillery greeted Temple as he passed from town to town.[15]

Even Macaulay concedes that this was a 'masterpiece of diplomacy'. Here, he asserts,

> there is no room for controversy. No grubbing among old state–papers will ever bring to light any document which will shake these facts; that Europe believed the ambition of France to have been curbed by the three powers; that England, a few months before the last among the nations, forced to abandon her own seas, unable to defend the mouths of her own rivers, regained almost as high a place in the estimation of her neighbours as she had held in the times of Elizabeth and Oliver; and that all this change of opinion was produced in five days by wise and resolute counsels, without the firing of a single gun.[16]

How can this be? How can the Dutch have been persuaded to overrule their constitution by a creature of 'rare caution'? How can the 'wise and resolute' counsellor be reconciled with the *gran rifiuto*? How can Temple the second be squared with Temple the first?

The fact is, Temple the second believed in what he was doing; Temple the first did not. Before his first mission, he had stated at court that England's interest lay with Holland and against France. It was for this reason, no doubt, that Arlington had issued his theatrical summons, with its pressures of urgency and opportunity, and hinted that acceptance might lead to something he would like better.[17] His second mission was exactly that: it was the realisation of his own ideal; and it brought out all his latent energy and determination.

Macaulay, however, insistently projects Temple the first over Temple the second. The years that followed at The Hague, he states, 'seem...to have passed very agreeably...He had no wearing labour, no heavy responsibility'.[18] The opposite, in fact, is the case. The ink was scarcely dry on Temple's treaty before he became aware of powerful forces working against it. There were those in England who continued to regard the Dutch less as allies in politics than as rivals in trade. Build more warships, growled Sir George Downing, later to be remembered in Downing Street, and 'Good night Amsterdam'.[19] The Dutch were then, writes C.R. Boxer, the 'greatest seaborne carriers of the world'. Temple saw sails turn the land into a sea, as they scudded over the country's network of canals; at Amsterdam, on its web of waters, he was overwhelmed by the smell of mace and nutmeg and clove. For these the Dutch sailed to the Cape and Ceylon, to China, Indonesia and beyond.[20] And on this trade Temple now found himself compelled to make demands that he considered unreasonable. As soon as one point was conceded, another appeared in its place: until he concluded that 'they who influence our merchants in this prosecution...have no meaning this treaty should end fairly'. This ominous prognosis was confirmed from Paris, where it was reported that the English court had come to an understanding with the French.[21]

Charles II used his ministers as he used his mistresses, with an easy affability that masked ruthless detachment. And so there was signed the secret agreement wherein Charles declared his Catholicism -- thus binding Louis to his interests; Louis offered Charles a subsidy -- thus easing the lot of a monarch chronically short of cash; and the two planned a descent on Holland -- thus removing an obstacle to Louis' ambitions, and offering spoils that would presumably reconcile Charles' subjects to the result. For their ideals he cared not in the slightest; his sympathy lay with the power and prestige, unfettered by any parliament, of his brilliant cousin of France.[22] And, as Louis' vista ran unobstructed at Versailles, so Charles employed French gardeners to lay out radiating avenues, a canal glittering along their central axis, in the Park.[23] Here Temple waited for him: he had been recalled, he was told for consultation; but after a few casual inquiries, the dark sardonic face moved on. Arlington kept him waiting an hour and a half, 'received me with a coldness that I confess surprised me', and turned his conversation elsewhere. Another, more forthright, of the king's ministers demanded that he impute bad faith to the Dutch. Temple refused, and retired to his garden.[24]

**iv**

TEMPLE's second garden has vanished even more definitively than his first. It lay on a bend of the Thames, where it was hemmed in on three sides by high walls, against which his fruit-trees were trained, but on the fourth ran down to the river. House, walls and garden have alike gone under the grass, and all that remains to suggest the 'sweetness and satisfaction' that he enjoyed at Sheen is a path by slow water, overshadowed by trees. It was from here that he had been summoned by Arlington, and here that he retired when, as he recorded bitterly, his alliance with Holland 'ended in smoke'.[25]

If Temple, then, retreated to his orchard at this time, it was hardly of his own volition; if he immured himself in his library, it was not for his own amusement. The 'great bulk of his writing during this period', his biographer observes, 'is intended...to make straight the path for a return to friendship with the Dutch'. This included a 'careful and sympathetic account of the Dutch people', finding affinities with the English in their language, descent and institutions. He claimed, indeed, that the book was written 'without other design than of entertaining very idle men, and, among them, myself'; but he could scarcely have avowed its conciliatory purpose towards a nation with which his own was by then at war. His declared idleness is belied by the printing of the book so rapidly that he had no time to revise the proofs; his alleged frivolity made so little impression that a new edition was called for within months; and his proclaimed innocence of design is contradicted by his reflections on the king's loss of credit in abandoning the alliance.[26] Retirement for Temple, clearly, was the continuation of diplomacy by other means.

The French moved into Holland in force; but, lacking knowledge of the waterline, allowed the Dutch to flood the country and hold up their advance. Their mere presence, however, spread panic. There was and is a glittering pool at The Hague, shadowed by medieval rooftops. To the north, van Leeuwenhoek would shortly see the teeming life in a drop of water; to the south, Vermeer had lately elaborated his lucid silence. It was the heartland of the Dutch enlighten–ment; and here de Witt suffered the death of a backwoods king. De Witt was nothing if not rational. He had written a book on conic sections which won the praise of Newton and Huygens; in the journal of his grand tour he achieved the same dispassionate impersonality; and his pioneering study of life expectancy, seen as a masterpiece of actuarial science, was to display all too vividly the gap between theory and practice. In his rule of the Netherlands on behalf of its merchant oligarchy, he consistently underrated the irrational attachment of the people to the living symbols of their liberation: to the Calvinist clergy and to the young Prince of Orange, both of whom he systematically excluded from power. Now the forces he had held down exploded, as he, and the brother he had associated in his regime, were mobbed at the edge of the pool, bludgeoned, stabbed, shot and dismembered. His brother's wife, escaping by water, saw one of her husband's fingers held up in triumph in the boat.[27]

The killers were protected and rewarded by the prince. William, born into a room hung with black for his father, who had attempted the subjugation of Amsterdam, was now unchallenged commander of a state at war. Here he found his métier. The sullen young man, it was observed, seemed to come alive only on the battlefield: recklessly exposing himself to enemy fire, the star of the Garter glittering on his shoulder, as if he defied his dark god to strike him down. But it was not so, of course: he believed himself protected by providence until the moment preappointed for his death.[28]

Winter came, and the French moved in over the ice. Amsterdam lay awake in arms, torches reflected from the canals making the city seem bright as day. Then there was a thaw, and the troops of the sun king struggled back through the water.

He also lost the English, as Charles' parliament prayed for delivery from popery and popish counsels, and refused him supply. He summoned Temple, who quickly concluded a treaty, and who was now offered the embassy to Spain, the 'highest diplomatic post in the king's gift'. On Macaulay's hypothesis, the combined attractions of status and security ought to have proved irresistible. Instead he asked to be sent again to Holland.[29]

But the years there which followed were no more agreeable than those which had gone before. Since Louis had now embroiled much of Europe in his quarrel, a conference was called at Nijmegen, with its Carolingian palace overlooking the wanderings of the Waal. But as the issues were hammered out on the battlefield, the delegates were thrown back on questions of pure, as opposed to applied, diplomacy. When carriages met in the narrow streets, who should give way to whom? Here was a delicious opportunity to establish a complex, convoluted and controversial order of precedence. But Temple suggested common courtesy; and the French, after applying to Versailles, reluctantly agreed. More intractable, perhaps, was the question of language. The French had taken to using their own, instead of the customary Latin; the Danes threatened to use theirs; and the cause of peace was not advanced when the French invited them to make use of Hebrew. Most delicate of all, however, was a question propounded by the Swedes: was the King of Denmark, as he claimed, King of the Goths and the Vandals; or merely, as they maintained, King of the Vandals and the Goths? *Vandalorum Gothorum*; *Gothorum Vandalorum*.[30]

Once again Temple accomplished prodigies of persuasion, only, once again, to have his credit annulled by the king. Nemesis, however, was waiting on the machinations of Charles. He himself had pursued policies favourable to Catholicism; his brother and heir openly avowed that allegiance. Now, all over England, armed papists were seen galloping through the night. None was ever apprehended; but they continued to be seen. Fishing-boats were reported to be disgorging Romish priests: some bearing papal bulls, some, inexplicably, without.

Vaults were ransacked, and coffins opened, in the search for arms. Charles watched, angry and frightened, as his Catholic queen was accused of plotting his murder 'to revenge the violation of her bed'; and evidence was placed before parliament of his underhand dealings with France.[31]

In the ensuing uproar, he appealed to Temple. He had no-one left, he complained, in whom he could confide. Arlington, tainted by association with the royal policies, had ceased to be useful. A time came when, to amuse the king, it was sufficient to totter about with a patch over one's nose; and the minister retired to his country villa to strut, in solitary pomposity, beneath the dead eyes of his alabaster Caesars. Temple, as always, went to the heart of the matter. A reformed privy council, which should represent both parliament and the king, would, he thought, bring the two into accord.[32] Macaulay agrees that the plan was the 'work of an observant, ingenious, and fertile mind':

> Town and country were in a ferment of joy. The bells were rung; bonfires were lighted; and the acclamations of England were echoed by the Dutch, who considered the influence obtained by Temple as a certain omen of good for Europe.

But the scheme was blasted before it could unfold by the 'perfidious levity of the king'.[33] Charles quickly made it clear that he regarded the council, not as an instrument of rule, but as an expedient to play for time. Temple sarcastically offered his 'humble advice' that he make some use of it: 'for to make counsellors that should not counsel, I doubted whether it was in his majesty's power or no'. When the commons began work on a bill to exclude his brother from the throne, Temple believed that the correct strategy was for the king to declare that he would answer any bills that came to him from both houses. As the lords were unlikely to agree to James' exclusion, this would avoid the appearance of a break with parliament. Charles, however, insisted on a flat refusal; and, since nobody else could be found to carry this provocative message to the house, Temple did so, 'to shew his majesty that I intended to play no popular games'.[34]

This would seem to dispose of that Temple who was 'most careful not to give offence' either to king or to parliament. Temple the opportunist is as much a figment of imagination as Temple the idler. From Sheen he sent word to Charles that he would 'never meddle any more with public affairs'. He had concluded, he said, that he could be of no further use to his king or country, 'whose true interests I always thought were the same'. Now he felt that, as he had written long before, 'the fruits of my garden...will preserve better than those of my embassies'.[35]

In this, however, he was mistaken.

## V

THE last of Temple's gardens would appear to have gone the way of the other two. The mansion, at Moor Park in the Surrey countryside, is Georgian; and the shadowed lawn behind it might seem to have obliterated all trace of the formal setting Temple knew. But the outline of his terraces may be distinguished under the grass; beneath the eighteenth-century masking stands the fabric of his house; while his arms, with the characteristic motto *DEUS NOBIS HÆC OTIA FECIT*, still hold their place over the door. Here Temple came when, abandoning Sheen, he made his retreat from the city absolute. And here he was visited by the Prince of Orange as King of England:[36] a transformation in which he himself had had no small share.

Temple had long and quietly worked for the marriage of William and Mary; and, when William discussed the possibility with him, it was, he said, 'as a friend...and not as the king's ambassador'. Temple initiated the formal negotiations; and when William came to London to complete them, served as intermediary. Charles, however, saw in this an opportunity to extract a peace favourable to France. William snarled that he would not sell his honour for a wife, and set a date for his return to Holland: an ultimatum that Temple brought to the king. 'He is the honestest man in the world', replied Charles, 'and I will trust him, and he shall have his wife, and you shall go immediately and tell my brother so, and that it is a thing I am resolved on'. Charles may have intended only to broaden his own room for manoeuvre through the outward forms of a Protestant alliance; but in these words he pronounced the doom of the Stuart line. James, with his square face and his immutable certainties, told Temple that he believed in absolute obedience to his sovereign, and so handed his daughter over to the man who, because he suffered no such scruple, would replace him as King of England.[37]

When that happened, William invited Temple to serve as secretary of state. Temple refused. 'He prized', says Macaulay, 'his ease and his personal dignity too much, and shrank from responsibility with a pusillanimous fear'.[38] That Temple prized his ease was hardly a secret: otherwise he would scarcely have blazoned it over his door. He was no less candid about his dignity: 'I could not', he says of his dealings with the court of Charles II, 'talk a language I did not mean'.[39] Temple prized his ease and his dignity; and this precisely is his defence. That a man so constituted should have endured his servitude so long speaks in the highest degree of his idealism. But idealism was necessarily circumscribed by integrity. Time and again, Charles had pressed him to accept the same office; time and again, Temple had refused. And the reason is clear. He could not have avoided, in office, what others of the king's ministers could not avoid: collusion in his intrigues with France. As it was, Charles sent the French ambassador to his door, and sulked when Temple refused to treat with him for a bribe.[40] Relentlessly, the king unravelled his every achievement; 'profound and bitter disappointment', in his biographer's phrase,[41] was the leitmotif of his career; and it was in the final, exhausted, recognition of futility that he promised Charles 'that I would never meddle any more with any publick affairs'.[42] He repeated the promise to James; and it was this that now stood in his way. 'His heart was a great deal broken', writes his sister, 'with the trouble & uneasiness the Prince and all his friends exprest at it'; but it was a thing that 'he had given his word never to doe'.[43] 'There are', Macaulay admits, 'perfectly honourable ways of quitting...politics'.[44] This would appear to be one of them: the *gran rifiuto* is a mirage.

And when one places the personal record of the accuser against that of the accused, the disproportion of the accusation becomes positively grotesque. 'I am sick', complained Macaulay, 'of the monotonous succession of parties, and long for quiet and retirement'. This was a few months before the appearance of his essay on Temple; and when, in the following month, he declined public office, it was on the grounds that 'a man in office, and out of the Cabinet, is a mere slave'. But it should not be imagined that his objection was to office without responsibility alone. Some years afterwards, he declined a seat in the cabinet, though the government sorely needed him, defending the decision as 'better for my reputation and peace of mind'.[45] Macaulay, then, placed as Temple had been, behaved precisely as Temple had done: except that he had not Temple's reasons for doing so. Is this the answer? Is the essay on Temple an attempt to exorcise through another what he found it impossible to excuse in himself? But the candour with which he avows his motives would seem to preclude that explanation. The solution will have to be sought elsewhere.

## vi

'I WILL try my hand on Temple', Macaulay had mused in advance of his essay; '...Shaftesbury I shall let alone'. This is extremely curious: Macaulay wrote for a Whig journal; he was the leading orator of the Whigs; and his party traced its descent to Shaftesbury, who had led the parliamentary opposition to Charles II.[46] 'Shaftesbury I shall let alone': strange veneration, this, for the founder of one's faith. But the dilemma of the historian of Whiggery is succinctly expounded by Acton:

> It is the supreme achievement of Englishmen, and their bequest to the nations; but the patriarchs of the doctrine were the most infamous of men.[47]

Here then is the key to Macaulay's statement: 'Shaftesbury I shall let alone'. But to let him alone was impossible: in a treatise of Temple's times which had omitted him, the silence would have screamed. How then to introduce him? In his essay on Temple, Macaulay does so as follows:

> It is certain that, just before the Restoration, he declared to the Regicides that he would be damned, body and soul, rather than suffer a hair of their heads to be hurt, and that, just after the Restoration, he was one of the judges who sentenced them to death. It is certain that he was a principal member of the most profligate Administration ever known, and that he was afterwards a principal member of the most profligate Opposition ever known. It is certain that, in power, he did not scruple to violate the great fundamental principle of the Constitution, in order to exalt the Catholics, and that, out of power, he did not scruple to violate every principle of justice, in order to destroy them.

There were those of Shaftesbury's time who would have tolerated Catholicism on principle and against the law; there were those who would have denied it toleration for its connection with continental absolutism:

> But Shaftesbury belonged to neither class. He united all that was worst in both. From the misguided friends of toleration he borrowed their contempt for the Constitution, and from the misguided friends of civil liberty their contempt for the rights of conscience.

Nor was it true that he atoned in opposition for his excesses in office:

> On the contrary, his life was such that every part of it, as if by a skilful contrivance, reflects infamy on every other. We should never have known how abandoned a prostitute he was in place, if we had not known how desperate an incendiary he was out of it. To judge of him fairly, we must bear in mind that the Shaftesbury who, in office, was the chief author of the Declaration of Indulgence, was the same Shaftesbury who, out of office, excited and kept up the savage hatred of the rabble of London against the very class to whom that Declaration of Indulgence was intended to give illegal relief.

Every attempt to free him leaves him only more hopelessly enmeshed:

> It is acknowledged that he was one of the Ministry which made the alliance with France against Holland, and that this alliance was most pernicious. What, then, is the defence? Even this, that he betrayed his master's counsels to the Electors of Saxony and Brandenburg, and tried to rouse all the Protestant

> powers of Germany to defend the States. Again, it is acknowledged that he was deeply concerned in the Declaration of Indulgence, and that his conduct on this occasion was not only unconstitutional, but quite inconsistent with the course which he afterwards took respecting the professors of the Catholic faith. What, then, is the defence? Even this, that he meant only to allure concealed Papists to avow themselves, and thus to become open marks for the vengeance of the public.

So often, accordingly, 'as he is charged with one treason, his advocates vindicate him by confessing two':

> They had better leave him where they find him. For him there is no escape upwards. Every outlet by which he can creep out of his present position, is one which lets him down into a still lower and fouler depth of infamy. To whitewash an Ethiopian is a proverbially hopeless attempt; but to whitewash an Ethiopian by giving him a new coat of blacking is an enterprise more extraordinary still.

Yet in the sentences that immediately follow, Macaulay performs, not one, but both of these seemingly impossible operations. First comes the whitewash:

> That in the course of Shaftesbury's dishonest and revengeful opposition to the Court he rendered one or two most useful services to his country we admit. And he is, we think, fairly entitled, if that be any glory, to have his name eternally associated with the Habeas Corpus Act in the same way in which the name of Henry the Eighth is associated with the reformation of the Church, and that of Jack Wilkes with the most sacred rights of electors.

Mild, meek, deferential and apologetic, Macaulay has here, with the utmost brilliance of advocacy, undone half of his former diatribe. He has damned Shaftesbury from every conceivable angle, and he does not absolve him now: he leaves it to the reader to do so. He merely whispers, as if thunderstruck by the thought, the possibility that out of the evil which was Shaftesbury some good may have arisen. He has taken a treasured icon of each of the historic political parties, and gently wondered how, if they will not find a niche for Shaftebury, they can continue to burn their tapers before the blaspheming reformer or the syphilitic defender of the faith.

So ends the first act; now comes the second, and the rest of the indictment is undone. For Macaulay's second argument proves unanswerable as the first. It is this: that Shaftesbury, so deep is the dye of his infamy, is sublime. Dryden's 'great portrait' is invoked, in which he appears as the embodiment of 'violent passion, implacable revenge, boldness amounting to temerity': he is 'one of the "great wits to madness near allied"'. Play is made with the 'audacity of his spirit', the 'fierceness of his malevolent passions'. Here is no squalid political turncoat; here is Satan in *Paradise Lost*. And it is against this background, of the heroic malevolence of Shaftesbury, that Temple is finally dismissed:

> It was his constitution to dread failure more than he desired success, to prefer security, comfort, repose, leisure, to the turmoil and anxiety which are inseparable from greatness; and this natural languor of mind, when contrasted with the malignant energy of the keen and restless spirits among whom his lot was cast, sometimes appears to resemble the moderation of virtue. But we must own that he seems to us to sink into littleness and meanness when we compare him, we do not say with any high ideal standard of morality, but with many of those frail men who, aiming at noble ends, but often drawn from the right path by strong passions and strong temptations, have left to posterity a doubtful and chequered fame.[48]

The two modes of defence may appear incompatible; but the conflict is only apparent. 'Chequered' is the clue. The darkness is deep; but it serves to accentuate the points of light. The highlights and the shadows combine, throwing Shaftesbury into powerful relief, as in the glare and the gloom of some great baroque portrait: *chiaroscuro*.

So impressive, indeed, is the effect that it is almost a pity that it is fiction. For Shaftesbury ended his career, not as the splendid demon of *Paradise Lost*, but as the shifty reprobate of *Paradise Regained*. To save his head, this 'keen and restless spirit' fled to Holland: to the land which, in the days of Temple's alliance with it, had been his *delenda Carthago*.[49] And it was Temple, not Shaftesbury, who negotiated the match through which his 'noble ends', insofar as he had any, were to be realised.[50] If Shaftesbury, then, is illuminated in history against the flickering fires of his incendiarism, Temple stands in the calm light of a steady, coherent, and ultimately triumphant purpose.

## vii

IT IS a purpose nowhere more eloquently celebrated than in Macaulay's great narrative. 'During many years', he observes,

> one half of the energy of England had been employed in counteracting the other half. The executive power and the legislative power had so effectively impeded each other that the state had been of no account in Europe. The King at Arms, who proclaimed William and Mary before Whitehall Gate, did in truth announce that this great struggle was over; that there was entire union between the throne and the Parliament; that England, long dependent and degraded, was again a power of the first rank; that the ancient laws by which the prerogative was bounded would henceforth be held as sacred as the prerogative itself, and would be followed out to all their consequences; that the executive administration would be conducted in conformity with the sense of the representatives of the nation; and that no reform, which the two Houses should, after mature deliberation, propose, would be obstinately withstood by the sovereign.[51]

'No character', comments Millgate, 'is more central' to Macaulay's conception of English history than the sovereign immediately in question.[52] William is central because of the revolution that accompanied his enthronement. And this is very strange: for the 'real hero', Woodbridge insists, of those memoirs of which Macaulay spoke with such contempt, is 'William Prince of Orange'.[53] It was unfortunate, therefore, that in this particular instance, the historian should have subordinated the integrity of his subject to the interests of party:[54] for Macaulay's political vision was Temple's, vindicated by hindsight. Temple's retreat from the world was as illusory at Moor Park as it had been at Sheen; and his tying up of apricots was no less deceptive than his writing of memoirs. For in the garden, as in government, he was to discern the kernel from which the future would unfold.

## viii

PENSHURST still has something of the air of a village suspended in time. A bell clatters the hours from the medieval church; beside it, the gardens of the manor have been restored to the simplicity of the Renaissance. Here Temple was educated by the gentle and scholarly uncle who was its rector; but the site was inhabited by shadows more potent than the living. In the park behind the manor stood the tree planted, according to Jonson,

At his great birth, where all the *Muses* met.

*All* the muses: for Sir Philip Sidney was England's Renaissance man, and so he appeared to Temple: 'a person born capable not only of forming the greatest ideas, but of leaving the noblest examples'. This combination of vision and realisation is the key to much that might seem incongruous in Temple: for he was to realise the Dutch alliance that was Sidney's vision, and in the cause of which he met his death at Zutphen; and his garden was a retreat, like Sidney's in the *Arcadia*, from a court in which vision was compromised.[55]

But the exemplary power of Penshurst was even yet not exhausted. Jonson was followed there by another poet, for whom the author of *Astrophil and Stella* was so far the supreme erotic celebrant of the language

That all we can of love, or high desire,
Seems but the smoke of amorous Sidney's fire.

Waller's pilgrimage was to the shrine of Lady Dorothy Sidney, whose image still simpers on the walls of the house as she clasps the rose to which he likened her. His devotion was shared by the young William Temple; and though she was married, in a ceremony which he may have witnessed, when he was eleven years old, it does not seem to have slackened. 'I have sent you my Picture', wrote the young woman, another Dorothy, whom he was himself to marry, in that sweetly sardonic tone which was so characteristic of her, '...but pray let it not presume to disturbe my Lady Sunderlands'.[56]

Their paths had crossed when Temple set out for the continent at the age of twenty. He paused on the way at the Isle of Wight, of which a cousin, Hammond, was governor, and held Charles I, then in the last summer of his life, in the commanding heights of Carisbrooke Castle. Meanwhile Dorothy Osborne and her brother, who were royalist, passed through the island; and in his indignation at seeing the king imprisoned, the young man cut the inscription: 'And Hamman was hang'd upon the Gallows he had prepar'd for Mordecai'. This perversion of scripture and language was taken most seriously, and the Osbornes pursued, overtaken and brought before the governor. The young man was released as a result of his sister's taking responsibility for the *graffito*: combined, it has been suggested, with intercession on the part of Temple. Certainly Temple was with them when they resumed their journey, and dallied with Dorothy on the coast of France.[57]

This came to the ears of his father, who peremptorily ordered him to Paris. Years of enforced separation followed; but if this was intended to create a rift between the lovers, it signally failed of its purpose. His side of their correspondence has all but vanished; but, as Virginia Woolf has pointed out, he is present by vivid implication in hers. Had he been pompous or frivolous or dull, she observes, that clear-eyed young woman would have had nothing to do with him; as it was, she wrote out her heart to him: her 'moodiness and melancholy; the sweetness of walking in the garden at night; of sitting lost in thought by the river; of longing for a letter and finding one'.[58]

The river flows through flat land in Bedfordshire: beside it stands the former convent that was the Osbornes' home and that, with its narrow windows and gloomy cloister, makes palpable the sense of oppression into which Temple's letters brought a quickening of hope. When she thought that the messenger brought none for her, 'it went Colde to my heart as Ice'; when one arrived, it was 'a pardon to one upon the block'. The solitude of the life she led, the opportunities for reverie, the part Temple played in these, and the intensity of her longing for him may be inferred from a scene in one of hers. It is an evening in late autumn, and she is dreaming by the fire, abstracted from a conversation between her brother and a friend:

> they fell into a discourse of fflyeing and both agreed that it was very posible to finde out a way that people might fly like Birds and dispatch theire Journy's soe. I that had not sayd a word all night started up at that and desyr'd that they would say a litle more in it, for I had not marked the begining.

But

> instead of that they both fell into soe Violent a Laughing that I should apeare soe much concern'd in such an Art; but they litle knew of what use it might have bin to mee. Yet I saw you last night but twas in a dream.[59]

Then he visits her, and she writes: "Tis but an howr since you went, and I am writeing to you already, is not this kinde?' Amazed disbelief still possesses her: 'good god, the fear's and surprizes, the crosses and disorders of that day, twas confused enough to bee a dream and I am apt to think somtimes it was noe more'. There were, indeed, formidable obstacles to be overcome, in the opposition of both their families; but they were married at the end of that year; and here, naturally, the regular correspondence ceases. In a series of undated notes, however, Dorothy tells Temple that if he would have 'such letters as I used to write before we were marryed, there are a great many such in y$^{r}$ cabinett y$^{t}$ I can send you if you please; but none in my head I assure you'. That this does not signal irretrievable breakdown is suggested by the later confession of the same note that since his going 'I am weary of my bed'; and by its valediction 'Good night to you my dearest'.[60]

## ix

'CAN there bee', Dorothy had asked, 'a more Romance Story then ours would make if the conclusion should prove happy?' In this she referred to the French tales of unhappy passion that were her preferred reading, and a series of which Temple translated during their years of separation. Having found it, he wrote, 'to no purpose to fly from my thoughts', he hoped to divert them 'by representing others misfortunes to them instead of my owne'. But in the alterations and additions that he made to his originals, the mask was cast aside. One of his heroines acquired the 'black eyes and dark curling hair of Dorothy Osborne'; in his observation that '*parents of all people know their children the least*' his own family is suggested; and, in his titling the series *A True Romance*, Temple underlined their personal application.[61]

Careless use of this word, writes Henry Knight Miller, 'confuses and conflates two utterly disparate, almost antithetical realms': that of 'medieval–Renaissance romance', which is aristocratic, public and unexpressive of personality; and that of 'nineteenth–century Romantic literature', which is non–hierarchical, private, and 'most frequently an expression of "personality"'.[62] The two realms, however, are not altogether distinct. '*Romantic*', observes Logan Pearsall Smith, 'like *romancy* and *romancical*, simply meant "like the old romances"'. For a contemporary of Temple's, a 'romantic object' was one that 'answers the most poetical description that can be made of solitude, precipice, prospect, or whatever can contribute to a thing so very like their' -- the romance–writers' -- 'imaginations'; and the word was applied in particular to the 'romancy plaines and boscages' of Sidney's *Arcadia*,[63] to which Temple had had such a privileged connection at Penshurst.

When Temple alludes, then, in Sidney, to 'romantic honour and love', he pays fealty to that 'medieval–Renaissance' domain which is interpenetrated with the usages of chivalry: that domain in which Sidney can write:

> Having this day my horse, my hand, my launce
> Guided so well, that I obtain'd the prize;

or:

> If I but stars upon mine armour beare...[64]

When Temple translates the French romances for his lover, he is still in that earlier world. But when he adapts these to their own situation, and titles them *A True Romance*, he has become a citizen of the state in which runs the writ of what is 'private' and an 'expression of "personality"'. And when he treasures up those letters of hers which are so vivid a manifestation of personal feeling, he proclaims that implicit valuation of the spontaneous and the natural through which he was to become the instrument of the later romantic thought.

## x

TEMPLE brought his bride to a garden where he had wandered disconsolately in the dark days of their courtship. As it was inhabited by a relative of hers, it may have given him a sense of vicarious contact with her. What it continued to mean to him may be guessed from the fact that he named his last garden, Moor Park, after it, and that he remembered it, across the space of thirty years, as 'the sweetest place, I think, that I have seen in my life'. He considered it, moreover, 'the perfectest figure of a garden I ever saw'. It stood out, to his mind's eye, as a house on a hillside from whose tree–lined terrace steps descended to another terrace on which cloisters flanked statues and fountains, and from this in turn to a shaded green 'wilderness'.[65] A 'wilderness' of this time was a grove, not necessarily informal -- one such is described as being 'cut and formed into several ovals, squares and angles, very well ordered' -- or, if it was, as an accent to an overall formality.[66]

The garden of Temple's day was still, in all essentials, the garden of Mediterranean antiquity. The formal layout of Egypt and Babylon was transplanted through Hellenism to Rome; the Roman villa crumbled; but its peristyle persisted in the cloister, with its simple *paradisum* of flowers and a well. The earlier, Florentine Renaissance retained its groundplan but removed its walls, so that square walks and outdoor rooms looked out from the hills above the city. In the later, Roman Renaissance, Bramante linked the Vatican to the Belvedere in a complex of stairways and balustrades: solving the problem of a garden on a slope, and re-emphasizing its status as architecture. Water fell in cascades from walls, rippled down staircases, and rose again out of fountains, in a concept derived from the desert-dwellers in Sicily and Spain. The cross canal of the Persian *pairidaeza*, carried west to the Alhambra, east to the Taj Mahal, and still central to Versailles, harks back to Babylonian irrigation. Ishtar and the land revive when she is sprinkled, in accordance with the notation still inscribed on circle and dial, sixty times. It is the regulation of water which makes the difference between death and life.[67]

In France, this garden had adapted itself to local circumstance. Here summers were spent, not in the hills, but on the plains, where the castle courtyard, patterned flat because seen from above, was imitated outside, multiplied, and ranged under Renaissance order into the logical coherence of linked parterres. The moat spread out into languid expanses of water; the vista followed the hunting-avenue down through the woods.

Under the baroque genius of Le Nôtre, these elements were combined into apotheosis. What the young Louis XIV found, when he visited his chief minister at Vaux-le-Vicomte, was a concentrated expression of personal greatness. Wherever he looked -- the terraces imperceptibly bevelled to carry off rain, the pools whose angle of refraction held the image of the house, the cascades whose murmur loudened as one advanced to the hidden canal, the great fountain balanced like a column of glass, the concave slope at the end from which the ensemble could be viewed anew, to culminate in the moated castle which was now a palace -- everything spoke of a subtle and coherent system of complete control; and it was wholly in character that the king should imprison the minister and appropriate the gardener.

Versailles shares with Vaux the elaborate parterres, the lavish pools, the gathering into a vista by woods on either side: though here the scale is vaster, and, amid the emblematic fountains, presumptuous commoners are transformed into frogs, or Apollo lashes his horses through a shattering brilliance of broken light. But it is not simply larger and more imperious; the most profound alteration at Versailles is not an addition, but an absence. There is no counterpart to the enclosing slope: no limit to the sweep down the green tapestry in the centre, and out over the long water to the horizon. And the central symbol of Versailles, rising and setting ceremonially, the light of his great gallery amplified and expanded by its walls of reflecting glass, multiplied by the thousands of candles and glittering back from the silver furniture, was the king himself.[68]

## xi

EUROPE caught its breath: Louis' splendour haunted the imagination; and the radii of Versailles reached out to Russia and to Ireland, to Sweden and to Spain.[69] But here, as elsewhere, Temple was to make Louis' ideas obsolete.

The natural garden, Miles Hadfield observes, had 'long been latent' in Europe.[70] It is implicit in the pastoral of antiquity, in which nature is superior to art;[71] and in the pastoral of the Renaissance, it resurfaces as if in a dream.[72] This was most immediately available to Temple through Sidney, who in the *Arcadia* had painted a setting which

> was neither field, garden nor orchard, or rather it was both field, garden and orchard; for as soon as the descending of the stairs had delivered them down, they came to a place cunningly set with trees...but scarcely had they taken that into their consideration but that they were suddenly stept into a delicate green; of each side of the green a thicket, and behind the thickets again new beds of flowers, which being under the trees, the trees were to them a pavilion and they to the trees a mosaical floor, so that it seemed that Art therein would needs be delightful by counterfeiting his enemy Error and making order in confusion.[73]

In the actual gardens of the time, however, it exists, where it exists, as a foil:

as a coign of wildness in thrall to architecture: as a dream half–remembered to the waking mind. Through the increasing elaborations of the baroque, it surfaces as a growing unease: as the recognition that nature ought indeed to be natural, and as the repeated cry for a return to it.[74] But the catalyst of the change, the crisis after which reality can no longer be held at bay, comes in Temple. Gardens 'wholly irregular', he writes, in an historic aside from his recollection of Moor Park, may 'have more beauty' than those of the regular kind. 'Something of this', he goes on,

> I have seen in some places, but heard more of it from others who have lived much among the Chineses; a people, whose way of thinking seems to lie as wide of ours in Europe, as their country does.

'Among us', he continues,

> the beauty of building and planting is placed chiefly in some certain proportions, symmetries, or uniformities; our walks and our trees ranged so as to answer one another, and at exact distances.

The 'Chineses', however,

> scorn this way of planting, and say, a boy, that can tell an hundred, may plant walks of trees in straight lines, and over–against one another, and to what length and extent he pleases.

The gardens of Europe, in this view, are mere mathematics; while those of the 'Chineses' involve a most subtle aesthetic:

> their greatest reach of imagination is employed in contriving figures, where the beauty shall be great, and strike the eye, but without any order or disposition of parts that shall be commonly or easily observed.

And 'though we', he concludes,

> have hardly any notion of this sort of beauty, yet they have a particular word to express it, and, where they find it hit their eye at first sight, they say the sharawadgi is fine or is admirable, or any such expression of esteem.[75]

## xii

*SHARAWADGI*, clearly, is the key to Temple's source; but no Chinese equivalent has been established for it. Instead the suggestion has been made that it stands for the Japanese *sorowaji*: which, in sound and sense -- 'not being regular' -- would correspond to Temple's word. There is, however, one apparently insurmountable objection to this hypothesis. Temple speaks, unequivocally as it would seem, of the 'Chineses': a fact that looms across the path like one of the towering precipices of Chinese landscape.[76] Viewed from the proper angle, however, a ravine can be seen to run through it to the other side.

That angle is the angle of context: the context of the geography of Temple's century: at the back of which still lurked the ill-defined notion of the 'Indies'. 'By the name of India', declared one contemporary, '...we comprehend all that tract between India...on the west...unto China eastward'; while another, still more generous, described as 'Indian' plants both from Barbados and Japan.[77] Yet another of Temple's contemporaries achieves a certain magnificence in his ambiguities. 'Went', records Evelyn,

> to visit our good neighbour, Mr. Bohun, whose whole house is a cabinet of all elegancies, especially Indian; in the hall are contrivances of Japan screens...the landscapes of the screens represent the manner of living, and country of the Chinese.[78]

Is 'Japan' used here in its sense of lacquer, though the screens are Chinese: Chinese japan, as one might speak of Japanese china? Or are they in fact Japanese, though depicting, as Japanese artists commonly did, Chinese land-scapes?[79] We cannot tell; and it scarcely matters: because Evelyn, before setting out his eastern wares, unfolds them from a wrapping of 'Indian' fabric. And Temple, in a similar context, makes the same equation:

> And whoever observes the work upon the best India gowns, or the painting upon their best skreens or purcellans, will find their beauty is all of this kind (that is) without order.[80]

Temple's 'Chineses', then, are not specifically Chinese; they are generically oriental, denizens of Cathay. Nor was he, in this instance, simply mistaken. The gardens of Japan were continually influenced by those of China,[81] and Temple was aware of the similarity. A book that he is known to have read shows a naturalistic Chinese garden, with pine–trees, waterfall and jagged stonework; and he knew, too, that the Chinese imperial palace was surrounded by 'large and delicious gardens', containing 'artificial rocks and hills'.[82] Temple, then, was aware from his reading that Chinese gardens were irregular; while on those of Japan he had access to more privileged information. For he was accredited to the one country in Europe to which Japan was still open by trade; that trade was conducted through Djakarta by the Dutch East India Company; and it was with this company that, in his trade negotiations in Holland, he had had to deal.[83]

At the foot of the hills that crowd into Nagasaki harbour, a dusty tramline curves parallel to a muddy canal; between them runs a laneway in a similar curve. These mark the outlines and the single street of Deshima: the artificial island, shaped like the paper of a fan, to which the Dutch were confined.[84] Here was the only gateway between Japan and Europe; and the tall brush of an araucaria, carried by the Dutch from Indonesia, still stands in one of its gardens.

Of this 'Dutch prison in Japan, for so I may deservedly call their habitation and factory at Nagasaki', Engelbert Kaempfer, the German naturalist who visited them there, speaks in considerable detail and with considerable disdain. Once a year, however, restrictions were lifted; the island was left behind; and the Dutch travelled upcountry to pay homage to the shogun at Tokyo. On their return, they were allowed to halt at the more gracious imperial capital of Kyoto, still the major locus of the Japanese garden, and were taken to see its temples. On two of these occasions, Kaempfer was with them. On the first, he observed 'a row of small hills artfully made in imitation of nature'; and on the second, 'a steep hill planted with trees and bushes in an irregular but agreeable manner'.[85] 'Irregular but agreeable'; 'artfully made in imitation of nature': Temple's *sharawadgi*.

## xiii

*SHARAWADGI* is a Japanese word connoting asymmetry; and no more characteristic concept could have arisen in that conversation reported to Temple. When the Chinese city of Chang–an was reproduced in Japan as Kyoto, its chessboard perfection soon fell apart. The western half of the quadrilateral, after devastation by earthquake and fire, was allowed to revert to wilderness, while the eastern flourished and overspread its original boundaries.[86] The Chinese temple complex, likewise, had its symmetry overruled, in accordance with the asymmetrical groundplan of traditional Japanese architecture. This contrast has been pondered by Singer, who attributes it to geography:

> Chinese civilisation seems one with China's wide plains. Its foundations were laid in the North, where the...evenly balanced structure of the open spaces, obviously orientated to the cardinal points of the compass, has a visual force.

Here the alternating sequences of heat and cold, of light and dark, of Confucian fixity and Taoist flow, were integrated into symmetrical patterns. 'The soil of Japan', on the other hand,

> essentially a world of thousands of great, small, and minute islands, bays and valleys, is as much partitioned off and irregular as the immense Chinese plains are open and uniform. The cross of the four cardinal points is everywhere overlaid by a graceful wilderness of hills, volcanic ranges, fields and forests.

With asymmetry, in contrast to balance, goes motion as opposed to equilibrium, the passing in place of the permanent. 'Chinese dwellings are cut into the soil, moulded from it, or joined to it in such a way that they appear to be part of the earth's crust'. The archipelago of Japan, on the other hand, 'is rocked by seismic shocks, invaded by storms, showered and pelted with rain, encircled by clouds and mists'; and its dwellings, accordingly, 'attach themselves only lightly to the soil'.[87] The contrast is immediately noticeable in the cities: where Suzhou is modelled in clay or carved in stone, Kyoto seems the same structure translated into the idiom of timber. So too with their gardens. In China, the trailing willows and blossoming plums, the curving waterchannels and lotus–covered pools, subsist within a framework of solidity: the stone–paved courtyards opening one out of another, the limewashed walls, the massive concatenations of rock. In Japan, however, where the sacred site was some numinous location in nature, the Taoist feeling for space and the spontaneous, for the understated and the inexpressible, given intense concentration by Zen, found a deeper echo.[88] Here a garden may consist of pools of sunshine on a flooring of moss, or the shadows of maples in an earthen yard, or light glittering through a grove of bamboo. And when rocks are clustered in scattered islands, they acquire a curious permeability from their setting in gravel or sand: becoming, as in some romantic adagio, suggestions of form floating over a sea of silence.

**xiv**

TEMPLE, then, could have spoken in Holland to men who had stood in the gardens of Japan; and that this indeed was his source is confirmed by the very anomalies of his information. By the time that he wrote, *sorowaji* was obsolete in the standard language; but it survived in the south, where the Dutch settlement lay. The trick of speech through which it became *shorowaji* is still characteristic of the region; while the further change to *sharawaji*, or *sharawadgi* as Temple spelled it, is consistent with its having been filtered through Dutch.[89] Deshima, too, unlocks the last of the word's enigmas. *Sorowaji* is a verb -- 'would not be symmetrical' -- and not a noun,[90] as Temple implied ('they say the sharawadgi is fine'); and here again the solution is provided by Kaempfer. The authorities, he explains, had provided the island with a disproportionate number of interpreters

> on purpose to make it needless for us to learn the language of the country, and by this means to keep us, as much as lies in their power, ignorant of its present state and condition...If there be any of our people, that hath made any considerable progress in the Japanese language, they are sure, under some pretext or

other, to...expel him the country.

But if the Dutch were limited in their Japanese, their would-be interpreters were scarcely more fluent in Dutch:

> the knowledge and skill of these people is, generally speaking, little else than a simple and indifferent connexion of broken words...which they put together according to the Idiom of their own tongue, without regard had to the nature and genius of the language out of which they translate, and this they do in so odd a manner, that often other interpreters would be requisite to make them understood.[91]

We have arrived at the terminal point of *sharawadgi*. A Dutchman of little Japanese stands awestruck before a garden 'irregular but agreeable'; 'artfully made in imitation of nature'. He enquires; and is answered in a 'simple and indifferent connexion of broken words'. But out of this babel of mutual incomprehension the essential fact filters through. Temple seizes upon it; and the European landscape is remade. *The sharawadgi is fine*.

## XV

TEMPLE did not recommend imitation of the gardens of his 'Chineses': 'they are adventures of too hard atchievement for any common hands'; but in placing them out of bounds, he merely added to their fascination. And with their underlying principle he was in inherent accord. Expenditure on gardens, he declared, was wasted

> if nature be not followed; which I take to be the great rule in this, and perhaps in everything else, as far as the conduct not only of our lives, but our govern ments.[92]

The secret, he wrote at the time of his alliance with Holland, of 'all that has seemed so surprising in my negotation' was

> that things drawn out of their center are not to be moved without much force, or skill, or time; but, to make them return to their center again, there is required

but little of either, for nature itself does the work.[93]

He would have understood this, from the *Tao Tê Ching*: 'The man of highest "power" does not reveal his "power"; therefore he keeps his "power"': it was what he had enjoined upon Charles II. He would have understood this: 'Tao never does; yet through it all things are done': it was how he had advised him to deal with his parliament.[94] Temple had grasped the principle of nature in government; he had grasped it in the garden. In retrospect, the next step is obvious: as in retrospect it always is. But at the time it requires a creative violence: the wrenching of ideas from their customary context; the discernment of likeness in what none had linked before.[95] Jung has written wryly of the disability of the discoverer, who ever 'stumbles through unknown regions...forever losing the Ariadne thread'.[96] Temple had isolated both of the elements; they would fuse in the crucible of another psyche.

## CHAPTER TWO

# THE FIREWORKS NIGHT OF JOSEPH ADDISON

'BUT the morning', recounts Macaulay,

> of Monday the fifth of November was hazy. The pilot of the Brill could not discern the sea marks, and carried the fleet too far to the west. The danger was great. To return in the face of the wind was impossible. Plymouth was the next port. But at Plymouth a garrison had been posted under the command of Lord Bath. The landing might be opposed; and a check might produce serious consequences. There could be little doubt, moreover, that by this time the royal fleet had got out of the Thames and was hastening full sail down the Channel. Russell saw the whole extent of the peril, and exclaimed to Burnet, 'You may go to prayers, Doctor. All is over'. But at that moment the wind changed: a soft breeze sprang up from the south: the mist dispersed; the sun shone forth; and, under the mild light of an autumnal noon, the fleet turned back, passed round the lofty cape of Berry Head, and rode safe in the harbour of Torbay.[1]

King James had once been a hero. In the war which was the setting of Temple's first diplomatic mission, he commanded, as Duke of York, the English fleet against the Dutch; and a Dutch settlement on the American coast, with its wall on the landward side, and its canal curved against the winds from the sea, was renamed New York. As lord high admiral, he distinguished himself by his faith in rules;[2] and as king, he seems to have expected a similar obedience from his subjects. But by imposing his fellow–Catholics on the army and the church, he alienated the bases of his own power, until the very bishops rose in revolt, and enjoyed for a moment the unwonted sensation of martyrdom. James put them on trial; and, on the day that they were acquitted, an invitation went out to William.

In the face of invasion, and the collapse of his authority, it quickly became apparent that James was a hero no more. As William marched on London, the king's nerve gave way, and he fled down the waterstairs, in heavy rain, to a life–long exile in France. The downpour continued as William entered the city; and, while his Blue Guards lined the streets, and the people waited patiently in orange ribbons and scarves, avoided them by a short–cut to the palace. On his and Mary's agreeing to rule in accordance with parliament, they were crowned king and queen; and 'Sir William Temple', writes Seeley, 'saw the union of which he had sown the seed become a mighty tree'.[3]

## i

THERE were few, perhaps, in the England of that day to whom its fruits were to fall in greater abundance than Joseph Addison. In the obscurity of studenthood when it occurred, he was to end his career, by virtue of the revolution, in the office which Temple had declined. He had meanwhile achieved another pre–eminence: his classical tragedy was so much the sensation of its decade that it seemed to debar him from any other form of applause. *Mais imaginés vous*, wrote the French ambassador, *ce qu'on aurait dit en France si l'on eut fait Mr. Racine Secretaire d'Etat*.[4] He enjoyed, moreover, a personal acclaim more telling than that of the playwright or the politician. 'I will venture to tell you a secret', wrote Jonathan Swift, a political opponent and no respecter of persons, on his promotion: that 'three or four such Choices would gain more hearts in three weeks than all the methods hitherto practiced, have been able to do in as many years'. It was, thought that veteran misanthropist, a 'prodigious singularity' to 'owe ones Rise entirely to Merit'.[5]

We think differently today. Today, scarcely anybody can compete with Addison for primacy in banality, blandness and boredom: a perception which induces rage, and the urge to deface so exasperating a monument to complacency. This attitude is most memorably embodied in Dobrée's excoriation of Addison as the 'First Victorian'. To be 'Victorian', in this view, is to 'do violence to one's own instincts'. Addison desires to dominate but fears to fail; and therefore takes refuge behind a mask of aloofness and perfection. His wish to 'count for something' is mysteriously inhibited; his reserve the result of an underlying conviction of worthlessness. And so he avoids women, and the equality of the bedchamber, because, it is alleged, they would have seen through his pretensions. Yet he needs to experience the pride of being approved; and translates this need into a small circle over which he can rule unquestioned.[6]

This picture of Addison as egregious moralist can be seen, on even the most cursory glance at the evidence, to be ahistorical and untrue. The reforming movement that he belonged to -- the reaction against Restoration licence which in turn was a reaction against Commonwealth repression -- began before him and continued after.[7] And in it, as Beljame long ago pointed out, his role was a humanising one: 'moderating its ruthlessness and guiding it into less narrow paths'; protecting all 'genuine manifestations of literature and art'; and, in the process, fusing the 'best qualities of Puritan and Cavalier'.[8] It was Swift, after all, and not Addison, who would have made it impossible for 'a *man of pleasure*, and a *free thinker*' to hold public office;[9] it was Addison, and not Swift, who was able to detach the public abilities of that same official from the fact that he had achieved notoriety as a rake, or for defecating in a pulpit.[10]

Still, trumpets Dobrée, 'better to err with Steele than shine in rectitude with Addison'; and this is heady stuff, no doubt, for those who do their dangerous living vicariously. The difficulty with it as history, however, is that Steele, too, appears to have harboured ambitions of shining in rectitude -- and some pages later is praised for this very fact. Steele, it appears, in sensing the reform of manners that was in the air, led the public in 'the way its best elements wanted to go'.[11] Strange, that what is reprehensible in Addison should be admirable in Steele; stranger still, that Steele seems not to have felt this chill, this shining in rectitude. There were, he acknowledged, differences in temperament between Addison and himself:

> the one, with Patience, Foresight, and temperate Address, always waited and stem'd the Torrent; while the other plung'd himself into it...

But this prudence of Addison's did not preclude compassion:

> ...and was as often taken out by the Temper of him who stood weeping on the Bank for his Safety, whom he could not dissuade from leaping into it.

And Steele had little patience with attempts to exalt him at his friend's expense: to hear himself placed above Addison, he wrote, moved him to 'Vexation, even to Tears'.[12]

## ii

THE modern defence of Addison, however, does not rest upon the deathless affection he evoked from his friends. It rests instead upon his writing; but it is of a very curious kind. Addison, states C.S. Lewis, is 'not attempting to write sermons or philosophy, only essays'. That is to say, his attitudes do not matter so very much, because his productions amount to so very little. He says so in as many words: they are 'rather small beer'. Yet this intellectual nonentity is to be redeemed by Chestertonian paradox: 'if I were to live in a man's house for a whole twelve–month, I think I should be more curious about the quality of his small beer than about that of his wine'. Addison's world, asserts Lewis, 'is a good one to fall back into when the day's work is over and a man's feet on the fender and his pipe in his mouth': he belongs among those who 'stand on the common ground of daily life and deal only with middle things'.[13] *Middle* things. The same ominous adjective is employed by more recent defenders, who speak of their subject's 'intellectual moderation'; of his feeling at peace in the 'middle station'; of his following the 'middle path'.[14] Addison, then, having been stripped and left for dead by his enemies, is in still worse case after the ministrations of his friends. He has been washed clean of a fascinating complexity to revel in an unimpeachable mediocrity.

And yet there are features in Lewis' portrait which he seems unable to integrate with the rest. 'In other respects', he admits, 'Addison' -- this avuncular mediocrity with his feet on the fender and his small beer at his elbow -- 'is a liberator'. There is the essay, than which 'no more classical piece of criticism exists', in which those songs which 'are the delight of the common people' are found to be 'paintings of Nature'. When did the keeper of the middle way step aside to listen to such songs? And why should he have valued what the 'common people' thought? How could the high priest of smugness have arrived at so unfashionable a judgement? And what has he, with his feet on the fender, to do with 'paintings of Nature'? Yet it is Addison who, in Lewis' words, stands 'exactly at the turn of the tide' between an age when 'men frankly hated and feared all those things in Nature which are neither sensuously pleasing, useful, safe, symmetrical, or gaily coloured', and one in which they 'love and actually seek out mountains, waste places, dark forests, cataracts, and storm-beaten coasts'.

How could the Addison of Lewis, who is 'above all else, comfortable',[15] have relished such uncomfortable surroundings? How could the Addison of Dobrée, who suffered from an 'almost morbid fear of failure and a horror of being made to look ridiculous',[16] have engaged in so quixotic a tilt against convention? If this is so, the individual dissected by the one, and bound up and laid to rest by the other, would seem a case of mistaken identity. They appear, both of them, to have got hold of the wrong body.

## iii

DESCENDING into the deep places of personality is now notoriously a matter of early and intimate relationships; but of these, in the case of Addison, we have scarcely any record. 'Not a single letter', writes his biographer, 'exchanged between Addison and his father, his wife, or his brothers is preserved, and those to friends about personal matters are few'. If, he goes on, 'there is any "black box" containing the key to Addison's private life waiting for discovery, it has so far eluded the search'.[17]

Most, if not all, of what is known of the early Addison can be given in rapid summary. At the time of his birth, his father was rector of Milston, in the wooded uplands above Salisbury; and, on his elevation to the deanery of Lichfield, the son attended the noted grammar school there. Later he moved to Charterhouse, where he attracted the idolatry of Steele, and from here went up to Oxford.[18] The history of the rest of his family is even sketchier. Of his mother, who died during his childhood, 'nothing of importance is recorded'. His brother Gulston became governor of Madras, and his brother Lancelot followed Joseph to Oxford and Gulston to India, where both died young. Of his sister Dorothy, Swift relates that she was a 'sort of wit', and 'very like' her brother.[19]

The only source for the tone of Addison's family life is Steele, who spent some Charterhouse holidays at the deanery,[20] and who later wrote:

> I remember among all my Acquaintance but one Man whom I have thought to live with his Children with Equanimity and a good Grace. He had Three Sons and One Daughter, whom he bred with all the Care imaginable in a liberal and ingenuous Way. I have often heard him say, He had the Weakness to love one much better than the other, but that he took as much Pains to correct that as any other Criminal Passion that could arise in his Mind. His Method was to make it the only Pretension in his Children to his Favour to be kind to each other; and he would tell them, That he who was the best Brother, he would reckon the best Son. This turned their Thoughts into an Emulation for the Superiority in kind and tender Affection towards each other...It was an unspeakable Pleasure to visit or sit at a Meal in that Family. I have often seen the old Man's Heart flow at his Eyes with Joy upon Occasions which would appear indifferent to such as

> were Strangers to the turn of his Mind; but a very slight Accident, wherein he saw his Children's Good–will to one another, created in him the Godlike Pleasure of loving them, because they loved each other.[21]

It is Steele's biographer who has noticed the oddity of the scene. 'Doctor Addison', writes Willard Connely, 'looked upon the lives of his three sons and daughter as a competition in kindness, with his own favour the prize. No kindness, no prizes'.[22] And indeed, to an age more accustomed to probe for ambivalence, the episode seems subtly unnatural. Unnatural in the parent, who enjoyed the 'Godlike Pleasure' of loving his children 'because they loved each other', and not as a matter of natural feeling. Unnatural in the children, who found in 'tender Affection' a matter of 'Emulation for...Superiority'. Steele, orphaned in early childhood,[23] his nose pathetically pressed to the window of this utopia, could scarcely be expected to look beyond the prospectus supplied by its founder. But to an observer less involved with its personalities, the scene seems ripe with the possibility of mistrust of self and of spontaneity. That this was so in fact is suggested by another scene recorded by Steele. 'Speaking obviously', writes Stephen,

> of Addison, he says that 'you can seldom get him to the tavern; but when once he is arrived to his pint and begins to look about and like his company, you admire a thousand things in him which before lay buried'. Addison, in fact, though not intemperate according to the standard of his time, sometimes resorted to stimulants to overcome bashfulness or depression of spirits.

In the single word 'buried', Steele has compressed an entire psychology. Stephen goes on:

> The charm of his conversation when once the ice was broken is attested by observers less partial than Steele. Swift, who never mentions him without praise, declares that, often as they spent their evenings together, they never wished for a third person. Lady Mary Wortley Montagu declared that Addison was the best company in the world...and even Pope admitted the unequalled charm of his conversation.[24]

It does not appear -- to answer Dobrée -- that the man who conversed so readily with Swift, Steele, Pope and Lady Mary Wortley was obsessed by insecurity: these would seem between them to have furnished at least one intellectual equal. What remains of his argument is that Addison indeed suffered from inhibition; but in this array of witnesses we have evidence scarcely to be questioned that it was the prison, and not the habitat, of the natural man. And there seems at least a *prima facie* case that its bars were forged in the deanery.

But the most extraordinary feature of that establishment has not yet been touched upon. Dean Addison was a lifelong royalist who, as a student under the Commonwealth, had 'lampooned the heads of the University, and was forced to ask pardon on his bended knees'.[25] Nor did this evangelist of charity and forbearance leave satire behind with his student days. Being rewarded at the Restoration with a chaplaincy in Tangier, his researches into local history were shaped into a narrative in which the pursuit of ecclesiastical power was lashed with the relish of a Gibbon, and with a wealth of circumstance that could not but recall to his readers the more intolerable manifestations of puritan rule. The ultimate consequence, as he described it, of 'high contemplative looks, deep sighs, tragical gestures, and other passionate interjections of holiness' was 'an armed hypocrisy'. And that the emotions of his earlier years were not recollected in tranquillity is evident from that fact that, when the revolution came, he opposed the sovereignty of William with so much vehemence that he lost, it was said, his prospects of a bishopric.[26]

One cannot but wonder whether the contrasts so obvious to us can have been lost upon a thoughtful member of his household. For the hater of hypocrisy had set up a system in which feelings must always come out in inverted form; the rebel against repression had set up a perfect regiment of the saints; and the unreconstructed royalist was lord protector of a functioning commonwealth.

Joseph Addison left no direct evidence of the feelings his upbringing may have prompted in him. Indirect evidence, however, does exist: it takes the form of a pair of anecdotes, each of which has a respectable provenance. Reference for the first is given to a 'tradition in the town where he was born', at a time when his contemporaries there would still have been alive. It is that, as a child, he 'ran away from his father's house and fled into the fields, where he lived upon fruits, and took up his lodging in a hollow tree': a tale which, while it may contain elements of romance, points to some profound mistrust in the young Addison of his family.[27] For the second, the source is Johnson, who went to the same school, and who is at pains to specify his informants. He was told that a rebellion there by the boys, where they 'barred the doors, and bade their master defiance from the windows', had been 'planned and conducted by Addison'.[28] It seems not unlikely that the Addison I have drawn above, forced into increasingly irksome conformity at home, should in the more robust surroundings of school have broken out -- surprising, it may be, even himself -- in an unmistakable rejection of authority.

We have, then, two pieces of information, each of which is consistent with the other, and both with the negative reading I have proposed of the fulsome narration of Steele. The black box exists: it is hidden within that grim and conventional item of furniture, the Victorian Addison. Certain panels in it fail to match; and when pressure is placed upon them, they open to disclose the most significant element of his character. For, in the year in which the Dean of Lichfield forfeited preferment by his opposition to the Prince of Orange, Joseph Addison hailed William as hero, deliverer and king.

## iv

'THE Revolution', records Macaulay,

> had just taken place; and nowhere had it been hailed with more delight than at Magdalen College. That great and opulent corporation had been treated by James, and by his Chancellor, with an insolence and injustice which, even in such a Prince and in such a Minister, may justly excite amazement, and which had done more than even the prosecution of the Bishops to alienate the Church of England from the throne. A president, duly elected, had been violently

> expelled from his dwelling: a Papist had been set over the society by a royal mandate: the Fellows who, in conformity with their oaths, had refused to submit to this usurper, had been driven forth from their quiet cloisters and gardens, to die of want or to live on charity. But the day of redress and retribution speedily came. The intruders were ejected: the venerable House was again inhabited by its old inmates: learning flourished under the rule of the wise and virtuous Hough; and with learning was united a mild and liberal spirit too often wanting in the princely colleges of Oxford. In consequence of the troubles through which the society had passed, there had been no valid election of new members during the year 1688. In 1689, therefore, there was twice the ordinary number of vacancies...

And one of these, in consideration of some Latin verses he had written, was given to Addison.[29]

In these verses, he brought the stately pastoral of Vergil to bear upon the English revolution; and when, in the first line, his shepherds meet *inter corylos densas*, we are prepared for the theme of restoration. Their song is an encomium upon those who have saved the land from ruin -- *qui dignabantur Regni fulcire ruinas* -- and who, in the end, are called upon by name:

> *Ipse Tuas, Gulielme, canam laudesque Mariae.*

And as Vergil, in the beautiful language of the ninth Eclogue, had placed Caesar's star above the older constellations --

> *Ecce Dionaei processit Caesaris astrum*

-- so Addison performs a similar service for William and Mary: he is the sun, she the moon:

> *Primus hic Imperio, nulli est Virtute secundus,*
> *Sic Sol, quam stellae, majori luce refulget.*
> *Sed qualis stellas micat inter luna minores,*
> *Talis, cum cincta est Sociis, Regina videtur.*

Inflated as these images may seem, at this distance from baroque apotheosis, there is every reason to believe their underlying feeling sincere; and, in the years that followed, Addison continued to paint William in heroic pose. In a further excursion into pastoral, James was declared guilty of that *mens laeva* of which

Vergil's shepherd had accused himself, and barred from his flock by a *non revocabilis ordo*; while a vernacular eulogy of the Dutch king declared that

> The Race of *NASSAUS* was by heav'n design'd
> To curb the proud Oppressors of mankind.[30]

One cannot but wonder at the reaction of the Dean of Lichfield as his son continued to stoke the bonfires of the opposite camp. 'For the period for which records are preserved', writes Smithers, 'Joseph was a regular resident' of his college 'even in summer time'. This failure to revisit his home suggests a coolness at the very least. Certainly the dean took the eclipse of his fortunes very badly; and it cannot have improved his temper to have set over him men associated with his son's apostasy. First Lloyd, 'one of the seven prelates put upon trial by King James II', and then Hough, who as President of Magdalen had resisted the king, was named Bishop of Lichfield; and a series of quarrels erupted between them and the dean which lasted for the rest of his life.[31] Addison afterwards wrote to Hough of his regret that his father had been 'so unhappy as to do some things, a little before he died, which were not agreeable to your Lordship'. However, he went on, 'in a Letter, not long before his death, he commanded me to preserve always a just sense of duty and gratitude for the Bishop of Lichfield, who had been so great a Benefactor to his family in general, and myself in particular'. That this was not written in bitter irony is evident from Addison's quiet remark that the advice was given 'at a time when men seldom disguise their sentiments';[32] while the reference to his 'family in general' no doubt alludes to the benefice which Hough had added to the elder Addison's deanery:[33] a gift, it may be, that called forth a corresponding generosity of spirit in its recipient. The evidence, then, for the relations between father and son suggests estrangement followed by reconciliation. But in politics, each remained immutable: as the elder Addison was steadfast in the royalism of his youth, the younger never deviated from the liberty of the revolution.

'Liberty' was a word which was then on the turn; but it still largely clung to its medieval connotation: of 'privilege held by grant or prescription'. The 'freeholder on the land', writes Ogg, 'and the freeman in the town were, each in his sphere, the accredited elements in society'.[34] It was this that was at issue in the resistance of Magdalen, as Macaulay reveals:

> The President defended his rights with skill, temper, and resolution. He professed great respect for the royal authority. But he steadily maintained that he had by the laws of England a freehold interest in the house and revenues annexed to the presidency.

And what was true of the Oxford college was true of the country as a whole:

> There was no prebendary, no rector, no vicar, whose mind was not haunted by the thought that, however quiet his temper, however obscure his situation, he might, in a few months, be driven from his dwelling by an arbitrary edict to beg in a ragged cassock with his wife and children, while his freehold, secured to him by laws of immemorial antiquity and by the royal word, was occupied by some apostate.[35]

It was by the resistance of such men, Tories by interest and inclination, that the revolution was set in motion. But its momentum was to work to the advantage of the Whigs. Those who had voted, writes J.R. Jones, for the exclusion of James from the throne 'were not going to be worried now by fears that the monarchy would become an elective institution, or by deviating from the strict line of hereditary succession'. The Tories, by contrast, were plunged into 'ideological difficulties' by the 'element of resistance involved in the Revolution, and the principles of the Settlement' of the crown upon William and Mary. It was the latter that turned resistance into revolution. The Declaration of Rights, while intended 'primarily to restore and perpetuate liberties...that were unquestionably assumed to belong to the nation', in effect 'subordinated the royal prerogative to the common law'. The suspending power of the monarchy was abolished, its prerogative courts declared illegal; martial law and the collection of revenue were subjected to the control of Parliament; and it was laid down that the election of this should be free.

All of this dovetailed into the ideology of the Whigs. 'Basic Whig principles', states Jones, 'justified resistance to a tyrant. Belief in the contractual basis of authority entitled them to remove an unjust ruler who disregarded the law'. Pamphlets of the time contended that 'both the exercise of authority and the duty of obedience were conditional since men were free–born and had instituted government for their own purposes'.[36]

These ideas received classic elaboration at the hands of Locke. In the first of his *Two Treatises of Government*, he challenged the pedigree of monarchy in parental authority, and in the second he held that authority to be no more than a 'temporary Government' necessitated by the 'imperfect state of Childhood'.[37] In the events of 1688, therefore, there was implicit a psychological no less than a political revolution. But it scarcely needed a Locke to expound this to Addison.

The young scholar's invocations of William can have had little effect upon that monarch: for, as Johnson sardonically observes, 'his study was only war'. However, he continues, 'by a choice of ministers, whose disposition was very different from his own, he procured without intention a very liberal patronage to poetry'.[38] Amongst these was Somers, who had served as counsel for the bishops tried by James, and Montague, who helped found the Bank of England to finance William's wars. Having attracted the attention of both, Addison received a grant from the Treasury: he was to travel abroad, and prepare himself for public office.[39]

## V

NOTHING that Addison wrote upon his travels, remarked an early biographer, could not just as well have been written at home, with the single exception of the description of San Marino.[40] But there is a sense in which it might be said that nothing was more emphatically written at home: that Addison's account of the mountain republic was the focal point of a pre–existing pattern.

Everything that he saw on the continent, he saw as a convinced Whig should.

Everywhere, Smithers remarks, 'the Protestant Establishment, the Revolution Settlement, and Whig economics were confirmed by observing their opposites'.[41] Italy, as the heartland of Catholicism, evoked such reflections as might have been expected from the supporter of a revolution that found the despotism of James indistinguishable from his religion, resolving it to be 'inconsistent with the safety...of this Protestant kingdom to be governed by a Popish Prince'.[42] Whig feelings, by contrast, found a peculiar satisfaction in the 'petty Republick' of San Marino, which 'has now lasted thirteen hundred years, while all the other States of *Italy* have several times changed their masters and forms of government'. Here might be encountered 'an Idea of *Venice* in its first beginnings, when it had only a few heaps of earth for its dominions, or of *Rome* it self, when it had as yet covered but one of its seven hills'. Its ultimate significance, however, lay in its contrast with the Papal States:

> Nothing indeed can be a greater instance of the natural love that mankind has for liberty, and of their aversion to an arbitrary government, than such a savage mountain covered with people, and the *Campania* of *Rome*, which lyes in the same country, almost destitute of inhabitants.[43]

Here Addison spoke in the voice of Whig theory. For Locke, 'all Men are naturally in...a *State of perfect Freedom*'; and the Williamite revolution had been an assertion of 'Natural Rights'.[44] For Addison, then, this propensity of human nature leapt out at San Marino over all the disadvantages of a 'savage mountain'. But another, and opposite, train of thought had begun to work in him, whereby the savagery of the mountain was to be be seen, not as an obstacle that liberty might overcome, but as its analogue and its visible sign. It was as if his early flight from a repressive household to the woods had established in him an identity, as yet inarticulate, between nature and freedom. It had been adumbrated in France, where, amongst Louis' gardens, he found himself

> so singular as to prefer Fontaine–bleau to all the rest. It is situated among rocks and woods that give you a fine varietie of Savage prospects. The King has Humourd the Genius of the place and only made use of so much Art as is

> necessary to Help and regulate Nature without reforming her too much...For my part I think there is something more charming in these rude heaps of Stone than in so many Statues and woud as soon see a River winding through Woods & Meadows as it dos near Fontaine-bleau than as when it is toss'd up in such a Variety of figures at Versailles.[45]

This contrast was defined with still greater emphasis when, on leaving San Marino, Addison stood before the great waterfall at Terni:

> It is impossible to see the bottom on which it breaks for the thickness of the mist that rises from it, which looks at a distance like clouds of smoak ascending from some vast furnace, and distils in perpetual rains on all the places that lye near it.

'I think', was his conclusion,

> there is something more astonishing in this *Cascade*, than in all the water-works of *Versailles*.[46]

Gradually, in the course of Addison's travels, a formula had been gathering force. It was this: as tyranny is to artifice, so is liberty to nature. And now he was ready to propose its corollary: if artifice was the fitting expression of continental despotism, nature was that of English liberty. In a poem of farewell to Italy, he wrote that, for all its native abundance, that land lay under a curse

> While proud Oppression in her vallys reigns,
> And Tyrannie devours her fruitfull plains.

His own country, by contrast, had been transfigured by its revolution:

> Tis Liberty that crowns Britannia's Isle,
> And makes her barren Rocks, and her bleak mountains smile.[47]

One does not think of Britain as predominantly barren or bleak: what has happened here, evidently, is that the sight of the Alps, in the transit of which the poem was composed,[48] has reawakened in Addison the memory of San Marino, which he has superimposed over the image of his own country. Britain, as the land of liberty, is accordingly seen as a wild landscape.

But at this point his reflections were interrupted. William died; Anne succeeded; the new queen favoured the Tories; and Addison's patrons fell from power.[49]

## vi

THE red columns wound southward, down the narrowing gorges of the Rhine; then, crossing the watershed, wheeled into the valley of the Danube. Here, on a vast stubble-field between the river and the forested hills, Marlborough met the French at a village called Blindheim: a name which, Trevelyan remarks, they were to earn the right to mispronounce.[50]

Marlborough commanded Queen Anne's armies as the result of an intense personal attachment. Anne, heavy, dull and taciturn, passed her existence in a state of tedium relieved by cards; while her husband, a silent kindly prince, liked to stand at the window, glass in hand, and look down at the passers-by. George was a being of her own kind; but there was another side to her nature, which was represented by Sarah. Sarah, so glowing, so definite, was a creature from another world: herself, perhaps, in a more favourable incarnation; and she poured herself out to her in the unfaltering accents of love. Sarah was not to dream of leaving her; she would drive to Jerusalem for a sight of her; she desired to possess her wholly. Sarah responded with calm friendship, and allowed herself to be worshipped.[51]

As she was, too, by her husband. John Churchill was the son of Winston Churchill: a soldier of sorts, a political reactionary, a family snob, a dabbler in history, and a lover of windy rhetoric. In the civil war Winston lost so heavily on the royalist side that he was obliged to take shelter with an imperious, grasping, parliamentarian mother-in-law; and it was here, it has been surmised, in a school of daily dependence and humiliation, that John Churchill learned the rudiments of his obsessive thrift, his smiling reserve -- and perhaps, too, his instinct for influential women. At the Restoration, Winston had his family arms augmented, and his daughter accepted at court, where she was speedily seduced by the king's brother. Tradition has it that a fall from a horse left her in such dishevellment as to inflame even the torpid imagination of James; certainly she became his mistress, and it was as James' favoured lieutenant that John Churchill rose to military command and a peerage. With the help of one of the king's mistresses, meanwhile, he laid the foundations of his fortune; and the story was told that Charles, walking in on the pair, offered young Churchill the ignominious forgiveness of knowing that he did it for money. Prudence, certainly, was a factor in his later successes: while his officers might complain of the barrenness of his table, his men were fed, clothed and paid with a punctiliousness then unusual, and repaid him in turn with their devotion. He rejected, moreover, the heiress that Winston had discovered for him, choosing instead relative poverty with Sarah. She did not make it easy for him. One of her portraits shows her clutching her severed blond hair: she had cropped it in a fit of pique, knowing how he admired it. She is barbarous, he tells her waiting-woman: she treats him like a footman; and 'yet', he cannot resist adding, 'I do love her with all my soul'. Her answer is unbending: 'If I had as little love as yourself, I have been told enough of you' -- a stab, no doubt, at the matter of the royal mistress -- 'to make me hate you, and then I believe' -- the hidden admission -- 'I should have been more happy than I am like to be now'.[52]

When William landed at Torbay, Churchill rode out from James' camp, followed by Prince George, while Princess Anne escaped from Whitehall in the company of Sarah: desertions which exacerbated the demoralisation in which James turned and fled.[53] She was not, however, to prosper under William. For it is one of the great ironies of history that the English revolution was carried out through the medium of a man who resented the restrictions that it placed upon him.[54] Temple had detected this tendency at an early age, recommending to him as a motto *potius inservire patriae liberae quam dominari servienti*.[55] He was now, it was remarked, stadtholder in England and king in Holland;[56] and at his palace at Het Loo, parterre followed patterned parterre, and fountain followed fountain, through a grandiose layout which underlined his monarchical status.[57] William was obsessed by rivalry: once for de Witt, always for Louis,[58] now for Anne, who had abdicated a prior claim on the throne in his favour, but was still next in succession to himself and Mary. Anne was repeatedly slighted, as was the inoffensive Prince George; and the Churchills shared their disgrace.

Then Mary died. Chattering and extravert, temperamentally alien to Anne, she had been a faithful minion to William in his persecution of her. Now, however, Anne was heiress apparent; she represented William's tie to legitimacy; and the lesser rivalry was swallowed up in the greater.[59]

When William's eagle nose and disappointed eyes were replaced on the coinage by the stately chins and downturned mouth of Queen Anne, there were few regrets. Her declaration to parliament that her heart was wholly English was met with a hum of applause; and in the gardens at Kensington the boxwood associated with the Dutch king was rooted out.[60] It was less simple, however, to make away with William's wars.

The English and Dutch had not at first felt threatened when the last of the Spanish Hapsburg bequeathed his empire to Louis' grandson. Had Louis at this juncture behaved with moderation, he would have listened to his best advisors; but he would not have been what he was. Instead, he declared his grandson eligible for the French crown, sent French troops into the Spanish Netherlands, and on the death of James, had his son proclaimed King of England. The Hapsburg emperor, excluded from the Spanish inheritance, was his chief continental opponent; Louis, accordingly, determined to take Vienna, place the Elector of Bavaria on the imperial throne, and then, with the greater part of Europe under his control, impose terms on the Dutch and deal with the English at leisure.[61] And so John Churchill, now Duke of Marlborough by the grace of Queen Anne, found himself at Blenheim.

In the army opposite, the command was divided. The French and Bavarians were drawn up separately, each in the classic formation of foot-soldiers in the middle and horsemen on the wings, so that the actual centre was weak in the staying-power of infantry.

All day long, the cannon roared; charges and countercharges induced exhaustion. Then, at five o'clock, Marlborough was ready. The French cavalry advanced; halted, as was customary, to discharge their pistols, and retired in disarray. Marlborough had forbidden his horsemen the use of firearms: their advantage was impetus. They advanced, with drawn swords, at a steady trot, increasing gradually in momentum, met, held, bent and broke the weakened centre of the enemy line. To the right, the Bavarians were held against the hills; to the left, the French cavalry pressed against the steep bank of the Danube. Men and horses hung, scrabbling and kicking, a moment, then fell into the morass that bordered the river. Their infantry, encircled, surrendered. *Oh*, cried the captured officers, *oh que dira le Roy!*

'If the battle of Blenheim', writes Trevelyan, 'had been won by Louis, no Voltaire could have made his system look ridiculous, no Rousseau could have made it seem irrational'. The French general was captured; and, over the years in England that followed, had the leisure to lay out a garden, in which the royal sunflower was inscribed in sand and brickdust and coal.[62]

## vii

QUEEN Anne received the news at Windsor, in a note pencilled on the field by Marlborough.[63] Her government needed a celebrant; and the chancellor of the exchequer climbed the three flights of stairs that led to Addison's garret. He had known financial anxiety, if not actual want, since his return to England; but again, as at the revolution, he was favoured by the course of events. The poem that resulted, *The Campaign*, was a triumph of journalism, in which he compared Marlborough's onslaught to the great storm of the previous year; and it was rewarded, appropriately, with a sinecure made vacant by the death of Locke.[64]

The Whigs floated back into office on the tide of the logic of the war. War enriched the financiers who leaned towards Whiggery, while it was paid for by a tax on the landed who tended towards Toryism; and the efforts of the more extreme Tories to block funds for it obliged Anne to turn to the Whigs. Addison was named undersecretary of state, then secretary to the Lord Lieutenant of Ireland: in effect becoming secretary of state for that country.[65]

The French court, meanwhile, had sneered itself back into confidence. Blenheim had been the result of chance; a second battle would certainly reverse its verdict. Louis' army, accordingly, positioned itself at Ramillies, in the Spanish Netherlands, on a plateau clothed in young corn and intersected by streams. One of these ran through a ravine, covering the French left; and it was here, against all expectation, that Marlborough attacked. As his men, under a heavy cannonade, slipped down the ravine, crossed the stream, and ascended the other side, the French, dismayed by their ferocity, gave way; and their general brought them large reinforcements from his more vulnerable right. Here Marlborough concentrated his forces, and the French broke and fled. Their confidence had been illusory: from the moment of Blenheim, wrote Napoleon's historian, *Malbrouck* had become a name of terror which 'the passage of a century has not effaced'.[66]

Louis, now desperate for peace, resolved to stake everything on the issue of a final battle. But when Marlborough began to cross the river beneath the towers and pinnacles of Oudenarde, the French command was divided as to whether to hold the hills above, or halt him in his advance. As they made their delayed descent, Marlborough flung his regiments forward in masterly improvisation, pressing them back from hedge to hedge, across fields and orchards and rows of poplars, while the sun went down.[67]

Versailles had always lacked water. Tens of thousands of soldiers laboured on a gigantic aqueduct; but these were withdrawn to be sent into the field, and it was never completed. The fountains played only at intervals; while the palace had dimmed, as its silver furniture was melted down to meet the cost of the war.[68] Versailles, arid and in eclipse, seemed a pointed image of broken empire; and Louis himself more Phaëthon than Apollo. He no longer even pretended to impose conditions: he was ready, he stated, to accept what his enemies should propose. But what they demanded -- that he compel his grandson to surrender the crown of Spain -- he could not give: the Bourbon prince had identified himself with his people, and they with him. And so the campaign went on to Malplaquet.

The French had now gone beyond despair to desperation. A half-starved army, working feverishly to block the way to Paris, linked streams, canals and marshes in a palisade of earthworks and felled trees. And when, combining a frontal with a flank assault, Marlborough forced his way through the woods of Malpalquet, the French, though pushed back, did not break. The road to Paris was still closed; and the cost had been immense. Now even Marlborough's men felt their lives were wasted, while in England the sense of futility had become pervasive. The tide had begun to turn against the Whigs; and the assault on them was launched to the slogan, 'unending, deafening', of 'High Church and Sacheverell'.[69]

## viii

HENRY SACHEVERELL, according to tradition, was Addison's room-mate at Oxford; certainly he is the 'dearest Harry' of a poem composed there.[70] Thereafter, however, their paths diverged, Sacheverell feeling obliged to hang out, as he put it, the 'bloody flag of defiance' against the 'damning Schism' represented by Protestant dissent. In this he struck a deep vein of national sentiment. Zeal for the Church of England, writes Trevelyan, was fed by 'two negative passions, anti–

Popery and anti–Puritanism', each based on 'bitter experience of the past and consequent fear for the future':

> The fires of Smithfield were the most living part of English historical tradit–ion...revived and strengthened by the recent action of James II in overthrowing the laws of the land in order to re–establish a Roman Catholic despotism in England, and by the renewal of an unprovoked, cruel and wholesale persecution of the Huguenots in France.

And fear of Rome was answered, at the other pole, by fear of Geneva:

> The overthrow of the Church and the aristocracy, the beheading of the King, and the rigid rule of the Saints had left a negative impression almost as formid–able and permanent...Animosity against the quiet business men who attended Nonconformist chapels was fostered on the ground that they were one and all 'fanatics', about to draw the sword and again destroy the Church...The Dissenters might seem humble and harmless burghers, but they were in alliance with the powerful and dangerous Whig lords.[71]

When Sacheverell, therefore, in an inflammatory sermon, denounced the government for its alleged betrayal of the church, he was indeed impeached and found guilty; but the sentence was a nominal one, and London meanwhile erupted into flame. Dissenters' chapels were wrecked, and their furnishings heaped up in pyres, round which the rioters rotated in ritual dance.[72] The scene was shortly echoed in the dismantlement of the ministry; and Addison found himself out of office once more.[73]

His feelings were expressed in an allegory in which he saw Britain as beset by two 'formidable Enemies'. When he identified one of these as Licentiousness, followed by Clamour, Confusion, Impudence, and Rapine, he reflected on what had already come to pass. But when he named the other as Tyranny, with its following of Barbarity, Ignorance and Persecution, he spoke to prospective fears. The 'bloody Flag' held up by Persecution, while it evidently referred to his erstwhile friend, happened also to be embroidered with 'Flower–de–Luces'. It was the belief of the Whigs that the now–Tory government would attempt to instal James' son, the client of France, as successor to Anne: a suspicion since confirmed by the papers of the French Foreign Office.[74]

For the trial of Addison's fellow-student had been, in effect, a trial of the revolution. Sacheverell, with provocative symbolism, had preached his sermon on the fifth of November, 'a day doubly sacred to the Whigs: as the day of Gunpowder Treason, and as the glorious day on which William of Orange had landed at Torbay'.[75] And that sermon had been an attack, not only on the government, but on the revolution.[76] The fundamental issue, therefore, in his impeachment was 'whether the British monarchy was based on hereditary or parliamentary right'; and on this point his conviction portended the ultimate victory of his enemies:

> The Whigs, united in their interpretation of the Glorious Revolution, argued that James II had broken his fundamental contract with the English people; resistance to his illegal acts, therefore, had been justified, and William and Mary owed their title, as did Queen Anne, to a decision of Parliament.[77]

In Addison's allegory, then, thrown up by turbulence and apprehension, there was a permanent element, and a prophetic one. Here, as in his poem on Italy, Britain was represented as a landscape transfigured by its values:

> There was a greater Variety of Colours in the Embroidery of the Meadows, a more lively Green in the Leaves and Grass, a brighter Chrystal in the Streams, than what I ever met with in any other Region. The Light it self had something more shining and glorious in it than that of which the Day is made in other Places. I was wonderfully astonished at the Discovery of such a Paradise amidst the Wildness of those cold, hoary Landskips which lay about it; but found at length, that this happy Region was inhabited by the Goddess of *Liberty*; whose Presence softened the Rigours of the Climate, enriched the Barrenness of the Soil, and more than supplied the Absence of the Sun.

This time, however, a further element is added:

> The Place was covered with a wonderful Profusion of Flowers, that without being disposed into regular Borders and Parterres, grew promiscuously, and had a greater Beauty in their natural Luxuriancy and Disorder, than they could have received from the Checks and Restraints of Art.[78]

The parallel of nature and liberty is now complete: it has been carried from the mountain landscape to the heart of the garden. It remained only to advocate it in practice; and this, too, would be the work of Addison. It would arise, as all the rest had done, out of his deepest needs, and in obedience to his inevitable impulses.

## ix

THE friendship of Addison and Steele was an attraction of opposites: Addison pale, English and reserved, Steele dark, Irish and ebullient. Addison followed a steady upward movement, like a barge through a series of locks on a canal; Steele shot the rapids of immediate experience. They had met in the hallways of Charterhouse, and gone on to the no less monastic purlieus of Oxford; but while Addison settled into his fellowship, Steele hankered after fellowship of another kind. When the trumpet rang out over the quiet cloister, Addison, one imagines, shut the window; but Steele exchanged his student's gown for the splendid uniform -- scarlet coat richly laced, white-plumed hat, jackboots and great sword -- of the Life Guard. The usual occupations of the military life followed: duty, a duel, a lover, a child; but Steele, in the midst of all this, somehow managed to compose what has been described as a 'serious manual of piety', *The Christian Hero*. This may not have made him the most popular officer in the mess; but it does seem to have made him the most amusing. The 'least levity' in him, he recalled, after the publication of this effort, was liable to call up some ironic reference to the *christian hero*. But he could scarcely complain: he had printed the tract, he confesses, under his own name, 'in hopes that a standing testimony against himself...might curb his desires'.[79]

Steele, then, was in sore need of inhibitions; Addison's problem was quite the opposite. And yet the attraction of opposites, one must presume, takes place within a framework of similarity. Both were Whigs and both were writers; and when the Whigs began their ascent under Anne, Steele was promoted editor of the official *Gazette*. His immediate impulse, to breathe life into its fusty mannerisms, drew down upon him a concerted howl of bureaucratic execration. The post, however, was a lucrative one; Steele's extravagance did not allow him to disdain ready cash; and so, in the years that followed, he was compelled to stumble where he wished to soar, and to stutter where he wished to sing. And it was this, it is scarcely possible to doubt, which was the origin of his most successful enterprise.[80]

At first sight, it must have seemed another of those madcap schemes which was to provide him with overnight solvency: like the alchemical experiment in which his money and his credit alike went up in smoke; like the unauthorised lottery over which the government brought him to heel pretty quick; like the project to build boats into which seawater might enter, and fish be carried 'alive, and in good Health', to the tables of London.[81] This time his commodity was himself: the English public was to be treated to his inexhaustible gift of the gab, heavily laced with his pipedreams of piety; and he called the project, with his usual unpretending effrontery, the *Tatler*.

Incredibly, it worked. Or perhaps it was not so incredible after all. For nothing that was human was alien to Steele. He understood the delicious prickings of sin and the profound comfort of repentance. He could be rake and reformer by turns, or the two at once. There was only one sensation he could not endure, and that was the absence of sensation. He suffered from an acute *horror vacui*; and in this sense the *Gazette* can be said to have stood midwife to the *Tatler*.

Addison was quickly pressed into service; and turned the paper, said Steele, into 'a greater thing than I intended': in the words of Beljame, 'made a clearance of the undergrowth and brought air and light to the saplings'. Here, in the form of the essay, Addison discovered his *métier*; and, to the spreading sails of Steele's imagination, lent gravity and balance. But it was inevitable that, with Steele at the helm, a course should sooner or later be steered for the rocks. This happened when, against all reasonable advice, he involved the paper in politics. Addison, accordingly, introduced its successor with the resolution to 'observe an exact Neutrality between the Whigs and Tories'. And the title of the new paper suggested, not only a greater restraint, but a shift in the balance of the partnership. If the *Tatler* was the work of Steele and Addison, the *Spectator* was the work of Addison and Steele.[82] But while the voice was the voice of Addison, the face was the face of Steele. In one of his *Spectator* essays, Addison sees his face in a glass, and is 'startled at the Shortness of it'.[83] This was Steele, as observed by an unfriendly critic: 'a short chin, a short nose, a short forehead' -- in short, 'the picture of somebody over a farmer's chimney'.[84] Yet it was this unprepossessing countenance which was both to filter and to free the spirit of Addison. It was his persona, in the most literal meaning of that word: not only a mask which provided anonymity, but one so fashioned as to enable his voice to resound, *personare*. And this Steele understood very well. Speaking long afterwards of Addison's 'superior Qualities', he observed that his 'Modesty would never have admitted 'em to come into Daylight, but under such a Shelter'.[85]

Here was the conveyance for a form of life both fleeting and fragile; here was the lottery that brought an unimaginable prize; here was the triumphant alchemical success. It was through the catalytic agency of Steele -- that improbable middleman, that mercurial impresario, that mad priest of the imagination -- that Addison was enabled, at last, to achieve an intimacy with his audience formerly possible only in the circle of his closest friends. His essays at their best, wrote Virginia Woolf, 'preserve the very cadence of easy yet exquisitely modulated conversation...bright, new, various, with the utmost spontaneity'.[86] 'The man and the author in him', declares Beljame, 'are one'.[87]

## X

NOT in general the most astute of biographers, Courthope has yet given a most eloquent account of the landscape that Addison escaped into if indeed he engaged on that early flight from his parents' home:

> No one who has travelled on a summer's day across Salisbury Plain, with its vast canopy of sky and its open tracts of undulating downland, relieved by no shadows except such as are thrown by the passing cloud, the grazing sheep, and the great circle of Stonehenge, will forget the delightful sense of refreshment and repose produced by the descent into the valley of the Avon. The sounds of human life rising from the villages after the long solitude of the plain, the shade of the deep woods, the coolness of the river, like all streams rising in the chalk, clear and peaceful, are equally delicious to the sense and the imaginat–ion.[88]

However hypothetical it may be that Addison enjoyed this sense of breadth and quiet in the vast reaches of the plain, a pattern is discernible in his writings whereby the open world of nature is set in opposition to a closed field in which artifice, and the repression of spontaneous feeling, prevail. It is in this spirit, and with a peculiar intimacy of feeling, that Addison commends the 'old Ballad of the *Two Children in the Wood*, which is one of the Darling Songs of the Common People'. It pleases, he asserts,

> for no other Reason, but because it is a Copy of Nature...The Condition, Speech, and Behaviour of the dying Parents, with the Age, Innocence and Distress of the Children, are set forth in such tender Circumstances, that it is impossible for a Reader of common Humanity not to be affected with them.

'Nature', then, is natural feeling. For though

> the Author of it (whoever he was) has delivered it in such an abject Phrase, and poorness of Expression, that the quoting any Part of it would look like a Design of turning it into Ridicule...the Thoughts...from one end to the other are natural; and therefore cannot fail to please those who are not Judges of Language, or those who notwithstanding they are Judges of Language, have a true and unpre–judiced Taste of Nature.

That Addison is moved by the tale is very obvious. At the same time he is apologetic about its deficiencies -- or rather solicitous, lest these be made a pretext for dismissal of the whole. And this he will not have: for his peculiar discovery is the power inherent in those 'Songs of the Common People' which

> because the Sentiments appear genuine and unaffected...are able to move the Mind of the most polite Reader with inward Meltings of Humanity and Compassion.

On this level, of feeling as opposed to form, there is nothing to choose between the 'abject' popular ballad and the most accomplished of classical verse:

> As for the Circumstance of the *Robin-red-breast*, it is indeed a little Poetical Ornament; and to shew the Genius of the Author amidst all his Simplicity, it is just the same kind of Fiction which one of the greatest of the *Latin* Poets has made use of upon a Parallel Occasion; I mean that Passage in *Horace*, where he describes himself when he was a Child, fallen asleep in a Desart Wood, and covered with Leaves by the Turtles that took pity on him.
>
> *Me fabulosae Vulture in Appulo*
> *Altricis extra limen Apuliae*
> *Ludo fatigatumque somno*
> *Fronde novâ puerum palumbes*
> *Texere...*[89]

Here is confirmation of the essential, psychological truth of the tale of the hollow tree. The citation, in an English context of orphanism and abandonment, of the Roman poet's protection by natural forces, is a convergence that powerfully illuminates Addison's inner experience. The retreat to the woodland stands for reversion to that primitive level of being which is also the locus of growth,[90] of the 'dark, hidden, near-impenetrable world of our unconscious',[91] the 'place of unconventional inner life',[92] which brings the rescue of those instincts that transcend 'conscious rationality and sensible rules',[93] and that, in the older tales, are commonly represented under the guise of animals, among which birds 'symbolise the higher aspirations'. 'Being lost in a forest', writes Bettelheim, citing the *Divina Commedia*, 'is an ancient symbol for the need to find oneself'.[94] Nature, then, for Addison, is human nature, imprisoned or unrealised. 'This Song', he writes of his woodland ballad, 'is a plain simple Copy of Nature, destitute of all the Helps and Ornaments of Art'.[95]

It was the distinction he had noted between Terni and Versailles, now applied to 'genuine and unaffected' feeling. So he had moved, through a series of interacting inner and outer landscapes, travelling all the while within himself. And, as his own liberation had been enacted in terms of landscape, he was in turn to free all nature, through the landscape garden, from its toils. 'I would rather', he was to write,

> look upon a Tree in all its Luxuriancy and Diffusion of Boughs and Branches, than when it is...cut and trimmed into a Mathematical Figure; and cannot but fancy that an Orchard in Flower looks infinitely more delightful, than all the little Labyrinths of the most finished Parterre.[96]

## xi

PORTRAITS of the Countess of Warwick reveal 'rather large eyes set far apart in her rounded face, a classic Greek nose, and a smallish, pretty mouth'; while her future husband, with his 'blond complexion, his blue-grey eyes, his classic features, and slender figure...was a handsome young man'. Amongst Addison's other advantages, we are told, was the fact that he had never 'wounded a hackney coachman, or killed his opponent in a duel'; and, bizarre as these qualifications may seem, they no doubt weighed with the countess: for her former husband had done both of these things: was indeed 'one of the wildest rakes in all England', whose early death has been blamed on his dissipation.

A curious sidelight on Addison's character, as conventionally interpreted, is that he apparently took the countess away from his patron Montagu:[97] yet another indication that he was neither so colourless nor so timid as has been supposed. It was over a decade, however, before the marriage took place; and amongst the causes assigned for the delay is, understandably, the countess' previous experience.[98] Other factors very probably contributed. It is suggested that Addison in his early years was not in a position to offer financial security;[99] and this receives indirect confirmation from a fable, otherwise meaningless, in the *Spectator*.

The setting is the era of ludicrous longevity before the flood. Hilpa's first husband had come to an untimely end 'in the 250th Year of his Age'. Shalum makes his addresses after her decade of mourning is at an end, and to such good effect that she answers him in 'less than a Twelvemonth'. She suffers scruples, however, on two accounts: first, that Shalum is 'secretly enamour'd' of her wealth; and second, that she may disrupt the quiet in which he lives. But Shalum's prosperity so increases through his dealings with Mishpach, a 'mighty Man of old', that his beloved, after a mere twenty years' hesitation, accepts him.[100]

Taken in isolation, the fable appears a pointless, if playful, fantasy; but read as a transposition of its author's personal life, would seem to offer considerable illumination. The countess might well wonder whether the relatively impoverished commoner loved her for her own sake, particularly as her fortune had helped rehabilitate the estate of her first husband;[101] and that Addison was intent upon removing this suspicion would explain his impatience at financial setbacks. She may also have hesitated to remove him from what appears to have been a well–adjusted bachelor existence.[102] The affluent widow, the husband who suffers an untimely demise, the impoverished suitor, the older and more powerful rival, all suggest the outline of Addison's own courtship; and, if Mishpach is Montagu, it was indeed through his dealings with him that he was in the end enabled to treat with the countess as an equal.[103] If this is so, and we have here the secret history of Addison's wooing, the exaggeration of its exasperations to antediluvian dimensions, with the promise of the beloved to return him an answer in 'less than fifty Years',[104] will have had a real, if wryly put, emotional meaning for him.

The factual ending coincided with that of the fable. Queen Anne died; King George succeeded; the Whigs returned to power; and Addison married his countess.[105]

## xii

IN a corner of the deerpark that lies behind Magdalen College, where the sound of the street is muted as to the hum of some distant shore, stands the gateway that once formed the entrance to Addison's garden. Here, through the *pietas* of his biographer, it has found an appropriate landfall:[106] here, where his liberation began.

In the iron of the structure are wrought the initials of Addison and his wife. The *A* of Addison intertwines with the *W* of Warwick; the *J* of Joseph overlaps with the *C* of Charlotte. It is a small signal, but a significant one: the cipher of a man who was neither domineering nor insecure; nor who feared, in the end, the equality of the bedchamber. The complacent modern portrayal of Addison, that 'love and anger seem to have been alike outside his range',[107] is thus seen, in combination with his early rebellion, to be false on both counts.

So far, indeed, was Addison from the Victorian stereotype that Victorian Saintsbury was appalled. 'Addison tells us', he protests,

> -- tells us over and over again -- that *all* the ideas and pleasures of the imagination are pleasures of sense, and, what is more, that they are pleasures of one sense -- Sight.

The fact that he 'rigidly excludes everything but Sense' is 'insuperable, irremovable, ruthless': a gesture that his critic finds 'strangely limited in range'.[108] Yet this limitation concentrates; Addison's vision, if narrow in range, is penetrating in depth: predicated upon, but not restricted to, sight. Sight he describes as 'the most perfect...of all our Senses': it 'furnishes the Imagination with its Ideas';[109] and these, insofar as they are pleasurable, 'proceed from the Sight of what is *Great*, *Uncommon*, or *Beautiful*'. The sense of beauty Addison sees as bound up with the instinct of sex -- yet another rude displacement of the Victorian imago -- and he offers a Latin poem of his own composing upon the sexual idiosyncrasies of birds: the blackbird lured by darkness, the nightingale by song, the owl by its own peculiarities of plumage and gaze. The appeal of the uncommon is no less natural, being rooted in curiosity; while that of greatness arises from the fact that the 'Mind of Man naturally hates every thing that looks like a Restraint upon it':[110] a familiar sensation for the Addison, repressed in childhood, whom I have posited here. The overall character, indeed, of Addison's aesthetic is the liberation of natural feeling. By its means, writes Walter Jackson Bate, 'both mind and emotions' are 'completely released from "restraint"'.[111]

'Among the many semantic accretions of the word romanticism', comments Harold March, 'two closely related ideas are the most fertile sources of implications: liberty and the emotions. Liberty covers individualism and rebellion against rules, authority, and tradition; the emotions seem to involve spontaneity, the subconscious, the springs of action and of artistic creation, and other human characteristics that are non–rational'.[112] On these criteria, the romantic movement had now begun.

As a system, concedes Clarence Thorpe, Addison's aesthetic may be open to all sorts of logical objection; but 'viewed as a set of tentative pronouncements charged with dynamic suggestion and exemplifying a method of almost illimitable possibilities of development, it is worthy to be classed as one of the great critical documents of all time'. It is a trusting 'not in reason and learning, but in natural response, in instinct, emotion, imagination, and original genius'.[113] By its means, states J.G. Robertson, Addison 'laid the foundation of the whole romantic aesthetics in England'.[114]

## xiii

IT is in terms of these aesthetics that Addison now reformulates a long–standing preference:

> If we consider the Works of *Nature* and *Art*, as they are qualified to entertain the Imagination, we shall find the last very defective, in Comparison of the former; for though they may sometimes appear as Beautiful or Strange, they can

> have nothing in them of that Vastness and Immensity, which afford so great an Entertainment to the Mind of the Beholder.
>
> When, therefore, we see nature
>
> imitated in any measure, it gives us a nobler and more exalted kind of Pleasure than what we receive from the nicer and more accurate Productions of Art.

It was the preference he had expressed for Terni over Versailles; had superimposed from San Marino over England; and, when this seemed threatened, formulated as the emblematic counterpart to its liberty. But when he completes the process, it is by grafting onto the stock of his own aesthetic the scion of an exotic prototype:

> Writers, who have given us an Account of *China*, tell us, the Inhabitants of that Country laugh at the Plantations of our *Europeans*, which are laid out by the Rule and Line; because, they say, any one may place Trees in equal Rows and uniform Figures. They chuse rather to shew a Genius in Works of this Nature, and therefore always conceal the Art by which they direct themselves. They have a Word, it seems, in their Language, by which they express the particular Beauty of a Plantation that thus strikes the Imagination at first Sight, without discovering what it is that has so agreeable an Effect.

*Sharawadgi*. It has travelled a great distance since Temple retrieved it from the Dutch of Deshima; and that distance is the measure of Addison's personal odyssey. It is as the result of this that he is now ready to advance upon Temple, boldly adopt the Asian prototype, and launch the landscape garden in England:

> Why may not a whole Estate be thrown into a kind of Garden by frequent Plantations, that may turn as much to the Profit, as the Pleasure of the Owner? A Marsh overgrown with Willows, or a Mountain shaded with Oaks, are not only more beautiful, but more beneficial, than when they lie bare and unadorned. Fields of Corn make a pleasant Prospect, and if the Walks were a little taken care of that lie between them, if the natural Embroidery of the Meadows were helpt and improved by some small Additions of Art, and the several Rows of Hedges set off by Trees and Flowers, that the Soil was capable of receiving, a Man might make a pretty Landskip of his own Possessions.[115]

## xiv

FOR Addison, as for Temple, insight outran application. Perhaps more so, indeed: for, unlike Temple, Addison was no gardener.[116] During his spell of comparative unemployment, he had bought an estate at Bilton, in Warwickshire, near the scenes of his early life, and gone about planting it with the antediluvian energy of his Chinese fable, setting a thousand trees as the target for his first year.[117] A series of letters of the following year, however, from the military relative he had put in charge of the place,[118] records the ignominious end of this venture. 'What you planted last year', writes Captain Edward Addison, 'are all dead, a few cherries and apples excepted, the Gardener says they were unscilfuly managed, sett too shallow by a foot, starv'd for water', and had in general suffered 'for want of being look'd after'.[119]

This last was hardly surprising: Addison in the intervening year had been active in pamphleteering and in parliament, on the death of Queen Anne had become secretary to the regency -- in which capacity, it has been observed, he was 'perhaps the busiest man in British public life' -- and was now again responsible for the administration of Ireland.[120] What emerges with equal force, however, from his relative's account is the ineptitude of his attempt at husbandry. 'I'le hint to you', writes the captain tactfully, 'the Gardeners maner of planting, for every tree he digs a hole 4 foot diameter and 2 foot deep, this he fills with fine good Earth, and then plants his tree'. Addison, then, that mighty planter of the imagination, was, it appears, utterly at a loss as to how a tree was to be put down in fact. Accordingly, declares the captain: 'your planting...I Intirely leve to your Gardener'; with mention also of 'your London oporator': presumably a professional nurseryman whose advice Addison had solicited, and who thought, reports his kinsman, 'Indiferently' of his plantations.[121]

The gardens at Bilton were never completed, have not survived, and are not recorded in any detail. What records exist, however, suggest a layout in which straight avenues, lined with hedges of yew, and with forest trees crowding behind, were disposed asymmetrically around a central axis.[122] How much of this limited exercise in irregularity was due to Addison, and how much to his collaborators, remains unknown; but the evidence suggests a compromise. That Addison desired to create an informal landscape appears indisputable: in an essay printed shortly before he purchased his estate, he sketched 'Compositions in Gardening' that ran into the 'beautiful Wildness of Nature, without affecting the nicer Elegancies of Art'.[123] Experience of his own limitations, however, with the increasing demands on his time, seem to have led him to leave the matter to experts, themselves constricted by traditional practices.[124]

The earliest practical ventures in the landscape garden were, in Horace Walpole's phrase, a 'twilight of imperfect essays': the efforts, as Christopher Hussey has observed, of 'author–amateurs and less original professionals';[125] and in retrospect Addison has invited the same ridicule as Temple, from those who, secure in the knowledge of later developments, seem imaginatively incapable of understanding the bewilderment of the innovator, for whom *sharawadgi* was a labyrinth without a magical thread.

## XV

BORGES has a tale of Averroes, puzzling over Aristotle among the cloistered water–gardens of the Guadalquivir, struggling to understand what drama might be without ever having seen a theatre, and deciding in the end that comedies were anathemas and tragedies panegyrics.[126] So it was with the English garden, as the unknown was translated into terms of the known. Such traditional features, note Hunt and Willis, as walks among woods, 'could be read as a significant exercise in a "natural" taste compared with the canal, basins, squared gardens and fountains round the house'. The evolution of the landscape garden, like all organic processes, was gradual: Temple's information 'shaped actual designs very slowly'. And, when more irregular plantations were attempted, these, 'often seemed ridiculously contrived...and just as artful in their wavering lines and random trees as the geometry retained in the main garden'.[127]

What role Addison might have played in these later developments must remain hypothetical. He had hoped to extend his estate, and evidently intended to continue planting it. Having reported the failure of his previous efforts, and the poor opinion his gardener and London 'oporator' held of them, his kinsman added hopefully: 'I have enlarg'd your Nursary nere one halfe, and have planted Ashes, and Elms, in it, that you may have trees of your own to transplant, when you have occation'.[128]

Such 'occation' as he did enjoy can only have been fleeting at best.[129] From now on he had little time left for his estate, or indeed for anything else. His work for Ireland grew heavier; he was a regular attendant at the frequent meetings of the Board of Trade; and he finally became senior secretary of state, at the time the highest administrative position in the land. From this he retired, his health devastated, to his wife's great mansion on Kensington hill, where he died some months after the birth of their daughter.[130]

In the continuing development of naturalism, however, Addison's influence remained pervasive. Already his ideas were part of the mainstream of gardening practice. This was the work of Stephen Switzer, who had been trained by the gardeners to King William and Queen Anne, and therefore in the formal style. Yet, in the year after the accession of King George, he quoted Addison's essay advocating informality, and adducing the Asian prototype, with approval.[131] Switzer was to express himself largely through writing; and his 'most constructive recommendations', observes Christopher Hussey, 'were those developing Addison's idea of a whole estate becoming a kind of garden'.[132]

It was Switzer's fellow–apprentice to the royal gardeners, and occasional collaborator, Charles Bridgeman, who, Hussey continues, was to be accepted as 'best able to give practical expression to the new ideas disseminated by Addison'.[133] This 'practical expression' is described by his younger contemporary, Horace Walpole:

> he banished verdant sculpture,...disdained to make every division tally to its opposite; and though he still adhered much to straight walks with high clipped hedges, they were only his great lines; the rest he diversified by wilderness, and with loose groves of oak, though still within surrounding hedges.

'As his reformation gained footing', Walpole goes on, 'he ventured farther, and...dared to introduce cultivated fields, and...morsels of a forest appearance':[134] at last producing a correspondence to Addison's recommendations.[135]

These later developments overlapped with the designs of William Kent. The two worked together;[136] and Kent's most significant layouts are palimpsests over those of Bridgeman,[137] breaking and blurring his lines: as an incoming tide will turn a castle in the sand into the semblance of a natural outcrop. This tendency has been attributed to his early training:[138] through the generosity of patrons, Kent had gone from painting carriages in England to painting canvases in Italy; and, on his return, brought the fluidity of the palette to plantation.[139]

Kent's 'new taste' in gardens was described by a contemporary as being 'to lay them out, and work without either level or line'. The result, it was stated,

> has the appearance of beautiful nature, without being told, one would imagine art had no part in the finishing, and is, according to what one hears of the Chinese, entirely after their models for works of this nature, where they never plan straight lines or make regular designs.[140]

*Sharawadgi*, clearly, was unforgotten:[141] an association deepened by the siting of *chinoiserie* features -- pavilions, pagodas and bridges -- in the English landscape garden.[142] That it was filtered through Addison is no less apparent: Kent's propensity to 'lay...out...without...level or line' is an unmistakable echo of his statement that the inhabitants of '*China*...laugh at the Plantations of our *Europeans*, which are laid out by the Rule and Line'[143]

This is scarcely to be wondered at. The original *Spectator* had reached an audience estimated at eighty thousand a day, from Edinburgh to Exeter, and from Massachusetts to Sumatra; and, in its collected format, soon acquired the status of a classic. It was translated into French, German and Dutch; Voltaire and Rousseau absorbed its ideas; Franklin used it as a manual for writing, and Boswell, hopefully, as a guide to life. Johnson considered Addison the standard of natural English; and now, when the English garden was firmly established, the *Spectator* was still, it was noted, 'in the hands of every one'.[144] The subscribers to the collected edition, meanwhile, had included Kent's most significant patrons.[145] Nor was Addison's earlier writing forgotten. The most influential, perhaps, of all Kent's designs, the meandering stream of the Elysian Fields at Stowe, was laid out in accordance with an allegory of his in the *Tatler*.[146] And Walpole's summation of Kent's achievement -- that he 'leapt the fence, and saw that all nature was a garden' -- is an indisputable realisation of Addison's proposal that the garden be extended to include meadows, marshes and mountains.[147]

## xvi

HAD Addison lived a normal lifespan, he would have witnessed this fulfilment of his dreams. But that he did not do so would not have distressed him unduly. 'A Man of a Polite Imagination', he had observed, '...feels a greater Satisfaction in the Prospect of Fields and Meadows, than another does in the Possession'.[148] His was the vision: the vision, when all is said, of what may well have been the most influential mind at work in the eighteenth century. He had assimilated the idea of the Japanese garden to the ideology of the English revolution; and, by mediating this through his own inmost needs, initiated the romantic return to nature.[149]

That this has not been acknowledged may be attributed to a number of factors. The personal quality of his thought was shadowed by the anonymity of its original publication;[150] later it paled in the very ubiquity of its success. Speaking of the aesthetic in which Addison 'founds art on the base of nature', Johnson sarcastically bade the 'profound observers of the present race', before allowing themselves to 'repose too securely on the consciousness of their superiority', to recollect that if they were in a position to criticise Addison, it was 'by the lights which he afforded them'.[151]

What Addison, then, afforded his century was not alone a vision but a medium of vision. He stands, said Lewis, at a 'very turning–point' in the history of feeling:[152] feeling itself, indeed, being his criterion. '*What is the Tree*', asks the emperor in his Persian fable,

> *that bears three hundred and sixty five Leaves, which are all Black on the one Side, and White on the other?*

So, too, behind the change wrought by Addison, shines the light of *magnus annus*, apocatastasis. And forces other than ubiquity or anonymousness have been at work in his subsequent eclipse. '*Sir*', said the imperial vizier, when he had given the expected answer,

> *permit me at the same Time to take Notice, that these Leaves represent Your Actions, which carry different Faces to your Friends and Enemies, and will always appear Black to those who are resolv'd only to look upon the wrong Side of 'em.*[153]

# CHAPTER THREE

# FAIR THAMES AND DOUBLE SCENES

POPE is the other half of the Victorian equation. If Addison is the first of Victorians, Pope is first amongst those who are deemed to need saving from them. And George Sherburn, when he undertook this task, singled out Leslie Stephen for having, in his biography of Pope, exhibited a lack of 'respect' for his subject.[1]

It is possible, certainly, to read Stephen in this way. Take, for instance, his account of Pope's correspondence with Swift. Pope wished to publish this; but to do so was to court the imputation of vanity. He therefore had it printed surreptitiously, and then blamed Swift for it, instancing the 'evil influence' of his family -- who, he suggested, stood to gain financially from the pirated volume -- and the decline of his mind. He took the attitude, says Stephen,

> of one who is seriously aggrieved, but who is generously anxious to shield a friend in consideration of his known infirmity. He is forced, in sorrow, to admit that Swift has erred, but he will not allow himself to be annoyed.

'I think', he wrote to a friend,

> I can make no reflections upon this strange incident but what are truly melancholy, and humble the pride of human nature. That the greatest of geniuses...may have nothing left them but their vanity. No decay of body is half so miserable.

'The most audacious hypocrite of fiction', comments Stephen,

> pales beside this. Pope, condescending to the meanest complication of lies to justify a paltry vanity...moralising, with all the airs of philosophic charity, and

taking credit for his generosity, is altogether a picture to set fiction at defiance.[2]

Extricating Pope from the implications of this account would, one presumes, form a central task for those who would restore him to respect; and Sherburn, when he edited Pope's correspondence, implied that this had been done. If the letters, he promised,

> are read without Victorian prejudice, the picture of his mind will be different in some respects from that which in many quarters has been current.

What this may mean is, I confess, unknown to me. Because Sherburn freely admits that it was Pope who was responsible for the surreptitious printing, and that the 'hypocritical suspicions' he cast upon others are 'painful to record'. So painful, indeed, does he find the recording that he sends us to the letters instead. But these do not suggest any mitigation of Stephen's judgement. 'When the Heart', wrote Pope to Swift at the conclusion of this intrigue,

> is full of Tenderness, it must be full of Concern...You are the only Man now in the world, who cost me a Sigh every day of my Life...I must confess a late Incident has given me some pain; but I am satisfied you were persuaded it would not have given me any: And whatever unpleasant circumstances the printing our Letters might be attended with, there was *One* that pleas'd me, that the strict Friendship we have born each other so long, is thus made known to all mankind. As far as it was Your Will, I cannot be angry, at what in all other respects I am quite uneasy under. Had you ask'd me, before you gave them away, I think I could have proposed some *better Monument* of our Friendship...Adieu. While I can write, speak, remember, or think, I am Yours.
>
> A. Pope.[3]

This was the man who discovered that Addison was a hypocrite.

## i

POPE's first major poem, the *Essay on Criticism*, contained an attack on John Dennis, the critic. Dogmatism was translated into physical description: a staring eye, a face that flushed angrily at contradiction, and a habit of intemperate speech.[4] Dennis responded in kind: wondering aloud, and with much wealth of detail, whether Pope, who suffered from arrested growth and severe curvature of the spine,[5] was 'a proper Author to make personal Reflections on others'.[6]

No respectable motive for Pope's attack has ever been established.[7] Dennis put it down to 'Envy and Malice': to an attempt, in a poem of which the subject was criticism, to supplant him in that discipline; and his modern editor is disposed to agree. 'As the most conspicuous critic then living in England', writes Hooker, 'Dennis was the obvious rival and the obvious target'.[8]

Addison reviewed the *Essay on Criticism* in a spirit very different from that of Dennis. Where the earlier critic had found nothing but 'Depravity of Genius and Tast',[9] he discovered 'Elegance and Perspicuity'. But on one matter Addison agreed with Dennis perfectly. So fine a poet as Pope, he declared, had no need of 'Envy and Detraction'; and he drove the point home with a citation from Denham:

*Nor needs thy juster Title the foul Guilt*
*Of Eastern Kings, who to secure their Reign*
*Must have their Brothers, Sons, and Kindred Slain.*[10]

To what did Addison refer? This is another question that has never been satisfactorily answered. But some of the most celebrated lines in the *Essay*, seemingly transparent, turn quite opaque when looked at more closely. When Pope derides as 'tuneful Fools' those who indulge in the repetition of rhyme, he gives two examples:

Where-e'er you find the *cooling Western Breeze*,
In the next Line, it *whispers thro' the Trees*;
If *Chrystal Streams with pleasing Murmurs Creep*,
The Reader's threaten'd (not in vain) with *Sleep*.[11]

What is strange about these lines is that the poem in which they occur is in flagrant breach of their doctrine: the *Essay* abounds in repeated rhymes -- ten on 'wit', and twelve on 'sense'.[12] What is still more strange is that Pope continued to employ the very repetitions he had parodied: the second occurs twice in a dozen lines in his *Iliad*, while the first not only recurs in his verse, but does so at moments of peculiar intensity. The erotic disturbance of his heroine in *Eloisa to Abelard* is mirrored by

> The dying gales that pant upon the trees,
> The lakes that quiver to the curling breeze;

while the divinity that interfuses the universe of his *Essay on Man*

> Warms in the sun, refreshes in the breeze,
> Glows in the stars, and blossoms in the trees.[13]

Either Pope was monumentally unaware of his own practice -- a possibility rendered unlikely by his habit of incessant revision[14] -- or the passage on rhyme has some irrational function, hitherto unrecognised. What it may be is suggested by this couplet:

> He then wou'd prune the tender'st of his trees,
> Chide the late spring, and lingring western breeze;

which occurs in the vicinity of this one:

> Like winds that softly murmur thro' the trees,
> Like flames pent up, or like retiring seas;

and this:

> All this is done, when first the western breeze
> Becalms the year, and smooths the troubled seas.

Here is the repeated rhyme which was the first of Pope's targets; and in the same place, too, is the second:

> Into their cells at length they gently creep,
> There all the night their peaceful station keep,
> Wrapt up in silence, and dissolv'd in sleep.

All of these lines occur in a poem by Addison;[15] and that this was not coincidence is evident from the fact that it was Pope's second attack upon him. Earlier, he had written of a garden demanding elaborate description that it was

> Enough to shame the boldest Bard that sings

Of painted Meadows, and of purling Springs.

This was a parody of Addison, who in a poem to his patron had written:

My humble verse demands a softer theme,
A painted meadow, or a purling stream.[16]

Addison had been ridiculed once, and held his hand. A second time begins to look like persecution. Nor was this all; consider the following:

As on the *Land* while *here* the *Ocean* gains,
In *other Parts* it leaves wide sandy Plains;

and compare it with this:

Wash'd with successive seas, the doubtful strand
By turns is ocean, and by turns is land.

The second of these couplets has a more assertive ring to it, certainly, than the first, and a more assured antithesis. But it is the second that is the original, by Addison, and the first which is its imitation, by Pope; and this, too, occurs in the *Essay on Criticism*.[17] Addison, then, in the mind of Pope, was by no means a contemptible poet: he evoked from him, at the same time, both imitation and ridicule. 'Envy and Detraction' was a reasonable inference.

## ii

A POSSIBLE motive for these assaults has been suggested by Sherburn: Pope's 'whole psychology', he writes, 'was that of physical inferiority'.[18] With this Norman Ault vociferously disagrees. 'It is not always necessary', he declares,

> either to condemn Pope's irritability when on occasion he seems to attack some one with rhyme but without reason, or to allude to the inferiority complex of a cripple psychology to explain or excuse it.

Yet he, too, on another page, feels compelled to appeal for understanding of

Pope's intrigues to his 'lamentable physical constitution'.[19]

Adler denied that there was anything psychologically predetermined about 'physical inferiority'. 'The outcome', he stated, 'depends on the creative power of the individual'; and this in turn depends upon 'the individual's own interpretation of his position'.[20] Of this, in Pope's instance, there is remarkable, though indirect, documentation. It may be questioned to what extent translations may be thought of as autobiography; but when these are found to consist of relatively brief extracts from lengthy works, and to be variations on a single, intensely personal, theme, the principle of choice would seem to function as a form of self-expression. Such is the case with the early translations of Pope, begun in the course of that tormented adolescence during which his body grew warped and stunted.[21]

The most immediate, and most pathetic, of these is the passage from the *Metamorphoses* in which Ovid recounts, with a sense of fatal inevitability, the transformation of Dryope:

> She feels th'encroaching bark around her grow
> By quick degrees, and cover all below...
> She ceas'd at once to speak, and ceas'd to be;
> And all the nymph was lost within the tree.[22]

It would be difficult to convey more vividly the feeling of being trapped in an alien body. Release from such a state can come only in fantasy, and this is the theme of *Vertumnus and Pomona*. Vertumnus is enabled to enter Pomona's walled orchard, and to win her love, through his ability to change himself, first into the guise of an elderly woman, then back again to his 'Native Form'.[23] And since in the original the old woman is described as *incurva*,[24] one may sense with what wistfulness the scene must have appealed to Pope. A third extract from the *Metamorphoses*, however, offers an altogether darker dénouement to bodily disadvantage. The cyclops Polyphemus, loving Galatea, is possessed of a delusive image of himself; and, when he realises the truth, and that her love is for a more fortunate youth, crushes his rival to death:

His body press'd beneath the stone, the blood
Flow'd from the marble in a crimson flood.

Pope failed to give this piece to the world:[25] suggesting an uneasy awareness of the application that might have been made of it. Polyphemus moreover was a poet, though an unsuccessful one; and Sappho, the subject of another of Pope's translations from Ovid, is, like him, conscious of a lack of physical attraction -- 'short my Stature' -- and like him, too, in being a rejected lover. And with her, while the pain of loss is turned inward -- murder being replaced by suicide -- the shadow of the enemy is still an implacable presence. Here Pope has added to his original the derision of the undamaged other:

My scornful Brother with a Smile appears,
Insults my Woes, and triumphs in my Tears;

and the diminutive poet's reaction is curiously heavy with obsession:

His hated image ever haunts my Eyes.[26]

This interpolation of Pope's is the central theme of his most elaborate translation from the Latin: an entire book of Statius' *Thebaid*. Here he takes up openly the topic of the conflict between brothers, the sons of Oedipus, for the kingship of Thebes: a tale of rivalry, animosity

And impotent Desire to Reign alone,
That scorns the dull Reversion of a Throne.

Curiously, the fantasy of the ousted brother echoes that of the love-torn Sappho: her 'daily Longing, and my Dream by Night' resurfaces as

His daily Vision, and his Dream by Night.

That is to say, the physically impaired poet, obsessed with hatred of an unmarked brother, overlaps with an equally obsessive prince who is excluded by a brother from the throne. The diminutive poet has an obvious parallel in Pope; has the princedom, too, an outside counterpart? The answer is suggested in the lines which set forth the spring of the action:

> Thy Curse, oh *Oedipus*, just Heav'n alarms,
> And sets th'avenging Thunderer in Arms

-- lines taken over from...Addison.[27]

## iii

WHEN, in the year of Pope's birth, James II was dethroned, 'every blossom of popish hope', says Johnson, 'was blasted...A papist now could be no longer Laureat'.[28] Dryden, who had converted to Catholicism, lost this position;[29] Pope, too, was Catholic;[30] and in the *Essay on Criticism*, as Dennis noted, identified with Dryden. Dennis pointed out too that the poem, while critical of the reign of Charles and of William, passed in silence over that of James.[31] In his translation of the *Thebaid*, Pope went still further, altering his original to vilify the reigning king and exalt his exiled rival;[32] and, as Addison's verses in praise of William and his ministers had led him to public office, Pope's first attack on him, appropriately, concentrated on these.

But Addison's offence, apparently, did not end with power: he had succeeded, not only to the rewards of poetry, but to its prestige. Pope's identification with Dryden went far deeper than Dennis supposed: he placed him on a list of departed relatives and friends as -- significantly, perhaps, in view of the struggle for the principate that is the theme of the *Thebaid* -- *poetarum princeps*.[33] But this dispossessed prince of poets had bestowed a splendid accolade on Addison. Always capable of friendship across the lines of party, the Whig scholar had helped the Catholic poet with his Vergil; and Dryden, when he came to publish, stated that the excellence of Addison's own translation had been 'troublesome' to him. 'After his Bees', he wrote, 'my latter swarm is scarcely worth the hiving'.[34]

This was the poem that Pope singled out for his second attack.

## iv

INFERIORITY, Adler thought, as a feeling which 'constantly presses towards its own conquest', was the source of any improvement in the human condition.[35] Something of this may be sensed in Pope's earliest translation from Homer: the passage in which he makes the Greek warrior speak of the glory of courting a death that is in any case inevitable, and of urging the 'Soul to War'.[36] Here is the essence of the Homeric heroism:[37] immortality gained at the expense of life in the body; and as such, it would seem, peculiarly appropriate to Pope. The *Iliad* was pre-eminently his epic; and one can see why his treatment of the *Odyssey* was by comparison so perfunctory.[38] For him no soft ways beckoned, no enchantresses lurked; no sirens tempted, nor Penelope intrigued for his love. His was a world of battle, not magic; he went into it armed at all points; and what he understood by an urging of the soul to war becomes apparent in the second of his Homeric translations.

In the *Odyssey*, George Lord has pointed out, the protagonist grows beyond the concept of the warrior, who 'with his narrow tribal loyalties, his jealous personal honour, and his fierce passions...is, whatever his motives, the foe of reason, order and civilisation'. As the bard at the court of Phaeacia sings the fall of Troy, and Odysseus' role in it, the still-anonymous hero, against all expectation, bursts into tears. 'His pride in his heroic accomplishments', observes Lord, 'is suddenly transformed into pity for his victims': it is as if he 'cannot arrive home in the profoundest sense until he has discovered the metaphysical order of the human community'.[39]

This was not the Odysseus that Pope admired. The episode he chose for early translation was that in which the hero, set ashore again on Ithaca, attempts to conceal his identity from Athena, and is praised by her for his cunning.[40] It is the residual trickster, and not the man enlarged by compassion, that appeals to Pope. And that this is so is confirmed in the passages he chose to modernise from

Chaucer. As Odysseus, in isolation from his nobler impulses, can be perceived as a mere schemer, so the Wife of Bath, removed from the humane irony that is the essence of her creator,[41] becomes simply another exemplar of the art of lying. The secret of this, she declares, is to carry it off with brazen conviction:

> Forswear the Fact, tho' seen with both his Eyes,
> And call *your Maids* to Witness how he lies.

It is to seize the initiative, imputing to the other what is true of oneself:

> I, like a Dog, cou'd bite as well as whine;
> And first complain'd, whene'er the Guilt was mine.[42]

This lesson is reinforced in the other of Pope's versions of Chaucer, in which the old knight's youthful wife is taken in adultery with his squire. Pope omits the reflections by which the narrator distances himself from the squire, and deepens and elaborates the mendacity of the wife.[43] By these means she is enabled to dislodge her husband from his first conviction --

> As with these Eyes I plainly saw thee whor'd

-- make him question the evidence of his senses --

> By Heav'n, I swore but what I *thought* I saw

-- and finally accept that all is an hallucination arising from his own nature:

> 'Twas You were jealous, not your Wife unkind.

Thus, by a mixture of lying, effrontery, ready tears, simulated affection, and expert knowledge of the borderlands of perception, reality is subverted:

> So just recov'ring from the Shades of Night,
> Your swimming Eyes are drunk with sudden Light,
> Strange Phantoms dance around, and skim before your Sight.

All of which is of more than passing significance. For it is the garden which is the setting of this episode that is declared to be

Enough to shame the boldest Bard that sings
Of painted Meadows, and of purling Springs.[44]

Pope's initial attempt to transfix Addison, then, takes place in a context, not only of displacement, but of categorical denial that such displacement took place, and of successful vilification of the victim.

Early opportunities were taken of putting these principles into practice. To Dennis' charge that he had been attacked 'in my Person, instead of my Writings',[45] Pope opposed a bland denial.[46] Then, in an anonymous pamphlet, he described the critic as

A baneful *Hunch-back'd Toad*, with look Maligne.[47]

Dennis had spoken of Pope as a 'hunch-back'd Toad';[48] Pope, at whatever cost in truth or plausibility, has flung the description back. The same manoeuvre was to be followed in the case of Addison. Addison had reproached him with seeking a reputation 'on lesser Ruins built';[49] Pope repudiated, with pious horror, any celebrity that might come to him over 'the fall'n Ruins of Another's Fame'. Denial had been accomplished; reversal must inevitably follow. Among the hazards faced by 'youthful Bards', Pope now discovered, was to have

All luckless Wits their Enemies profest,
And all successful, jealous Friends at best.[50]

Dennis had described Pope as a hunchbacked toad; it was Dennis who was the hunchbacked toad. Addison had described him as bearing no brother near the throne; it required no gift of prophecy, for anyone familiar with Pope's mental processes, to discern the form in which Addison would finally appear.

## v

THE difficulty was that Addison's praise of him had been, as Pope admitted, 'lavish'. It would have been a trifle inappropriate, therefore, to plunge at once into open vendetta. Instead a spell of apparent peace succeeded, in which Pope ostentatiously behaved himself for an entire year. 'Of every one's esteem', he burbled of Addison to Steele, 'he must be assur'd'.[51] It testifies, one imagines, to the shock he had felt at being found out in Addison's review. The following year, however, was to provide him with opportunities to be himself, and show how much his professions of admiration were to be trusted.

The most elaborate of Pope's pastoral poems commemorated the setting of his childhood; but *Windsor–Forest* also celebrated the Tory peace with France. It was felt that the treaty was favourable to Louis, and therefore to James' Catholic son; and Pope signalised his share in the resulting euphoria by dedicating his poem to a leading Jacobite, and attacking the revolution.[52] This he did through yet another parody of Addison: taking his description of Catholic Italy, and applying it, at considerable cost to the facts, to Williamite England.[53]

Herein lies the key to three puzzles which have greatly vexed Pope commentators, and which may be described, respectively, as the Case of the Invisible Caesura, of the Missing Signatures, and of the Unaccountable Missive.

The hunt for the caesura was set on foot by Pope. Years afterwards, he claimed that *Windsor–Forest* was made up of two distinct parts 'written at two different times': an early pastoral, and a celebration of the peace. The problem is that this is contradicted, not only by the poem as it stands, but by all of the evidence, including the manuscript.[54] And this is very strange: the disjunction of a unified poem is asserted by the person who, one would suppose, had the greatest interest in promoting its integrity.

The matter of the signatures is no less provocative. Two sets of pages are missing from a volume containing poems by Pope, and, it is suggested, edited by him, in the year before the publication of *Windsor–Forest*. In a second edition, two years afterwards, these signatures are inserted, and they contain that poem. No satisfactory explanation for the earlier omission has been found.[55]

The missive, finally, is a note from Addison to Pope, thanking him for the 'noble entertainment' a certain unnamed poem has afforded him. As it dates from the month before the publication of *Windsor-Forest*, it is argued, plausibly, that that is the poem.[56] On the face of it, this seems impossible. How can Addison's warm response to the piece be reconciled with the fact that it parodied himself?

Individually inexplicable, these three puzzles, when fitted together, form a pattern which is continuous and coherent. Pope prints a sneaking gibe at Addison; it passes unchallenged, and he feels he may safely venture another. This time he is answered, shatteringly, in public, and is reduced to mumbling denials and expressions of esteem. A third parody, however, is in the press, which would tend to give the lie to these assertions. Drastic action, accordingly, follows. Out come the signatures carrying the poem; and when, after the space of a year, Pope thinks it safe to confide it to Addison, he asserts that the offending passage was written long before: a statement that he repeats in public when he is busy covering up his earlier attacks. Addison, meanwhile, not wishing to question this show of good will, gravely accepts the explanation and praises the poem.

I do not insist upon this solution: I merely note that it covers the facts. But this much may be taken as certain. The assaults of the Whig writers on the author of *Windsor-Forest* need not be put down either to innate depravity or to some secret, directing malevolence on the part of Addison.[57] Pope had launched the attack, and they were returning his fire.

Addison, meanwhile, had been placed in an impossible position. From either direction, shot hurtled through the air. Some of it struck glancing blows at himself: intensifying, no doubt, the amazement of his political allies at his association with Pope.[58] But for now he was held immobile under a tattered flag of truce.

Relief, however, was at hand. Pope's ruling passion was to rule. Given his compulsion to assault those whom he identified as rivals, a direct hit was sooner or later to be expected; given his obsession with Addison, it may be said to have been inevitable. And when that happened, the charade would be at an end.

It came over Addison's tragedy of *Cato*. With the Whigs at their lowest ebb, he called to mind a similar conjunction in classical history: when the republican party, reduced to a remnant by the dictatorship of Caesar, reproduced on the shores of Africa the democratic institutions of Rome. The Whig half of the house burst into a frenzy of applause; the Tory half, refusing to accept the imputation, joined in; and the script was so much in demand that it was hawked by the fruit-sellers. It was a critical as well as a popular success: Berkeley, who sat in a box with Addison, thought the play 'most noble', and its author 'a great philosopher'.[59] Pope claimed to have wept over it in manuscript; and, in the prologue which Addison invited him to provide for it, asked:

> While *Cato* gives his little senate laws,
> What bosom beats not in his Country's cause?[60]

Addison's triumph, however, aroused other sensations. Dennis put out a pamphlet in which he undertook to demonstrate the play's 'Faults and Absurdities' under three heads: those which arose from neglect of Aristotle, those which remained in spite of Aristotle, and those which subsisted in their own right, without reference to Aristotle at all.[61] Pope responded with an assault on Dennis, depicting him in the pose of an outrageous lunatic;[62] but since, as Johnson remarks, he 'left the objections to the play in their full force', he 'discovered more desire of vexing the critick than of defending the poet'.[63] And Dennis years afterwards published a startling account of the episode. His pamphlet, he explained, had been the inspiration of Pope:

> The great Success of Mr. *Addison*'s *Cato* fermented his Envy, and provok'd his Malice exceedingly. To discharge some Part of his Spleen, he goes to...the Bookseller, and persuades him to engage me to write some Remarks upon Mr. *Addison*'s Play. He prevail'd upon the Bookseller, and the Bookseller upon me:

an accusation that Pope was never able to refute.[64]

Addison replied to Dennis in the *Spectator*: appealing, as might have been expected, from the critic's 'Rules' to 'Nature', and alluding to his disastrous career as a dramatist, together with his pioneering in stage effects, in a description of

> Showers of Snow, which, as I am informed, are the Plays of many unsuccessful Poets artificially cut and shreaded for that Use.[65]

With Pope, too, Addison settled his accounts. 'As a satirist', observes Macaulay, 'he was, at his own weapons, more than Pope's match';[66] and on this occasion he made devastating use of them. He wrote of a dream in which Jupiter proclaimed that 'every Mortal should bring in his Griefs and Calamities, and throw them together in a Heap'. A Bosch-like scene ensues in which the 'whole human Species' converges for the purpose of discarding 'red Noses, large Lips and rusty Teeth', and in which the Spectator divests himself of the short broad face of Steele. Not all the humour, however, was so kindly:

> Observing one advancing towards the Heap with a larger Cargo than ordinary upon his Back, I found upon his near Approach, that it was only a natural Hump.

Worse was to follow. A second proclamation allowed the sufferers to exchange afflictions, as a result of which

> I could not for my Heart forbear pitying the poor hump-back'd Gentleman...who went off a very well-shaped person with a Stone in his Bladder; nor the fine Gentleman who had struck up this Bargain with him that limped through a whole Assembly of Ladies who used to admire him, with a Pair of Shoulders peeping over his Head.

This scarifying portrait was intensified by its moral, which -- a reiteration of his review of the *Essay on Criticism* -- was not to 'envy the Happiness of another'.[67] Addison has no doubt etched Pope's likeness in acid; but he had for several years now been the object of a petty, persistent and almost insane persecution; and 'it is intolerable', said Wilde, 'to be dogged by a maniac'.[68]

## vi

WHEN Pope signed a contract to translate the *Iliad*, an associate of Addison's, Tickell, contracted for a rival version; and Pope ever afterwards laboured to prove that this was the work of Addison. The overall evidence of character would in itself cast heavy doubt on such a statement. Pope's whole life, observes Macaulay, 'was one long series of tricks, as mean and as malicious' as that of which he tried to convict Addison, or as that of which he tried to convict Swift. 'Nothing', the historian goes on, 'was more natural than that such a man...should attribute to others that which he felt within himself'.[69] Pope's previous relations with Addison would turn this supposition to near-certainty; and final confirmation is provided by the documented facts.

Tickell left to his descendants both the contract by which he bound himself to translate the *Iliad*, and a manuscript in which he describes the author of that translation as 'Tickell'.[70] Tickell, then, was under the impression both that he intended to make his own translation, and that this was what he had done: a conclusion, it may be allowed, that he had some right to reach.

The same conclusion, indeed, is suggested by Pope. There had been, he says with fine understatement, a 'coldness' between them, when one evening Addison, meeting him at the coffee-house, took him aside and told him

> that his friend Tickell had formerly, whilst at Oxford, translated the first book of the *Iliad*, that he now designed to print it, and had desired him to look it over. He must therefore beg that I would not desire him to look over my first book, because if he did it would have the air of double dealing. I assured him that 'I did not at all take it ill of Mr. Tickell that he was going to publish his translation, that he certainly had as much right to translate any author as myself; and that publishing both was entering on a fair stage'. I then added that 'I would not desire him to look over my first book of the *Iliad* because he had looked over Mr. Tickell's, but could wish to have the benefit of his observations on my second, which I had then finished, and which Mr. Tickell had not touched upon'. Accordingly I sent him the second book the next morning; and Mr. Addison a few days after returned it with very high commendations.[71]

The crime of Addison, then, resolves itself into this: that he did for Tickell what -- on Pope's own admission -- he did for Pope.[72] Pope's account, moreover, contains a detail which is the most extraordinary feature of the whole episode, and which, if carefully unravelled, provides the clue to the rest. Pope here betrays the fact, which he elsewhere 'industriously suppressed',[73] that Tickell printed only one book of his *Iliad*, though he had contracted to translate all twenty-four.[74] Pope's adversary, says Johnson, 'sunk before him without a blow';[75] and this strange surrender prompts a number of questions. Who initiated the rival translation? Who called it off? Were they one and the same? If so, why? If not, what took place behind the scenes?

The supposition that Addison was the translator runs at once into insuperable difficulty. Shortly after Tickell signed his contract, Addison revived the *Spectator*, this time without the collaboration of Steele, and produced what were, in Macaulay's opinion, 'perhaps the finest essays...in the English language'.[76] This was scarcely the action of a man embarking upon a project which took Pope six years, and gave him nightmares of an interminable journey.[77] It was a situation, moreover, with which Addison was familiar: years before, he had discontinued a similar project on Herodotus.[78]

A theory has been put forward, however, according to which Addison, if not the actual author of the translation, was still its originator, engaging Tickell to 'spoil Pope's triumph in the *Iliad*'. In this theory, which also derives from Pope,[79] may be seen the pattern whereby he himself had egged Dennis on to attack Addison. Nevertheless, it has its adherents. Tickell 'erred', suggests Sherburn, 'because an older and highly influential friend urged him into error'. The reason given for this suggestion is extremely odd: it is Tickell's 'reputation for integrity'. This 'reputation' derives from Pope, who declared him a 'very fair, worthy man' when he was labouring to assert the opposite of Addison.[80] How, then, was this 'fair, worthy man' urged into 'error'? Says Sherburn: 'Addison could aid Tickell to a career: in fact he was doing so'.[81] Strange integrity. In fact Addison advanced

Tickell's career *after* he had withdrawn his translation.[82] On this supposition, he was rewarded for having backed out of the plot.

Other factors combine to reduce this theory from the improbable to the ludicrous. If Addison was about to launch an underhand attack on Pope, it was in his interest to dissimulate his dislike of him. Instead he portrayed him in a blistering satire. Still more imperative was it to conceal his own involvement. Instead he went and told Pope: or so at least Pope informs us.

The same evidence which falls to pieces against Addison falls perfectly into place around Tickell. Tickell was a young Oxford scholar who had attached himself to Addison by what Johnson describes as 'the most elegant encomiastick strains' in praise of his verses;[83] and he was later, as Addison's editor, to burst into injudicious anger when he felt him to have been slighted.[84] It must have been with a sense of growing indignation that he witnessed Pope's relentless attempts to discredit his idol, and with considerable excitement that he accepted the publisher's offer -- for his publisher and Pope's were competitors of long standing; and this, it was long ago pointed out, is the most likely source of the rival translation.[85] He was a better poet than Addison and a better scholar than Pope: at one stroke, it must have seemed to him, he could secure his reputation and exact vengeance for his friend.

Addison will have seen the matter in a different light. He knew that, in the words of Johnson, the 'first excellence of a translator' was to be 'read with pleasure by those who do not know the originals';[86] and that, in this respect, Pope was unlikely to be faulted. He did not love Pope; he did not allow injuries to pass unpunished; but his practice with his enemies was to go for a clean and a quick kill. To engage in tortuous animosity, after the fashion of Pope, was not his method. He was, moreover, a man of the world, as Tickell was not; and to combine a protracted public vendetta with a demanding literary project can scarcely have seemed to him a very intelligent undertaking.

Tickell appears to have given up his project with reluctance. In his note of surrender, he declared that he had found it 'fallen into a much abler Hand';[87] but in private, it is clear, he felt no such diffidence: in a manuscript comparison of the two versions, he argues the superiority of his own.[88] For Tickell, then, to have retreated from the contest with a statement that he feared comparison with Pope, when in fact he did not, argues that he acted under some powerful outside influence. Only one such influence is known: that of Addison.

The entire transaction, then, suggests the uneasy terms of a compromise, Tickell agreeing to a humiliating retreat, and Addison to what must have been no less distasteful: the carrying of excuses to a man he despised. This, too, explains Addison's promotion of Tickell, in the course of which he encountered considerable opposition.[89] It makes sense to think of it, not as a reward for unaccomplished villainy, but as compensation for a painful sacrifice.

Tickell afterwards seems to have suffered remorse for having embroiled Addison in his scheme. In the elegy which he composed upon him, he wrote:

> Oh, if sometimes thy spotless form descend,
> To me thy aid, thou guardian Genius, lend!
> When rage misguides me, or when fear alarms,
> When pain distresses, or when pleasure charms,
> In silent whisperings purer thoughts impart,
> And turn from Ill a frail and feeble heart.[90]

It is tempting to see in these lines a reference to the matter of the translations: to regret at having allowed Pope to goad him -- 'rage misguides' -- into striking back at him with his own degraded weapons. However this may be, they are proof positive, from the central character in the episode, that Addison's influence over him was not such as 'urged him into error', but calculated instead to turn him from 'Ill'.[91] With all the other evidence, they point to the fact that Tickell's 'older and influential friend', far from having instigated his translation, was instrumental in having it withdrawn: that, in Stephen's words, the 'whole affair, so far as Addison's character is concerned', is a 'gigantic mare's nest'.[92]

## vii

'I AM more joy'd at your return', writes Pope to Addison, 'than I should be at that of the Sun'. 'I must e'en', he exclaims on another page, 'be contented with telling you the old story, that I love you heartily'. 'I am conscious', he declares yet again,

> I write with more unreservedness than ever man wrote, or perhaps talk'd to another. I trust your good nature with the whole range of my follies, and really love you so well, that I would rather you should pardon me than esteem me.

It seems almost a pity that Addison did not learn of the love, rejoicing and spontaneity that he elicited in his admirer. He never did: because all of these effusions are part of an elaborate forgery that Pope concocted after his death.[93]

John Caryll was a Catholic squire who had generously encouraged the young Pope. His house was dismantled in the later eighteenth century;[94] but about the middle of the nineteenth, a priest who had charge of a farmhouse on the property communicated with Dilke, the noted scholar and friend of Keats. There were, the priest informed him,

> some documents, relating to the Caryll family, stored away in a half–ruined outhouse attached to this building, in a state of decay which made it desirable if possible to destroy them. Mr. Dilke requested that before this was done he should be allowed to see them. Leave having been obtained, he proceeded to examine the papers, set by set, and, where they were useless, to burn them in a bonfire in the court–yard of the farm–house. In the midst of a quantity of uninteresting MSS. at last appeared a letter–book in Caryll's hand containing copies of Pope's letters to him.[95]

From these it became apparent that letters originally sent by Pope to Caryll had been printed by him as to others; and that, in the words of another nineteenth–century scholar, 'the whole of the letters to Addison are an absolute fiction'.[96] In epistles dated to the time when he had engineered the attack on him by Dennis, Pope condoles with Addison over it, laments the fact that 'so many mischieveous insects' (i.e. the likes of Dennis) 'are daily at work to make people of merit' (i.e. Addison and Pope himself) 'suspicious of each other'; and comforts him with the reflection that 'all the great men and all the good men that ever liv'd' have had their share of 'Envy and Calumny'.[97]

Pope, then, fabricated a correspondence which showed him in warm friendship with Addison at a time when he had betrayed whatever trust existed between them, and earned a contemptuous repudiation. This he did in order to shift the location of the break, and to reverse their roles in it. Where in fact he had schemed to subvert Addison's success, in the fictitious correspondence he made it appear that Addison -- to his amazement, horror and shock -- had done this to him. In a series of letters incompatible with what genuine documents have survived, Pope takes the battle of the translations to Addison's door. Addison is here portrayed as trembling lest it be known he does not care for Pope, expressing perfect satisfaction with his politics, and great anxiety to serve his interest. To this Pope replies with dignity, scorning to owe anything to one who could think him 'capable of maligning or envying another's reputation as a Poet'.[98] Here, as Stephen remarks of another of his exercises in epistolary fiction, Pope 'precisely inverts the relation which really existed between himself and his correspondent'.[99] He had impinged upon Addison by means of underhand attack; this had been answered by open rebuke, which he had never dared to contradict. In the imaginary correspondence, all this is reversed. Here it is Addison who launches the attack, and Pope who delivers the rebuke, which is received in silence.[100]

It must have been a weight from the heart for Pope to realise in fiction what he had feared to do in fact. Even here, however, he was aware of one great obstacle: that, as Johnson later noted of Addison,

> amidst that storm of faction in which most of his life was passed, though his station made him conspicuous and his activity made him formidable, the character given him by his friends was never contradicted by his enemies.[101]

Pope felt this difficulty keenly. Accordingly, after informing another correspondent that Addison had engineered the rival translation, he asserts the astonishing improbability that 'there is no rupture between us'. After assaulting

Addison, as he made it seem, to his face, he laments that '(to say the truth) all the world speaks well of you'.[102]

Here for a moment in these winding corridors of deceit, a window opens fleetingly on reality. Soon after the contracts for the *Iliad* had been signed, Queen Anne died, and Addison became secretary to the regency:

> At the centre of preparations for King George's arrival, he also held in his hands the threads of national strategy and diplomacy which ran to every capital in the Western world.[103]

This is the man who is deemed to have been obsessed by Pope, as Pope undoubtedly was by him. In the year in which the translations appeared, the Princess of Wales, who had been at the head of Pope's subscription, wrote of Addison to Leibniz: *Sa tragédie est très-belle, et Caton luy-même ne se plaindroit pas des sentiments nobles et dignes d'un homme comme luy, qu'il luy a donnés.*[104] And when he was named secretary of state, Tom Burnet, a scurrilous young Whig envenomed against him by thwarted ambition,[105] was forced to concede: 'he has the Character of an incorrupt man, which is no little matter now a days'.[106]

One of Addison's first tasks in his new position was to discipline the firebrand Earl of Peterborough, later the boasted friend of Pope. It may well be imagined that the man whom the Duke of Marlborough feared to offend, who challenged the Earl of Chesterfield over a slight, who extracted an apology from the papal court, and in whose honour Louis XIV set his fountains playing,[107] was not to be cowed by any common functionary. Yet Peterborough wrote to Addison, after he had transmitted the royal rebuke: 'It is a satisfaction to receive it from your hands, being confident my answer will be fairly represented'.[108]

Pope's vast fabric of mendacity was put together, it is impossible to doubt, in order to form a setting for the caricature in which Addison, as the sinister Atticus, ruthlessly excludes all rivals from the throne. And this is equally at odds with contemporary evidence: those who had known both men closely recording their disbelief in it. Lady Mary Wortley Montagu, who had not always agreed with Addison, felt 'indignation', she said, 'when he is abus'd'; and she sensed that Pope's correspondence was 'wrote by himselfe and falsly ascrib'd' to others.[109] Swift, a reliable witness reports, had 'no Esteem for Mr. Pope', on account of his 'jealous...Temper'; and was 'particularly offended' by his 'satire upon Mr. Addison, for whose Integrity, Generosity, & other amiable Qualities, the Doctor always declar'd the highest Regard'.[110]

Tickell went still further. When the caricature appeared, he wrote a reply to it, in which he stated that it was so untrue as to be mindless, and that the character it portrayed was Pope's own. In it, he wrote,

> Ironies Reverst right Virtue show,
> And point which Way true Merit we may know.

And he well understood the psychology behind it:

> So the skill'd Snarler pens his angry Lines,
> Grins lowly fawning, biting as he whines.

Tickell, clearly, had read his Pope with attention, not mistaking the autobiographical significance of:

> I, like a Dog, cou'd bite as well as whine;
> And first complain'd, whene'er the Guilt was mine.[111]

And the motive for the assault was unfalteringly recognised:

> Exert your utmost Energy of Spite,
> And as each envious Hint arises, write.[112]

As a record of the inner history of the relations of Pope and Addison, by a witness in an unrivalled position to know of them, these lines are of the utmost value. And it may be that, in the relative crudity of their carving, the primitive image of Pope, arrested in the very motion of hypocrisy -- 'lowly fawning, biting as he whines' -- glimmers with greater force.

## viii

JOHN Lord Hervey was a reputed bisexual:[113] so that Pope, in his portrayal of him as Sporus, the catamite of Nero,[114] found him an easy target. 'Sporus', Dustin Griffin has pointed out, functions as a 'kind of antiself', whereby Pope can more clearly define his own 'manly virtue'. But on a deeper level, Griffin suggests, Pope recognises in Hervey another version of himself: a '"little man", never physically manly', he called himself 'abhominably epicoene'.

Other aspects of 'Sporus', however, suggest pure difference. Hervey was not noted for personal uncleanliness -- was not, as Pope called him, a 'Child of Dirt'; but Pope's weakness, as Johnson reported, 'made it very difficult for him to be clean'. Nor was he noted for 'Smut' or 'Blasphemies'; while Pope was. In fact, Griffin observes, a major source for the character of 'Sporus' would 'appear to be the printed attacks on Pope'.[115]

I would carry this argument further. Another manifestation of 'Sporus' is his indulgence in 'Lyes': in an earlier version, significantly, 'unmanly' lies.[116] And, while it would be superfluous to comment on Pope's mendacity, Hervey was the very antithesis of a liar. His memoirs depict his actions, and even his most secret thoughts, without mercy.[117] 'He had the Roman fashion', writes T.H. White, 'which refused to pity or to distort'.[118]

Still less was he a coward. When Pulteney, an associate of Pope's, made a printed reflection on his masculinity, he responded with a challenge. His wife, who knew nothing of this,

> observed that Hervey was so cheerful that she thought he would simply write a reply to Pulteney's 'monstrous' attack. He drank his chocolate with her, gave her 'a ridiculous paper of verses' to copy, and then as he left for the House of Commons, said he would dine that afternoon with some members.

Hervey and Pulteney, with their seconds, met in the park; and, although

> it was a frosty day, with snow covering the ground, the duellists stripped down to their shirts. As they were drawing their swords Hervey told Pulteney that in

his pocket he had a paper

> stating that the duel was at his instigation and asking the King to protect Pulteney from the consequences of killing him if that should happen.[119]

Hervey, then, used the influence at court for which Pope derided him to protect a man who had insulted him and might take his life; while Pope, who was protected by nature from any such challenge, could repeat Pulteney's insults with impunity.[120] It was in fact in his masculine role that Hervey appears to have given greatest offence to Pope: as the friend, defender, and perhaps suspected lover of Lady Mary Wortley Montagu.[121]

The great emotional crisis of Pope's life, alone of equal import with his hatred of Addison, was his infatuation with that brilliant Whig aristocrat;[122] and the terrible satirist, in love, showed himself quite as foolish as any other mortal. When she left England on her husband's embassy to Turkey, he wrote of her destination as the 'Land of Jealousy, where the unhappy Women converse with none but Eunuchs'. Who one such eunuch might be was suggested in another letter, where Pope declared himself capable

> of following one I lov'd, not only to Constantinople, but to those parts of India, where they tell us the Women best like the Ugliest fellows, as the most admirable productions of nature, and look upon Deformities as the Signatures of divine Favour.

He had spoken after her departure of passing her house with the 'same Sort of Melancholy that we feel upon Seeing the Tomb of a Friend'; and later sent her a poem which, he hinted, had a personal application. This was *Eloisa to Abelard*; and here all the preoccupations he had woven about her absence -- desire and the shadow of death, passion and physical impossibility -- combined in the breathings of an erotic landscape. And when, after her return, he arranged for her to become his neighbour at Twickenham, this was projected over the garden he had begun to plant there, and which in her absence seemed void of meaning:

> In vain fair Thames reflects the double scenes

Of hanging mountains, and of sloping greens...[123]

But his feelings suffered a violent inversion when he discovered that his fantasy was baseless. Now he launched a series of attacks on her in terms of deceit and sexual disfunction, which reached their hysterical climax in the injunction to expect

From furious *Sappho*, scarce a milder Fate,
Pox'd by her Love, or libell'd by her Hate.[124]

'Sappho' was brilliant. Pope's erstwhile idol was not only a writer of verse, but had visited the Aegean islands, there to identify herself with the ancient poet.[125] But 'pox'd' was more cunning still.

Pope's 'satiric' method, at its most sophisticated, consists in selecting a surface detail which, while wholly or partly true, can be made to suggest depth after depth of mendacity. 'The mumbling spaniel', observes Griffin, 'who dares not bite, whose smiles betray "Emptiness", makes wonderfully witty fun of Hervey's false teeth'. But the 'implied charge of sexual impotence' is 'patently ridiculous. Hervey married the beautiful Molly Lepel, sired a large family...and carried on -- apparently with some success -- an affair or two'.[126]

On the slender peg of this factual detail, then, could be hung the voluminous mantle of Pope's own sexual fears and frustrations. The same technique was followed with the woman he had aspired to in vain. Lady Mary's face had been ravaged by smallpox; and after she had learnt of inoculation in Turkey, she became celebrated as its advocate in England. Pope has taken this public fact, and invested it with sinister significance.[127] Again, as with Hervey, the surface truth is made to serve a deeper untruth, and the distortion to disguise a situation the direct antithesis of what is asserted. It is Pope, and not Hervey, who spatters filth from behind safe cover; it is he, and not the woman he adored, who is 'furious' and who libels out of hate.[128]

And the twisted tale of Pope's amour has a dimension which links it with another and an older obsession. As in his early writings the theme of the rejected lover had been intertwined with that of the successful rival, so now the presence of the one conjured up the shadow of the other. Addison had married his countess just after the Wortleys set out for Constantinople;[129] and it comes as no surprise to learn that the legend that the marriage was unhappy -- the origin of that fictitious figure who feared the equality of the bedchamber -- can be traced to Pope.[130] Addison had been for him the ultimate rival, to be discredited even while he was compulsively imitated. But Addison had proved a maddeningly elusive target: he had passed from celebrity in verse to unprecedented popularity in prose; from this to acclamation on the stage; and from here to a position in which he exercised regal functions. His achievement had been crowned with acceptance by the aristocratic woman he had aspired to: a conclusion Pope could not hope for with any confidence. It was a close friend and political associate of Addison's, moreover, who engrossed the woman he loved.[131] And so the old rivalry welled up again at the close of the poem into which he poured all the fears and doubts of his frustrated passion:

> And sure if fate some future Bard shall join
> In sad similitude of griefs to mine,
> Condemn'd whole years in absence to deplore,
> And image charms he must behold no more,
> Such if there be, who loves so long, so well;
> Let him our sad, our tender story tell;
> The well-sung woes will sooth my pensive ghost;
> He best can paint 'em, who shall feel 'em most.

This last line, in which poetic pre-eminence is asserted, is taken over from Addison; and from that poem which first had thrust him into public office.[132]

## ix

AMONG the Pope manuscripts in the British Library, scribbled on the backs or the covers of letters, still heavy with the original seals or glittering with the mica of the sand used to dry the ink, is a page of jottings in which the workings of Pope's mind can be followed as he attempts to fashion his fictional Addison. Of these the opening couplet runs:

> But our Great Turks in Wit must reign alone:
> & ill can bear a Brother on y$^{e}$ throne.

This was to remain the basic thrust of the assault: to invert the image that Addison had applied, with such devastating accuracy, to himself. This fact is underlined in another couplet:

> wits starve as useless to a Common weal
> while Fools have places purely for their Zeal

-- a comforting explanation for Addison's success; while the self-pity that informs the reflection whines still more plaintively in a cancelled version of the first line:

> Poor Wits deserve more of y$^{e}$ Common weal.[133]

Here is the original grievance -- envy of Addison -- out in the open. How to make it seem the opposite was the problem. It did not long remain so.

'Addison', writes C.S. Lewis, 'is not a simple man; he is, the older sense of the word, "sly"': the sense, that is to say, of which the nominal form is 'sleight', and which is closer to dexterity than disingenuousness. For the Tories of the time, explains Lewis, for a Pope or for a Swift,

> every enemy...becomes a grotesque. All who have, in whatever fashion, incurred their ill will are knaves, scarecrows, whores, bugs, toads, bedlamites, yahoos; Addison himself a smooth Mephistopheles. It is good fun, but it is certainly not good sense; we laugh, and disbelieve. Now mark Addison's procedure. The strength of the Tory party is the smaller country gentry with their Jacobite leanings and their opposition to the moneyed interest. All the material for savage satire is there. Addison might have...painted merely the block-headed, fox-hunting sot, the tyrant of his family and his village. Instead, with the help of Steele, he invents Sir Roger de Coverley. The measure of his success is that we can now think of Sir Roger for a long time without remembering his Toryism; when we do remember it, it is only as a lovable whimsy.

The point is illustrated from the *Spectator*:

> In all our journey from London to his house, we did not so much as bait at a Whig inn...This often betrayed us into hard beds and bad cheer; for we were not so inquisitive about the inn as the innkeeper; and provided our landlord's principles were sound, did not take any notice of the staleness of his provisions.

'As a natural consequence', Lewis goes on,

> Mr. Spectator soon 'dreaded entering into an house of any one that Sir Roger had applauded for an honest man'. It is so beautifully done that we do not notice it. The enemy, far from being vilified, is being turned into a dear old man. The thought that he could ever be dangerous has been erased from our minds; but so also the thought that anything he said could ever be taken seriously.[134]

'Sir Roger', observes Stephen, 'is the incarnation of Addison's kindly tenderness, showing through a veil of delicate persiflage'.[135] Addison, in a word, was an ironist; and it 'would be too much', states Macaulay,

> to say that he was wholly devoid of the malice which is, perhaps, inseparable from a keen sense of the ludicrous. He had one habit which both Swift and Stella applauded, and which we hardly know how to blame. If his first attempts to set a presuming dunce right were ill received, he changed his tone, 'assented with civil leer', and lured the flattered coxcomb deeper and deeper into absurdity.[136]

Steele was as little disposed to blame it as were Stella or Swift, speaking affectionately in retrospect of 'that smiling Mirth, that delicate Satire, and genteel Raillery which appear'd in Mr. *Addison* when he was free among Intimates'. He was 'above all Men', says Steele, 'in that Talent we call *Humour*';[137] and it is here, precisely, that Pope has found his detail to distort. It takes only the slightest of strokes to turn a smile into a grimace; and when Pope had thickened 'smiling Mirth' into 'civil leer', 'delicate Satire' into 'teach the rest to sneer', and 'genteel raillery' into 'hint a fault, and hesitate dislike' -- all in the interest of domineering and the discrediting of rivals[138] -- his demonic Addison had begun to take shape.

Maynard Mack accuses Addison of failing to apply his sense of absurdity to himself;[139] but it is Pope, as Ehrenpreis points out, who regularly excludes himself from his own satire.[140] Addison, on the other hand, had an acute awareness of what we should nowadays describe as unconscious motivation. 'I would have every zealous Man', he wrote,

> examine his Heart thoroughly, and, I believe, he will often find that what he calls a Zeal for his Religion is either Pride, Interest, or Ill–Nature.

He was, in fact, a better psychologist than those who have so complacently sat in judgement upon him. He felt, following Hobbes, that there was in laughter an element of malice; but at the same time regarded the opinion that it was the 'effect of Original Sin' as decidedly odd. Sanity, he decided, was a matter of balance:

> For tho' Laughter is looked upon by the Philosophers as the Property of Reason, the Excess of it has always been considered as the Mark of Folly. On the other Side, Seriousness has its Beauty whilst it is attended with Chearfulness and Humanity, and does not come in unseasonably to pall the good Humour of those with whom we converse.[141]

This is the much–maligned 'moderation' of Addison. It is a moderation, not of lukewarmness or mediocrity, but of basic forces deeply felt, and of the attempt to fuse them. It is not the hysterically asserted surface perfection of a Pope, nor the superficial sort, with which he is commonly credited, of the smoothly functioning moral machine. It is a clear–eyed acceptance of contradiction: integrity lived under its dynamic aspect, as the attempt to integrate. 'When a Man is made up', he wrote in a characteristic reflection,

> wholly of the Dove, without the least Grain of the Serpent in his Composition, he becomes ridiculous in many Circumstances of Life, and very often discredits his best Actions. The *Cordeliers* tell a Story of their Founder St. *Francis*, that as he passed the Streets in the Dusk of the Evening, he discovered a young Fellow with a Maid in a Corner; upon which the good Man, say they, lifted up his Hands to Heaven with a Secret Thanksgiving, that there was still so much Christian Charity in the World.[142]

A passage of this kind raises, or ought to raise, troubling questions for the proponents of the Victorian Addison. Sherburn, alluding to some sexual innuendo by Pope, declares that it was 'exactly the sort of vulgarity that Addison would find intolerable'.[143] Mack chimes in: 'being the man he was, Addison undoubtedly found Pope's ribald streak offensive in itself' -- even, he claims, in its milder manifestations.[144] They are not supported by the facts. One of Addison's papers depicts the 'Tantalism, or *Platonick* Hell' of the Frenchman who saw 'a couple of the most beautiful Women in the World undrest and abed with him, without being able to stir Hand or Foot'. Another tells of the temple dogs who could discern unchastity, and who, on the return of a priest who had been 'making a charitable Visit to a Widow', set upon him with 'so much Fury, that they were all of them hanged, as having lost their original Instinct'. Yet another illustrates the theory of transmigration with a 'Town-Rake' who 'did Penance in a Bay-Gelding for Ten Years'.[145]

Addison understood sexual intimacy as well as sexual innuendo. He relates with great sympathy -- born, perhaps, of his own courtship -- the tale of the secretary who spent the night with his emperor's daughter, 'resolving to hazard all, rather than live deprived of one whom his Heart was so much set upon'.[146] Such was the Addison of fact. But when one knows so 'exactly' and 'undoubtedly' the man that he 'was', it must assuredly be unnecessary to read him.

## X

IT WAS by picking on straws, and weaving them together with plentiful helpings of mud, that Pope gave an appearance of solidity to his caricatures. Steele had written that Addison, in conversation, 'frequently seems to be less knowing to be more obliging'; that 'he chuses to be on a level with others rather than oppress with the Superiority of his Genius'.[147] Pope has taken the word 'obliging' and inverted its meaning. 'It is not merely unjust', said Macaulay, 'but ridiculous, to describe a man who made the fortune of almost every one of his intimate friends, as "so obliging that he ne'er obliged"'.[148] Amongst these were Gulston and Lancelot Addison, Gulston's widow writing of her regret that 'her husband had not been able to express to...Joseph the deep sense of gratitude which he felt for "all the pains you took to advance him"'.[149] If Addison was determined to bear no brother near the throne, it is curious that his own brothers were not apprised of the fact.

Swift, one imagines, would have been a major irritant to a man bent on exclusive dominance. Yet Addison dedicated the volume of his travels to Swift as 'the most agreeable companion, the truest friend, and the greatest genius of his age'.[150] Thus the first Victorian to the author of the *Tale of a Tub*. Swift was not slow to reciprocate. 'I believe', he wrote to Stella, 'if he had a mind to be chosen king, he would hardly be refused';[151] and, after political differences had temporarily overclouded their relationship,[152] wrote him an affectionate letter of congratulation on his promotion to secretary of state. 'I examine my Heart', he said, 'and can find no other Reason why I write to you now, beside that great Love and Esteem I have always had for you'.[153] Addison in turn stated that he and a mutual acquaintance had often spoken of Swift, 'and when I assure you he has an exquisite taste of writing I need not tell you how he talks on such a Subject'.[154] Addison's 'jealousy of kindred genius and accomplishments', in the words of a nineteenth-century biographer, 'appears nowhere but in the lines of Pope'.[155]

Pope's malicious transvaluation of surface truth appears most effectively in his distortion of an entire scene: that scene which, inverting his earlier compliment to *Cato*, he described as a 'little Senate'.[156] Addison, writes Willard Connely,

> provoked mirth at the coffee-house; and wonderful mirth it was, to captivate unfailingly the lofty-witted Swift; he let go his satire on gauzy wing, his raillery like polished gems through one's fingers...[157]

Addison's kingship was one of acclamation, not autocracy; his audience captivated, not captive. He was, says Lady Mary Wortley simply, 'the best company in the world'.[158] Pope himself had stated that 'no people are to be so little feared...as those of the highest pitch of understanding...I should not else talk at random, or sleep, in the company of Mr. Addison'.[159] He then took this easy dominance, and twisted it into domineering; and his own account suggests how he may have been prompted. He nodded in company, and dozed over his wine.[160] On some such occasion, a shout of laughter. He starts out of sleep, to see Addison in triumph. Immediately there falls across his vision a shadow without sound. It is the shadow from his own *Thebaid*: the rival brothers waking to envy, hatred

> And impotent Desire to Reign alone,
> That scorns the dull Reversion of a Throne.[161]

For Pope, this will have been linked with another scene:

> You who would know him better, go to the Coffee-house...and you shall find him holding forth to half a score young fellows...puft up, and swelling with their praise.[162]

So Dryden, as seen by Shadwell. And Addison, as seen by Pope, is the most elaborate of all his psychological inversions. Behind it, as always, is that which he professes to abhor. It is Addison seen with a jaundiced eye: Addison, unbearably, on the throne of Dryden. So the deep untruth depends, not only on the surface truth which vouches for it, but on its own internal consistency. Pope speaks of what he knows: it is the source of the persistence of his caricatures, and their power.[163] Addison's 'great figure', writes Thackeray,

> looks out on us from the past -- stainless but for that -- pale, calm, and beautiful: it bleeds from that black wound. He should be drawn, like Saint Sebastian, with that arrow in his side.[164]

But the arrow is a *trompe l'oeil*, appearing to pierce where it glances away; and the wound is the shadow of the hand that has released it.

## xi

WHEN Pope was accused of having written his caricature of Addison after his death, he cited witnesses to the effect that he had handed it about in his lifetime: thereby establishing that, as Dennis sardonically remarked, he had 'libell'd him in Manuscript while he liv'd, and in Print after he died'.[165]

Pope always maintained that this was printed against his will, by ruthless pirates and gutter publicists. But the invisible pirate was, once again, himself.[166] Meanwhile, he had provided a complimentary poem for Tickell's edition of Addison's works; and it is, claims Ault, 'highly improbable' that 'the satire and the eulogy derive from the same period, like two sides of the same medal'.[167] Inconvenient it may be; but hardly improbable in a man who had wept over Addison's tragedy, and then whipped up an attack on it.

This zigzag motion was repeated in the years that followed. When Pope at last acknowledged the caricature, it was with what Ault describes as a 'sort of semi–apology'.[168] This is most judiciously put. It took the form of a wish that his 'Resentment, though ever so just, had not been indulged'. The sincerity of this desire may be judged from the fact that the volume in which it appeared contained a sly insinuation that Addison was the author of Tickell's *Iliad*.[169] If Pope believed this, he had no cause for apology: sort of, semi–, or otherwise circumscribed. And if he regretted what he had written, he would scarcely have placed it, as he did, at the heart of what has been called his *Apologia pro Vita Sua*.[170]

Still he persisted in the dirty dance. In this fresh promulgation, he changed the subject's name to 'Atticus'; but in a footnote made it clear that it was Addison he meant, and that the 'occasion of writing it was such, as he could not make publick in regard to his memory'.[171] It is edifying to see Pope point the finger at an individual while alleging to have made him anonymous, and take credit for concealing misdeeds that he does not specify. And, a few months afterwards, these invented offences were advertised in the pages of a fictitious correspon–

dence.[172]

Nor had he finished even yet. A couple of years later, we find Pope asserting that, of all contemporary writing, 'no whiter page than Addison remains'. He, he goes on,

> from the taste obscene reclaims our Youth,
> And sets the Passions on the side of Truth;
> Forms the soft bosom with the gentlest art,
> And pours each human Virtue in the heart.[173]

Here, it can scarcely be doubted, is the source of the Victorian Addison. Here is the wholesome influence on youth, the Sunday-school paragon, the plaster saint who turns out, not very surprisingly, to be a hypocrite. Pope has whitewashed him in order to spatter him the more effectively; has placed him on a pedestal so that he can be toppled with a more satisfying crash.

And to disguise his own management of the demolition. Public Pope regrets and affects solicitude over what private Pope, under the guise of anonymity, relentlessly reveals. The split in the presentation of the subject becomes a split in its perception: Addison, in the iconography of Pope, is a being vastly reverenced but sadly flawed.

For the art of the liar involves layer after layer of deception. The first stage is to take some truth, and twine one's falsehood around it. The second is to confuse. Apparent evidence is multiplied, its elements individually improbable, but in combination serving to induce doubt and obscure the facts. The third stage, after one has set up one's scarecrow and thrown one's smokescreen about it, is to stand back, wailing and wringing one's hands:

> Who would not weep, if *Atticus* were he![174]

The tone is one of infinite sadness. 'It is penetrated', wrote Chesterton, 'with sorrow and a kind of reverence';[175] or, as Mack prefers to gloss it, with 'disappointment...a certain tenderness...a degree of respect' for 'Addison as a young man's hero and role model, a figure of magisterial powers crippled by a single frailty, a type of the lost leader'.[176]

> Where have we heard these accents before?
>
> When the Heart is full of Tenderness, it must be full of Concern...
> You are the only Man now in the world, who cost me a sigh every day of my Life...
> I must confess a late Incident has given me some pain...
> Had you ask'd me, before you gave them away...

To be sure: that last, appalling letter to Swift. Another lost leader. Another magisterial cripple. Another young man's role model. Who filched Pope's letters, even as Addison pre-empted his epic. So strange a coincidence, and so sad. Sad.

It was his masterpiece of illusion. For a quarter of a century, through ambuscade and apology, through mendacity and moralisation, through feigned concern and fictitious correspondence, he had advanced imperceptibly on his target, like the moving forest in *Macbeth*. From time to time the protective covering was shaken. It was recognised that his tale of a betrayed friendship was full of oddities and inconsistencies;[177] it was realised, even, that his accusations against Addison might with justice be applied to himself;[178] but the evidence which would strip away the camouflage still slumbered on a Sussex farm. For now he seemed perfectly safe. He had hidden his leaf in a forest; his dead leaf in a dead forest; had planted a dead forest in which to hide his dead tree.

## xii

THE consequences were incalculable. For Pope's project was not only to make over Addison in his own image, but his own in the image of Addison. And by so doing, he falsified a cardinal transition in intellectual history.

Pope's '"rules" of gardening', complains Morris Brownell, 'have rarely been distinguished' from those of his predecessors.[179] What these rules may be, and how it might be possible so to distinguish them, one is not informed. Certainly the editor of Pope's gardening poem has been unable to do so. The landscape movement, states F.W. Bateson, 'was initiated by Addison's essays': in them, Pope's views are 'all anticipated'.[180]

These however are dismissed by Brownell as 'speculative', 'tactful', replete with 'equivocation' and 'vague notions' of Chinese and other prototypes. This is not Addison; this is Atticus. This is the figure advanced by the bogus correspondence, who stands by in a tactful, vague and equivocal silence before the honest, forthright and daring assertions of Pope. Of these two, clearly, only the fictitious Pope was capable of the boldness demanded by original thought; and in him, accordingly, is discovered the 'adaptation of a classical idea by a modern sensibility for the picturesque'.[181]

In Pope, it is true, both a classical idea and a modern sensibility are to be found. But the sensibility is borrowed; and the idea is wrong.

A year after Addison, in the *Spectator*, had invented the English landscape garden, Pope, in Steele's *Guardian*, invented it again. Here he described a garden of his own -- as yet imaginary[182] -- resembling that of the poet Martial, which

*rure vero, barbaroque laetatur.*

All the Roman poet is saying, however, is that his garden is rustic; not that it is irregular.[183] So much for the classical idea.

The modern sensibility is equally well grounded. Pope goes on to observe that there is

> something in the amiable Simplicity of unadorned Nature, that spreads over the Mind a more noble sort of Tranquility, and a loftier Sensation of Pleasure, than can be raised from the nicer Scenes of Art:[184]

which is a conflation of statements from Addison.[185]

When he came to lay out his own garden, the same influence was apparent: a fact that has induced great perplexity. For the 'new fashion', as Miles Hadfield observes, 'was essentially Whig'.[186] 'Informal gardens', agrees Michael Reed, 'were associated with liberty in general, and with the Whig version of it in particular'.[187]

Christopher Hussey, accordingly, draws attention to the strange phenomenon of 'Tory Pope enunciating the identity, which Whig amateurs of gardening constantly stressed, of Nature with Liberty'. This he discovers in the 'precocious *Essay on Criticism*', from which he quotes:

> *Nature*, like *Liberty*, is but restrain'd
> By the same Laws which first *herself* ordain'd.

If Pope indeed expressed this view in the *Essay on Criticism*, as originally printed, he was more than precocious; he was incomprehensible. For this was a poem, as Dennis had noted, of which the political vision was Jacobite. And in fact it was '*Monarchy*', and not '*Liberty*', which at this time was declared to be absolute; the about–face came in a revision made decades afterwards.[188] The Jacobite euphoria faded as the Tory ministers quarrelled, and vanished when, at the Hanoverian succession, they fled into exile or were incarcerated in the Tower: as was the suspected Jacobite to whom *Windsor–Forest* had been inscribed.[189] Self–interest now suggested that Pope dissociate himself from the cause he had so lately glorified; and he moved from Windsor Forest to the riverside at Twickenham, there placing himself, as Erskine–Hill observes, 'under the protection of the Whig Lord Burlington': a protection under which he was to shelter for the rest of his life.[190]

The manoeuvre was abetted by the age in which he lived. The triumph of the Hanoverian succession had petrified to the frieze of a monolith; the resulting concentration of power ranged disappointed Whigs alongside disaffected Tories;[191] and the combined opposition was formidable. The 'Tory gentleman', writes Macaulay,

> fed in the common–rooms of Oxford with the doctrines of Filmer and Sacheverell, and proud of the exploits of his great–grandfather, who had charged with Rupert at Marston, who had held out the old manor–house against Fairfax, and who, after the King's return, had been set down for a Knight of the Royal Oak, flew to that section of the Opposition which, under pretence of assailing the existing administration, was in truth assailing the reigning dynasty. The young republican, fresh from his Livy and his Lucan, and glowing with admiration of

> Hampden, of Russell, and of Sydney, hastened with equal eagerness to those benches from which eloquent voices thundered nightly against the tyranny and perfidy of courts.[192]

On which side was Pope? On the evidence, both. He has been declared, with equal conviction, to have been both an unrepentant Jacobite and an ardent upholder of liberty.[193] But it was the latter role that he now chose to emphasize: to such effect that Courthope was able to state, without conscious irony, that 'Pope was the poet of the Revolution of 1688'.[194]

This newfound ideal was appealed to on personal, no less than political, grounds. 'If our Principles be well consider'd', he exclaims in the bogus correspondence,

> I must appear a brave *Whig*, and Mr. *Tickel* a rank *Tory*; I translated *Homer* for the publick in general, he to gratify the inordinate desires of One man only. We have, it seems, a great *Turk* in Poetry, who can never bear a Brother on the throne; and has his Mutes too, a sett of Nodders, Winkers, and Whisperers, whose business it is to strangle all other offsprings of wit in their birth. The new Translator of *Homer* is the humblest slave he has, that is to say, his first Minister; let him receive the honours he gives him, but receive them with fear and trembling: let him be proud of the approbation of his absolute Lord; I appeal to the People.[195]

Pope here completes his reversal of personalities. Not content with imputing his own tyranny of temperament to Addison, he now attributes Addison's psychological liberation to himself. This illusory freedom was put forward with the most relentless deliberation, the most rigid obsession, all concealed under an apparent spontaneity. In the preface to his fabricated letters, he rested their authenticity on the claim that an 'Author's Hand, like a Painter's', was 'more distinguishable in a slight sketch than in a finish'd picture'.[196]

So too, at Twickenham, he splashed the brushwork of *sharawadgi* over the groundplan of the *hortus conclusus*. Pope's was a garden in which the central axis ran between a balanced arrangement of urns and statues, with some 'pleasing intricacy...in the far corners of the plot'.[197] Here the trees grew, it seemed to one visitor, 'with as much freedom as in a forest'.[198] But this apparent liberation was deceptive. It was a space, said Horace Walpole, 'enclosed with three lanes and seeing nothing'.[199] On the fourth side, leading under the house to the river, was the tunnel, or grotto, that could be shut off at will;[200] and in Pope's *apologia*, in which substance and setting coincide, this is what occurs. The poem opens with the poet's cry for closure:

> Shut, shut the door, good *John*!

It is to be shut against the irruption of other poets who, professedly contempt–ible, yet loom with some mysterious sense of threat:

> What Walls can guard me, or what Shades can hide?
> They pierce my Thickets, thro' my Grot they glide.[201]

The threat was of invasion of the circuit within which the poet was secure; and, at the 'turning point of the poem...precisely at its centre'[202] -- corresponding to the psychological need that he fulfilled -- was the mythic figure of Atticus.

For Pope had assumed in his garden the disguise of his lifelong rival; and beneath the interlocking spaces of the lawns that, in Horace Walpole's phrase, he had 'twisted and twirled and rhymed and harmonised',[203] was the evidence of a crime that would not let him alone. The elimination of Addison was vital to his self–image: it was only in his ritual crucifixion that he could seem to himself to live.

A sense of self so fragile was inevitably fractured. At the entrance to the tunnel which led into Pope's garden, and which is all that remains of it, are carvings of the hands, feet and heart of a dismembered Christ. So was Pope's psyche dissociated, locked in an entombment without hope of resurrection, unliving because fixated on the moment of its dispossesion. For the *arma Christi* are completed by the crown of thorns, the cipher of *Jacobus Rex*, and the year which saw a failed uprising for James, a failed assassination attempt on William, and the turning of the royal exile inward and away from the world.[204] Thus Pope's secret landscape was a species of funerary baroque: lamenting, in the passing of the last of the Stuart kings, the death of his hopes.

## xiii

POPE appears to have realised that his entire fabrication, like an inverted pyramid, rested on a single point. All the inventions and accusations; all the tangled tales and bogus papers; all the sighs and tears and shakings of the head: all of these collapsed without a motive. That a man who lived a whole life should have envied an embittered invalid; that a cabinet minister should have envied a political outcast; that a talker who captivated the most brilliant wits of his day, and a writer who enjoyed a string of dazzling successes, should seriously have envied anybody at all, was on a rational motive unbelievable. Pope had therefore to invent an irrational one; and this he did with his customary glibness. Though Addison, he declared, wrote 'with so great ease, fluency, and happiness', though his 'prose character' was the 'chief point of his excellence', he 'did not think so'. *Cato*, he claimed, 'his *Campaign*, and some other little things in poetry were what he thought he was to be immortalised by'.[205]

The inversion, once more, is obvious: these were the writings which had exposed him to Pope's envy. And the charge is opposed, as usual, by all of the evidence. Long before his encounter with Pope, Addison had described himself as a 'lesser Muse', and declared his intention of leaving verses to 'them that practise 'em with more success'.[206] And, by the time he did meet him, he had done so.[207] The essay, says Beljame, revealed to him the shape of his 'true vocation'.[208] Virginia Woolf agrees: 'if anything is perfect', she writes, 'the exact dimensions of its perfection become immaterial'; and the essay, for Addison, was the 'shapely silver drop, that held the sky in it'.[209]

'With his readers, as with his friends', declares Beljame, 'he had only to be himself to win their ears and their affections';[210] and of this he was perfectly well aware. 'It was said of *Socrates*', wrote Addison,

> that he brought Philosophy down from Heaven, to inhabit among Men; and I shall be ambitious to have it said of me, that I have brought Philosophy out of Closets and Libraries, Schools and Colleges, to dwell in Clubs and Assemblies, at Tea–Tables, and in Coffee–Houses.[211]

It is perhaps the utmost reach of the art of the liar to fuse two truths and forge a falsehood. It was true that Addison felt himself below Pope as a practitioner of verse: he had implied as much when he spoke of the latter's craving for a fame 'on lesser Ruins built'.[212] It was also true that he was lacking in confidence of a certain kind: his sense of self–worth had been damaged in youth, and his spirit never wholly emerged from the shadows which had occluded it. This was apparent in his helplessness before a large audience: a fact that his cousin Budgell confirms.[213] In this, however, he was hardly unique. Horace Walpole was a diffident speaker in Parliament; Gibbon, by his own confession, a 'Mute'. Yet Walpole had a very just idea of the value of his letters, and Gibbon felt even the minor details of his life to be of interest insofar as they had helped to shape the historian of the Roman empire.[214] For Addison, too, lack of confidence in public did not extend to his most personal expression. It is Budgell, again, who supplies the evidence: Addison, he says, compared a failed imitation of the *Spectator* to the 'Attempt of *Penelope*'s Lovers to shoot in the *Bow* of *Ulysses*; who soon found that no body could shoot *well* in that *Bow* but the *Hand* which used to *draw* it'.[215]

If Budgell invented or exaggerated, it is strange that he should have done so in two such opposing directions. But in fact these two accounts chime perfectly with the evidence of the *Spectator*. For Addison constructed his greatest triumph around the core of his most notable infirmity. 'I had not', recounts his tongue–tied persona, 'been long at the University, before I distinguished my self by a most profound Silence'. The mute Spectator, however, was endowed with strange possibilities of development:

> when I consider how much I have seen, read and heard, I begin to blame my own Taciturnity; and since I have neither Time nor Inclination to communicate

the Fulness of my Heart in Speech, I am resolved to do it in Writing.[216]

So well did he acquit himself that at the end of the original series, on the death of Sir Roger and the breakup of his club, Addison gave notice of a new gathering where the Spectator intended to abandon his former passivity and 'shew the World how well I can talk if I have a Mind':

> I design upon the first Meeting of the said Club to have *my Mouth opened* in Form, intending to regulate my self in this Particular by a certain Ritual which I have by me, that contains all the Ceremonies which are practised at the opening the Mouth of a Cardinal. I have likewise examined the Forms which were used of old by *Pythagoras*, when any of his Scholars, after an Apprenticeship of Silence, was made free of his Speech.[217]

When the paper resumed, this ritual was represented as having taken place; and its consequences were described by Addison with his customary irony:

> I used, for some time, to walk every Morning in the *Mall*, and talk in Chorus with a Parcel of *Frenchmen*. I found my Modesty greatly relieved by the communicative Temper of this Nation, who are so very sociable, as to think that they are never better Company than when they are all opening at the same time...I therefore threw my self into an Assembly of Ladies, but could not for my Life get in a Word among them; and found that if I did not change my Company, I was in Danger of being reduced to my primitive Taciturnity.

He repaired, accordingly, to the coffee-houses, where he made a habit of courting disputation:

> I was a Tory at *Button*'s and a Whig at *Childe*'s; a Friend to the *Englishman* or an advocate for the *Examiner*, as it best served my Turn: Some fancy me a great Enemy to the *French* King, though, in reality, I only make use of him for a Help to Discourse...I was asked the other Day by a Jew at *Jonathan*'s, whether I was not related to a dumb Gentleman who used to come to that Coffee-house?

Irony, however, was deceptive: for the burden of the Spectator's tale was that

> I am quite another Man to what I was.
>
> *...Nil fuit unquam*
> *Tam dispar sibi...*;

and the fundamental theme of transformation was pointed at still more meaningfully in the epigraph. Here was the Vergilian serpent, held underground throughout the winter; then, renewed in springtime, and rising towards the sun, brandishing the weapon of its tongue:

*Qualis ubi in lucem coluber, mala gramina pastus,*
*Frigida sub terra tumidum quem bruma tegebat;*
*Nunc positis novus exuviis, nitidusque juventa,*
*Lubrica convolvit sublato pectore terga*
*Arduus ad solem, et linguis micat ore trisulcis.*

The image in context has still more potent overtones of aggression; for it is used of the Greek invader, poised at the approach to the palace of Troy. And these implications were not lost upon Addison:

> since I have now gained the Faculty I have been so long endeavouring after, I intend to make a right Use of it...While a Man is learning to fence, he practises both on Friend and Foe; but when he is a Master in the Art, he never exerts it but on what he thinks the right Side.[218]

Of what side he thought this Addison promptly gave proof: within a week he had savaged Pope.[219] When his persecutor, then, set out to displace him, bombarding him with ridicule and appropriating his outworks, it was to find that the heart of the kingdom lay elsewhere. Pope was besieging an abandoned city.

It was thus through the silent Spectator, in whom he magnified his most humiliating weakness, that Addison reached the fullness of his powers. And this metamorphosis was bodied forth, not only in ritual and symbol, but in a code which has hitherto remained unread.

When Steele came to the end of the original *Spectator*, he attributed to Addison all those papers

> marked with a C, an L, an I, or an O, that is to say, all the Papers which I have distinguished by any Letter in the name of the Muse *C L I O*.

This would seem to be perfectly straightforward; yet its meaning was missed from the start. Steele was writing, suggested an eighteenth-century editor, *currente calamo*, and without 'intention or authority to explain the meaning of Addison's signatures'.[220] If this was so, he hit upon an extraordinary coincidence. For the letters appear in the order in which he cited them, and Clio is the muse of history, and by extension of all writing in prose.

When Addison years earlier had embarked upon his translation of Herodotus, it was as if driven by some inkling of his ultimate vocation. For each is the chronicler of the age in which he lives. With Addison we are hushed in the gloom of the Abbey, or hear the hum of the coffee–house in the wars of the King of France. With Herodotus we take a coracle to Babylon, or look down in wonder on the canals and the great trees of the temple of Bubastis. But Herodotus is more than the traveller and the teller of tales; he is the historian of Salamis and of Plataea, of Marathon and of Thermopylae. He is the historian of the liberty of the Greeks; and Addison is more than that of the English. For he has taken the moment of the English revolution, the moment that transformed his own existence, and out of it fashioned an aesthetic of liberation: that liberation, both external and internal, which we know as romanticism.

Yet it is Addison himself who has confounded the code of his achievement. When only the *C* and the *L* of the muse's name had appeared, he took note of the curiosity they had aroused, and studiously misdirected inquirers. Running these together with the *X* of cousin Budgell, which he professed to take as the number ten, he implied that they, too, were to be considered under their numerical aspect.

For this he had excellent reasons. He was aware of the animosity with which he was regarded by one closed and cunning mind; and he was aware too, as it seems probable, that whatever was openly asserted could as openly be distorted or denied. It was for this reason, one presumes -- or perhaps from some sense of premonition -- that he referred his readers, for a 'full Explication' of these 'obscure Marks', to 'Time, which discovers all things'. They were, he suggested, 'little Amulets or Charms', designed to preserve his creation from the 'Fascination and Malice of Evil Eyes'.[221]

So they have. For a quarter of a millenium, while in the world above his monument was defaced, they have preserved their secret unbroken: like the seal on a pharaonic tomb.

## xiv

ROMANTICISM, in its immediate origins, is the aesthetic manifestation of the English revolution. It was Temple who, through his diplomacy in Holland, made that revolution possible; and who, through his discovery there of the naturalist gardens of Japan, brought these as well within the English ambit. These two achievements were fused by Addison in the course of an extraordinary inward journey. The revolution had brought him liberation; and in the thought of a lifetime this came to pervade every aspect of psychic life, in a return to nature of which the landscape garden was both embodiment and symbol.

The same revolution had dispossessed Pope, and his resentment was concentrated on its most effective celebrant. His slander of Addison, and appropriation of his achievement, detached this from its roots in personality, and reduced its history to fragments. But Addison had already unleashed the energy of the romantic movement, which is emotional liberation, with its drive to psychic wholeness. So it was that the chief architect of romanticism remained buried in his handiwork: as the tree which upheld the palace of Byblos became, in the interval of his death and resurrection, the living coffin of Osiris.

PART TWO

# THE TREE OF KNOWLEDGE

## Implications of Romanticism

*Dost thou ask proof? Our tree yet crowns the hill,*
*Our Scholar travels yet the loved hill–side.*

ARNOLD

## CHAPTER FOUR

# THE SINGULAR DEMON OF DR. BENTLEY

IN HER castle at Windsor, on its cliff overlooking the Thames, Queen Anne gave audience, a macaw perched behind her on an 'Indian' screen. A middle-aged parson wrote corrections for her speech. The lord treasurer spoke to him familiarly, playing with an orange; and he warned another minister never to treat him like a schoolboy, for he had had too much of that in his life already: 'meaning from sir William Temple'.[1]

A world had passed away for Swift since he had entered under the Vergilian doorway, or transcribed his master's essays by the quiet garden. When Temple died, at the end of the old century, he felt that with him had gone 'all that was great and good among men'. But now he wrote, 'don't you remember' -- to that other inmate of Temple's household whom he knew as Stella -- 'don't you remember how I used to be in pain when Sir William Temple would look cold and out of humour for three or four days?' It was what he would hardly bear, nowadays, from a crowned head.[2]

### i

WAS it simply the passage of time? Had Swift, now himself an intimate of the great, lost his awe of them? Or, deep down, had it always been so? It was at

Sheen and Moor Park, thought Thackeray,

> as he was writing at Temple's table, or following his patron's walk, that he saw and heard the men who had governed the great world -- measured himself with them, looking up from his silent corner, gauged their brains, weighed their wits, turned them, and tried them, and marked them. Ah! what platitudes he must have heard! what feeble jokes! what pompous common-places! what small men they must have seemed under those enormous periwigs, to the swarthy, uncouth, silent Irish secretary.[3]

It was inevitable, perhaps, that the savage satirist should be seen as dancing in chains to another man's tune. There is, however, an opposite opinion; and it comes from a hostile source. Macaulay no more held a brief for Swift than he had for Temple: for him, the Dean of St. Patrick's was

> the apostate politician, the ribald priest, the perjured lover, a heart burning with hatred against the whole human race, a mind richly stored with images from the dung-hill and the lazar-house.[4]

Yet Macaulay was convinced that Temple's influence on Swift was beneficent. The 'judicious reader', he observes,

> may possibly think Johnson a greater man than Swift. He may possibly prefer Johnson's style to Swift's. But he will at once acknowledge that Johnson writes like a man who has never been out of his study. Swift writes like a man who has passed his whole life in the midst of public business.

And it is, he asserts,

> impossible to doubt that the superiority of Swift is to be, in a great measure, attributed to his long and close association with Temple.[5]

Time passes; the polarity continues.[6] Between the two, no rapprochement seems possible. But it is the latter which would seem to be justified by the *Battle of the Books*.

## ii

'A MOST idle and contemptible controversy', states Macaulay, 'had arisen in France touching the comparative merit of the ancient and modern writers'.[7] As the challenge took the form that the age of Louis surpassed those of Augustus and Pericles,[8] it was hardly surprising that Temple was on the side of antiquity. His praise of the letters of Phalaris led to the demand for a new edition; the young Oxford scholar who undertook it supposed himself deprived of a manuscript by Bentley, keeper of the royal libraries; and he attributed this, with searing irony, to the librarian's inimitable courtesy: *pro singulari sua humanitate.*[9]

Bentley was the greatest textual scholar of his time. 'Hopeless nonsense', writes his biographer, 'under his touch, became lucid and coherent'. He proposed emendations to a Greek inscription copied by travellers: when the original marble, years later, was brought to England, he was found to be correct in every detail. It was left, however, for later ages to appreciate him: he was a Gulliver in Lilliput in his own. The trouble was that he knew it. 'He would be the most extraordinary man in Europe', an early patron is said to have declared, 'had he but the gift of humility'.[10]

If the imputation of discourtesy had initially been unjust, Bentley now proceeded to earn it. Temple had had nothing to do with the attack on him; yet it was Temple whom he chose for his target. 'With all Deference', Bentley snarled, 'to so great an Authority, and under a just Awe of so sharp a Censure', he believed it might be demonstrated 'that the *Epistles* of *Phalaris* are Spurious'.[11]

And demonstrate it he did. The letters, he pointed out,

> mention towns which, at the supposed date, were not built, or bore other names. Phalaris presents his physician with the ware of a potter named Thericles, -- much as if Oliver Cromwell were found dispensing the masterpieces of Wedgwood. Phalaris quotes books which had not been written; nay, he is familiar with forms of literature which had not been created. Though a Dorian, he writes to his familiar friends in Attic, and in a species of false Attic which did not exist for five centuries after he was dead.

All of this, however, was so far beyond contemporaries that it was largely disregarded;[12] while its method provided an opening for parody. The real Bentley, as 'a Scholar, a Courtier, and a Divine', was presumably a gentleman; while the attacker of Temple, a person of 'Extraordinary Services' to the 'Protestant Interest, to the English Nation, and the King', clearly, was not. One would rather, like Cicero on Plato, be 'Handsomly mistaken' than be so 'Rudely...in the right'.[13] This was the contrast that Swift adopted, and expressed in unforgettable imagery: Bentley, as unclean and insidious spider, turning knowledge into a trap; Temple, in the Vergilian susurrus of the hive, enriching existence with the 'two Noblest of Things': with honey and beeswax, '*Sweetness* and *Light*'.[14]

## iii

THIS phrase of Swift's was for Arnold the very touchstone of civilisation;[15] it is difficult to imagine how praise could run higher; and yet there are indications that what the secretary gave with so much ceremony in the *Battle of the Books* was, in the *Tale of a Tub*, surreptitiously withdrawn. Here reality, and the means of knowing it -- reason, sanity, or what you will -- are split into shining fragments that glitter, momentarily, in the brilliance of that mocking mind. The glimpse of definition passes; the kaleidoscope turns once more; certainty slips beyond recall. 'In the Proportion', declares the author -- or the demon who has taken hold of his pen --

> that Credulity is a more peaceful Possession of the Mind, than Curiosity, so far preferable is that Wisdom, which converses about the Surface, to that pretended Philosophy which enters into the Depth of Things, and then comes gravely back with Informations and Discoveries, that in the inside they are good for nothing.

There is here, then, stated, ironically or otherwise, a preference for surface over depth: for that wisdom which accepts things as they seem rather than spending itself in metaphysics. Upon which the satirist, or his mouthpiece, concludes:

> And he, whose Fortunes and Dispositions have placed him in a convenient Station to enjoy the Fruits of this noble Art; He that can with *Epicurus* content his Ideas with the *Films* and *Images* that fly off upon his Senses from the *Superficies* of Things; Such a Man truly wise, creams off Nature, leaving the Sower and the Dregs, for Philosophy and Reason to lap up. This is the sublime and refined Point of Felicity, called, *the Possession of being well deceived*; The Serene Peaceful State of being a Fool among Knaves.[16]

Who can this be but Temple? Temple, citing the Spanish proverb that 'a fool knows more in his own house than a wise man in another's',[17] had retired from the undoubted knavery of the Stuart court to the peaceful possession of what he called, in the essay that celebrated them, the 'Gardens of Epicurus'.

## iv

LAMB found in this essay of Temple's the 'plain natural chit–chat' of the former statesman, devoted now to 'garden pedantry':[18] the jottings of an innocuous potterer. It was an attitude Temple encouraged. 'I may perhaps', he says of gardening, 'be allowed to know something of this trade, since I have so long allowed myself to be good for nothing else'.[19] But one learns to be wary of Temple's negligence: his volume on Holland, professedly the entertainment of a 'very idle' mind, had for its urgent object an alliance against France; his fragmentary history of England, left lying among his works like an abandoned project, aims, without mention of James II, to justify his supersession.[20] These, like his walking in upon a stranger, and sitting down unintroduced, are the casual means to a calculated end. So, too, the garden essay is full of the apparent inconsequence that Lamb admired: of his orange–trees, or the grapes on his eastern wall, or the curious fashions of the 'Chineses'[21] -- but it was here that, confounding the wisdom of his age, he set another worldview in motion. It is worth asking, then, whether the throwaway casualness, here as elsewhere, is not the last and most deliberate disguise of a carefully calibrated purpose.

The opening, certainly, is extraordinary:

> The same faculty of reason, which gives mankind the great advantage and prerogative over the rest of the creation, seems to make the greatest default of human nature; and subjects it to more troubles, miseries, or at least disquiets of life, than any of its fellow creatures: 'tis this furnishes us with such variety of passions, and consequently of wants and desires, that none other feels; and these followed by infinite designs and endless pursuits, and improved by that restlessness of thought which is natural to most men, give him a condition of life suitable to that of his birth; so that, as he alone is born crying, he lives complaining and dies disappointed.[22]

Here is immediate and complete refutation of Macaulay's glib assertion that he had 'no call to philosophical speculation'.[23] Humanity, for Temple, is the species tormented by thought. It is a torment that cannot be stilled, but only tempered, either by discipline or by diversion.

Diversion is 'the common business of common men, who seek it by all sorts of sports, pleasures, play or business'. Sport and pleasure are soon exhausted; play grows dull if unenlivened by gain: leaving only business, which is glossed as 'the pursuit of riches in one kind or another'. And the end of this, even for kings, is frustration: 'none ever yet thought he had power or empire enough'; or, if they did, fell into the same pursuits as their subjects. Of these, they sought the pleasures of imagination in the embellishment of their surroundings, and the 'most exquisite delights of sense' in the 'contrivance and plantation of gardens'. Thus, for Temple, the avenue of diversion leads inevitably to the garden.

The other avenue, that of discipline, is the path of philosophy, of which the goal is happiness. This may be defined in terms either of virtue or pleasure:

> yet the most reasonable of the Stoics made the pleasure of virtue to be the greatest happiness; and the best of the Epicureans made the greatest pleasure to consist in virtue; and the difference between these two seems not easily discovered.

Temple however finds in the Stoic objective, to be 'not only without any sort of passion, but without any sense of pain', the demand that 'a man, to be wise, should not be a man'. This leaves the way open for the Epicurean ideal: the placing happiness 'in the tranquillity of mind, and indolence of body'; for, 'while we are composed of both, I doubt both must have a share in the good or ill we feel'. And, since no other abode conduces more to these virtues than the garden, Epicurus passed his life wholly in his: 'there he studied, there he exercised, there he taught his philosophy'.[24] Thus the second of Temple's lines of escape from the ravages of thought converges, no less inexorably than the first, upon the garden. Epicurus teaches in a garden; it is the garden that is the teaching.

## V

TEMPLE's identification with Epicurus becomes apparent in his singling out the poet Horace from among his disciples. 'It was no mean strain of his philosophy, to refuse being Secretary to Augustus, when so great an emperor so much desired it'. As Temple himself had declined similar office, one begins to discern, behind the horticultural smalltalk, the lineaments of a personal apologia.

It is amplified by its surroundings. Horace was but a one star in a singularly brilliant constellation. Together with him Vergil and Lucretius, Maecenas, Atticus and Caesar, all disciples of Epicurus, were 'admirable in their several kinds, and perhaps unparalleled'; while the age which they inhabited was the greatest of which there is record, 'both as to persons and events'. And this is very strange. For this is the century immediately before the birth of Christ: about which there hovers a most peculiar silence. Temple's essay, after all, is an attempt to come to terms with an existence viewed manifestly as absurd. And in that effort, it appears, the religion of his time and place has nothing to offer. Epicurus openly denied the intervention of divinity in the world; yet Temple specifically acquits him of impiety, wondering how such 'sharp and violent invectives' came to be made against him by, among others, 'the primitive Christians'.[25]

Here was no antiquarian controversy; in the lifetime of Temple, the arguments of Epicurus had returned with new and terrible force. Events had occurred in his century of such a nature that, while an intelligent person could not fail to respond to them, a prudent one could not but do so obliquely. For the penalties for speaking one's mind were severe enough to intimidate some of the greatest intellects of the time. We are presented, then, with a movement of unprecedented velocity -- a hurricane or a tidal wave -- yet concerning which witnesses have been suborned or silenced.[26]

The evidence, however, was incapable of being concealed. Everywhere, in the landscape of the century, we discern its wreckage. And, as with that prehistoric cataclysm in the sunken lands off Schleswig-Holstein, the storm has left its buried trees all pointing in the same direction.[27] It is impossible to ignore a catastrophe of such dimensions: a catastrophe, that is to say, for authority. For the emptying an institution of its moral validity is, as Jung discovered in the presence of Freud,[28] no less irreversible than instantaneous.

The tidal wave of the thought of the seventeenth century, diverse as were its manifestations, is dominated in the end by a single factor. This was not a theory or an idea; it was something irrefutable, since visible and palpable: it was a fact. It arose from the combination of two lenses, said to have occurred from the play of children in the shop of a spectacle-maker in Holland. Certainly it is documented for that country, where it was taken up for the war against Spain; and soon after, the telescope was on sale in England and France. More significant by far, however, was its arrival in Italy, where Galileo came to hear of it, and constructed one of his own: with the result that

> many noblemen and senators, although of great age, mounted the steps of the highest church towers at Venice, in order to see sails and shipping that were so far off that it was two hours before they were seen steering full sail into the harbour without my spyglass, for the effect of my instrument is such that it makes an object fifty miglia off appear as large and near as if it were only five.

Doubt had not yet appeared; only the dissemination of its instrument, in a spirit of magic and wonder. But early in the following year, Galileo looked outward into space, saw the mountains and valleys of the moon, and far beyond; and he published his findings in *Siderius Nuncius*.[29] Certain of his discoveries might be questionable, his priority in others not without challenge; but their scope, and the exultation with which he proclaimed them, were irresistible. He had added thirty-six stars to the Pleiades, eighty to the belt and sword of Orion, and in the orbit of Jupiter had found 'four planets, never seen from the very beginning of the world up to our own times'.[30]

On the day on which *Siderius Nuncius* appeared, the English ambassador to Venice sent to King James I what he considered the 'strangest piece of news' that his majesty 'hath ever yet received': that a local professor, with the help of an optical instrument 'which both enlargeth and approximateth the object...hath discovered four new planets rolling about the sphere of Jupiter'; and that, in so doing, Galileo had 'overthrown all former astronomy'. The ambassador was Henry Wotton; he was the lifelong friend of John Donne;[31] and it was in the following year that Donne's lamentation appeared:

> And new Philosophy calls all in doubt,
> The Element of fire is quite put out;
> The Sun is lost, and th'earth, and no mans wit
> Can well direct him where to looke for it.[32]

Donne, with the intuition of the poet, had immediately grasped the implications of the vision compelled by the telescope: that, in exploding the traditional cosmos, it had revealed a chaos of peculiar horror:

> And freely men confesse that this world's spent,
> When in the Planets, and the Firmament
> They seeke so many new; they see that this
> Is crumbled out againe to his Atomies.[33]

Here was the terrible, unspeakable secret: that the heavens, as now first encountered in actuality, appeared to vindicate the materialist philosophy, in which the world was created from a random collocation of atoms, propounded by Epicurus.

## vi

SO it was that, in the seventeenth century, Epicurus again became a viable philosopher. The French priest Gassendi attempted to housebreak him by accepting his atoms, while attributing their creation to God: thereby, as a commentator observes, turning his philosophy into 'the antithesis of itself'.[34] But the commoner reaction was denial. John Dryden, an almost exact contemporary of Temple's, expressed it with more piety than poetry when he exclaimed:

> No Atoms casually together hurl'd
> Could e're produce so beautifull a world.[35]

The Cambridge Platonists adopted a more oblique approach. The appeal to Plato was to an order behind appearances: the outer world desacralised, they turned within. Human reason implied transcendent reason, and therefore design in nature. This was expounded by Ralph Cudworth in his *True Intellectual* -- as opposed to material -- *System of the Universe*[36] And Cudworth was Temple's tutor at Cambridge.[37]

Temple, then, was introduced at a formative stage to the doubt disseminated by the new cosmology; and it is clear that he was intrigued by it. In an essay written while he was still evidently under Cudworth's influence, he asserted:

> sure hee were a wise man would conclude there were no sea further than hee could see, or there were no bottome because his line were at an end; never any huntsman said the hare was vanish'd where his hounds came to a loss; what hounds are wee that with our noses groveling on the earth and sensible objects presume to trace that eternall order and series of thinges, which though it soone leaves us at a loss, yet mounts up by the linkes of a continued chaine the end of which is in the hand of its maker.[38]

Here is the thought of his tutor; but the style, it has been noted, is that of Sir Thomas Browne. Browne's work had been greatly popular while Temple was at Cambridge;[39] but it was not until some years afterwards that there appeared the most splendid of his meditations on this subject.

*The Garden of Cyrus* has long been admired for the haunting cadences of its prose. What has not been equally recognised is the *gravitas* of its purpose. 'Sir Thomas', writes a sympathetic student, William P. Dunn, 'serene and dreamy as a hermit in the seclusion of Norwich, produces...a mystical little fantasy on the quincuncial arrangement of trees as practised by the ancients'. The quincunx, or five of dice, is

> the pattern of trees planted in slanting rows so that the intersecting lines form lozenges. Browne pursues the lozenge, the five points, the cross, all of which are involved in the pattern, into the four corners of the earth. The feature of it most necessary to his symbolism, however, is the decussation or intersection -- the four corners and cross in the middle, which 'makes up the letter X, that is the emphatical decussation or fundamental figure'. He seems to consider this endless Pythagorean excursion a very modest one. He will 'decline the old theme of crosses and crucifixions', we are asssured at the outset, but he lingers a moment on it nevertheless, with the antiquarian's reluctance to put away such a temptation.

'Every one', comments Dunn,

> knows Coleridge's protest that the book finds 'quincunxes in heaven above, quincunxes in earth below, quincunxes in the mind of man, quincunxes in tones, in optic nerves, in roots of trees, in leaves, in everything'. We might reply that this ought not to be a difficult thing to do, considering that the figure X, which is the essential feature of the quincunx, certainly can be found in almost anything in the universe. Anyone will admit, however, that Browne rides the quincunx to the farthest edge of thought. Gosse is right when he calls this a 'radically bad book'.[40]

Another student writes in similar vein. Quoting Johnson's remark that *The Garden of Cyrus* is little more than 'a sport of fancy', Joan Bennett agrees that Browne's intention in it is not very serious.[41] 'The work', explains Dunn, 'is partly a *tour de force* of antiquarian learning, partly pure delight in inventing the variations to such an air...Here speaks the placid delver into old books, safe anchored and out of the current of his tremendous century'.

Nothing could be further from the truth. For, as if involuntarily, and in contradiction to conscious thought, Dunn writes of the *The Garden of Cyrus* that

> it has a contact with the coloured, pulsing life of nature that is nowhere else revealed in his writings. It seems to brood over a half–disclosed secret whose splendour calls out the most magnificent passages he ever wrote.[42]

Bennett agrees. 'Enhancing the wonder for Browne', she writes,

> ...is the conviction that what he sees is the controlled design of the great Artificer. When...he writes of the sensuous effects of the quincuncial disposition of trees, he more than once declares this faith; the prose glows with it: 'And therefore providence hath arched and paved the great house of the world, with colours of mediocrity, that is, blew and green, above and below the sight, moderately terminating the *acies* of the eye'.[43]

And this, surely, is the key: 'the controlled design of the great Artificer'. For the quincunx, writes Jung, is the combination of quaternity with unity,

> the four forming, as it were, a frame for the one, accentuated as the centre. In the history of symbols, quaternity is the unfolding of unity. The one universal Being cannot be known, because it is not differentiated from anything and cannot be compared with anything. By unfolding into four it acquires distinct characteristics

-- as in 'the division of the horizon into four quarters, or the year into four seasons'.[44] The one, then, 'is the quintessence of the four':[45] as for Browne the framework of the world bears the indelible markings of its maker.

Now, however, he exclaims, 'the Heavens are not only fruitful in new and unheard–of stars', but 'mens minds also in villainy and vices'.[46] Here the new astronomy is, as with Donne, linked with new possibilities of depravity. And so, beneath what may seem the tedious iterations of a baroque conceit, is a determination to find order in all things, even the smallest, after the greater ordering of the heavens has been disallowed. 'Brown never states in so many words', declares Lytton Strachey, 'what his own feelings towards the universe actually are'. No, not in so many words; but in every word it is implicit. In what Strachey describes as his 'magnificent brushwork', comparable to that of a Rubens or a Velasquez, in the phrase that he chooses to walk for miles with, ringing and ringing on the inward ear -- 'according to the ordainer of order and mystical mathematicks of the City of Heaven' -- there is implied that all-encompassing architecture: that framework which he wills still to prevail, in spite of the new heaven and the new earth. Or take the other, the 'astonishing sentence': 'meanwhile Epicurus lies deep in Dante's hell';[47] suddenly, when given context, this switches aspect from quaint inquiry to contemporary issue. No, there is no irrelevance in *The Garden of Cyrus*: least of all in that which its author alleges for 'crosses and crucifixions'. He has put the cross of Constantine back in the sky, in the hope that in this sign faith once again will conquer.

> But the Quincunx of Heaven runs low, and 'tis time to close the five ports of knowledge; We are unwilling to spin out our awaking thoughts into the phantasmes of sleep, which often continueth præcogitations; making Cables of Cobwebbes, and Wildernesses of handsome Groves.[48]

Which is precisely what the eighteenth century, through the medium of Temple, set itself to accomplish.

## vii

GILBERT Burnet, who had sailed with William to England, persuaded Mary to surrender her authority to him, and been rewarded with the see of Salisbury, declared that Temple 'was an Epicurean both in principle and in practice', who 'seemed to think that things were as they are from all eternity...'[49]

This certainly was the teaching of Epicurus: that the universe was matter in motion, uncreated and indestructible;[50] and this it was which earned him his place in Dante's hell, where those for whom the soul perished with the body were, considered as his followers, laid living in the tomb:

> *Suo cimitero da questa parte hanno*
> *con Epicuro tutti i suoi seguaci,*
> *che l'anima col corpo morta fanno.*[51]

Temple's essay on Epicurus appeared in the same volume as his defence of the ancients; and Bentley, like Burnet a cleric of the Church of England, soon afterwards delivered a series of sermons defending 'the Christian religion against notorious infidels, viz. Atheists, Deists, Pagans...': the ultimate target of which has been seen as Epicurus.[52] The discrediting of Temple's classicism, then, will have appeared in the light of a duty, whatever incidental satisfaction it may have afforded that sardonic spirit.

As Temple's thought evolved, however, ultimate questions had come to seem unanswerable: questions such as

> whether the world were eternal, or produced at some certain time? whether, if produced, it was by some eternal Mind, and to some end, or by the fortuitous concourse of atoms, or some particles of eternal matter? whether there was one world, or many? whether the soul of man was a part of some etherial and eternal substance, or was corporal? whether, if eternal, it was so before it came into the body, or only after it went out?

All attempts at solution, he considered,

> seem to agree but in one thing, which is, the want of demonstration or satisfaction, to any thinking and unpossessed man.[53]

Here the atomic cosmology -- 'the fortuitous concourse of atoms' -- is dissolved in the scepticism into which it dissolves all else. What is left is Epicurus as guide to existence; and here he is found supreme. His attitude, as Temple sees it, is this:

> neither to disquiet life with the fears of death, nor death with the desires of life; but in both, and in all things else, to follow nature.[54]

And it is this quietism which is the target of the *Tale of a Tub*. At its centre is the word '*Superficies*': the satirist's commendation is of him

> that can with *Epicurus* content his Ideas with the *Films* and *Images* that fly off upon his Senses from the *Superficies* of Things.[55]

The term relates to a key concept in Epicurus.[56] Lucretius in his exposition of the master's doctrine speaks of *simulacra* -- the *eidola* of his original:[57] atomic particles discharged from the surface -- or '*Superficies*' -- of visible objects, which form themselves into -- Swift's phrase again -- '*Films* and *Images*':

> *quae, quasi membranae summo de corpore rerum*
> *dereptae, volitant ultroque citroque per auras.*

And it is this process, Lucretius goes on to assert, that accounts for the belief in spirits. We ought not therefore, he insists, to imagine that there are souls which can escape from any underworld, or shadows that flit about among the living:

> *ne forte animas Acherunte reamur*
> *effugere aut umbras inter vivos volitare.*

Swift, then, has taken the physics of Epicurus, and reflected it back over his philosophy.[58] By his refusal to adhere to the orthodox theology, Temple is, the *Tale* implies, a dweller on the surface of things. Swift, like Bentley, was an Anglican cleric: and it is now apparent how he could break a lance against him in the *Battle of the Books*, and embrace him as brother in the *Tale of a Tub*.

## viii

BURNET coupled his denunciation of Temple as Epicurean with the assertion that he was 'a great admirer of the sect of Confucius in China, who were atheists themselves but left religion to the rabble'.[59] This is a caricature of what Temple wrote. Their 'gross and sottish idolatry', he had stated, 'is only among the vulgar or illiterate'; but 'the learned adore the Spirit of the world, which they hold to be eternal; and this without temples, idols, or Priests'.[60]

Burnet's distorting rage is impelled, perhaps, by this questioning of a clerical monopoly; but it is intriguing that he should have connected the two. For Confucius was indeed for Temple a kind of eastern Epicurus. 'The chief principle', he reports,

> he seems to lay down for a foundation, and builds upon, is, that every man ought to study and endeavour the improving and perfecting of his own natural reason to the greatest height he is capable, so as he may never (or as seldom as can be) err and swerve from the law of nature...[61]

This, however, does not belong to Confucianism proper, but to the Neo–Confucian syncretism which, in the words of Needham,

> set, by a prodigious effort of philosophical insight and imagination, the highest ethical values of man in their proper place against the background of non–human Nature.

This philosophy of nature was taken over from the Tao,[62] in which Needham finds a 'close and unmistakable' parallel with the Epicurean quietism;[63] and with which, certainly, Temple's affinities are to be found. 'His life', it is said of the sage in *Chuang Tzu*, 'is like the drifting of a boat'. For the Tao is the way of water,[64] the philosophy of continuous flow;[65] and it is this living line that is manifest in the Chinese, and through it the Japanese, garden. In the landscape arts of Japan, writes R.H. Blyth, 'the aim is to reduce the complexity, the wild lawlessness of the material, to that point, and not beyond it, where the true nature of the thing is revealed to the poetic eye'.[66] This might be a paraphrase of Temple's *sharawadgi*: 'where the beauty shall be great, and strike the eye, but without any order or disposition of parts that shall be commonly or easily observed'.[67]

Temple, then, had discovered, not only the aesthetic of *sharawadgi*, but the world–view that it implied. And this was no coincidence. Macaulay, for all his professed contempt of him as a thinker, yet acknowledges in his early essays 'a mind habituated carefully to reflect on its own operations'.[68] 'I find', Temple had written,

> soe little ease and satisfaction by giving my thoughts full scope and liberty of rambling that I must een recall them, but they are past it allready, noe sooner out of hand but out of sight, besides they take such ayery pathes and are soe light themselves leaving neither impression nor sent behind them that tis im–possible to follow them by the track of either, well let um goe they are not

> worth an hue and cry...I put my selfe upon this taske of writing not out of a desire to preserve my fancyes but to destroy them...life is theire death, order and continuance dissolves theire being, theire independency will suffer nothing of law nor constraint...[69]

A young man -- he was twenty-four when this was written[70] -- whose reveries took such 'ayery pathes' that they would 'suffer nothing of law nor constraint' was already predisposed towards a pattern of garden design in which neither logic nor constriction was apparent. He had found, as the dominant principle of his own mind, the fluid universe of Epicurus.

And, as it was lacking in a centre, the Epicurean world-picture was limitless in extent.[71] So it was too in the thought of China. 'It is as if', stated one of its writers, 'the whole of empty space were a tree, and heaven and earth were one of its fruits'.[72]

## ix

THIS was the vision that had swum back into the sights of the seventeenth century; and those in the eye of the storm were torn between exultation and terror. 'Even Kepler', it has been observed, 'was frightened by the wild perspective opened up by Galileo's spyglass: "The infinite is unthinkable", he repeatedly exclaimed in anguish'.[73]

Swift suffered terribly from waves of dizziness that enveloped him like 'a hundred oceans rolling in my ears',[74] in the disorder known as labyrinthine vertigo. The term is medical; but no more appropriate metaphor could have been devised for the being set adrift on the 'ayery pathes' of the new astronomy.[75] And when Swift traces his malady to a surfeit of the fruit of Temple's garden,[76] it is tempting to take this, too, as metaphorical. For here, as it would seem, the bottom fell out of his world; and he was never able to put it together again. Temple had initiated him into the causes of things; had pointed out to him

Where all the fruitful atoms lie,
How some go downwards to the root,
Some more ambitiously upwards fly,
And form the leaves, the branches, and the fruit.[77]

Swift refers ostensibly to politics; but the imagery is ominous. Temple's garden essay had gone to the press in his hand;[78] and here, it is difficult to doubt, he had discovered how

> Fancy, flying up to the Imagination of what is Highest and Best, becomes over-shot, and spent, and weary, and suddenly falls like a dead Bird of Paradise, to the Ground.[79]

Temple in his garden had given him to eat of the fruit of knowledge; and he struggled to tell himself that, if paradise had been blasted there, it was as prelude to its eventual restoration:

Hence mankind fell, and here must rise again.[80]

But he determined to quit the garden. Being, as he says, 'inclined to take orders', but having a 'scruple of entring into the church meerly for support', he extracted from Temple the promise of a sinecure in his gift:

> Whereupon Mr Swift told him, that since he had now an opportunity of living without being driven into the church for a maintenance, he was resolved to...take holy orders.

Upon which he reports:

> He was extremely angry I left him.[81]

But the stratagem in which Swift involved Temple was a mere externalisation of the dilemma of his own mind. No sooner had the *Tale* been published than it was denounced as 'one of the Prophanest Banters upon the Religion of *Jesus Christ*, as such, that ever yet appeared', and -- supreme irony -- its authorship attributed to Temple.[82] Swift was never able to shake off its implications. He believed -- and current scholarship is disposed to agree with him -- that the *Tale* affected his chances of preferment;[83] and, when he became dean of St. Patrick's, another Dublin cleric claimed to have fixed these verses to the door:

> This place he got by wit and rhyme
> And many ways more odd
> And might a bishop be in time
> Did he believe in God.[84]

It is difficult to doubt that, on one level, Swift was indeed the _hypocrite renversé_ that a friend discerned: possessed in secret by fear and trembling, yet taking an impish delight in concealing his religious observances from the world.[85] But there are elements that will not fit into this synthesis. The _Tale of a Tub_ and the _Battle of the Books_ appeared in the same volume as _The Mechanical Operation of the Spirit_, which is the key to the other two. Materialist reductionism is the generic method of Swiftian satire: in the _Tale_, it takes the form of exposing religious disturbance as physiological disorder. The ostensible target is false religion; but that it could be applied to all religion was as obvious to Swift's startled contemporaries as it has since been to the psychoanalysis to which he is a hero and a pioneer.[86] And it is a remarkable fact that the fundamental allegory of the _Tale_ is that of religion as a coat: precisely that analogy of surfaces which it execrates in Temple.

Consider the passage in which Swift's narrator, having promised to unravel the cause of madness, goes on:

THERE is in Mankind a certain * * * * *<br>
* * * * * * * * * *<br>
* * * * * * * * * *<br>
* * * * * * * * _Hic multa_<br>
* * * * * * * * _desiderantur._<br>
* * * * * * * * * *<br>
* * * And this I take to be a clear Solution of the Matter.

It 'were well', comments his hypothetical editor, 'if all Metaphysical Cobweb Problems were no otherwise answered':[87] so echoing the attitude of Temple. And is there not significance in the invasion of the text by asterisks: coherence undermined by a field of stars? Is this not the mirror at the heart of the labyrinth?

*Hic multa desiderantur*: to be desired, indeed.

Temple had shown Swift the view into the abyss; but he could not contemplate it with Temple's equanimity. He attempted to exorcise the vision; but it stole up behind him in ever more atrocious shapes. He remained obsessed with infinity: with the infinitely large as revealed by Galileo's telescope; with the infinitely little as revealed, in Temple's Holland, by van Leeuwenhoek's microscope:

> So, naturalists observe, a flea
> Hath smaller fleas that on him prey,
> And these have smaller yet to bite 'em,
> And so proceed *ad infinitum*.[88]

Gulliver's world is that of a humanity quartered between absurdities: the monstrously great and the monstrously small, the analytical mind that floats above the earth, and the animal body that riots in its mire. Swift is the surrealist of the new philosophy.

## X

FOR he was nothing if not ambivalent. Ehrenpreis has discovered, in the gigantic visage of the king of Brobdingnag, the humane features of Temple;[89] and, at the end of the day, it was Temple's vision that prevailed. In St. Patrick's Cathedral in Dublin, from the spot where adjoining tablets in the floor mark the presumed resting-place of Swift and Stella, may be seen the black marble tablet on which is inscribed what a character in Yeats describes as 'the greatest epitaph in history';[90] and in which Middleton Murry has noted a curious omission:

> It is silent on any Christian hope. It might be the epitaph of one of his Roman heroes -- a Brutus or a Cato: except perhaps for the fierce indignation that tears at his heart no more. Death is not the opening of a gate, but the closing of a wound.[91]

It is glossed by another inscription, in another church, in another city. The city is London, the church Westminster Abbey. Temple gave orders that his heart was to be buried by his sundial at Moor Park, and his body here, with those of the three women he loved: his daughter, his wife and his sister; and the inscription simply records that fact:

*SIBI SUISQUE CARISSIMIS*
*DIANÆ TEMPLE DILECTISSIMÆ FILIÆ*
*DOROTHEÆ OSBORNE CONJUNCTISSIMÆ CONJUGI*
*ET MARTHÆ GIFFARD OPTIMÆ SORORI*
*HOC QUALECUMQUE MONUMENTUM*
*PONI CURAVIT*
*GULIELMUS TEMPLE, BARONETTUS*[92]

It is an extraordinary statement: it speaks of his affections, but says nothing of his beliefs. Swift, then, as he faced the ultimate mystery, took his mode from Temple: the mode of silence.

Temple might be thought of as the first romantic, Lawrence the last;[93] and Lawrence at the end can add nothing to Temple at the beginning. 'Live and let live', he writes, in a formula that R.H. Blyth equates with the Japanese attitude to nature,[94]

> love and let love, flower and fade, and follow the natural curve, which flows on, pointless.[95]

Apart from that last, dogmatic adjective, this is identical with Temple's summation of Epicurus:

> Neither to disquiet life with the fear of death, nor death with the desires of life; but in both, and in all things else, to follow nature.[96]

This is what he lived by, and he died as he had lived. His tomb is inscribed to the unknown god; and his heart is in his garden.

## CHAPTER FIVE

# THE SPACIOUS FIRMAMENT ON HIGH

'I WAS yesterday about Sun–set', wrote Addison,

> walking in the open Fields, till the Night insensibly fell upon me. I at first amused my self with all the Richness and Variety of Colours which appeared in the Western Parts of Heaven: In Proportion as these faded away and went out, several Stars and Planets appeared one after another, till the whole Firmament was in a Glow.

Faced with this infinite vista, Addison was assailed by the panic, or as he phrases it, 'secret Horror' that preyed on the mind of Swift:

> I was afraid of being overlooked amidst the Immensity of Nature, and lost among that infinite Variety of Creatures, which in all Probability swarm through all these immeasurable Regions of Matter.

To which he replied with a consideration of the divine omnipresence:

> There is nothing he has made, that is either so distant, so little, or so inconsiderable, which he does not essentially inhabit...In short...he is a Being whose Centre is every where, and his Circumference no where.[1]

### i

THE friendship of Swift and Addison was immediate and lifelong; but it was a bridge across a chasm of difference. The 'new natural philosophy', writes Ehrenpreis, was a 'current that Addison wished to deepen but Swift to diminish'.

Swift 'yearned for boundaries and Addison for expanses'.[2]

In this he had had a privileged apprenticeship. The master of Charterhouse, still an island of the middle ages in the roar of the City of London, was obsessed with the new cosmology. Thomas Burnet, like Temple, had been a student of Cudworth's at Cambridge, and so exposed to the attempt to combine the outer vista of Epicurus, or his mentor Democritus, with the inner vision of Plato. In the year that Temple left the university, Cudworth's associate Henry More, in a volume aptly titled *Democritus Platonissans*, exclaimed:

> Wherefore with leave th'infinite I'll sing
> Of Time, of Space: or without leave; I'm brent
> With eagre rage, my heart for joy doth spring,
> And all my spirits move with pleasant trembeling.

'The striking and appalling thing, to a medieval man', comments Tuveson, 'about this passage would be that the "pleasant trembeling" is inspired by the infinity not of the divine Spirit but of space and time'; and Burnet gave this infinity aesthetic formulation. It was he, Tuveson continues, who, in his *Sacred Theory of the Earth*, expressed 'what amounted to a new sensibility'.[3] 'The greatest Objects of Nature', stated Burnet,

> are, methinks, the most pleasing to behold; and next to the great Concave of the Heavens, and those boundless Regions where the Stars inhabit, there is nothing that I look upon with more Pleasure than the wide Sea and the Mountains of the Earth. There is something august and stately in the Air of these things, that inspires the Mind with great Thoughts and Passions.

Had he confined himself to this aspect of his theme, Burnet's later career might have been happier; but, being no less 'brent' than More with the fervour of the new vision, he attempted to reconcile it with the Bible. For, while its infinity inspired him, he was dismayed by its irregularity, his preconceptions being those of the geometrical garden. And so, though he found the earth even enough in places,

> yet if we consider the whole Surface of it...'tis a broken and confused Heap of Bodies, placed in no Order to one another, nor with any Correspondency or Regularity of Parts: And such a Body as the Moon appears to us, when 'tis

> looked upon with a good Glass, rude and ragged...such a Thing would the Earth appear if it was seen from the Moon.[4]

Such disorder, clearly, was the result of sin. The original earth, by contrast, had been a regular sphere, without mountains or seas, spread over an inner sphere of water, from which rivers flowed from the poles to the equator. The biblical deluge occurred when the earth collapsed into the abyss of waters, and the land and the sea, as we know them, formed.[5]

When it was objected that Genesis described a terraqueous globe, Burnet replied that Moses 'did not Philosophize or Astronomize'; that his was 'a narration suited to the capacity of the people'.[6] The literal tale of the Garden, with its talking snake, was ludicrous: a point he underlined by a lively retelling, in which a courtly serpent accosts Eve, as she gazes in wonder at the Tree, and assures her of the virtue of its fruit:

> Serp. *Salve pulcherrima, Quid rerum agis sub hâc umbrâ, sola et seria?*
> Ev. *Ego hujus Arboris pulchritudinem contemplor.*
> Serp. *Jucundum quidem spectaculum, sed multo jucundiores fructus...*[7]

The result was uproar, as Burnet's theory took to the streets in the form of a ballad explaining

> That all the books of Moses
> Were nothing but supposes...
> That as for Father Adam
> And Mrs. Eve, his Madame,
> And what the devil spoke, Sir,
> 'Twas nothing but a joke, Sir,
> And well-invented flam.

If, as was reported, he was considered for the see of Canterbury, that had now become unthinkable.[8]

## ii

WHILE Burnet languished in a limbo between ridicule and obscurity, his former pupil did not desert him. Addison published an ode in his praise, titled, tellingly, *Ad Insignissimum Virum D. THO. BURNETTUM*; and, as if to remove any doubt as to the character of his mentor's distinction, he added *Sacrae Theoriae Telluris Autorem*. The body of the poem was equally forthright. Here Addison spoke of Burnet as one who, uncompromising in his quest into the unknown, was no less uncompromising towards the herd mentality and its received untruths:

*Dum veritatem quaerere pertinax*
*Ignota pandis, sollicitus parum*
*Utcunque stet commune vulgi*
*Arbitrium et popularis error.*

'*Popularis error*' is a daring stigmatisation of the literal interpretation of the Bible: all the more so in a young man who still had his career to make, and who depended for it upon his patrons at King William's court. But Addison addresses Burnet, his biographer observes, in 'superlatives unusual in his writing';[9] and it is not difficult to see why. In the course of his ode, Addison revisits the scenery of his mentor's cosmology, placing himself at that moment when the earth, collapsing, revealed to the inhabitants of the water, previously shut up as in a prison, the vision of the sun, or left them marvelling, as they swam, at the stars, and the tremulous image of the moon:

*Nunc et recluso carcere lucidam*
*Balaena spectat solis imaginem,*
*Stellasque miratur natantes*
*Et tremulae simulacra lunae.*[10]

It was as if Burnet had impelled an equal release to Addison's own vision. Certainly freedom from incarceration was the dominant image of his oration at the Sheldonian Theatre, where he defended the thesis that the new philosophy was to be preferred to the old. His method was clever and paradoxical. 'Shall we', he queried, 'stigmatise with the name of novelty that philosophy, which, though but lately revived, is more ancient than the Peripatetic, and as old as the matter from whence it is derived?':

> *Si vero Philosophiae isti Novitatis nomen tribuendum sit, quae quanquam jam primum innotuerit, vel Peripateticam Antiquitate superat, & ipsi materiae, a quo derivatur, extitit coaetanea.*

But the peculiar attraction of this philosophy was hinted at in his contempt for its opposite. It was a scorning 'to be any longer bounded within the straits and crystalline walls of an Aristotelic world':

> *inter mundi Aristotelici angustias & moenia chrystallina diutius coarctari.*[11]

If Addison's experience of his home was one of emotional claustrophobia, it is not surprising that he should have spurned the enclosing walls of a limited world; or that a mentor who stood up to irrational authority should have meshed with his own inner needs. This collocation of psychology and cosmology was to take definitive shape in that vision of landscape which was the culmination of his quest for coherence. And, as in every quest, monsters lurked along the way.

### iii

ADDISON was equally loyal to another unlucky cleric. William Whiston had succeeded Newton at Cambridge, and Burnet in investigating the relations between science and scripture. But when he lost this position over his theological opinions, Addison, who was, he says, 'my particular Friend', arranged for him to deliver a series of lectures on astronomy at his coffee–house near Covent Garden, 'to the agreeable Entertainment of a good Number of Curious Persons'.[12]

Amongst the curious persons was Pope; and the consequences were more curious still. Pope had previously regarded Whiston as disreputable;[13] attendance at the coffeehouse, however, placed him, in his own estimation,

> above the stars, with a thousand systems round about me, looking forward into the vast abyss of eternity, and losing my whole comprehension in the boundless space of the extended Creation, in dialogues with Whiston and the astronomers.

This letter, originally addressed elsewhere, was in Pope's printing of it readdressed to Addison. This served a double function. It enabled him to present himself as, lost in a cosmic vastness, holding Addison's friendship 'one of the best comforts I have for the insignificance of my self',[14] at a time when he was egging Dennis on to discredit *Cato*; and it enabled him to inform Addison about matters in which the latter had been the means of instructing him.[15]

'Every hour of my life', Pope declared in this epistle, 'my mind is strangely divided';[16] and, when he came to share his insights with the world at large, he gave ample evidence of this predicament. 'If', writes Leslie Stephen of the *Essay on Man*,

> he had fairly grasped some definite conception of the universe...he might have given forcible expression to the corresponding emotions...He might again conceivably have written an interesting work, though it would hardly have been a poem -- if he had versified the arguments by which a coherent theory might be supported. Unluckily, he was quite unqualified for either undertaking, and, at the same time, he more or less aimed at both.[17]

The verdict of later scholarship is not significantly different, detecting in the poem a radical ambivalence.[18] This was anticipated in its opening image, where the universe was described as

A mighty maze! but not without a plan.

In an earlier printing, however, it had appeared as

A mighty maze of walks without a plan.

That Pope, in two editions of the same poem, could describe the universe both as with and without order suggests the dichotomy that he manifested elsewhere; and it is significant, in this respect, that the image is taken from Addison:

The ways of Heaven are dark and intricate,

Puzzled in Mazes and perplex'd with errors:
Our understanding traces 'em in vain,
Lost and bewilder'd in the fruitless search;
Nor sees with how much art the windings run,
Nor where the regular confusion ends.[19]

These lines appear in *Cato*: it was characteristic of Pope that he should borrow a critical passage in his poetry from a work on which he had strained to bring ridicule. Characteristic, too, that where Addison had created a synthesis, Pope should institute a split. For where Pope wavers between cosmos and chaos, Addison sees the first behind the appearance of the second.[20] He had derived the concept from Temple's *sharawadgi*, in which nature conceals the reach of a subtle and hidden art;[21] and applied it to the order which by now had been rediscovered in the universe.

## iv

FOR the Epicurean moment had not endured. The frightening, chaotic prospect opened up by Galileo was returned to order by Newton. 'No other work', states A.R. Hall,

> in the whole history of science equals the *Principia* either in originality and power of thought, or in the majesty of its achievement...Order could be brought to celestial physics only once, and it was Newton who brought order.[22]

Newton, observes Koestler, 'was to do in imagination what history had failed to achieve: to bring Kepler and Galileo together'. Galileo had established that a projectile once placed in orbit would move perpetually in a circle; Kepler, that the actual orbit of the planets was an ellipse. Newton identified the source of the disparity as the power of the sun's attraction, or gravity. This, however, required rigorous mathematical corroboration, to provide which it was necessary to develop the infinitesimal calculus. Once he had done so, Newton had accounted for all observable motion in the universe; and so, at the end of the century of Donne, coherence was restored.[23]

It was such a coherence, moreover, as allayed the fears of the devout. For Newton, gravitation was not a physical, but a metaphysical force. 'It is inconceivable', he wrote to an inquiring cleric,

> that inanimate brute matter should, without mediation of something else which is not material, operate upon and affect other matter without mutual contact, as it must be if gravitation, in the sense of Epicurus, be essential and inherent in it.[24]

The villain is Epicurus, the cleric Bentley, the year the year after Temple's Epicurean essay has gone into its third printing; but for Addison, now, there is no contradiction. 'Others', he writes,

> have considered infinite Space as the Receptacle, or rather the Habitation of the Almighty: But the noblest and most exalted way of considering this infinite Space is that of Sir *Isaac Newton*, who calls it the *Sensorium* of the Godhead.[25]

Any conflict, then, between the religious and the revolutionary Addison is illusory: the 'strain of mysticism' in him, notes Smithers, is only 'apparently anomalous'.[26] The key to the connection is to be found in that passage where he declares that of 'all Hardnesses of Heart, there is none so inexcusable as that of Parents towards their Children'. The man, he goes on, 'who, notwithstanding any Passion or Resentment, can overcome this powerful Instinct, and extinguish natural Affection, debases his Mind even below Brutality'. Here Addison is a rebel, and a romantic rebel, founding his condemnation of the abuse of authority on natural feeling. He, he goes on, who can

> extinguish natural Affection...frustrates, as much as in him lies, the great Design of Providence, and strikes out of his Nature one of the most Divine Principles that is planted in it.

The 'Love, Tenderness, and Compassion', declares Addison, 'which are apt to arise in us towards those who depend upon us, is that by which the whole World of Life is upheld':[27] *l'amor che move il sole e l'altre stelle.*[28]

## V

AND so it was inevitable that where Louis XIV had laid down despotism, Addison should discover liberation. Louis always refused to have any terminal point to his great avenue.[29] It was to be a vista without limit; and there could be little doubt as to whose pretensions it expressed. Versailles, writes Christopher Thacker, was 'a gesture of arrogance':

> Félibien, the royal historiographer, writes succinctly of the use throughout the château and the gardens of the sun-motifs, linked with that of Apollo: 'It is proper to point out that, since the Sun is the king's device, and since poets identify the Sun with Apollo, there is nothing in this superb edifice which is not linked to this divinity'. There is in the gardens of Versailles an extraordinary and intended emphasis on the Apollo-sun-god allegory: not only are there many features related to different aspects of the mythology connected with Apollo, but they dominate the gardens, from the statues of Apollo and Diana set by the central window of the Galerie des Glaces to the group of Apollo and his chariot at the head of the Canal, and the Latona fountain midway between the château and the Canal (Latona or Leto was Apollo's mother). The east-west axis of the gardens, marked by these memorials of the sun god's power and progress, seems to be united to the axis of the sun itself, as it rises beyond the château, and sets at the far end of the great Canal. It is curious that at Versailles the *temples* of love, friendship, music, wisdom and the like, so frequent in great gardens from the Renaissance onwards, just are not there. They would have been a distraction from the Apollo-sun-Louis symbolism, an impertinence even. Versailles is firmly dedicated to this one cult.

But of course. With an arrogance of cosmic dimensions, he had translated the new astronomy into terms of himself.[30] And Addison, when his career with the Whigs brought him in course of time to Versailles, was undeniably impressed. 'I cou'd not believe', he wrote of the royal gardens, 'it was in the power of Art to Furnish out Such a variety of noble Scenes':[31] what Saint-Simon described as the king's *plaisir superbe de forcer la nature*'.[32] And yet, as he formulated his native preference for freedom in terms of nature, he was to invert Louis' cosmology. A 'spacious Horison', he wrote, 'is an Image of Liberty'.[33]

## vi

'IT was Addison', states Tuveson,'that representative man, who succeeded in fitting sensibility and theory together'.[34] This he did, gathering it into a coherent system, in the form of his aesthetic. Each of the three categories he had distinguished -- the Uncommon, the Beautiful, the Great -- was founded on a psychological response. But behind each, in a equally coherent theodicy, he discerned an aspect of divine purpose. The Uncommon, he suggested, had been made attractive to encourage the 'Pursuit after Knowledge'; the Beautiful, that 'all Creatures might be tempted to multiply their Kind'; while the source of the delight in Greatness, he thought, was this: that the 'Supreme Author of our Being has so formed the Soul of Man, that nothing but himself can be its last, adequate, and proper Happiness'.[35]

Addison's description, Tuveson declares, 'of the response to the vast is new in its consistency and its lack of self-consciousness and of a sense of conflict of values';[36] and its integrative function is formulated 'with characteristic incisiveness' in the sentence:

> Such wide and undetermined Prospects are as pleasing to the Fancy as the Speculations of Eternity or Infinitude are to the Understanding.[37]

Here, Tuveson concludes, '*Weltanschauung* and sensibility...are in perfect balance and harmony'.[38] *Weltanschauung* it is, indeed, in the truest sense: a vision of the world both literal and metaphorical, which concentrates the insight of a lifetime:

> The Mind of Man naturally hates every thing that looks like a Restraint upon it, and is apt to fancy it self under a sort of Confinement, when the Sight is pent up in a narrow Compass, and shortnd on every side by the Neighbourhood of Walls or Mountains.

It is here, by way of antithesis, that Addison turns the 'spacious Horison' -- the infinite vista of the new western cosmology, which had come to resemble that of the east -- into another paradigm of liberation -- here, in the same place, and to the same end, as he advocates the adoption of *sharawadgi*.[39] The two main features, then, of the revolutionary English garden -- internal liberty and external freedom from constraint -- had been brought together by Addison out of the needs of his own nature.

The change of taste in gardening, wrote Lovejoy, involved 'a change of taste in universes'.[40] A change in universes, certainly; yet not, after all, so much a matter of taste. The English landscape garden evolved under the changing shadow of that mythic tree, the body of which was the *axis mundi*, and its fruits the scattered stars.

# CHAPTER SIX

# IL RIPOSO DI CLAUDIO

WHEN Addison invented the English landscape garden, giving it internal liberty and external freedom from constraint, one factor remained to complete it; and this, too, was implicit in his thought.

Already, on his travels, he had exulted in distant prospects,[1] of a kind evocative of the new astronomy. At Capri, he had seen 'a vast extent of seas, that runs abroad further than the eye can reach'; while at Tivoli was a vista which 'opens on one side into the *Roman Campania*, where the eye loses it self on a smooth spacious plain': which, he observed, the '*Roman* Painters often work upon'.[2]

Though the reference is generic, none of the Roman painters worked upon that landscape with greater intensity than Claude Lorrain; and the 'real subject', writes Marcel Röthlisberger, of Claude's early paintings,

> is the dramatic effect of the sun, the atmosphere as it changes from hour to hour, and what can truly be claimed Claude's greatest invention -- the painting of the sun itself...Strange as it may seem, this is unprecedented.[3]

The strangeness may abate a little when it is recalled that Claude lived in the Rome of Galileo, being already settled in the area of Trinità dei Monti when the astronomer was lodged there during his trial:[4] a trial which revolved around the centrality of the sun. It may not be thought coincidence, either, that the Sun King showed himself avid for the paintings of Claude, that the creator of his vistas had some in his possession, and that Louis appropriated them.[5]

But Claude brought to his landscapes a vision more resonant than any new world could offer: for him, it reopened the portals of the old. Rome's greatest poet had derived, from the Lucretian exposition of Epicurus, a radiant vision of unlimited space and fluid light;[6] and Claude's paintings, it has been observed, 'are saturated with the Vergilian spirit':[7] of pastoral feeling for the Italian landscape,[8] rendered numinous by a sense of vast distances beyond.[9]

So it was that, in Claude's Campagna, the classical temples stand among trees, their shadows framing some exquisite morning, where the hills retreat into a lucid void; or cluster round a seaport at the fall of night, ships silhouetted at anchor along a lane of fire.

## i

ADDISON's aesthetic theory, in its visual dimension, reads like a transcript of Claude. Of Greatness, he declared that 'wide and undetermined Prospects' conduce to a 'delightful Stillness and Amazement in the Soul'; while of Beauty, which diffuses a 'secret Satisfaction and Complacency thro' the Imagination', he wrote: 'we no where meet with a more glorious or pleasing Show in Nature, than what appears in the Heavens at the rising and the setting of the Sun'; and of the Uncommon he stated:

> There is nothing that more enlivens a Prospect than Rivers, Jetteaus, or Falls of Water, where the Scene is perpetually shifting, and entertaining the Sight every Moment with something that is new.[10]

This was a variant of his recollection of Tivoli, explicitly connected with landscape painting:

> But the most enlivening part of all is the river *Teverone*, which you see at about a quarter of a mile's distance throwing it self down a precipice, and falling by several Cascades from one rock to another, 'till it gains the bottom of the valley, where the sight of it would be quite lost, did not it sometimes discover it self through the breaks and openings of the woods that grow about it. The *Roman* Painters often work upon this Landskip, and I am apt to believe that *Horace* had

> his eye upon it in those two or three beautiful touches which he has given us of these seats.[11]

'Mr. Addison', observed Horace Walpole, 'travelled through the poets, and not through Italy';[12] and in so doing he exemplified what Lionel Trilling has described as the *'other culture*, the ideal culture, that wonderful imagined culture of the ancient world': which, he goes on, 'no one but schoolboys, schoolmasters, scholars and poets believed in'.[13] In the eighteenth century, however, politicians believed in it; or thought it expedient to appear as if they did. The elder Pitt, dying in a season of disaster for England, asked that there be read to him, from the final lines of the Iliad, the stately obsequies of Hector and Troy's despair. And his son in turn, when he faced the mockery of parliament for having concluded peace with Bonaparte, answered in the words of Aeneas that he had not consulted his own desires. *Me si fata meis*, he began,

> *paterentur ducere vitam*
> *auspiciis et sponte mea componere curas,*
> *urbem Troianum...*

Somewhere around here he faltered; and Fox, his lifelong rival, prompted him through the rest:

> *...primum dulcisque meorum*
> *reliquias colerem, Priami tecta alta manerent,*
> *et recidiva manu posuissem Pergama victis.*[14]

Even the ferocious practicality of Johnson was stilled before that compound of majesty and magic. 'All the modern languages', he declared, 'cannot furnish so melodious a line' as

> *formosam resonare doces Amaryllida silvas.*[15]

So it was that, when Addison liberated the English landscape, it was by the invocation of classical authority. 'The Beauties of the most stately Garden or Palace', he wrote,

> lie in a narrow Compass, the Imagination immediately runs them over, and requires something else to gratifie her; but, in the wide Fields of Nature, the Sight wanders up and down without Confinement...

'For this Reason', he went on, 'we always find the Poet in love with a Country–Life': a contention he illustrated from Horace and Vergil.[16]

And so it may be taken as inevitable that the romantic English garden, with its vista of illimitable woodland, should be set with the temples of antiquity.[17]

## ii

ANTHONY Ashley Cooper, third Earl of Shaftesbury, had impeccable Whig credentials. Grandson of the party's founder, his education had been supervised by Locke, theorist of the revolution;[18] and, in the year of Addison's garden essay, Shaftesbury declared to Addison's patron, Somers, that this had created an ideal aesthetic ambience. 'Nothing', he wrote, 'is so improving, nothing so natural, so congenial to the liberal arts, as that reigning liberty and high spirit of a people, which from the habit of judging in the highest matters for themselves, makes them freely judge of other subjects'.

Despotism, on the other hand, worked to the opposite effect: 'since it is not the nature of a court (such as courts generally are) to improve, but rather corrupt a taste'. Even the genius of Christopher Wren, it appeared, could not redeem the inherent viciousness of that courtly idiom, the baroque:

> Hardly, indeed, as the public now stands, should we bear to see a Whitehall treated like a Hampton Court, or even a new cathedral like St. Paul's;

while the churches still a–building in London to the designs of Wren and his associates, 'the many spires arising in our great city', might

> be the occasion perhaps that our immediate relish shall be hereafter censured, as retaining much of what artists call the Gothic kind.[19]

How baroque could be classed as Gothic might at first sight appear something of a puzzle. Both, however, had arisen from Catholicism, the first from its medieval regime, the second from the Counter-Reformation; and it was the latter, in the person of James II, which had been the target of the revolution. Both, therefore, were associated, in the Whig mind, with the elaboration, and therefore corruption, of an original simplicity.

This association, as it applied to the medieval style, was eloquently glossed by Addison. 'Poets', he wrote, 'who want...that majestick Simplicity to Nature, which we so much admire in the Works of the Ancients, are forced to hunt after foreign Ornaments'. 'I look', he went on,

> upon these Writers as *Goths* in Poetry, who, like those in Architecture, not being able to come up to the beautiful Simplicity of the old *Greeks* and *Romans*, have endeavoured to supply its Place with all the Extravagancies of an irregular Fancy.[20]

The same held true of the baroque. 'When King James II', writes Simeon Potter, 'observed that the new St. Paul's Cathedral was *amusing*, *awful*, and *artificial*, he implied that Sir Christopher Wren's recent creation was "pleasing, awe-inspiring, and skilfully achieved"'.[21] For Shaftesbury, on the other hand, the new cathedral was *amusing*, *awful*, and *artificial* in precisely the modern senses of these words: he found it risible, unsightly, and unnatural.

And so there arose the apparent paradox noted by Wittkower: that

> in the reign of Queen Anne...Baroque houses were placed in 'unnatural', formal gardens derived from France, while in the reigns of George I...and his successors classical houses were given 'romantic' landscape-garden settings.

The paradox, however, was only apparent: garden and house were subsumed in a higher ideal; or, as Wittkower phrases it, were 'two sides of the same medal inscribed "LIBERTY"'.[22] 'All that was ever desirable', wrote the republican martyr Algernon Sidney, 'or worthy of praise or imitation in Rome, proceeded from its liberty, grew up, and perished with it'.[23] And the classical house, as then understood, traced itself to republican Rome, as recreated by Palladio.

Palladio had in fact, with great originality and imagination, invented a style in which classical motifs were gathered into unity within a Renaissance order. The interior of the villa was harmonised into 'subtlety of proportion, composition and equilibrium' through the Pythagorean theory of number as music: room opening out of room in a continuing chordal echo. The exterior, meanwhile, was centralised around the temple portico, and linked to its outbuildings by colonnades.[24] For the church, the problem of pagan facade over Christian function was resolved by placing a tall temple front over the nave, and a lower one, split into two, over the flanking aisles, the two superimposed in a contrapuntal relief that echoed the structure within: in which simplicity of surface, punctuated by great windows, shaped the light into clear–cut masses: a formula, notes Ackerman, which held an inherent appeal for the 'cerebral, abstract' element in Protestantism.[25]

Soon after Richard Boyle, Earl of Burlington, returned from his grand tour to find Queen Anne succeeded by King George, two books of architecture, dedicated to the king -- and 'thus', comments Summerson, 'stamped as Whiggish products' -- appeared.[26] One illustrated the designs of Palladio; the other urged imitation of his 'antique simplicity' in England. Burlington, finding in the classical master the counterpart of his own austere formality, was a man possessed. He set out again for Italy, and, annotating his text as he went, traversed the languid canals and muddy fields to the blinding facades and cool interiors of the Palladian villas; or stood entranced in Venice, where in the floating blaze the lines of San Giorgio are edged and lucid as an antique gem. Returning to England, he took the theme of the domed cube of the Rotonda, on its sun–drenched hill outside Vicenza, and played a set of learned variations on it along the soberer reaches of the Thames. Chiswick was not a mansion, it was a manifesto: England would abide no longer in the Pandaemonium of the baroque.[27]

## iii

'HANDSOM, luminous, disencumbered' was Addison's response to the Palladian style.[28] In the word 'disencumbered' lurk the Puritan ancestors of the Whigs; and in Shaftesbury's loathing of the baroque, they return to life. His 'moral and aesthetic philosophy', remarks Christopher Hussey, gave 'to an architectural style the added prestige of moral rightness'.[29]

Shaftesbury's classicism, however, did not confine itself to architecture. His was a critique so radical, so absolute, that it undermined the foundations even of the puritan creed. When the church, writes C.A. Moore, 'was compelled to defend herself against a growing suspicion that Christian dogma was incompatible with recent discoveries in natural science', her apologists 'at the outset allowed almost equal weight to natural revelation and supernatural', the natural being regarded as a 'faithful record of the Creator's power and beneficence'. This side of the argument, however, developed so convincingly as to make the other seem obsolete:

> The extreme, or deistic, view was that human reason requires no other revelation than the outward and visible world. Even those rationalists who still accepted the Bible held its utterances to be merely a confirmation of universal truths already set forth to the reason of man in the Book of Nature. The line between these two positions -- the heretical and the orthodox -- was not always clearly marked...the difference was one, not of kind, but of degree.[30]

While Addison stood on the orthodox side of this spectrum, Shaftesbury 'took the heretical stand that the Deity has written himself so plainly in the Book of Nature that further revelation would have been superfluous'. Nature, to him,

> was not merely the 'objective and phenomenal' demonstration of the Creation, but was itself an emanation of the Deity; and although he actually accepted the doctrine of a personal God, his phrasing...constantly hovers on the verge of pure pantheism.[31]

Shaftesbury's sense of horror in the gloom of the mountain forest, therefore, is 'blended with a strange, religious pleasure',[32] in which

> Mysterious voices are either heard or fancied, and various forms of deity seem to present themselves and appear more manifest in these sacred silvan scenes, such as of old gave rise to temples, and favoured the religion of the ancient world.[33]

Here Shaftesbury's philosophy of nature and his programme for architecture would seem to coincide. When he refers to 'temples' in sites whose aura evokes the 'religion of the ancient world', it is as if, with the restoration of its sanctuaries, he advocated the renewal of its worship. And there is, indeed, striking evidence for this view. When he condemned baroque architecture as 'Gothic', he did not merely reject its elaboration; he repudiated its very essence. In the Christ of religious art he found a

> Barbarian. No form, no grace...Lank clinging hair, snivelling face, hypocritical canting countenance.[34]

What is extraordinary about this vision is how exactly it corresponds to the figure described by Macaulay:

> The extreme Puritan was at once known from other men by his gait, his garb, his lank hair, the sour solemnity of his face, the upturned white of his eyes, the nasal twang with which he spoke, and, above all, his peculiar dialect. He employed, on every occasion, the imagery and style of Scripture. Hebraisms violently introduced into the English language, and metaphors borrowed from the boldest lyric poetry of a remote age and country, and applied to the common concerns of English life, were the most striking peculiarities of this cant, which moved, not without cause, the derision both of prelatists and libertines.

'The learning and eloquence', Macaulay notes,

> by which the great reformers had been eminently distinguished, and to which they had been, in no small measure, indebted for their success, were regarded by the new school of Protestants with suspicion, if not with aversion. Some precisians had scruples about teaching the Latin grammar, because the names of Mars, Bacchus, and Apollo occurred in it. The fine arts were all but proscribed.[35]

Shaftesbury thus reverses the rule of the saints who were his political ancestors; and the sign under which he does so is no less significant. The saviour of conventional iconography, he goes on, is

> at best melancholy, mad and enthusiastical in the common and lower way...not so well even as the Bacchanals and Bacchantes;

while the uncommon and higher way, one is given to understand, is that of the 'true antique figures', which have a

> deep, eager, severe, ecstatic or enthusiastic air.[36]

'Enthusiasm', the term applied to the puritan sectaries, is here restored to its original context:[37] of that paganism against which the puritan most passionately inveighed. Shaftesbury, writes Martin Price, desires to attain release from the 'Calvinistic emphasis on human depravity'; and to that extent inverts the basis of puritan thought. When he 'argues down the evidence' for it, or 'traces it to self-disgust and the perversion of the natural', he does so, says Price,

> with the defiance...of a man seeking to uncover an important truth the world has conspired to conceal. But the defiance takes the form of therapy, a summoning up of the powers man has relinquished or guiltily suppressed.[38]

This talk of a summoning is deeply eloquent. When the Roman general had doomed a city, he called upon its gods to transfer their dwelling to Rome. This summoning, this *evocatio*, was the promise of a more centred sanctuary. And this is the ultimate significance of Shaftesbury: that he represents, in the history of puritanism, the return of the repressed.

## iv

HORACE WALPOLE remarked that Milton seemed to have anticipated the irregular garden in those lines in which, describing Paradise, he spoke of

> How from that Saphire Fount the crisped Brooks,
> Rowling on Orient Pearl and sands of Gold,
> With mazie error under pendant shades

Ran Nectar, visiting each plant, and fed
Flours worthy of Paradise which not nice Art
In Beds and curious Knots, but Nature boon
Powrd forth profuse on Hill and Dale and Plaine...[39]

Walpole's editor, however, noted Milton's antecedents in Spenser and Tasso: in both of whom art vies with nature in a garden of temptation, which in Tasso also takes the form of a maze.[40] For Milton, too, while the artless garden is unfallen nature, it carries ominous intimations of that fall in 'mazie error'. Donne's lament, likewise, over the disproportion of the heavens had found the indirect line sinister, observing of the sun that

where he rose today
He comes no more, but with a couzening line,
Steales by that point, and so is Serpentine.[41]

'Serpentine' carries inevitable overtones of the serpent in paradise, reinforced by the furtive motion of 'steals'; while 'couzening', with its connotations of deceit and seduction, calls up the curving line of Epicurus' atoms, as opposed to the geometrism inherent in Plato.[42]

Milton, too, C.S. Lewis remarks, was sensitive to the feelings of 'lost bewilderment, loneliness and agoraphobia' aroused by the new astronomy, which appear in his description of the moon drifting

Like one that had bin led astray
Through the Heav'ns wide pathles way.[43]

At the same time, as with Kepler, terror was blended with exultation. He had prepared for his journey to Italy with an introduction to Donne's friend Wotton, who had written that letter of astonishment about the telescope; and he secured a meeting there with Galileo, whom he was to place, alone amongst contemporaries, three times in *Paradise Lost*.[44] Here, Lewis observes, the two visions overlap. The traditional universe

> was both unimaginably large and unambiguously finite. It therefore had shape...The old *kosmos* humbled you by its size, but exhilarated you by its

> symmetry; the mind could rest in it with full satisfaction. The Newtonian model is less like a building than a forest; illimitable, without horizons...Milton felt a strong need to express the new sort of space-consciousness. But he also wanted to retain a good deal from the old walled and elegant *kosmos* which is so much richer in plasticity, in associations, and indeed in everything except one particular (and romantic) species of sublimity. His solution was to enclose his *world* (*kosmos* or *mundus*) in an opaque spherical shell, hang this from the floor of his *heaven* by a golden chain, and surround it with illimitable *Chaos*.

Inside his *world*, comments Lewis, 'safe inside the shell', Milton 'can still enjoy the old beauties', while outside, 'in the pathless, the waste infinity', he becomes 'the poet...of space'.[45]

There were those who from the outset sensed ambivalence in the poem; and of these the most uncompromising was Bentley. Bentley, as his treatment of Temple showed, had an inquisitorial nose in such matters; and, when he set out to edit *Paradise Lost*, posited an earlier editor who, taking advantage of the poet's blindness, had fatally corrupted the text.[46] This enabled him to dismiss some of the most glorious episodes in the poem as 'silly thought', 'meanness of Stile contemptible', and -- significantly -- 'Romantic Trash'.[47] In these deletions, therefore, a later critic has found a genuine, if grotesquely expressed, sensibility. 'He may only', comments Empson, 'produce a trivial piece of nagging, but he has a flair for choosing an important place to do it'.[48] And one such locus, inevitably, is Paradise:

> Not that faire field
> Of *Enna*, where *Prosperpin* gathring flours
> Her self a fairer Floure by gloomie *Dis*
> Was gatherd, which cost *Ceres* all that pain
> To seek her through the world; nor that sweet Grove
> Of *Daphne* by *Orontes*, and th'inspir'd
> *Castalian* spring might with this Paradise
> Of *Eden* strive; nor that *Nyseian* Ile...

Upon which Bentley is scathing: '*Not Enna*, says he, *not Daphne, nor Fons Castalius, nor Nysa, nor Mount Amara could compare with Paradise*. Why who, Sir, would suspect they could; though you had never told us it?'[49] 'A man who had given his life to the classics', replies Empson quietly, 'might easily have suspected it'. 'Milton's use of the pagan', he goes on, 'seemed to Bentley to imply a doubt of the Christian mythology; and for myself I think, not only that he was right, but that the reverberations of this doubt are the real subject of the descriptions of the Garden'.[50]

This sense of a lost perfection, says Empson, is concentrated onto the sexual situation of Adam and Eve:

In shadier Bower
More sacred and sequesterd, though but feignd,
*Pan* or *Silvanus* never slept, nor Nymph,
Nor *Faunus* haunted.

Bentley is scandalised: 'their wild Grottos forsooth are *Sacred*';[51] and Empson again is in agreement:

> Surely Bentley was right to be surprised at finding Faunus haunting the bower, a ghost crying in the cold of Paradise, and the lusts of Pan sacred even in comparison to Eden. There is a Vergilian quality in the lines, haunting indeed, a pathos not mentioned because it is the whole of the story. I suppose that in Satan determining to destroy the innocent happiness of Eden, for the highest political motives, without hatred, not without tears, we may find some echo of the Elizabethan fulness of life that Milton as a poet abandoned, and as a Puritan helped to destroy.

For Satan is, among other things, writes Empson, 'Milton as rebel, and also the paganism Milton had renounced':[52]

As when farr off at Sea a Fleet descri'd
Hangs in the Clouds, by *Æquinoctial* Winds
Close sailing from *Bengala*, or the Iles
Of *Ternate* and *Tidore*, whence Merchants bring
Thir spicie Drugs: they on the trading Flood
Through the wide *Ethiopian* to the Cape
Ply stemming nightly toward the Pole. So seem'd
Farr off the flying Fiend.[53]

'They carry spices', Empson comments, 'like those of Paradise, because they stand for paganism and earthly glory, for all that Milton had retained contact with after renouncing and could pile up into the appeal of Satan; Satan is like a merchant because Eve is to exchange these goods for her innocence; and like a fleet rather than one ship because of the imaginative wealth of polytheism and the variety of the world'.[54]

A fleet that the eighteenth century was to bring to port.

## V

NOTHING distinguished Protestantism more clearly from that against which it protested than the conviction that the papacy was, in the unforgettable phrase of Hobbes, 'no other, than the *Ghost* of the deceased *Romane Empire*, sitting crowned upon the grave thereof'. Nor was it alone in its Pontifex Maximus that the religion of antiquity remained; Catholicism had perpetuated the icons of its gods, it 'being easie, by giving them new names, to make that an Image of the *Virgin Mary*, and of her *Sonne* our Saviour, which before perhaps was called the Image of *Venus*, and *Cupid*'.[55]

Burton, in the *Anatomy of Melancholy*, agreed:

> 'Tis the same devil still, called heretofore Apollo, Mars, Neptune...Jupiter and those bad angels are now worshipped and adored by the name of St. Sebastian, Barbara, etc.; Christopher and George are come in their places. Our Lady succ–eeds Venus...[56]

It was this hatred of idolatry that particularly marked the puritan revolution:[57] Cromwell was appealed to to 'demolish those monsters' –– the antique marbles at Hampton Court –– as a matter of religious urgency: 'for whilst the groves and altars of the idols remained untaken away in Jerusalem, the wrath of God continued against Israel'.[58] Yet it was these very groves that the puritans' descendants now set themselves to restore. Venus, for Burton, was a 'notorious strumpet';[59] but for Shaftesbury she was again an object of reverence. Everyone, he insisted, 'courts a Venus of one kind or another'. The admirers, he conceded,

> of beauty in the fair sex would laugh, perhaps, to hear of a moral part in their amours. Yet what a stir is made about a heart! What curious search of sentiments and tender thoughts! What praises of a humour, a sense, a *je ne sçai quoi* of wit, and all those graces of a mind which these virtuoso-lovers delight to celebrate! Let them settle this matter among themselves, and regulate, as they think fit, the proportions which these different beauties hold one to another. They must allow still, there is a beauty of the mind, and such as is essential in the case.[60]

For Addison, also, the antique deities have been stripped of taboo. Burton had characterised Flora as

> a rich harlot in Rome; and for that she made the commonwealth her heir, her birthday was solemnised long after; and to make it a more plausible holiday, they made her goddess of flowers, and sacrificed to her amongst the rest.[61]

Addison saw beyond such reductionism to the living force of the myth. For his association of nature with liberty, he created a corresponding visionary landscape:

> The Place was covered with a wonderful Profusion of Flowers, that without being disposed into regular Borders and Parterres, grew promiscuously, and had a greater Beauty in their natural Luxuriancy and Disorder, than they could have received from the Checks and Restraints of Art.

'I descended', he continues,

> into the happy Fields that lay beneath me, and in the midst of them, beheld the Goddess sitting upon a Throne. She had nothing to enclose her but the Bounds of her own Dominions, and nothing over her Head but the Heavens. Every Glance of her Eye cast a Track of Light where it fell, that revived the Spring, and made all Things smile about her.[62]

Here, though he calls her Liberty, is the goddess condemned by Burton: but so far from mere harlotry, though her flowers grow 'promiscuously', that she renews the earth. And he was no less appreciative of the pagan eroticism in Milton:

> *Thammuz* came next behind,
> Whose annual wound in *Lebanon* allur'd
> The *Syrian* Damsels to lament his fate
> In amorous dittyes all a Summers day,
> While smooth *Adonis* from his native Rock
> Ran purple to the Sea, suppos'd with blood

Of *Thammuz* yearly wounded: the Love-tale
Infected *Sions* daughters with like heat,
Whose wanton passions in the sacred Porch
*Ezekiel* saw, when by the Vision led
His eye survay'd the dark Idolatries
Of alienated *Judah*.[63]

The adjective that Addison applies to this passage is peculiarly appropriate: it is, he says, 'finely Romantick'.[64] It is fitting that Addison, who initiated romanticism in the garden, and who did so in a context of emotional release, should have invoked it in this fashion: for the romance of pagan antiquity, with all its orgiastic overtones, is the romance of landscape itself: of nature, and with it human nature, in its cycle of regeneration.

## vi

WHEN Temple lived at Carlow under Cromwell, he felt himself, as he was later to feel in the England of Charles II, under siege by Catholicism.[65] And in the western hills that bounded his vista, beside a gorge through which a stream cascades or gathers into pools, stands a church connected, by Catholic assimilation, with the name of the Celtic Adonis.[66]

Temple was cut off by his own traditions from the lore of the land; but it was available to him, under another aspect, in his library. Here he translated the plangent lamentation of Horace over the passing moment of spring:

The nymphs and graces naked range
About the fields, who shrunk before
Into their caves. The empty grange
Prepares its room for a new summer's store.

The caves are absent from the original, as is the grange made ready for a land come back from the dead. And among his translations from Vergil is the descent into the underworld of Orpheus,[67] involvement in the dark ways of the irrational and unknown. It was a quest that was to bring forth a strange and yet familiar harvest when he encountered irreducible nature in the gardens of Japan. In the romantic landscape which derived from him, and which took the form of the antique sanctuary, it was as if that belief had at last been made visible in which Flora was the secret name of Rome.[68]

All history is psychic history. Judaism fulminated against the rituals of nature;[69] but the *Song of Songs* re-echoes with the love of Thammuz and Ishtar.[70] Catholicism prohibited similar worship; but the gods returned under the habit of its saints.[71] Protestantism hammered these figures out of carven niche and painted window; but its children surrendered in turn to the same compulsion. A curious instance is provided by just these years. Cromwell died; his effigy, crowned and sceptred, assumed the royalty he had declined in life;[72] and an elegy identified him with the king as sun, descending at night to his marriage with earth.[73] For nothing which inhered in the psyche could permanently be repressed: the dream would recur until its meaning was recognised. That which had been denied, dismembered or dispossessed would return in new and irresistible form: as the phoenix sang in the flame of the juniper tree.

For Milton, the Tree of Life was the locus of natural alchemy:

> High eminent, blooming Ambrosial Fruit
> Of vegetable Gold;

while its apparent opposite, with its forbidden secret, cast a shadow of fear:

> and next to Life
> Our Death the Tree of Knowledge grew fast by.

Yet this, too, held out the promise of regeneration:

> Knowledge of Good bought dear by knowing ill.[74]

It is in the risk to the *hortus conclusus* that the world becomes human: in the dance of the labyrinth, the leap into chaos: there, where life and knowledge are one and the same.

# PART THREE

# IMPERIAL PARADISE

## Ramifications of Romanticism

*The tree of man was never quiet:*
*Then 'twas the Roman, now 'tis I.*

HOUSMAN

## CHAPTER SEVEN

# THE GARDEN INVADES THE HOUSE

EVERYWHERE he travelled, on that first migration, doors opened along the way. He was the son of England's prime minister: he was Walpole's son; and 'though I am harmless in my nature, my name has some mystery in it'.[1]

### i

OVER the character of Robert Walpole there still hangs an air of enigma. Was he in fact the unpretentious squire -- enormous, redfaced, foulmouthed -- he seemed to be: who noisily munched apples from home during Commons debates; of whom it was reported that he opened his bailiff's letters before state dispatches; whose deepest aspiration seemed to be the lowest denominator of the men he led? If so, who was it that reared the great Palladian mansion in Norfolk, and adorned it with its exquisite paintings?[2] The appetite of a squire, and the taste of a connoisseur? But that would be to impute duality to him; and few have been so single in their purpose.

Walpole managed parliament for two kings who, though father and son, were opposites in temperament: it is wholly appropriate that their common musician should have linked one with water and the other with fire.[3] George I arrived from Germany with a sinister reputation: a wife divorced for adultery, her lover believed murdered, and accompanied by two women, one of whom was, and the other confidently asserted to be, his mistress. There was moreover another kind of queerness about him: something subtly unnatural, inexplicable but pervasive, like settled malevolence or a secret disease. Yes: he was a foreigner; and, as he was not heard to speak the language of his subjects, and did not seem to care for their company, it was clear that he must be a blockhead.[4]

Subsequent research has shaken this comfortable doctrine. Documents that he read and wrote, supported by the accounts of witnesses, suggest a perfectly adequate command of English. It does not seem to have occurred to his mocking subjects that their shy and complicated king might not have wished to risk his dignity by speaking their language imperfectly; or have seen a certain advantage in appearing not to understand it. His portraits, meanwhile, show a face that while guarded is aware and sensitive, as befitted the enlightened ruler who conversed with Leibniz and was the patron of Voltaire.[5]

George II, by contrast, was an explosive little man whose great desire was to command an army. As his subjects, however, did not seem inclined to give him one, he had to content himself with a minute study of regiments, orders and uniforms, and with hectoring those about him.[6] Chief among these was his flaxen, handsome, ample wife, on whom he was hopelessly dependent; and, perhaps for this reason, paraded his visits to a mistress for whom he did not give a straw. When evening came, he would pace up and down, watch in hand, with the obsessive exactitude of the martinet, until the hour struck, and he plunged into her apartments.[7]

As Prince and Princess of Wales, George and Caroline were voluble in their adopted language, though not always to fortunate effect. Caroline, it was said, wished a newly-promoted cleric joy of his bishopric with an inordinate stress upon the final syllable;[8] while her husband, in the course of a dispute with his father, was reported to have shrieked at the royal emissary: 'Rascal! I fight you out!' So the Duke of Newcastle heard; and, being a very timid man, shuddered and drooled all the way back to his master, gasping that he was to be fought out. The king asked if this were true: had his son issued a challenge? By no means, answered the prince: he did not fight social inferiors; what he had said was, he *find* him out. *FEINDT. FEINDT.* Not *FEIDT.* The quarrel was composed;[9] but when George I died suddenly on the road to Hanover, it boded ill for his chief minister. At the very mention of his prospects, Walpole broke into tears.[10]

He was saved by Caroline. In her, Walpole had cultivated the true source of power. It had not been difficult: both were plainspoken, realist, with a relish for influence and a hearty appetite for life. Caroline, on her deathbed and in great pain, was convulsed with laughter when one of the solemn professional faces bending over her brought its wig too close to a candle, and burst into flames.[11] She was quick–witted enough to see what Walpole could do for her husband; and so, eventually, did the king. When Walpole drew up a generous civil list that only he could steer through parliament, George saw how he was placed. 'Consider, Sir Robert', he said, 'that what makes me easy in this matter will prove for your ease too'. He was as good as his word; and Walpole wielded the royal power in the reign of George II as he had in that of George I.[12]

For, if the revolution had underlined the king's dependence on parliament as an institution, as individuals its members were still dependent on the king. From him flowed titles, honours and place; and this current was now controlled by Walpole. Commoners pleaded with him for promotion; earls and bishops abased themselves in his anterooms. He combined the two great forces in the state: he wielded the power of the king in relation to parliament, and the power of parliament in relation to the king. He fulfilled the desires of each through his influence over the other.[13] So successfully did he accomplish his work for the king that he received the coveted star and ribbon of the Garter. He was exultant: he had the decorations painted into his portraits, and plastered into the walls of his house; his installation seemed a royal pageant; his feast at Windsor outshone that of any of the nobility. And in this lies the resolution of his apparent enigma. Distinction and display were all one to him, as they had been to an older tradition of aristocracy: one characterised, not by restraint, but by largesse.[14] The massive feasts and the splendid paintings; the roaring laugh and the flaunted order of chivalry: all were varying inflections of the single language of power. His was the truly regal presence of his time: both the sovereigns that he served stood in awe of his powers.[15] And so, while George I cut out paper figures with his mistress, or George II pursued his exact researches into uniforms, Walpole marshalled his battalions in the Commons, and made or unmade whole benches in the Lords.[16] It was hardly to be wondered at, then, that his own head in marble should dominate those of the Roman emperors in the great classical palace that stood in the winds from the German Ocean.[17]

## ii

AND so, for his son, doors opened everywhere; but for Horace Walpole, they seemed to open into nothing. At Florence he was presented to the last of the Medici; but the Renaissance city palled. Its sculptures seemed no more than a 'good sort of people, that I have a great deal of unruffled regard for'. What did they signify? Human nature was everywhere the same: everywhere the same passions, the same compulsions: politics, intrigue and the permutations of sex. *Everybody does everything, and nothing comes on't.*[18]

Florence was excessively boring; and Rome was falling apart: a city dilapidated, with palaces in disrepair, and families in decline. Here lived 'Mr. Stuart', 'a good deal resembling King James the Second', and looking much like an idiot when he laughed or prayed.[19]

There was, indeed, an excursion to an underground town: a temple quite perfect, houses painted with architecture against a background of red. It was the only uncorrupted Roman city: buried, it held a strange fascination. But the one above ground lacked meaning. What was the Pantheon but 'a strange mass of light poured perpendicularly into a circle of obscurity'? Classicism left one cold. 'Am not I a very Goth?'[20]

And one's companion made it infinitely worse: Gray, with whom one had shared sympathies at Eton, though not of one's own class -- sent thither out of a shop in London -- Gray, with his Latin hexameters, his dutiful journals, his accumulated notes -- 'what a vile employment 'tis, making catalogues!' But Walpole was paying his way, and accompany him he must. 'Left Rome!' exclaimed Gray, in an agony of disbelief.[21]

At Florence one had revelled in the carnival, when the stone city stirred into life. One did nothing but slip out of one's domino into bed, and out of bed into one's domino. It was 'frantic', cried Walpole, 'Bacchanalian'. And now it was summer, and there was music, evenings, on the bridge, while the sun hung over the water, dying and calm, and one lingered in the scented gardens through the warm nights: 'an excellent place', murmured Gray, 'to employ all one's animal sensations in'. Gray, in his own eyes, was annihilated: reduced to an 'O, and the motto *Nihilissimo*'. There was a furious quarrel; and he went home alone. One saw oneself, years afterwards, with shame and remorse: 'insensible to the feelings of one I thought below me; of one, I blush to say it, that I knew was obliged to me...I have since felt my infinite inferiority to him'. One had been 'intoxicated', at the time, by 'indulgence, vanity, and the insolence of my situation, as a prime minister's son'.[22]

But that was about to change.

## iii

HE returned to find his father in the twilight of his power. For years the opposition to him had steadily grown. He had eliminated all rivals; grown coarser and more careless in the exercise of power. Those who opposed him were peremptorily deprived of court place and military commission; and amongst these was Cobham, veteran of Marlborough's wars and master of Stowe.[23]

Stowe is the great political landscape of the eighteenth century. An equestrian George I dominates the approach to the house,[24] which, in the course of the century, was recast into a purer classicism, while the pools and plantations behind were released into irregularity.[25] It was here, in Kent's Elysian Fields, that Addison's allegory was realised: a Temple of Ancient Virtue stood circular and intact, while beside it lay a ruin emblematic of its modern counterpart.[26] Across the stream curved an exedra holding the busts of Milton, Locke and William III: amidst whom glowered the implacable features of Pope.[27] For here was the context, of antagonism to Walpole, in which he discovered his devotion to liberty.

This the prime minister was held to have undermined, both by his projection of power at home, and by his failure to project it abroad. He appealed to landed society through the avoidance of war, recalling too vividly how this had brought down the Whigs in the reign of Anne. But the young men in parliament could scarcely remember Queen Anne, and to them, with their connections in the merchant community, Walpole's appeasement on the Spanish Main seemed ignominious and unprofitable.[28] At their head stood Frederick, Prince of Wales, whose stirring anthem 'Rule, Britannia' rhymed 'slaves' with 'waves'; who was applauded at Addison's *Cato*; and who, having quarrelled bitterly with his parents, was the focus of opposition to their minister. It pleased him to think that, when he fought a fire in the city, he heard cries of 'crown him, crown him!' He was commemorated, certainly, among the monuments of Stowe, and gave Pope some urns for his garden. The poet, for his part, presented the prince with a pup: whether with satiric intent or not, does not appear.[29]

Frederick, at Temple Bar, toasted the war which Walpole, against his will, was at last obliged to declare. But, weakly waged, it lacked conviction; and an election reduced his majority. As he waited for parliament to open, Walpole lay sleepless at night, or, his casual jollity gone, stared vacantly at the dinner-table. So Horace observed as, 'up to the...ears, in dirt, straw and unpacking', he fitted up an apartment in the house the king had given his father at ten Downing Street.[30]

His tenure there was to be brief. After the session had begun, the minister's majority dropped inexorably, until at last, after twenty years of power, he went down in defeat. 'You have no idea', said Horace, 'of their huzza!' And now Sir Robert was no more: he was to ascend to the Lords as Earl of Orford. He communicated his resolution to Frederick, who assured him of his safety; and those who had purchased window-seats on the way to the Tower were disappointed.[31]

So were those who expected change. The opposition leaders, among them the master of Stowe, compounded for place with Walpole's heirs. Pope sketched a satire on his former associates; but he was aged beyond his years now, and ailing, and his admiring audience had gone. 'The fall of an unpopular Minister', smiled a later historian, 'was not succeeded, according to general expectation, by a millenium of happiness and virtue; some Courtiers lost their places, some patriots lost their characters. Lord Orford's offences vanished with his power'; and the government was fixed again 'on the old basis of the Whig Aristocracy'.[32]

For Horace, through the worst of the turmoil, there had been the consolation, 'very sweet, though very melancholy': that his mother was 'safe, secure and above the rage of confusion: nothing in this world can touch her peace now!' He had come to consciousness in a household shadowed by his parents' estrangement: the prime minister lived openly with his mistress; and Horace all his life was to feel a peculiar sympathy for dispossessed queens, for a Catherine of Aragon or an Anne Boleyn.[33]

For himself, wrote Horace, 'all the grandeur, the envied grandeur of our house will not cost me a sigh'; and he was as good as his word. After the final years in which he kept his father company in the deserted palace of Houghton,[34] he moved to a house of his own.

## iv

'LORD God! Jesus! what a house!' cried Lady Townshend. 'It is just such a house as a parson's, where the children lie at the feet of the bed!'[35]

'Why will you make it Gothic?' asked a friend in Italy. 'I know it is the taste at present, but...' the taste, he thought, was uncouth: '*mi pare...un gusto gotico*'.[36] For the Goth was silhouetted in history against the glare of the destruction of Rome; the lament of the psalmist, invoked by Jerome on the wreck of the city -- *deus venerunt gentes in hæreditatem tuam* [37] -- was re-echoed at the Renaissance over the ages which had gone between; and, once the medieval idiom had been labelled 'Gothic', it became visual shorthand for barbarism.[38]

Yet Gothic, however discredited, never quite died. It was intertwined too closely with the fabric of English history. Churches, colleges, country houses were repaired and added to, even built anew, in the idiom prescribed by tradition.[39] And, as restoration merged into imitation, and survival into revival, Walpole touched the movement with imaginative life: not, indeed, the life from which it had arisen, but one deriving from the preoccupations of his time. 'I am almost as fond', he wrote, 'of the *Sharawaggi*, or Chinese want of symmetry, in buildings, as in grounds or gardens'.[40]

There was, in fact, a received connection between the two. To Renaissance Italy the Gothic style, with its 'pointed arches and overshading rib vaults', suggested an origin in the forests of the north: a view that was echoed in England. The 'idea of it', it was confidently asserted, 'is taken from a walk of trees, whose touching heads are curiously imitated by the roof'. 'For this northern people', it was surmised, 'having been accustomed, during the gloom of Paganism, to worship the Deity in groves,...when the new religion required edifices they ingeniously projected to make them resemble' them.[41] To the Renaissance eye, Gothic lacked 'everything that can be called order': King's College Chapel, asserted Walpole as an undergraduate, was from a time before Palladio had 'methodised the Vandal

Builder's hand'.[42] One could hardly expect it to be recognised, from so disparaging a perspective, that Gothic in fact had been drawn out in obedience to the most exhaustive of schemata: to the *summa* of scholastic theology, which attempted to combine all knowledge, divine and human, into a single structure of unparalleled clarity, coherence and completeness, in what has been described as 'visual logic'.[43] So the medieval architect, taking the pointed arch as module, had woven it into an echoing and interacting structure that articulated, in high severe sculpture and glowing glass, in masonry that appeared 'weightless and shot through with visible energy', the lineaments of an otherworldly order.[44] Nothing could have been more ethereal in effect, or more rational in foundation.

There was this much, however, to be said for the delusion: as the medieval centuries wore on, and philosophy grew less assured of the universal, reason dissolved into the subjectivism of 'private sensory and psychological experience',[45] and architectural statement was replaced by an 'endless pursuit of ambiguity'. Pinnacles were suggested on the lower levels of buttresses, confounding above and below; gables were placed over interior arches, confounding within and without. When a *continuum* replaced the 'independent validity of each particular member', the hierarchy of scholasticism had been dissolved; when a tower was composed entirely of 'open–work tracery and stone filigree', wall surface had become a 'tenuous web'. What was left was 'ebullient linear energy', which expressed itself in vegetative ornament.[46] And so there was a certain fitness in the fact that, as Lovejoy declares, it was 'clad in the mantle of "Nature"' that 'the great art of the Middle Ages...regained aesthetic respectability'.[47]

Walpole's house at Strawberry Hill, accordingly, evolved in organic fashion, culminating in an ample round tower, beside which a pointed one rose in studied asymmetry; and it was this 'deliberate irregularity', writes Summerson, that was 'architecturally, its most important innovation'.[48] And, as Addison had connected the irregular with psychological liberation, Gothic, for Walpole, was freedom of emotion. 'One must have taste', he declared, 'to be sensible of the beauties of

Grecian architecture; one only wants passions to feel Gothic'.[49] As emotion, moreover, was irrational, he refused to justify it on rational grounds. 'I do not', he stated, 'mean to defend by argument a small capricious house'.[50] It was caprice, indeed, that was its essence. Strawberry Hill had evolved from the home of a toyshop owner, and it pleased him to describe it as a 'play–thing'.[51] But if his building was entered upon with the inconsequence of child's play, it would soon acquire its intensity. With the elaboration of fantasy goes the fascination of the forbidden: that intimation of reality which leads the child into the world of darkness: of disaster and pestilence; of the fall of a cradle and the doom of a royal line; of the collapse of a bridge and the destruction of a city.

## v

> *THE first thing that struck Manfred's eyes was a group of his servants endeavouring to raise something that appeared to him a mountain of sable plumes...an enormous helmet, an hundred times more large than any casque ever made for human being, and shaded with a proportionable quantity of black feathers.*[52]

*The Castle of Otranto* had come to him through the secret door of dreams; and he sat down that evening, he recalled, 'without knowing in the least what I intended to say or relate'.[53] Like all dreams, it was a compound of memory and impulse. In the domineering ruler, the neglected wife, the sought–after mistress, the son who is crushed by the father's excesses, may be recognised themes from the Walpole family romance; while in the avenging presence of the lord of Vicenza, the city of Palladio, there runs a lingering sense of Gothic as the transgression of order. And, while he recognised that certain of its features had other sources -- as when, years afterwards, returning to Cambridge, he found himself in the courtyard of Otranto[54] -- in outline the imagined castle and his own house were the same. As his narrative took form, he drew the one in terms of the other,[55] and he indicated in his preface that the scene was 'undoubtedly laid in some real castle'; that the author 'had some certain building in his eye'.[56] In private, he was still more explicit. When he acquired a suit of armour for Strawberry, he said: 'It will make a great figure here at Otranto'.[57]

In essence, indeed, they were identical. Walpole was fully aware of what he called 'the wildness of the story'.[58] This he justified by inverting a line from his classical namesake, Horace, who had written that incongruity of form was like a feverish dream, in which head and foot belonged to different bodies:

> *vanae*
> *fingentur species, ut nec pes nec caput uni*
> *reddatur formae.*[59]

Walpole altered this to read *tamen ut pes, et caput,*[60] indicating that the poet's 'unmeaning visions' -- *vanae species* -- might well possess an order of their own. This, indeed, is virtually a summary of the story: the gigantic helmet, which crashes into the courtyard of Otranto, is found to belong to the same wearer as the outsized foot in the 'great chamber next to the gallery'.[61]

Incongruity, then, was quite deliberate. 'I wrote it', he said, 'in spite of rules'.[62] More specifically, 'my rule was nature'; he had been 'desirous of leaving the powers of fancy at liberty'.[63] Nature, once again, was liberty; it was the rejection of classical order; it was that which, seemingly formless, had a form not immediately discernible, which was the expression of its own inherent energies. It was, in a word, Temple's *sharawadgi,* which he had transposed from the garden to the building, now applied to imagination in general; and to the imagining of nature in its most apocalyptic forms.

## vi

DANTE, to Walpole, was 'a Methodist parson in Bedlam'.[64] Nothing could illustrate more luridly the meaning of the middle ages to the eighteenth century: they were an underworld of unreason, an inferno of the emotions. For they were pervaded with that species of enthusiasm which had provoked the English revolution.

Monks were considered 'fanatical enthusiasts';[65] and Gothic buildings viewed accordingly as 'heavy, dark, melancholy and *Monkish*'.[66] And as the religious orders were seen as excrescences on an originally simple system, so in medieval thought, while there was 'a kind of quickness of life and spirit', an 'infinite agitation of wit', there was 'no soundness of matter or goodness of quality'. It was overrefined and flimsy: 'cobwebs of learning, admirable for the fineness of thread and work, but of no substance or profit'.[67]

Such was the initial reaction of the young Horace Walpole. At Paris, on the Rue d'Enfer, was a convent that seemed to combine every aspect of 'melancholy, meditation, selfish devotion, and despair'. It was 'old and irregular', with a gloomy chapel from which dark passages led into 'a large obscure hall, which looks like a combination–chamber for some hellish council'. The large cloister contained the tombs; and in the lesser was pictured a 'dead man who spoke at his burial', portraying 'all the strongest and horridest ideas, of ghastliness, hypocrisy discovered, and the height of damnation; pain and cursing'.

And yet...and 'yet 'tis pleasing'. The monk was robed in white, and had his apartment and his garden, his library and his gallery, all disposed in the greatest order. Far from being sinister, he was extremely civil. 'Soften the terms, and mellow the uncouth horror that reigns here, but a little, and 'tis a charming solitude'.[68]

As time went on, Walpole slipped ever more deeply into this mood. He was drawn to Gothic by its atmosphere -- 'the gloomth of abbeys and cathedrals'; by its effect -- 'magnificent, yet genteel, vast, yet light, venerable and picturesque'; and, ultimately, by its very connection, which the rational part of his century, and his own mind, abhorred, with darkness and unreason: with a priesthood that exhausted its 'knowledge of the passions in composing edifices whose pomp, mechanism, vaults, tombs, painted windows, gloom, and perspective' induced 'sensations of romantic devotion'. The Gothic, he averred, came 'nearer converting one to popery than all the regular pageantry of Roman domes'.[69]

This was the ambience which he aimed at in his own dwelling; and he was so far successful that a French aristocrat, thinking himself in a chapel, pulled off his hat.[70] He spoke, indeed, quite explicitly of the 'popery of my house'; and it was so in more senses than one. It stands a little upriver from the site of Pope's; he liked to imagine, when he first moved into it, that he had seen the recently deceased poet's ghost flit by in the moonlight; and within a few years he was able to write:

> my house is so monastic that I have a little hall decked with long saints in lean arched windows and with taper columns, which we call the Paraclete, in memory of Eloisa's cloister.[71]

Here he alludes to the poem in which Pope dramatised his doomed obsession with Lady Mary Wortley: in which his impotence was represented by Abelard, and his frustration by Eloisa. Death is the only hope held out to her in her setting of tombs, presided over by Melancholy, whose

> gloomy presence saddens all the scene,
> Shades ev'ry flow'r, and darkens ev'ry green,
> Deepens the murmur of the falling floods
> And breathes a browner horror on the woods.[72]

In this funereal landscape, the flowers themselves are shadowed, as if in some garden of Persephone, lost in the underworld. And it is rendered still more ominous by the presence of Gothic, whose 'awful arches make a noon-day night'. This perception, too, was rooted in the style. In its later manifestations, observes Henderson, the 'flurry of curves and spikes, by which the physical presence is gradually withdrawn, and the dense material mass...dissolved into the empty air', architecture has reached 'a fantastic and ingenious compromise between the two poles of being and non–being'. Here creation, it appears, is undone, 'and chaos renewed'.[73] And so, in the final scene of *Otranto*, the castle is shattered by the avenging spirit whose dissociated limbs had inhabited it, and left in ruin.[74]

For nature was destructive as well as creative; and Gothic was linked with its darker aspect. The irregular line of *sharawadgi* became the meandering pathway of a maze; and at the heart of the labyrinth lurked horror. If the garden was the dream of the eighteenth century, Gothic was its nightmare.

## vii

WALPOLE'S earliest alterations were still in progress when he received a letter from Gray, enclosing a poem he had recently completed. It was called *Elegy, wrote in a Country Church–yard*.[75]

Gray had made his way home by slow stages after their quarrel. He was aware of the difficulty of his temperament, suffering, as he said, from a 'frightful' melancholy, only tempered by a 'Leucocholy' which, 'though it seldom laughs or dances', was 'a good easy sort of a state'.[76] He had settled in Cambridge: residence in college suited his limited means, and might even, he thought, bring scholarly companionship. But of this he had no great hope, and he addressed the university in a Hymn to Ignorance, in which its medieval outlines were associated with darkness, decay and mental torpor:

> Hail, horrors, hail! ye ever–gloomy bowers,
> Ye gothic fanes, and antiquated towers...[77]

He spent his summers at Stoke Poges, then a secluded village among winding lanes, the small church standing in untidy turf under ancient elms and yews, from where his letter to Walpole was written, and where his tomb now stands.[78]

For the elegy is his apologia: it is the epic of the obscure. Every mortification he had suffered on that harrowing journey had deepened his sense of difference from his fashionable friend: the son of his country's ruler, shining in every company, showed up in striking contrast his own insignificance and introversion.[79] Robert Walpole had been repeatedly attacked by the opposition, Pope among them, for corruption and extravagance;[80] and Gray now reflected on the power of such figures

> The struggling Pangs of conscious Truth to hide,
> To quench the Blushes of ingenuous Shame,
> Or heap the Shrine of Luxury and Pride
> With Incense, kindled at the Muse's Flame.[81]

But Gray had gone far beyond satire. The focus shifts from society; the level of discourse is no longer extravert, the persona of a Pope, bragging of aristocratic acquaintance or posturing public indignation. From the first, astonishing peroration, of the world's being left 'to Darkness, and to me', the protagonist is romantic solitude personified, and in the obscure dead of the churchyard he discovers its correlative. Amid their inarticulate epitaphs, he finds his own:[82] throughout the poem, he weaves a dance between 'thy' and 'their';[83] and in its passionate depth of feeling he wrote perhaps the best-loved lines in the language.[84]

It was, ironically, his celebration of obscurity that was to bring him fame. An acquaintance had interposed, Walpole written in conciliatory fashion, and a visit to London followed. The man of fashion spoke of 'the Town & this & that & t'other' for the space of three hours to his largely silent interlocutor, who took his leave 'very indifferently pleased, but treated with wondrous Good-breeding'. Walpole, for his part, found Gray 'the worst company in the world', but his writing most admirable; and it was his excited handing about of the poem that made its author a celebrity.[85]

Among the most eloquent scenes in it is the elegiac evocation:

> The breezy Call of Incense-breathing Morn,
> The Swallow twitt'ring from the Straw-built Shed,

The Cock's shrill Clarion, or the ecchoing Horn,
No more shall rowse them from their lowly Bed;

and this is matched by the equally desolate vision in which

For them no more the blazing Hearth shall burn,
Or busy Huswife ply her Evening Care:
No Children run to lisp their Sire's Return,
Or climb his Knees the envied Kiss to share.[86]

And the latter is an almost literal translation of Lucretius:

*iam iam non domus accipiet te laeta, neque uxor*
*optima, nec dulces occurrent oscula nati*
*praeripere et tacita pectus dulcedine tangent.*[87]

Gray has returned, then, in allusion, to the universe of Epicurus; and the poem originally ended on this note:

Hark how the sacred Calm, that broods around
Bids ev'ry fierce tumultuous Passion cease
In still small Accents whisp'ring from the Ground
A grateful Earnest of eternal Peace.[88]

It was a universe in endless becoming, that offered nothing but the prospect of dissolution: reduced to an 'O, and the motto *Nihilissimo*'.[89]

## viii

MELANCHOLY was the specifically English disorder: 'spleen' was adopted into French as *maladie hypochondriaque propre aux Anglais*. It was an affliction noted by visitors at every level of English society, from atrabilious milords to funereal boors. Nor did the inhabitants dispute the diagnosis: it was, said Addison, 'a kind of Demon that haunts our Island'. It was the weather, it appeared, that was to blame. The islanders were constantly immersed, wrote the Abbé le Blanc, in impenetrable fogs. 'Tis necessary', declared Lady Mary Wortley, 'to have a very uncommon constitution not to be tainted with the distempers of our climate'. Gray trembled at an east wind; Walpole expected, as a matter of course, a wave of suicides as winter set in.[90]

The national melancholia had now deepened to despair for the nation. Bourbon Spain had been joined in the war by Bourbon France; and the Irish in French service, invoking ancient wrong, inflicted a crushing defeat on British arms at Fontenoy. And as if to heighten the sense of atavistic nightmare, the white–haired boy that Gray and Walpole had seen in Rome descended on Scotland in the final flourish that converted the Stuart cause from futility to romance. When the Hanoverian king's son crushed the rebellion, he was seen first, in relief, as the conquering hero of the Bible; and only later, in revulsion, as the butcher of Culloden. As Gray, anonymous in Westminster Hall, watched a doomed Jacobite play with the tassels of the axe, Charles Edward and Cumberland must alike have seemed remote to one whom destiny

> Forbad to wade through Slaughter to a Throne,
> Or shut the Gates of Mercy on Mankind.[91]

But Walpole could not muster any such detachment. A Jacobite revival had been a constant dread of his father's;[92] through him, he enjoyed a substantial income from crown sinecures;[93] and he could imagine all too readily the consequences of a Stuart return:

> Now comes the Pretender's boy, and promises all my comfortable apartments in the Exchequer and Custom House to some forlorn Irish peer...I shall wonderfully dislike being a loyal sufferer in a threadbare coat, and shivering in an antechamber at Hanover.[94]

And for the nation at large, the overwhelming sensation was self–doubt. If a band of motley clansmen could march unchallenged into the kingdom, the nation, it was clear, suffered more than a malady. It was a malaise; and it was now devastatingly diagnosed. Liberty, wrote John Brown in his *Estimate of the Manners and Principles of the Times*, was indeed rooted in the soil and climate of England; but it might as easily rot there. The danger was not from despotism, but from a decadent people. He traced the blight to Walpole; but 'bribery in the minister supposed a corrupt people': he had been obliged to practise corruption for good measures as well as bad. And these 'seem generally to have aimed no higher than to secure present Expedients, to oblige his Friends and Dependants, and provide for his own Safety'. England had not yet arrived at the 'last period of degeneracy' of a Carthage or a Rome; but the signs were ominous. Youths of quality were flung into 'premature, and indigested, travel', exposed to 'every foreign Folly, Effeminacy, or Vice', their supreme concern being to 'trifle agreeably'.[95]

It was hardly to be expected that Horace Walpole should welcome these explicit criticisms of his father's policies and provision for himself, or the implicit strictures on his own travels and tastes. He spoke of Brown's 'vanity and insolent impertinence', and of his mental disorder, which some years later led to his suicide.[96] But his book was now, says Macaulay,

> universally read, admired, and believed. The author fully convinced his readers that they were a race of cowards and scoundrels; that nothing could save them; that they were on the point of being enslaved by their enemies, and that they richly deserved their fate.[97]

The book's most terrifying aspect, indeed, was prognosis. The French, declared Brown, however 'contemptible in private life', were 'in public, formidable'. Their youth, unlike those of Britain, devoted themselves to the state. So it was that on land they were 'far our superiors', on sea 'making large and dreadful strides', and, if the 'unperceived decline' of England were not arrested, would pursue the matter on Salisbury Plain.[98]

What in fact emerged from Salisbury Plain was a very different phenomenon. William Pitt sat in Parliament for the ghost–town of Old Sarum, marked by the cruciform foundations of a vanished cathedral. Pitt was an advanced specimen of the national melancholy: landscape, for him, was a remedy for depression. 'Come and hunt prospects with me', he cried to a cousin, 'and keep me from hanging myself'. His own grounds were, throughout life, his greatest extravagance. As his 'impatient temper', Horace Walpole recalled, 'could brook no delay', he would plant them, when the fit came upon him, by torchlight. And then, the work having been done and undone by turns, and the grounds, as he considered, improved to the limit of their capacity, he peremptorily abandoned them.[99]

Pitt's melancholia and his mania were played out most completely in parliament, as he alternated between despair for his country and demonic energy in its cause. 'Is this', he cried over Walpole's accommodation with Spain, 'is this any longer a nation?' He was related by marriage to the master of Stowe, and given a commission in his regiment; but, after a speech in which he praised Prince Frederick at the expense of the king, was deprived of this by the prime minister. 'We must muzzle', Walpole had stated, 'this terrible cornet of horse'; but, his biographer observes, 'no more effective way of unmuzzling the cornet, and giving him the prominence his ambition sought, could have been devised by Pitt's greatest friend'. He was taken into Frederick's household, and his importance in parliament intensified, as did his involvement in the clamour for a commercial war.[100]

It was an arena for which he had an hereditary affinity. His grandfather had gone from being a ruthless interloper on the trade of the East India Company to its president on the Coromandel Coast. Nicknamed for the enormous gem he had acquired there -- snatched, some said, from the eye of an Indian god, or, said others, from a slave whose ghost continued to haunt his gallery -- Diamond Pitt singled out young William as a 'hopefull lad'; and there were to be provocative parallels between the two. 'When Trade is at stake', exclaimed the grandson, 'it is your last Retrenchment; you must defend it, or perish'. 'These words of Pitt's', says J.H. Plumb, 'thrilled the nation', giving voice to an 'active and expanding commercial imperialism' which was at the same time felt to be both 'necessary and righteous', as the conflict with Spain readily took on overtones of armada and inquisition.[101]

Walpole's fall brought him little advantage, and he continued to harry ministers and king. George II at last had his opportunity to lead his troops into battle, displaying an exultant contempt for danger; but the admiration of his English subjects was tempered by the fact that he had done so wearing the Hanoverian colours. Pitt's reputation for patriotism was not impaired by his contention that 'this great, this powerful, this formidable kingdom is considered only as a province to a despicable electorate'. It was enhanced, even, by his attacks of the gout: the crutch, the flanelled foot, the face drawn with pain as he dragged himself into the Commons, all gave dramatic representation to the image of a man suffering for his country. At last the ministry felt compelled to reckon with him: the king was told that it was the 'only probable measure to carry on his business effectually in parliament'; but George refused to have him in attendance on himself, and Pitt, barred from being secretary at war, accepted a sinecure instead.[102] 'Patriotism', sneered Horace Walpole, 'has kissed hands on accepting a place'.[103] But when Pitt went on to become paymaster of the forces, and renounced the large perquisites of the office, which had formed the basis of Robert Walpole's fortune, criticism was disarmed.[104]

He was no less resolute in the principle for which he had clamoured in opposition. When Pitt welcomed the end of the war, it was not because he doubted the need for another -- which the defiant rattle of the kettledrums in Handel's music for the occasion seems to prefigure -- but because he thought it had been fought on the wrong lines.[105] For European diplomacy was in process of revolution.

## ix

THE Karlskirche in Vienna exemplifies to perfection that species of architecture known as imperial baroque, the *Kaiserstil*. Like a condensed silhouette of the city of Rome, as befits the capital of a Holy Roman Empire, it combines a high dome reminiscent of St. Peter's with an idiosyncratic doubling of the column of Trajan: a feature which gives it a peculiarly personal significance. For the Emperor Charles had been the unsuccessful English candidate for the crown of Spain; and, draped in Spanish black, still projected an unsmiling claim to the Pillars of Hercules.[106]

His death left his daughter's inheritance, in the absence of a full treasury and a strong army, protected only by a piece of paper. Maria Theresa spent her reign on the defensive; and her characteristic monument is still more inward–looking than her father's. Originally designed, like Versailles, to stand on a hilltop, Schönbrunn had instead been built at its foot: so that where Versailles dominates all of visible space, Schönbrunn holds the glowing sky at a distance through the colonnade of the Glorieta.[107]

At Berlin, the triumphal avenue marches steadily through the woods. Brandenburg had begun as a German colony; so had Prussia, a region of trackless forest and hidden lake, of sandy plain and silted estuary, converted and conquered by the Teutonic Knights. Their lives on the frontier 'imposed sobriety, duty, precision and clarity of purpose', in a land that demanded a 'fierce and unending struggle' against 'sun, wind, mist, and a bitter soil'. And when, at the Reformation, the order of the black cross was secularised by a Hohenzollern grand master, Prussia passed to Brandenburg.[108]

The Great Elector made Brandenburg Prussia formidable in battle; his son, in return for assistance against Louis XIV, wrested from the emperor recognition as sovereign outside the empire, *König in Preußen*.[109] Frederick I gloried in his new status, and patronised the arts which enhanced it. Poets celebrated his capital in the form of an anagram: *Berolinum*, as *Lumen orbi*, was to give light to the world.[110]

His son, however, had, before the king was buried, drawn a line through the list of officials meant to emphasize the royal dignity. It was, says Vincent Cronin, 'one of the symbolic lines of history, dividing two epochs: behind lay the pretentiousness of a petty German Court; ahead the powerful efficiency of Prussia'.[111] Frederick William, reclaiming waste land, improving agriculture, cutting roads and canals, trebled state revenue, and increased his army to a size then considered a portent: a process epitomised by his regiment of giants.[112] He made his garden into a parade–ground and his palace into a barracks, where he caroused with his officers, deriding philosophy as a breaking of wind, and turning verse to the purposes of a single–minded parsimony:

*Gold kann ich nicht scheißen*
*Friedrich Wilhelm, König in Preußen.*[113]

Aloof from all this stood his own son, the future Frederick II. The boy's mother, daughter of George I of England, contrasted the refinement of the court of Hanover with the coarseness of Berlin; and he in turn affected French, warbled on the flute, and wore his hair long -- in defiance of military regulations. The king sank into a chronic state of sullen rage. He saw his life's work threatened with ruin; and there were those about him who thought he would go mad. At a review before the princes of Germany, the king caned young Frederick, taunting him at the same time with his cowardice; and the prince, at last humiliated beyond endurance, planned his escape. He intended -- or so he asserted -- to run away to his uncle, that frustrated martinet George II: perhaps the one man in Europe who would happily have changed places with him. But he dressed for his attempt in flaming red, and when he arranged for horses was reported immediately. The king's fury was unmeasured: the prince was imprisoned, and forced to watch as the friend who had been his associate was executed. Frederick fainted away before the head fell on the bloodied sand.[114]

Frederick William never again had to strike his son. The young man was allowed to exchange his cell for a government office, where he studied regulations, made tours of inspection, kept strict accounts. After a suitable hiatus, he was readmitted to uniform. Step by step he was inducted into his dynastic duties, and into a marriage which was but one more of them. 'I have drilled', he groaned, 'I drill, I shall drill'; and when, in the tenth year of this, his father died, it seemed that at last he was free.[115]

In Frederick's villa at Potsdam, his flutes remain under glass. The walls of his mirrored music–room reflect the park, over which float distant clouds. His music was to earn him the accolade of Bach; his apparent enlightenment had already won him the admiration of Voltaire. But Frederick was not what he seemed. His apprenticeship had taught him dissimulation, to placate his tormentor; his torment had taught him ruthlessness. In his patronage of the arts -- the palaces, the public buildings, the processional avenues -- he reverted, indeed, to the programme of his grandfather. But in projecting, through this, the power of the state, he continued his father's policies. What he deplored in these, indeed, was not their excess but their inadequacy. Frederick William's regiment of giants was, after all, merely another manifestation of that ostentatiousness against which, in other respects, he had reacted. While building up the war machine of Prussia, he had never ventured to set it in motion. This made him ridiculous in the eyes of Europe; and Frederick, while disbanding the giants, added sixteen new battalions to his infantry. For, while realising the aims of two of his immediate ancestors, he was to be remembered in terms of a third: like his great–grandfather, the Great Elector, he was determined to win glory through war.[116]

And so, when news came of the death of the emperor, he informed Maria Theresa that he would support her husband's election in his place, and guarantee the rest of her inheritance, on condition she part with Silesia, the province immediately to his south. This 'proposal of robbery, punctuated by blackmail', having been scornfully rejected, Frederick urged his officers 'to the rendezvous of fame'.[117]

*C'est un fou, cet homme là est fol,* drawled the languid Louis XV; but in this, his first war for Silesia, Frederick easily seized the territory from Maria Theresa, as she considered temporarily. The second, however, brought out that quality in him which seemed greatness to contemporaries -- the ability to force victory from desperation -- and confirmed him in possession. The imperial idea had been weakened: he had established a second pole for Germany. He instanced the 'dangerous policy of the House of Austria' of 'enslaving forever Germanic liberty'; but an English visitor to his dominions reported nothing there but an 'absolute Prince and a People, all equally miserable, all equally trembling before him, and all equally detesting his iron government'. Already there was an intimation of the isolated old man, his blue coat stained yellow with snuff, at whose passing there was no sorrow, only stunned relief:[118] of the sharp and almost otherworldly asceticism which is concentrated in the death-mask: of the selfless, ceaseless, loveless will to power.

Maria Theresa, writes Acton, was a 'sensible and reasonable woman', but 'without culture or superior talent', and her husband was 'not able to supply the deficiency'. So it was that she turned to her chancellor, the brilliant and devious Kaunitz, whose aims were realised in the alliance of Austria with France. This was balanced by that of Prussia with England, so that, within the diplomatic revolution, the fundamental antagonisms remained: Briton being leagued against Bourbon, and Hapsburg against Hohenzollern.[119]

Frederick's third and final war over Silesia began in disaster. 'It is a time for stoicism', he declared; 'the disciples of Epicurus would find nothing to say'. But when all was at its darkest came Rossbach. Here Frederick, though outnumbered five to two, engaged the French army on the march: his infantry, marching parallel, formed themselves, with clockwork discipline, into attacking echelons, confusing their enemy, who were then routed by his cavalry. France never afterwards risked an army in his presence: it was the battle, thought Bonaparte, which began the collapse of the Bourbon monarchy.[120]

On the German side, its impact was no less decisive. 'Never', wrote Macaulay,

> since the dissolution of the empire of Charlemagne, had the Teutonic race won such a field against the French...The fame of Frederick began to supply, in some degree, the place of a common government and of a common capital...Then first

it was manifest that the Germans were truly a nation.[121]

In England, inns repainted their signboards to honour the King of Prussia. Pitt described his victory as a happy turn for liberty and Protestantism: a sentiment reinforced by Leuthen. Here Frederick defeated the Austrians, drawn up in strength on higher ground, by making for their centre before suddenly reforming and taking them in the flank. Afterwards, while campfires illuminated the bloodstained snow, a voice was raised over the groans of the wounded and dying, in moments the entire army had taken up the hymn, and *Nun danket alle Gott* became *der Choral von Leuthen*.[122]

Frederick, sniffed a later historian, was acclaimed the Protestant hero though neither a hero nor a Protestant. But a simpler epitaph was pronounced by the avenger of Rossbach. After Jena, the victorious French commander visited the garrison church where Frederick's coffin lay beside that of his father. But if his generals expected some memorable gibe, his reaction took them by surprise. 'Hats off, gentlemen', barked Napoleon. 'If he were alive, we should not be here'.[123]

## X

THE English war began in America, with an assault on a French fort by a keen young colonel of militia. His name was George Washington. Another British officer wrote to the secretary of state that it was the 'being actuated by your spirits that now makes us masters of the place'; and he renamed it, accordingly, Pittsburgh.

When Pitt at last assumed direction of affairs, his demonic energy was reflected in the conduct of the war. An ambassador claimed to be able to detect his presence from the style of dispatches alone. An admiral who complained of an impossible task was shown his crutches and told: 'Sir, I walk on impossibilities'. There was ample reason, certainly, for gloom: a British army had been neutralised, a British fleet disabled. 'It is time for England', wrote Horace Walpole, 'to slip her own cables, and float away into some unknown ocean...'[124]

But unknown to all in England as he wrote, the balance had already turned. A few months earlier, in a monsoon downpour, an entire cycle of history had come to an end.

The early British presence in India was under the rule of the great Moghuls: Babur, descending from the mountains, conquering the hot plains, and on the site of his victory designing a garden; Humayun, gentle and inept, buried under a pointed dome that is a lesser anticipation of the Taj; Akbar, the universal mystic, whose rose-red throne was a Hindu, Buddhist and Christian, as well as Islamic, tree of life; Jahangir, whose fascination with nature was reflected in a great school of painting; Shah Jahan, whose quadripartite garden, squares subdividing into squares within the framework of a cross canal, is hovered over by the most ethereal of all buildings. Then came the puritan Aurungzeb, who erected a pinched and narrow parody of his father's creation: whose reign, like that of his contemporary Louis XIV, was a succession of expansionary wars; and who left, like him, a sense of emptiness and exhaustion.[125] He was followed by a succession of wraiths, under whom the throne of Delhi was carried off to Persia, and the city left strewn with corpses, it was said, 'as the walks of a garden with dead flowers and leaves'. The wraiths continued to succeed one another; and, where viceroys ruled in their name, they were, says Macaulay, 'no longer lieutenants, removable at pleasure, but independent hereditary princes'. Here the English found their opportunity.[126]

They had come to India to trade, silver for cotton and silk, fabrics of 'perfect Coal Black, pleasant grass greens and carnations', of the kind that Temple admired; and, by the end of William's reign, had established three presidencies there: to the west Bombay, the fair haven or *bom bahia* of the Portuguese; to the east Madras, between dark foliage and a white line of surf; and to the north Calcutta, on a crescent of the river that gave access to the rich plain of Bengal, and that took its name from Kali, goddess of the destruction and renewal of life.[127] Here, on the anticipation of war, both French and English began to extend their fortifications. When the nawab, or nabob, of Bengal, ordered them to halt, the French answered tactfully that they were carrying out repairs; but the English governor, a man both arrogant and weak, was offensive. The nawab jumped from his seat in a fury, marched on Calcutta, and confined his unruly captives in their own lockup. In the course of a stifling summer night, some were asphyxiated, others were trampled to death, and others still grew mad and died in delirium.[128]

The Black Hole of Calcutta seemed a glorious opportunity to Robert Clive. As a clerk at Madras for the East India Company, Clive had neither the training nor the appearance for a military role. Corpulent, awkward and morose, he was said to have attempted suicide, and to have told a man he had insulted, and who had a pistol pointed at his head, to 'fire and be damned'. But the lack of value he placed on his life had taken another form in a series of reckless escapades against the French, which led the directors of the company to reward him with a diamond-studded sword. Now he was commissioned to take Calcutta, and re-establish its privileges to the 'full extent granted by the Great Mogul'.[129]

Clive, having joined in a plot to replace the nawab with one of his generals, marched his men at night, in heavy rain, through flooded fields, to Plassey. He made his headquarters in a brick hunting-box of the nawab's, from which, at daybreak, he saw a lush green plain, over which black monsoon clouds stood out against the rich blue of the sky. Against him the nawab's army, in appearance, said an eyewitness, 'most pompous and formidable' -- its elephants covered in scarlet cloth, the drawn swords of its cavalry glittering -- advanced. Its French gunners opened a cannonade, against which the English, with their lighter artillery, could not contend. But at noon, the bulbous rainclouds opened; and, to the sound of thunder, unleashed a torrent on the battlefield. The English gunners who, unlike their opponents, moved quickly enough to cover their ammunition, cut down a charge by the nawab's forces, which now began to disperse. The nawab was murdered; and Clive, bringing French influence in India to an end, ruled through his successors.[130]

Clive confirmed Pitt's distrust of conventional commanders; and in this spirit he dispatched young Wolfe to Canada. Ungainly and excitable, in action Wolfe had shown a combination of daring and deliberation which set him apart from the indecision of his seniors. But when he sailed to Quebec, high on its wooded promontory over the river, he found a French force stronger than his own, and in an entrenched position. His efforts to dislodge them were futile; and, stricken by fever, he sent a despondent letter to Pitt, who gave up hope for the expedition. Meanwhile, however, Wolfe had noticed a steep and narrow pathway leading up a ravine to the plateau. Drifting downriver under cover of darkness, his advance force scrambled up the path, followed by the remainder of his troops, who in the morning light took up position on the Plains of Abraham. The French, hurriedly gathered, were scattered, though not before Wolfe had been fatally wounded; and Quebec, and ultimately Canada, fell into English hands.[131]

The story later grew that, on the night before the battle, Wolfe declared that he would prefer to have written Gray's Elegy than defeat the French; that he had, even, recited it as his boat drifted down: a tale that no doubt drew strength from the poem itself:

The Paths of Glory lead but to the Grave.[132]

But Walpole, as the roll–call of conquest continued, was exultant. 'You would not know your own country again', he told the British envoy in Florence. 'You left it a private little island, living upon its means. You would find it the capital of the world'.[133]

## xi

HE had spoken jestingly, while a French invasion seemed imminent, of placing guns upon his battlements. For, as he continued to build, though it never quite lost its playfulness, his house became increasingly splendid. In the glass of his great gallery are displayed his ancestral arms. Light streams through the escutcheoned windows into coloured pools on the floor, while on the opposite side the room floats into infinity through alcoves of looking-glass under a running network of gold. The library, too, approached through an armoury, showed the family bearings, in 'supreme expression', writes his biographer, of 'pride of ancestry'. So in *Otranto,* the gigantic helmet, the mailed hands and feet that emerged from the walls of the castle, were those of an avenging ancestor.[134]

For the Goth was a figure of radical ambivalence. Destroyer of Rome, it was a decadent Rome that he destroyed. And what made this view the more authoritative was its sanction by Rome itself. The Germans, wrote Tacitus under a senate subservient to autocracy, limited the power of their rulers: *nec regibus infinita aut libera potestas*. These were listened to by right of persuasion rather than command: *auctoritate suadendi magis quam iubendi potestate*; and, while they were permitted to decide on lesser matters, the greater required the deliberation of all: *de minoribus rebus principes consultant, de maioribus omnes*.[135]

The English were heirs to this Germanic liberty. The Goths, wrote Temple, were 'our ancestors'; and the constitution 'universal among these northern nations', and 'so well known in our island', was a 'government of freemen'. To seventeenth-century England, these immemorial institutions lived on.[136] The 'Grounds of our Common Laws', Parliament was informed, 'were beyond the Memory or Register of any Beginning, and the same which the Norman Conqueror found within the Realm'.[137]

Scholarship, on the other hand, argued that the common law, as a regulation of tenure, presupposed the Norman feudalism: so that, the king was told, there was no particle of land which was 'not held in fee of your Majesty'. The summons to Parliament was based upon tenure from the crown: it was a feudal *curia*, in which the barons, as vassals, met their royal lord, and out of which the subordinate knights and burgesses had evolved into a separate house. Scholarship, however, was no match for tradition, still less for events. In the debates on the Williamite settlement, it was asserted that the 'original of government came from Germany'; and this was received doctrine to the eighteenth century.[138] 'No Nation', it was stated under George I, 'has preserv'd their Gothick Constitution better than the English'; while, under George II, a Gothic temple was set up at Stowe, with statues of the Anglo–Saxon deities:

> Gods, of a Nation, valiant, wise, and free,
> Who conquer'd to establish Liberty![139]

For Walpole, too, his house was a Germanic temple. 'I...am always', he wrote, 'impatient to be back with my own Woden and Thor, my own Gothic Lares'.[140] It was a realisation of mythic origins; for, as Tacitus had stated, the temples of the Germans were woods and groves: *lucos ac nemora consecrant*; as they scorned to confine their gods within walls: *nec cohibere parietibus deos*.[141] And so, for Walpole, the Gothic building breathed and moved. It was organic nature -- branch, leaf and flower, still in motion though transposed into stone -- which continued the life of the forest, and embodied the energies of its inhabitants. *Ce beau système*, declared Montesquieu of the English constitutional arrangements, *a été trouvé dans les bois*.[142]

'Heroic German ancestors', comments Pocock, 'had brought their free institutions, already ancient, out of the forest to overthrow a Roman Empire corrupted by tyranny'.[143] In Frederick's English garden stands a pavilion of *chinoiserie*, within which, under the overhanging trees, the light is green; while on the far side of his villa the view bears down to a ruined Rome. In Walpole, Pitt's victories induced a comparable sensation. 'I shall burn all my Greek and Latin books', he declared. 'They are histories of little people'.[144]

# CHAPTER EIGHT

# THE ETERNAL MOMENT

THE Pantheon is still there, floating, on the lake in the western hills. The wind stirs, and it vanishes. It is still, then, in the sunlight, and Rome is back again, solid.

Stourhead is the most perfect of classical gardens. Here is the Vergilian circuit: the command for reverence at the entrance to a sacred site -- *procul o, procul este, profani* -- the descent into an underworld -- *facilis descensus Averno* -- and the ascent again, round the rim of the lake, to the hillside temple of Apollo.[1]

While all this was conjured into existence, Edward Gibbon came here as a schoolboy. In the house behind, he found a volume on the Roman empire; and, when the dinner-bell rang, was crossing the Danube with the Goths.[2]

## i

HE was born by Putney Heath, where in winter the trees are ghostly in the mist that drifts up from the river. He did not remember his mother very well; but he recalled her telling him, as they crossed the heath in a carriage, that he must learn to think for himself. Few injunctions have been more faithfully followed.[3]

Her place was taken by her sister, who unlocked for him the magical cave of his grandfather's library, and to whom he ascribed that 'early and invincible love of reading, which I would not exchange for the treasures of India'.[4]

His father stares in puzzlement from his portrait. Hardly knowing what to do with a lad who was kept awake by problems of biblical chronology, and to whom the dynasties of Assyria and Egypt were 'top and cricket-ball', he sent him to Oxford.[5] Here the fellows treated him with the deference befitting a gentleman commoner, whose silk gown and velvet cap proclaimed the superfluity of intellect; and he continued his reading alone. The 'blind activity of idleness urged me to advance without armour into the dangerous mazes of controversy; and...I bewildered myself in the errors of the Church of Rome'. If it was an error, it was an ominous one: he had reasoned himself to Rome on the basis of what he took to be historical evidence.[6]

The elder Gibbon was a churchgoer, as a matter of course: he was a landed gentleman. But to take the business seriously...He introduced his son to a deist friend; and, when this failed, packed him off to a clergyman at Lausanne, in a dark house by the cathedral that clings to the slope above the lake. The pastor, more subtle than the parent, left books lying about. These vanished, were absorbed and discussed, until the 'Romish creed disappeared like a dream'. So did his English: 'I am now', he declared, 'good protestant'.[7]

He was permitted riding, fencing and dancing: though he never did become a horseman, remained clumsy with the foil, and, while he could walk a minuet, was defeated by the country-dance. None of this, however, mattered to Suzanne. She admired his fine hands, his deep-red hair, his features *si spirituelle*. And for him, in turn, the striking and scholarly parson's daughter was 'the most beautiful soul I know'. Now, though he still desired to bring 'clarity into the shadows of antiquity', she held out to him the prospect of a happiness 'above Empire'.[8]

It was empire, however, that was to win the day. His father had remarried, and the son was recalled in a letter that spoke of making him happy. 'He desires my happiness', he told Suzanne, 'and if he desires it, he will not think of separating me from you'. By his father, he was treated with 'easy and equal politeness'; while his stepmother took 'assiduous care to study and gratify my wishes'. 'The priests', he reflected afterwards, 'and the altar had been prepared, and the victim was unconscious of the impending stroke'. His twenty-first birthday gave him the power to break the entail on the family estate; his father's debts made the decision pressing; and the young man's acquiescence left him with an income adequate either for scholarship or for marriage, but not both.[9]

The father was unsympathetic. Such a marriage would send him to an early grave: had he not sufficiently trampled on his country? Yet he would not stand in his way. 'Marry your *foreigner*, you are independent'. He was not: there would be no increase in his income should he marry without consent.[10]

'I sighed as a lover, I obeyed as a son'. Suzanne was contemptuous. Was he attired for ambition? Favoured by tenderness? Married? Or about to be? *Seriez vous attiré par l'ambition? favorisé par la tendresse? Marié? ou prêt à l'être?* 'Will the chains be of flowers or solid gold?'[11]

## ii

WHILE Pitt was writing his biography in the history of the world, Gibbon was a captain of militia; and at Sissinghurst, where roses now climb among the ruins, guarded French prisoners amidst 'dirt most excessive'. Becoming 'sick of so hateful a service', he opened Cicero *de Natura Deorum*, and began once again to 'taste the pleasure of thinking'. And now, with the war at an end, came fulfilment of a long-cherished project: he was to journey to Rome.[12]

At Paris, he laid in a supply of 'Cloaths, ruffles, silk stockings &c', including a suit of 'velvet of three colours, the ground blue', allowed himself to be engaged by a sympathetic Frenchwoman in warm discussion of the pleasures of the senses, and, on arriving again at Lausanne, received a letter of angry reproach. Suzanne, it was true, had consorted with other men -- had even been engaged to one for a time -- but her heart, she insisted, had never wavered. 'Must you always', sighed Gibbon, 'offer me a happiness which reason obliges me to renounce?' There was a meeting, at which he affected detachment; and she redoubled her reproaches. He had amused himself by ravaging her soul with tortures 'most deliberately conceived and carried out'; he had brought her *au bord du tombeau. Fille dangereuse et artificielle*, he warned himself through his journal.[13]

But they were, it seemed, to be friends. When they spoke, it was with 'all the freedom of people who have understood one another'. Yet he could not help thinking of her, and 'ventured to call'. Next day, again, he gave way to this 'inclination'. He felt nothing for her, he assured himself; but he continued to call. At last he acknowledged the truth: 'my senses were stirred and hers were not at all undisturbed'. It was time to resume his journey.[14]

'The pilgrimage of Italy, which I now accomplished, had long been the object of my curious devotion'.[15] The religious imagery did not belie his feeling. In the summer heat of Florence, he stood with a 'secret respect' at the tombs of Michelangelo and Galileo, 'the restorer of the arts and of philosophy'. As he passed in autumn through Viterbo, with its papal palace and shadowed alleyways, with their echoes of medieval riot and assassination, his thoughts were on the region in classical times. And now at last he found himself in Rome, 'in a dream of antiquity'.[16]

A dream it was. He experienced the city in the double exposure of the Renaissance, as in the great image invoked by Freud. 'Let us suppose', writes the analyst, 'that Rome is not a human habitation but a psychical entity': as indeed it is.

> In the place occupied by the Palazzo Caffarelli would once more stand -- without the Palazzo having to be removed -- the Temple of Jupiter Capitolinus.

For

> in mental life nothing which has once been formed can perish...everything is somehow preserved, and...in suitable circumstances...can once more be brought

to light.[17]

So it was for Gibbon. On the evening on which he 'sat musing amidst the ruins of the Capitol, while the barefooted fryars were singing Vespers in the Temple of Jupiter', the twin images momentarily coalesced, and 'the idea of writing the decline and fall of the City first started to my mind'.[18] But it was the church that was the dream, and the temple that was the reality:

> Those gods and those men had long since vanished; but, to the eye of liberal enthusiasm, the majesty of ruin restored the image of her ancient prosperity.[19]

In Paris, the life that might have been had passed away. Suzanne had gone there as companion to a woman in whom a millionaire banker had shown an interest; but he had married her instead. Gibbon's pen slipped badly as he wrote of her: in attempting to say that she was 'handsome as ever', he reduced her to 'handsome as every'; while a summons to supper exalted itself into an invitation to 'summer'. Turning elsewhere, he resumed his discussions on the pleasures of the senses, proceeding as it would seem from theory to practice; until, at last relinquishing 'the embraces of Paris', he found himself once more driving 'through the summer dust and solitude of London' on his return to the family manor.[20]

Buriton is set within a last wave of wooded hill before the downs plunge to the sea: bordered, in the massive fortress of Portchester, by the futile defences of the Saxon shore. Here, each Sunday, Gibbon crossed with his father and stepmother to the medieval church, in the family pew of which he had deposited the Greek scriptures. 'Since my escape from Popery', he wrote, 'I had humbly acquiesced in the common creed of the Protestant Churches'. But the text sent him to the commentators, the commentators to the sources; and these now forced him to draw his own conclusions 'on the miraculous darkness of the Passion' from 'the silence of an unbelieving age'.[21] His conversion to the empire was absolute, his vision on the Capitol complete.

He sat down to its transcription in London, in a house off the Roman road of Oxford Street, where his library was light blue with a gold border, and his bookcases white with a classic frieze. Here, one morning, 'about half an hour after seven as I was destroying an army of Barbarians, I heard a double rap at the door'. A cousin offered him a seat in parliament; Gibbon accepted, and within a fortnight was a member of the British senate. 'It is more tremendous than I imagined; the great speakers fill me with despair, the bad ones with terror'. And they plunged every day 'deeper into the great business of America'.[22]

## iii

WHEN George II was buried, half of Pitt's authority went with him. The new king took his ideas from the opposition to his grandfather, who, his mother considered, counted for no more in the affairs of state than 'one of the trees we walked by'. On the premature death of his father Frederick, his role was taken by one of his associates, the proud and pedantic Earl of Bute, who encouraged the insecure youth to assert himself, and for whom the problems of politics were to be resolved by a virtuous sovereign.[23]

Virtue, however, was sorely tried as the prince arrived at manhood. He suffered 'the greatest temptation to be gallant with the young ladies', who, it was said, 'lay themselves out in the most shameful manner'. With one of them he fell passionately in love, and was kept to the path of rectitude only by the severest strictures of his mentor.[24] Such was the situation when he became king, and one of his earliest actions was to peruse a list of suitably Protestant princesses. Of these, seven had been located; but three were instantly rejected. Brandenburg's mother was rumoured to have had an affair; Anhalt Dessau's grandfather had married an apothecary's daughter; Saxe Gotha was addicted to philosophy. There remained Brunswick Wolfenbuttel, Brandenburg Schwedt, Hesse Darmstadt and Mecklenburg Strelitz. Points against three of these were soon discovered: Brunswick Wolfenbuttel was only fifteen; Brandenburg Schwedt was good–looking but bad–tempered; Hesse Darmstadt added stubbornness to unacceptable size. Thus, by a rational process of elimination, Charlotte of Mecklenburg became queen of England. She was not, the young king confessed, 'in every particular as I could wish'; but in every vital respect she was perfect. She was not difficult; she was not disreputable; and she was not an intellectual. In the course of her voyage, she practised 'God save the King' on the harpsichord, along the road was 'extremely courteous to an incredible number of spectators', and on arrival at St. James' was walked across the road to be married.[25]

George III had now imposed virtue on himself; it remained only to impose it on his kingdom. 'As I mount the throne', he had declared, 'in the midst of a bloody war, I shall endeavour to prosecute it in the manner most likely to bring an honourable and lasting peace'. Pitt insisted upon changing 'bloody' to 'expensive but just and necessary'; but there were many besides the king who, appalled by its expense, no longer thought it necessary or just; and Pitt, though he comported himself 'like a Lucifer', at last felt compelled to resign.[26]

Pitt's defiance of royalty in the abstract was equalled only by his deference in its presence. In the same room as majesty, it was said, his eagle nose was to be seen between his legs; and when the king now offered him any reward in the gift of the crown, he was overcome by tears at this 'gracious goodness' . The result was the barony of Chatham for his wife, and an annuity for three lives. The royal goodness was further attested by the publication of these details in the *Gazette*, a step without precedent.[27]

Consternation followed. The coffeehouses fell silent, as at some national calamity. 'Am I not an old fool?' cried Horace Walpole. 'Here have I fallen in love with my father's enemies, and because they served my country, believed they were the most virtuous men upon earth'. But at a banquet in the City, Bute was mauled by the crowd, and Pitt overshadowed the king. Shame had set in as he justified his reward: 'Is it not bestowed upon me for signal and important services?' No–one, writes his biographer -- not Caesar, not Alexander -- had 'changed such national dejection to such national triumph in so brief a space'.[28]

The peace, however, was carried; but an attempt to recoup the costs of the war by taxation in America precipitated, says Ian Christie, 'an imperial crisis of major proportions':

> To British politicians it was axiomatic that Parliament exercised sovereign powers in all respects over all British subjects in the king's dominions.

The colonists, on the other hand, insisted that

> their legislatures were miniature parliaments with full and exclusive powers over their internal policy, and that the colonial inheritance of all the rights and liberties of Englishmen precluded their property being subjected to taxation except by an assembly in which they were represented.

Pitt agreed. It was, he told the Commons,

> a subject of greater importance than ever engaged the attention of this House; that subject only excepted, when nearly a century ago, it was the question whether you yourselves were to be bond or free.

'If liberty', he thundered, 'be not countenanced in America it will sicken, fade and die in this country'. Across the Atlantic, toasts were drunk to him, and his statue, in a toga, was set up on Wall Street.[29] But when he agreed to take office again, his friends were dismayed, and his enemies sneered. For he had ascended to the Lords as Earl of Chatham. The City, which had ordered illuminations for his return to power, cancelled them. 'His titles', it was claimed,

> are his epitaph,
> His robes his winding-sheet.

So they were: he had surrendered, with the Commons, his influence over 'the only branch of the legislature that could compete with the power of the crown'; and in the Lords was bluntly informed that the hereditary legislators of the realm 'would not be browbeaten by an insolent minister'. The great orator became tongue-tied. 'Like oracles and groves', wrote Horace Walpole, 'whose sanctity depended on the fears of the devout, and whose mysterious and holy gloom vanished as soon as men dared to think and walk through them, Lord Chatham's authority vanished with his popularity, and his godhead, when he had affronted his priests'.[30]

Walpole was no less disillusioned in another erstwhile idol. Frederick of Prussia, after his defeat of France and Austria, had found his greatest threat in Russia. For the empress Elizabeth, daughter of Czar Peter, the desire to limit a growing power on the Baltic was deepened by personal dislike, certain gibes of his having been repeated about her fondness for strong drink and strong men. Frederick came close to annihilation: the bullet is still shown that flattened itself against the snuff-box in his pocket; but he was saved by the accession of Elizabeth's nephew Peter, who regarded him with idolatry. The play of Peter's bedchamber had consisted in the manipulation of toy soldiers; now he could command troops in person. In the square before the Winter Palace, he set them wheeling, marching, and counter-marching, until at the moment of climax, all the cannon in the citadel and the admiralty went off with a monumental bang. And after he had been murdered and replaced by his wife, the Prussian general's daughter known to history as Catherine the Great, the collusion continued. Frederick linked his possessions in Brandenburg with those in Prussia by persuading Catherine and, much against her will, his former victim Maria Theresa, to join him in detaching portions of the intervening state. 'The King of Prussia', wrote Walpole, 'the hero of the last war, has only been a pickpocket in Poland'.[31] And at home, the prospect was scarcely less dismal:

> We sanctify such violences and iniquities, that one should think the House of Commons was composed of three hundred and sixty-five Empresses and Kings of Prussia.[32]

Pitt's ministry had become, by his own admission, 'a ridiculous phantom'. As he lay immobilised, his chancellor discovered a perfect solution to the American problem. It would raise revenue from the colonies; and, since it transferred an existing duty from England to America, but at a lower rate, would assert authority without causing offence. It was a tax on tea.[33]

In the shots that rang out on a village green, or across a bridge over a winding river, resistance turned to revolution. Pitt thought the American congress 'the most honourable assembly of statesmen since those of the Greeks and Romans in their most virtuous times';[34] and, in the year in which, behind the Palladian window at Philadelphia, it declared its independence of Britain, there appeared the opening volume of the *Decline and Fall of the Roman Empire*.

## iv

'YOU have unexpectedly', wrote Walpole, 'given the world a classic history'. He was 'in no light profound enough to deserve your intimacy'. He felt no envy now, though he had for a moment; and if there was one quality in the author which he particularly admired, it was

> your amiable modesty. How can you know so much, judge so well, possess your subject and your knowledge and your power of judicious reflection so thoroughly, and yet...betray no dictatorial arrogance?[35]

But when Gibbon called about his second volume, he was slighting. There was so much that was tiresome -- the contrast, for instance, 'between Roman and Gothic manners' -- and 'though you have written the story as well as it could be written, I fear few will have patience to read it'. Claimed Walpole:

> He coloured; all his round features squeezed themselves into sharp angles; he screwed up his button–mouth and rapping his snuff–box, said: 'It had never been put together before' -- so *well* he meant to add -- but gulped it.

'Well', he concluded,

> from that hour to this I have not seen him, though he used to call once or twice a week; nor has he sent me the third volume, as he promised. I well knew his vanity, even about his ridiculous face and person, but thought he had too much sense to avow it so palpably.[36]

'Ingenious trifler' was Gibbon's judgement on Walpole;[37] and in his third volume, after recounting some Germanic atrocities, he commented: 'Such were those savage ancestors, whose imaginary virtues have sometimes excited the praise and envy of civilised ages'.[38] His contempt for the medieval interlude was genuine. Venice appeared to him a collection of 'stinking ditches dignified with the pompous denomination of Canals...and a large square decorated with the worst Architecture I ever yet saw'; while the Sainte-Chapelle he found hugely amusing as a receptacle for bogus relics. The classical palace of Theodoric, he declared, in an ironic tilt at Walpolean notions, 'represents the oldest and most authentic model of Gothic architecture'.[39]

For Gibbon, it has been observed, saw everything from the standpoint of Rome.[40] He 'identified himself with his subject', writes Dawson,

> as no other historian has done. A contemporary...said of him that he came at last to believe he was the Roman Empire, and though this was said in jest by an unfriendly critic it contains a real element of truth. For this...absurd little man...with his pug face and his pot belly, was possessed and obsessed by the majestic spirit of Rome...He felt as a Roman; he thought as a Roman; he wrote as a Roman.[41]

Gibbon denied the continuity of Parliament with Germanic institutions,[42] preferring to find its prototype at Rome:[43]

> The temperate struggles of the patricians and plebeians had finally established the firm and equal balance of the constitution; which united the freedom of popular assemblies with the authority and wisdom of a senate and the executive powers of a regal magistrate.[44]

And this fusion of commons, aristocracy and king was vindicated by its capacity for empire. Gibbon's triumphal Rome marched in step with his triumphal England. Of Trajan, the last great Roman conqueror, he wrote: 'Every day the astonished senate received the intelligence of new names and new nations that acknowledged his sway': a passage, notes Swain, which must have recalled Pitt's victories; while the senate to which they were reported delighted equally in the image of liberty.[45] Had that image become reality, wrote Gibbon, in an evident parallel with England,

> the privileges of the subject would have secured the throne of the monarch; the abuses of an arbitrary administration might have been prevented, in some degree, or corrected, by the interposition of these representative assemblies; and the country would have been defended against a foreign enemy by the arms of natives and freemen. Under the mild and generous influence of liberty, the Roman empire might have remained invincible and immortal...[46]

But it had not done so; and in its fall he saw 'the greatest, perhaps, and most awful scene in the history of mankind'.[47]

## v

LYTTON STRACHEY considered it an 'extreme improbability' that the 'gigantic ruin of Europe through a thousand years' should have been 'mirrored in the mind of an eighteenth–century English gentleman'.[48] On the contrary, nothing was more probable -- indeed, inevitable. For the eighteenth century was *par excellence* the age of the ruin. 'The inheritance of humanism', writes Laurence Goldstein, carried with it 'an entail of doom'.[49]

The lament for Rome had begun with its fall; throughout the middle ages, the site evoked sadness and awe; and, as the hopes of the Renaissance were clouded, and the painters of the baroque absorbed themselves in divagations from the ideal, dead cities appeared in their canvases whose 'wild and irrationally decadent towers, spires, palaces and statues tumble so startlingly yet exquisitely on to strange quays, in an elegant nightmare of decay'.[50] But the great poet of ruin was Claude; and in the English vision of landscape, his influence was ubiquitous. 'The solemn scene', intoned Dyer,

> Elates the soul, while now the rising Sun
> Flames on the ruins in the purer air
> Towering aloft, upon the glittering plain...[51]

In Claude's landscapes, however, the Roman edifices as they were in his own day -- ruined, or with medieval additions -- stand side by side with their imagined restoration, in 'an idealised Campagna...enhanced by the dimension of the antique'.[52] For the ultimate subject of Claude is not the past in itself, but in its relation to the present. The juxtaposition of the two creates depth in time, as his perspective creates depth in space, with the lengthened vistas of dawn or sunset adding a further suggestion of transience. He was supreme, said Constable, in the 'evanescent character of light'.[53]

All this was glossed most completely by Keats, setting out from his meditation on Claude's 'Enchanted Castle': its casements opening from a delicate Roman facade, shadowed by Gothic tower and battlement, while behind over the sea glimmers the chill light in which Psyche appears forlorn. And he went on, in the great odes, to tease out its ramifications: of melancholy over perfection that must pass; of the luxury and impending desolation of autumn; of desire arrested, and so capable neither of fading nor fulfilment, in the eternal present of an antique urn; of all history encompassed in a nightingale's song, at the timeless instant before the epiphany passes; of Psyche, who, though she inhabits no temple, lives on in the landscape of the mind, still dreaming of transformation within the magical palace of Eros.[54]

The Claudian moment, then, is one of exquisite intensity, at the same time haunted by the intimation of mortality. It is a moment such as that in which his master, Vergil, has Aeneas return to life from shipwreck and simultaneously, through the medium of art, apprehend his own past:

*constitit et lacrimans, 'quis iam locus', inquit, 'Achate,*
*quae regio in terris nostri non plena laboris?*
*en Priamus! sunt hic etiam sua praemia laudi,*
*sunt lacrimae rerum et mentem mortalia tangunt.*[55]

Troy is evoked for Aeneas on his voyage to refound it in Rome; Rome in turn has fallen; and this is the epic subject of Gibbon. He sees the imperial capital, after its capture by the Goths, in a Claudian vista of desolation -- 'the vacant space of the *eternal* city' -- and everything in his vast panorama speaks of time and its silent passage. 'Insensible' and 'imperceptible' are favourite adjectives. The 'nations of the empire insensibly melted away into the Roman name and people'; under this uniform government, the provinces 'insensibly sunk into the languid indifference of private life'; and, in a discouraged populace and an undisciplined military, the empire's greatness was 'insensibly undermined'. The church, meanwhile, 'imperceptibly changed the language of exhortation into that of command'; and, after the closure of the temples, the people, again 'insensibly', imbibed the doctrines of the new religion. And this unperceived progression of the city is linked explicitly with the life of the individual. Of the fable of the Seven Sleepers, Gibbon declares:

> We imperceptibly advance from youth to age, without observing the gradual, but incessant, change of human affairs, and, even in our larger experiences of history, the imagination is accustomed, by a perpetual series of causes and effects, to unite the most distant revolutions. But, if the interval between two memorable æras could be instantly annihilated; if it were possible, after a momentary slumber of two hundred years, to display the *new* world to the eyes of a spectator, who still retained a lively and recent impression of the *old*; his surprise and his reflections would furnish the pleasing subject of a philosophical romance.[56]

It was this poetry of passage that he found wanting in Byzantium. To Gibbon, the history of the eastern empire seemed a 'dead uniformity' of 'spiritual despotism': like one of its own icons, remote from human drama or passion: lacking in emotion as it appeared to lack motion.[57] Small wonder, then, that he should have criticised it in the most devastating imagery his century could afford. As the France of Louis XIV had once seemed the embodiment of the artificial and the unnatural, so now for Gibbon was the domain of the eastern emperors. 'The coasts and islands of Asia and Europe', he wrote,

> were covered with their magnificent villas; but...the marble structure of their gardens served only to expose the riches of the lord and the labours of the architect.

And these were contrasted with the 'modest art which secretly strives to hide itself and to decorate the scenery of nature'.[58] *Sharawadgi.*

## vi

BUT if Rome had declined and fallen, it had, like the 'scenery of nature', revived. Waiting at the gates of the corrupted city Gibbon saw, with Tacitus, a 'hardy race of barbarians, who despised life when it was separated from freedom'. And it was they, now, who embodied what had once been represented by Rome. 'The most civilised nations of modern Europe', he declared, 'issued from the woods of Germany'.[59]

England, Germanic by origin, was Roman by achievement. Walpole emphasized the first of these aspects, Gibbon the second. Their differences were differences of standpoint within a common historical vista. And so the quarrel between them was of short duration. When he came to the end of Gibbon's history, Walpole declared himself 'extremely pleased'. 'Mr. Gibbon', he now asserted, 'never tires me'. He was to revise, even, his opinion of his character: 'vanity', he reflected, 'is not vice'.[60]

In the English revolution, Goth and Roman had combined to create a new order of the ages; and in the English garden, following Claude, medieval and classical buildings stood side by side.[61] But the process would, inevitably, continue: it was inevitable because the principle of nature. The Goth, too, was subject to the depredations of time, and Gothic ruins also found a place in the landscape vista. The meaning of the ruin, wrote Diderot, was this: 'everything perishes, everything passes, only time goes on...I walk between two eternities'.[62]

And so, while the American colonists sought to assert a 'political liberty threatened by the apparent corruption of the constitution' -- an issue expressed in terms of Cato and Tacitus -- while, in their words, the 'BRITISH CONSTITUTION seems fast tottering into fatal and inevitable ruin'[63] -- a morning and evening scene of Claude's were printed as emblematic of the 'rise and fall, or ascendancy and decline of the Roman Empire'.[64] In Gibbon's history, Walpole noted a passage which 'I believe the author did not intend to be so applicable to the present moment': 'the Imperial ministers pursued with proscriptive laws, and ineffectual arms, the rebels whom they had made'.[65] And, as his father's policies, perceived as the corruption of a people, had been commemorated by a ruin at Stowe,[66] so now, when they seemed to the colonists to live again in the 'adroit manipulation of Parliament by a power–hungry ministry',[67] the Whig Duke of Norfolk set up ruins to mark the British reverses in America.[68] Franklin, reported Walpole, 'said he would furnish Mr. Gibbon with materials for writing the History of the Decline of the British Empire';[69] Washington was inspired by Addison's *Cato* to resist the despotism, no longer of a Louis XIV, but of a George III;[70] Jefferson combined authorship of the Declaration of Independence with the construction of a house that he named, after Palladio's account of his Villa Rotonda, Monticello.[71] And America went on to create its own Capitol, its own monumental classicism, its own myth of morning and the unlimited vista. It was a cycle that had long before been anticipated at Rome:

*atque iterum ad Troiam magnus mittetur Achilles*.[72]

'Worlds succeed to worlds', wrote Horace Walpole, 'in which the occupiers build the same castles in the air. What is ours but the present moment?'[73]

## vii

HE has no news, writes Walpole to a friend abroad; 'but when chaos is come again, what would signify a courier from Paradise?'[74]

In this he expressed, as Gibbon had, the central myth of his century. The 'period in the history of the world', stated Gibbon in a defining passage, 'during which the condition of the human race was most happy and prosperous', was that 'golden age' of Rome under its benevolent emperors, when the 'increasing splendour of the cities' was set within 'the beautiful face of the country, cultivated and adorned' -- inevitably -- 'like an immense garden'.[75]

In that other epic of the century, *Tom Jones*, the same equation is found. Fielding anticipated Gibbon in his statement that the Roman empire between Nerva and the Antonines enjoyed the 'only golden age, which ever had any existence, unless in the warm imaginations of the poets, from the expulsion from Eden down to this day';[76] and it is this loss of Eden, and its restoration, that is enacted in his novel. Fielding's epic is set, on one level, within the English garden of his own day, in which, he exclaims, 'days are too short for the ravished imagination'; but on another, it is an account, not of *a* garden, but of *the* garden. Its movement of exile and return is inscribed around a point named Paradise Hall.

Insofar as the site had a factual reference, it was to a garden attributed to Lancelot Brown.[77] Brown first exercised his capabilities at Stowe, where he absorbed the painterly idiom of Kent; and through his connections there attained an unprecedented position in English society. 'He shares the private hours of the King', observed Pitt, '...and sits down at the tables of all the House of Lords'. And it was Brown who, in the American crisis, acted as intermediary between these two. He represented Pitt to the king as having acted 'for the dignity of the crown, the happiness of his Majesty and the royal family, and the lustre of the whole empire'; and was able to report that he had been 'heard favourably'.[78]

Brown's unique achievement is a reflection of the place of the garden in the eighteenth–century imagination: a place identified, with great precision, in Walpole's epitaph:

> With one lost Paradise the name
> Of our first ancestor is stained;
> Brown shall enjoy unsullied fame
> For many a Paradise regained.[79]

Brown worked for old families and new fortunes, for the king and for Clive, for Pitt and for his nemesis Bute.[80] His effect was unvarying: a pastoral vista of meadow, wood and water; but his broad flowing easy lines rose sometimes to dramatic magnificence. At Marlborough's Blenheim, he flooded the valley, turning its monumental Roman bridge into a causeway, and creating an appropriately lavish setting for the massive silhouette of the house;[81] while at Prior Park, the concave hillside is edged by trees whose shadows fall across it, the pool at its foot reflecting a Palladian bridge that echoes the great mansion curving along its summit.[82]

This was the basis for Fielding's Paradise Hall; but a major dislocation between fiction and fact is the absence of the vista so prominent in the novel.[83] While the Avon can be seen, observes Wilbur Cross, in the valley below, there is no sign of its meandering '"through an amazing variety of meadows and woods, till it emptied itself into the sea, with a large arm of which, and an island beyond it, the prospect was closed". Extensive as is the view from Prior Park, there is no sight of the sea; nor, near at hand, of "an old ruined abbey, grown over with ivy"'. Coleridge, Cross goes on,

> wondered from what point of vantage Fielding saw a 'ridge of wild mountains, the tops of which were above the clouds', and remarked that the clouds must have been 'uncommonly low', for the so-called mountains of Somersetshire are only hills. Of later date, Thomas Keightley, who once made a study of the topography of *Tom Jones*, came to the conclusion that 'the real site...' was not Prior Park at all, but Sharpham Park near Glastonbury, the home of Fielding's grandfather. Had Keightley visited Sharpham, he would have discovered that the manor house and the prospect in no wise correspond with the description...; but a walk of a few miles would have brought him to the very place which was in Fielding's mind. Had Keightley climbed Tor Hill, to the northeast of Glastonbury, the magnificent panorama for which he was searching would have opened full upon his view.

Here are the river, the hills with trailing clouds, the arm of the sea, with the island standing out in it; while close at hand is the ruined abbey: Glastonbury. And the 'whole district from Glastonbury to Sharpham', Cross observes,

> once surrounded by water or deep marshes, was formerly called the Isle of Avalon, and became associated in Celtic romance with the land of immortality.[84]

The scene at the same time, it has been observed, is Claudian:[85] still further intensifying its status as a pagan elysium.

## viii

FOR Sir Thomas Browne, in the previous century, 'the delightful World comes after Death, and Paradise succeeds the Grave'.[86] Now all this was reversed.

That the inversion of the biblical myth was latent in the English garden was obvious to contemporaries. For this we have the evidence of one of its most articulate enemies. At Stowe, John Wesley wrote: 'it was ominous for my lord to entertain himself and his noble company...on the bank of Styx; that is, on the brink of hell'; while in the classical statuary at Stourhead, he found himself unable to 'admire the images of devils'.[87] It was no less apparent to its advocates. If Rome was a garden to Gibbon, the garden was Rome to Walpole; and Rousham, with its roistering and erotic deities, he found 'as elegant and antique as if the Emperor Julian' -- who as the restorer of paganism was of intimate concern to Gibbon[88] -- 'had selected the most pleasing solitude about Daphne to enjoy a philosophic retirement'.[89]

But the most explicit of these landscapes of inversion was Wycombe, home to the Hell-Fire Club. The classical house is set beside a broadening of the river Wye into an islanded lake, the whole overlooked by a hilltop church in which the dominant figure is Judas. At the nearby abbey of Medmenham, meanwhile, an authentic medieval foundation was enhanced by an ivy-covered cloister, a ruined tower, and a stone madonna in a niche; but that this was meant to heighten the sense of transgression was indicated by an inscription celebrating penile tensions over penitentials -- *PENI TENTO NON PENITENTI* -- while burlesque rituals in the chapel were accompanied by couplings between the members, robed as monks, with habited 'nuns': by some said to have been prostitutes, by others society women who arrived at the abbey masked.[90]

One of the participants was John Wilkes. Gibbon had met him in the militia, and found him an incomparable companion, though of infamous character, openly boasting that 'in this time of public dissension he was resolved to make his fortune'. Wilkes carried on a brilliant press campaign against the ministry, amongst whom was the master of the Hell–Fire revels; and, finding him immune from arrest for libel as a member of parliament, it became their object to have him expelled. Their instrument was the eponymous Earl of Sandwich, another of the Wycombe orgiasts. Sandwich had a nervous defect which made him look, it was said, as if he were walking down both sides of the street at once: an operation which he now proceeded to carry out. While pausing to utter expressions of the deepest horror, he recited to the House of Lords, with obvious relish, an *Essay on Woman* which had been found amongst Wilkes' papers, and which was a close parody of Pope's *Essay on Man*. 'Let us', sang Pope,

> (since Life can little more supply
> Than just to look about us and to die)
> Expatiate free o'er all this scene of Man;
> A mighty maze! but not without a plan.

'Let us', smirked Sandwich,

> (since life can little more supply
> Than just a few good Fucks, and then we die)
> Expatiate free o'er that lov'd scene of Man;
> A mighty Maze! for mighty Pricks to scan.

Bishop Warburton, Pope's editor, was beside himself; there was an appeal for the recital to cease; but the lords roared 'Go on!', then voted the piece 'most scandalous, obscene, and impious'. Wilkes was expelled from the Commons; and though he continued to win re–election, was denied the right to sit. He was now perceived as the victim of an assembly corrupted by a tyrannical ministry; and 'Wilkes and Liberty' became inseparable concepts.[91]

Wilkes in time resumed his seat in parliament, as he did his revels in the golden sphere which glitters above the tower of Wycombe church. Beneath this lies a hexagonal mausoleum, built in imitation of Rabelais' Abbey of Thélème –– that anti–monastery, imagined at the moment when the middle ages turned into the

Renaissance, of women and men living together in natural spontaneity. The doorway at Medmenham Abbey is inscribed with its motto, *FAY CE QUE VOULDRAS*, as the house at Wycombe is declared sacred to liberty. It was liberty as licence, freedom in its age-old recollection of saturnalia. Wilkes claimed that, far from being mere burlesque, the abbey rituals were a conscious reversion to the religion of nature, 'English Eleusinian Mysteries' that included libations to the *Bona Dea*. And when he visited the Grande Chartreuse, he wrote:

> The savageness of the woods, the gloom of the rocks, and the perfect solitude, conspire to make the mind pensive, and to lull to rest all the turbulent guilty passions of the soul.[92]

For Gibbon, too, the religion of nature was a return to radical innocence. His monumental history, observes Harold Bond, was the eighteenth-century *Paradise Lost*: the epic of a fall from 'intellectual, spiritual, and political freedom into the darkness of barbarism and servitude'.[93] Decline, notes G.M. Young, was intertwined for him with a 'general collapse of the intellect under the pressure of a world-tyranny': the church. This had been implicit in his original vision: in the chant of friars in a former temple; and when, now, he attributed the spread of Christianity to earthly causes, he shattered forever the *hortus conclusus* of sacred history.[94]

But *Decline and Fall* is a poetics, as well as a politics, of paradise. Over against that 'savage enthusiasm which represents man as a criminal and God as a tyrant', he placed the 'rational enthusiasm' which reveres the 'God of nature'; and in this discrimination of enthusiasms lay his ultimate critique of the churches. Of the supreme monument of Byzantium, Haghia Sophia, he observed that an 'enthusiast' might be

> tempted to suppose that it was the residence, or even the workmanship, of the Deity. Yet how dull is the artifice, how insignificant is the labour, if it be compared with the formation of the vilest insect that crawls upon the surface of the temple![95]

Gibbon's 'master-stoke as a historian', declares Young, is his placing of the

Council of Chalcedon:

> In A.D. 600 the Eastern Empire is still standing: the West an almost unrelieved spectacle of ruin and desolation. But look a little closer...all the forces which are shaping the future West are shown incorporate in Gregory, pontiff, missionary and feudal lord. In the East there is no corresponding principle of vitality to sustain the splendid but exhausting victories of Heraclius.

And at this, 'the most difficult point he had reached', Gibbon 'quietly turns back to trace the history of the theological doctrine of the Incarnation'. The religious unity of the East was shattered by the acceptance of the Roman formula at Chalcedon, 'and Islam entered by the breach'.[96] And from here, under the keystone of his great edifice, Gibbon paints the vista from the site of the council:

> A quarter of a mile from the Thracian Bosphorus, the church of St. Euphemia was built on the summit of a gentle though lofty ascent; the triple structure was celebrated as a prodigy of art, and the boundless prospect of the land and sea might have raised the mind of a sectary to the contemplation of the God of the universe.[97]

### ix

THE large tolerance of the age is reflected in a session of whist in which Walpole, the most republican of Whigs, was paired with Lady Bute, and Gibbon with the 'Archbishopess of Canterbury'.[98] Elsewhere, too, polarities were resolved. Suzanne, after years of silence, recovered her old adoration. She had read with delight, she said,

> that history where I see the intelligence of so many centuries concentrated in one intelligence, the judgements of all the nations coming together in one judgement, which illuminates them and gives them back to us with all the grace of novelty and with none of their ancient, noble fashion lost.

And for Gibbon, in turn, her friendship *fait le consolation et la gloire de ma vie.*[99] He recalled that it was in Paris that the last pagan emperor had spent his winters:

> That splendid capital, which now embraces an ample territory on either side of the Seine, was originally confined to the small island in the midst of the river...The severity of the climate was tempered by the neighbourhood of the ocean...But in remarkable winters the Seine was deeply frozen; and the huge pieces of ice that floated down the stream might be compared, by an Asiatic, to the blocks of white marble which were extracted from the quarries of Phrygia.

So he had condensed from the fluidity of time the substance of his monumental history. 'Our most beautiful and aristocratic ladies', wrote Suzanne, 'first wished to know him out of curiosity and then could not part from him for real liking'. He was presented at court, and introduced at her house to the Holy Roman Emperor.

> If Julian could now revisit the capital of France, he might converse with men of science and genius, capable of understanding and of instructing a disciple of the Greeks; he might excuse the lively and graceful follies of a nation whose martial spirit has never been enervated by the indulgence of luxury; and he must applaud the perfection of that inestimable art which softens and refines and embellishes the intercourse of social life.[100]

He retired to Lausanne, for which he felt, as he had said of Julian, 'that tender regard which seldom fails to arise in a liberal mind from the recollection of the place where it has discovered and exercised its growing powers'. His house was 'connected on the north side with the City, and open on the south to a beautiful and boundless horizon'.[101] And when he came to the last volume of his history, he described how Saint Bernard had journeyed through this same country, and how, when his companions towards evening commented on the splendour of the lake, he claimed not to have noticed it:

> To admire or despise St. Bernard as he ought, the reader, like myself, should have before the windows of his library the beauties of that incomparable landscape.[102]

Landscape and library formed a unitary metaphor for him: 'the freedom of the mind'.[103] From the site of his terrace, the view sweeps down to the water; and here, when the sun is from the south, the mountains on the far shore are lost in the light. Here Gibbon wrote the last line of his last page. It was an enchanted moment:

> The air was temperate, the sky was serene, the silver orb of the moon was reflected from the waters, and all Nature was silent.[104]

Yet completion brought fragility as well as fulfilment: in the intensity of the moment, a thought for the passage of time:

> I feel, and with the decline of years I shall more painfully feel, that I am alone in paradise.[105]

# CHAPTER NINE

# A VISTA TO THE GALLOWS

'NOR can our telescopes', reported Gibbon,

> discover the tricolor banners on the other side of the lake...The whole horizon is so black that I begin to feel some anxiety for England, the last refuge of liberty and law...If England...should now be seduced to eat the apple of false freedom, we should indeed deserve to be driven from the paradise which we enjoy.[1]

## i

IN THE autumn after he had finished his history, bonfires roared over the river in Paris; a royal minister writhed in effigy in the flames.[2] In London, during the winter that followed, the newly-founded *Times* commended the 'noble struggles' of the French 'in the cause of liberty'. It was the English, the paper reminded its readers, who had discovered the principles of nature -- physical, psychological and political -- and the country was now at the pinnacle of its power.[3]

For the American revolution, it became apparent over time, had not weakened England; it had weakened France. Support for the rebellious colonists brought the country's financial difficulties, exacerbated by the privileges of clergy and nobility, to a point of crisis; but the opposition to new taxation, which would have overridden these privileges, had obliged the king to summon the Estates General, which had not met since before the time of Louis XIV. And this summoning unleashed demands, dreams and desires which had troubled the national psyche since the Sun King's reign,[4] and which were intimately associated with England.

In the libertine days of the regency which followed the death of Louis XIV, a daring young poet was applauded in the salons of power. But he mistook the nature of his acclaim: when he returned an aristocrat's insults, and was thrashed by his lackeys, he received, instead of justice, imprisonment in the Bastille. On his release, Voltaire went to England. And here he found a land where, he wrote, 'one thinks freely and nobly': a land, moreover, where intellect translated into influence: where a M. *Adisson* could become a minister of state, and a Newton be accorded the burial of a king. And in, says Peter Gay, 'the first radical critique of the Old Regime' -- the *Lettres philosophiques* -- he illuminated, through his glowing portrayal of the English constitution, the shadows of that of France. 'I have been', he told Horace Walpole long afterwards, 'your apostle and your martyr'.[5]

Of that *anglomanie* which Voltaire boasted, the most visible sign was the *jardin anglais.* Voltaire claimed to have introduced France to the English fashion, of which he considered his own garden, formal except for its vistas, an example; and his English visitors, swallowing their astonishment, politely agreed.[6] But the most celebrated example was that described in the *Nouvelle Héloïse*. Rousseau had, as he confessed, been influenced by the *Spectator*; and his imaginary garden is planted on the principle of *sharawadgi*. Here symmetry, Eva Neumeyer observes, 'is declared "an enemy of nature"': which, it is stated, *ne plante rien au cordeau*. The protagonist thinks himself on a desert island amid *allées tortueuses et irrégulières*, which he then discovers to be the result of hidden deliberation: a skill which, it is conceded, is practised in the gardens of China, *faits avec tant d'art que l'art n'y paraissait point.* Yet both Chinese and English gardens are denounced for their magnificence: Stowe, with its *ruines*, its *temples*, its *anciens édifices*, being singled out for particular condemnation.[7] For to Rousseau, the return to nature involves a rejection of history: a repudiation of the artifice of society to recover a primordial sensibility.[8]

This did not seem unattainable. Had not the Americans created a new and virtuous society in the wilderness?[9] Their Declaration of Independence was greeted with exultation in France. The young French nobility burned to join their cause with Lafayette; in the classroom, he and Washington shared attention with Cicero and Horace; and the American minister in Paris, Benjamin Franklin, seemed to unite the simplicity of a Rousseau with the wisdom of a Voltaire.[10]

Now that American independence had been recognised by Britain, the tension between past and possibility was centred on France. Were its estates to assemble separately, according to historical precedent, allowing the two privileged orders, clergy and nobility, always to outvote the commons? Or was the balance to be evened, as was now demanded, by a double representation for the third estate? The controversy was spoken of as a war between the orders: 'the press teems', wrote an English witness, 'with the most levelling...principles'.[11] And at the centre of the maelstrom was Suzanne.

## ii

ON THE eve of her wedding, she had written to her future husband: 'The anguish of my heart, and the funereal images by which it is agitated, may prevent me from satisfying you'. In the same letter, however, she promised: 'you must never tire of a feeling which my heart makes inexhaustible'; and this was a sentiment to which the rest of her life bore witness.

Jacques Necker, Swiss like herself, had made a fortune speculating in French and English treasury bonds at the time of the war with Frederick and Pitt. This left him gleaming with self-made satisfaction; and the gaze into space through half-closed eyes, the ponderous incoherence -- the sphinxlike smile and the sphinxlike silence -- made him seem conceited to some, and to others profound.

Jacques, wrote Suzanne with grim humour, was 'so completely persuaded of his own superiority that he does not even see mine'.[12] But in combining the superiority of both, she brought to his minimalism of expression the sounding–box of her formidable articulacy.

She conferred the same benefit on their daughter. Suzanne had been attached to the circle of Rousseau;[13] and little Germaine was brought up in obedience to his doctrine of natural sensibility.[14] Jean–Jacques had refrained from applying it to his own children, who were promptly dispatched to the orphanage. This was undoubtedly the result of sensibility: sensibility concerning his own inadequacy; sensibility concerning his lover's reputation; and sensibility concerning the children themselves, who were thus, he insisted, exposed to a more bracing lifestyle. At the same time, he wept piteously over the episode: still further evidence of sensibility.[15] In Suzanne, however, sensibility was combined with steel. One contemporary described her as being starched stiff both inside and out; and with this her daughter would have agreed. After a visit to the theatre, Germaine was commanded to set down her natural reactions: exactly, she noted, as when she returned from church. When, in an attempt to encourage some symptom of affection, she simulated coughing–fits, Suzanne saw through it, and said so. The child wrote: 'My heart is drawn tight; I am sad; and in this large house...I see...only a desert'. 'Your style', commented the mother, 'is...high–flown'.[16]

With her father, there was no such difficulty. To his daughter at least, Jacques' silences were balm. He listened to her, applauded her, and left her 'content and with refreshed spirits'. One morning, a visitor recollected, when Suzanne had been called from the table, Germaine threw a napkin at Jacques, who wound it about his wig in a turban; and the two danced around the table, in wordless happiness, until footsteps were heard outside, and Suzanne re–entered to find them intent on their meal.[17]

Germaine in after years lamented that she had not been born earlier, so that, having been her father's lover, she would have known true joy. But the shrine at which she worshipped was the creation of Suzanne. Suzanne had fixed her salon on Friday, conferring immediate popularity on a household that, being Protestant, did not observe the fast; raved over philosophers; and achieved the final cachet of fashion when, having set up a subscription for Voltaire's statue, she received the great man's verses in return. The praises of her salon, in which the sphinx was lauded as a worker of miracles, were re–echoed outside, and eventually reached Versailles.[18]

## iii

JACQUES's news was excellent: while the state was poor, the country was rich. All that was needed was confidence, and order in the public finances. He was taken at his word: loans were oversubscribed; foreign capital poured in; and even during the vast expense of the American war, no new taxes were levied. The public debt rose alarmingly; but Necker published a glowing statement, which also reported on his domestic happiness with Suzanne. Nothing like it had ever been seen: it reduced an archbishop to tears. Necker, who as a Protestant could not be naturalised, and as a foreigner could not sit in the cabinet, nevertheless demanded a seat. Instead, he was invited to resign; but in the years that followed, he was courted by priests and peasants, by prelates and princes. He was a man designed by heaven, declared Catherine of Russia, 'to occupy the most glorious position in Europe'.[19]

A successor, indeed, was indiscreet enough to suggest that Necker's surplus was a deficit; but it was he whose effigy crumpled in the fire.[20] And his successor in turn, he who had wept over Necker's treatise, in desperation announced the summoning of the Estates, and resigned. The state was on the verge of bankruptcy, the nation on the verge of revolt; and Necker was restored to the direction of finance. The public joy was 'very great indeed', reported the

American minister in Paris, Thomas Jefferson. And now, it was remarked, 'American principles are bursting forth in Every quarter'. A new dawn was in the air; but to Germaine it was a chilling one. 'The ship has been placed under his command', she wrote of her father, 'at so desperate a moment that all the admiration I have for him is barely enough to inspire me with confidence'.[21]

Her apprehensions were to be fulfilled. As she stood at a window in Versailles, watching the representatives of the three estates file into church -- the nobles in lace and silver, the clergy resplendent in their robes, the commons in simple black -- she was struck by the pockmarked Mirabeau. 'His huge head of hair', she wrote, 'distinguished him from all the others. It was as if his strength derived from it, like Samson's. His face gained in expression from his very ugliness, and his whole person suggested a strange power'. She felt a sickening fear, by contrast, at the sight of the weak-faced king and the death-pale queen. It was dispelled by the huge ovation which greeted her father. Great things were expected of him. He had tided the nation over the previous winter when, declining a large salary, he had raised enough in loans to continue the administration. But the faces of the deputies lengthened as they listened to three hours of statistics, and he lost the chance to turn his popularity into a programme. His ideal, shared by his wife and daughter, was a system based on the English: a bicameral parliament under a constitutional monarchy. But the royal family had no interest in such a plan; and the only hope of its acceptance lay in an alliance with the Third Estate. Mirabeau, who saw an 'impending invasion of democracy', expressed an interest in the popular minister, but was met with sphinxlike hauteur, and turned on his heel. 'Your man', he told his intermediary, 'is a fool. He'll have news from me'. He had: the third estate proclaimed itself the National Assembly.[22]

Necker warned the king that, with the army disaffected, force was out of the question; and when Louis ordered the estates to meet separately, his seat was significantly empty. The deputies marched to the minister's quarters, a frenzied crowd crying 'Long live Monsieur Necker!' He was summoned to the palace, begged by the royal couple to remain at his post, and carried back to his house on the shoulders of the crowd. Germaine was ecstatic. 'The intense enthusiasm', she wrote a quarter of a century later, 'is still present to my memory, and revives the emotion it stirred up in me in those happy days of youth and hope. All those voices repeating the name of my father seemed to belong to a crowd of friends who shared my respectful love'.[23]

On Necker's advice, Louis summoned the estates to meet jointly as the National Assembly. But he ringed Versailles and Paris with troops, and sent his minister orders to leave the country at once and in secret. The family were outside France when the news came that, on July 14th, the people, incensed by Necker's dismissal, had taken the Bastille.[24]

Once more he was recalled by the king. Suzanne was apprehensive; he himself felt he was on the edge of an abyss; but Germaine exulted in his triumph. Along the road, the workers in the fields fell on their knees as his carriage passed; the inhabitants of the cities unyoked his horses to pull it through the streets. In Paris, where the population packed the windows and rooftops, Germaine, in an ecstasy, swooned. The 'inconceivable electricity' of the event, she wrote, made her soul succumb to 'emotions that exceeded its strength'. But Necker, once again, squandered the irreplaceable moment. Instead of calling for a meeting of the powers of France, he asked for the release of a fellow–Swiss who had fired into a crowd. The assembly refused, and he remained in the shadows while, with Jefferson's assistance, it formulated its Declaration of the Rights of Man.[25]

This Louis refused to accept. He was answered by a crowd of women and children, of soldiers and a rabble in arms, marching in the rain from Paris, and camping in the assembly–hall, where the women removed their clothes to dry, and those among them who were prostitutes prepared for a busy night. Germaine was woken at dawn by a cry that a mob had invaded the queen's antechamber, murdering her guards. Necker had already gone to the king; as Germaine and Suzanne hurried through the corridor to the palace, they heard musket–shots, and on the floor of the gallery saw pools of blood. In the grand salon, they found the court. Below, in the courtyard, the crowd howled for the queen. Marie–Antoinette walked calmly to the balcony; the shrieks turned to acclamations, and the shout went up: 'The king to Paris!'

It was all wrong, thought Germaine, as they moved through the Bois de Boulogne. The sky had cleared, and the weather was 'exceptionally splendid. The air barely stirred the trees, and the sun's radiance dispelled all darkness from the landscape. Not a single external object corresponded with our sadness'.[26]

In London, a dissenting preacher rejoiced that he had seen a French king led captive by his people. In a sermon commemorating the hundred and first anniversary of the English revolution, he described that in France as its fulfilment.[27] He was to receive a most memorable reply.

**iv**

IF, for some reason, you were to journey between Temple's Carlow and Swift's Dublin, and turn off the road after a dozen or so miles, you would come to the mound, or rath, under which the Wizard Earl of Kildare is believed to sleep, and once in seven years to ride a white horse, shod with silver, to his ancestral castle of Kilkea. Beneath the mound lies the village of Ballitore, in the eighteenth century a settlement of the Quakers, lauded by Voltaire for their discarding of clergy and aristocracy;[28] and the people of the village will still show you in their houses the broad window seats, facing westward, in which these industrious folk made the most of the evening light. This combination of tradition and enlightenment is to be found in the career of the most celebrated pupil of their school: Edmund Burke.

After he had moved to a Dublin in which Swift was now silent, Burke's continuing correspondence with Ballitore shows him preoccupied with the treatise which was to make his name: the *Philosophical Enquiry into...the Sublime and Beautiful*.[29] The Greek treatise on the sublime, *Peri Hypsous*, rediscovered at the Renaissance, had intrigued the psychological interest of the England of Hobbes and Locke. *To hypsos*, in its original connotation, refers to height; it was appropriate, therefore, that John Dennis should experience the sublime in his crossing of the Alps; and that he should describe it, with characteristic vehemence, as 'a delightful Horrour, a terrible Joy'.[30] Addison, when he followed Dennis over the Alps, confessed, too, to 'an agreeable kind of horror';[31] but when he came to construct his aesthetic theory, found no place in it for this experience. He was unlikely to value ambivalence after an upbringing in which repression and affection, hostility and love, were confounded; and in place of the sublime, therefore, he substituted the '*Great*':[32] the open vista as freedom from constraint. The '*Uncommon*' appealed to another form of liberty, exploration or the indulgence of curiosity; while '*Beauty*' was freedom from the straight line, or *sharawadgi*.[33] The English garden, as it developed under his influence, embodied all three of these aspects. In its layout of lawn, trees and water it achieved the beauty of the irregular; in its openness to the horizon, it exhibited greatness; and in its disposition of emblematic buildings, it intrigued the sense of curiosity.

Burke followed Addison in his definition of the beautiful: 'our gardens, if nothing else, declare, we begin to feel that mathematical ideas are not the true measures of beauty'. In the overall structure of his theory, however, he rearranged Addison's categories. Curiosity he dismissed on the first page: some degree of novelty, he held, was inherent in 'all our passions'. And these he divided, with a decisiveness that aroused comment both then and after, into two. On the one side he put beauty, which he linked with pity; on the other, he placed the sublime, which he connected with power. These he had detected, he claimed, by working 'beyond the surface of things': it was the sublime as subliminal; and all of his theory was derived, as he acknowledged, from the analysis of his own feelings.[34]

This is scarcely to be wondered at. Burke was the son of a Protestant father and a Catholic mother in a land in which the latter were deprived of power: yet, constituting a majority, posed a constant threat to it.[35] All of his efforts in relation to Ireland were an attempt to impress this insight upon its English administrators. Similarly, he had warned that continuing English rule over America depended on the colonists' perceptions. 'If that sovereignty', he queried, 'and their freedom cannot be reconciled, which will they take?'[36] And he was no less tireless in asserting what he believed to be the inalienable rights of the Indian peoples.[37] On 'Ireland, America, and India', wrote Harold Laski, Burke 'was at every point upon the side of the future'.[38] Then came the French revolution; and it found him on the side of the past.

## V

THE simple solution is to suppose that Burke saw where his principles had been leading, and backed away: that he turned reactionary. But the difficulty with this is that to react is to respond to an event which, by definition, has already occurred; Burke reacted against things which had not yet happened. Perhaps this is what it means to be an Irish reactionary; or perhaps there is some other explanation.

Such as context. No passage in Burke, perhaps, has earned him more scorn than that in which he reads such ominous implication into that scene which Germaine had witnessed with so much foreboding: the invasion of Versailles and the attempt on the life of the queen.[39] But after the queen and king had been forcibly returned to Paris, and were subjected, in the Tuileries, to another invasion, an eyewitness wrote: 'This is unconstitutional and a very dangerous example'. The writer was a young officer from the provinces: his name was Napoleon Bonaparte.[40]

What appealed to Burke in fact was, in Eliot's phrase, not the pastness of the past but its presence.[41] What had begun as base matter, he believed, might be transmuted by the alchemy of time. Hereditary kingship, which had no doubt originated as despotism, was by now a principle of stability; while elective monarchy, however admirable on paper, in practice was a formula for chronic civil war.[42] Aristocracy, likewise, might have begun with the barbarian invasions; but by now it served as a counterforce both to royal arrogance and to popular agitation.[43] The commons, meanwhile, provided an energising element, and a point of contact with public opinion.[44]

Burke, then, saw England as possessed of a tripartite constitution, composed of prince, peers and people, valuable not so much for its individual components as for the balance which subsisted between them; and his apologia was that he constantly brought his weight to bear on behalf of that component which needed it most.[45] In this he was not alone. A contemporary described the English constitution as 'the most perfect combination of human powers in society which finite wisdom has yet contrived...for the preservation of liberty and the production of happiness'. This was John Adams, future President of the United States.[46]

Burke believed that a similar balance might have been established in France. Instead, the representation of the third estate had been doubled, swamping the other two, reducing the king to a cipher, and leaving a single, unrestricted source of power.[47] What had happened in America, in Burke's view, was altogether different. There, the balanced English system had been reconstituted, with a two-tier legislature echoing lords and commons, and a president replacing the king.[48] The French saw it otherwise. For the English, the American was a prodigal son; for the French, a noble savage. For them, the transatlantic state was an altogether new creation, carefully constructed from first principles.[49] It was an irresistible exercise in Cartesian logic; and this was what worried Burke. He recalled how, formerly, the French had represented their monarch as a far more glorious sovereign than the English, being freer of restrictions.[50] This despotic attitude had simply been transferred, in his view, to an absolute assembly.

## vi

BURKE validated his political vision through the imagery of the English garden. As Temple had perceived the Japanese aesthetic as anti–mathematical, and Addison had adopted it as a symbol of liberty, in conscious opposition to the sweeping, ruthless, mathematical approach to nature of Versailles, so Burke now saw the framers of the new French constitution as 'clearing away as mere rubbish whatever they found, and, like their ornamental gardeners, forming everything into an exact level'.

He referred in particular to the plan to abolish the historic provinces, and redivide the country into equal *départements*. It was boasted that with what he called this 'geometrical policy', all 'local ideas should be sunk, and that the people should no longer be Gascons, Picards, Bretons, Normans, but Frenchmen, with one country, one heart, and one assembly'. But instead, Burke warned, 'of being all Frenchmen, the greater likelihood is, that the inhabitants of that region will shortly have no country. No man ever was attached by a sense of pride, partiality, or real affection, to a description of square measurement'.

In obliterating local, particular attachments, Burke informed the French, 'you have industriously destroyed all the opinions, and prejudices, and, as far as in you lay, all the instincts which support government. Therefore the moment any difference arises between your national assembly and any part of the nation, you must have recourse to force. Nothing else is left to you; or rather you have left nothing else to yourselves'. And it was in this context that Burke made his most extraordinary prediction, one that in later years seemed to make his inflammatory rhetoric glow with the coals of fire of the authentic prophet. 'In the weakness of one kind of authority', he foretold, 'and in the fluctuation of all, the officers of an army will remain for some time mutinous and full of faction, until some popular general, who understands the art of conciliating the soldiery, and who possesses the true spirit of command, shall draw the eyes of all men upon himself'.[51] These words were printed fourteen years before the coronation in Notre-Dame.

The *Reflections on the Revolution in France* are studded with such predictions. 'A king', he wrote, while the King of France was still its nominal head of state, 'is not to be deposed by halves'. 'There must', he warned, three years before the Terror, 'be blood'.[52] And, 'in the groves of *their* academy', he intoned, in the uncanniest of all examples of what a French historian has described as his *clairvoyance*,[53] 'in the groves of *their* academy, at the end of every vista, you see nothing but the gallows'.[54] For Louis XVI in fact was executed on the avenue of a French formal garden: the Champs-Élysées, laid out for his sun-king ancestor through the groves of the Tuileries.[55]

The French, then, for Burke, had merely cast absolutism into a new form: as Napoleon was to crown the Champs-Élysées with the arch commemorating his triumphal armies.[56] It was here that Burke saw the contrast with England. The framers of the English revolution, he conceded, might indeed have had the right, in the abstract, to reinvent the state; but abstract principles in actual life, like light through water, are, he says, 'refracted from their straight line'. Again, mathematics versus *sharawadgi*. The French had been possessed of a 'noble and venerable castle', dilapidated it was true, but capable of being restored. 'A disposition to preserve', wrote Burke, 'and an ability to improve, taken together, would be my standard of a statesman'. The true lawgiver, he thought, 'ought to love and respect his kind, and to fear himself'. For 'power', he wrote, 'will survive the shock in which manners and opinions perish; and it will find other and worse means for its support'.[57] This echoed the unflattering view of human nature he had expounded in the *Sublime and Beautiful*. There he had written of how, in the 'shouting of multitudes', the 'best established tempers can scarce forbear being borne down, and joining in the common cry'.[58] It was an insight combined by a later poet with the climactic scene of the revolution.

**vii**

EXECUTION
OF
LOUIS XVI
KING OF THE FRENCH

> The greatest tranquillity prevailed in every street through which the procession passed. About half past nine, the King arrived at the place of execution, which was in the *Place de Louis XV*, between the pedestal which formerly supported the statue of his grandfather, and the promenade of the Elysian Fields. LOUIS mounted the scaffold with composure...the trumpets sounding and the drums beating during the whole time...His executioners then laid hold of him, and an instant after, his head was separated from his body; this was about a quarter past ten o'clock.

It was said that, as the dripping head was held above the crowd, a voice called out that the blood of the last Grand Master of the Templars, executed by a French king centuries before, had at last been avenged.[59] This was what Yeats fused with the clamour that, in Burke's view, arose from unreason in the moment of collective derangement: his protagonist, in spite of himself, almost joining in the cry of 'Vengeance for Jacques Molay'.[60] *The Times* carried news of the scene in a black border;[61] it completed English revulsion with the French experiment.

Gibbon had had early doubts. 'They have the power', he had mused, 'will they have the moderation to establish a good constitution?'[62] But as the excitement of the revolution spread to England, hearts 'beat high with great swelling sentiments of Liberty'. 'Everything', wrote a man who had been a boy at the time, 'everything, not this thing or that thing, but literally everything, was soaked in this one event'. 'A new world was opening', recalled Keats' fellow–Claudian, Hazlitt, 'to the astonished sight. Scenes, lovely as hope can paint, dawned on the imagination; visions of unsullied bliss lulled the senses, and hid the darkness of surrounding objects...'[63]

Now Gibbon considered wearing mourning for the king. If the French, he sighed, 'had been content with a liberal translation of our system...' -- the French revolution, for Gibbon, was a mistranslation from the English -- '...if they had respected the prerogatives of the crown and the privileges of the Nobles, they might have raised a solid fabric on the only true foundation the natural Aristocracy of a great Country'. In this he aligned himself with Burke, a fact of which he was aware: 'I am as high an Aristocrate', he declared, 'as Burke himself'.[64]

Burke, indeed, represented a new national consensus. 'Men and women', comments Ketton–Cremer, whom Walpole had 'known familiarly, with whom he had talked and supped in Paris, were dragged through yelling crowds to the guillotine...The old Whig, who had watched with sympathy the progress of the American Revolution...turned in despair from the spectacle presented by France'.[65] Walpole now considered Burke's *Reflections* 'the wisest book I ever read in my life'.[66] He defended, even, its apotheosis of Marie–Antoinette:

> glittering like the morning–star, full of life, and splendour, and joy...But the age of chivalry is gone...[67]

'It paints her exactly', wrote Walpole, 'as she appeared to me the first time I saw her when Dauphiness. She was going after the late King to chapel, and shot through the room like an aërial being, all brightness and grace and without seeming to touch earth -- *vera incessu patuit dea!*'[68] And when she, too, was sentenced to the guillotine, and was asked what she had to say, he thought her reply -- *rien* -- 'the most sublime word that ever passed through human lips'.[69] She had become the last of his tragic queens.

'It remained', he concluded bitterly, 'for the enlightened eighteenth century to baffle language and invent horrors that can be found in no vocabulary'.[70] 'I will tell you', said the poet Cowper, who had at first thought the revolution 'wonderful', 'I will tell you what the French have done: they have made me weep for a king of France, which I never thought to do, and they have made me sick of the very name of liberty'.[71]

## viii

IT IS appropriate that Tom Paine should have come into contact with Burke over his design for an iron bridge:[72] the shortest distance between two points, forceful, geometrical, owing nothing to the past. Paine trusted in reason, as Burke did not. The son of a staymaker, who had run away to sea, he had found, in Franklin's Philadelphia, an ambience answering to his own uncompromising pragmatism. 'Of more worth is one honest man to society...', he declared in *Common Sense,* 'than all the crowned ruffians that ever lived'; and it was *Common Sense*, says Leonard Woolf, which 'made...republicanism inevitable' in America.[73] And when, in his *Rights of Man*, he predicted that government would change all over Europe as well, he asserted, in answer to Burke, that it 'certainly may be done without convulsion or revenge'.[74] But when he voted in the French assembly against the execution of the king, he barely escaped the guillotine himself.[75]

Burke could have told him so. But as Leslie Stephen has pointed out in this connection, 'popular instinct sometimes outruns philosophical insight';[76] and on one, fundamental issue, Paine's instinct was sound. He claimed that, with the American and French revolutions, a new mode of being had begun, 'a renovation of the natural order'.[77] The English revolution had been made in the name of liberty; but it was a liberty that was Janus–headed, one face modern, the other medieval. Franchise, freehold, the freedom of a city: all these were, not human rights, but historic privileges; and England in the eighteenth century enjoyed the benefit of that ambiguity.[78] But the American Declaration of Independence, the French Declaration of the Rights of Man, both linked liberty with equality.[79] However this ideal might be retreated from in practice -- and it very quickly was[80] -- the two could never after be seen apart.

Meanwhile, however, Burke's vision prevailed. 'The *distinguishing* part of our Constitution', he acknowledged, 'is its liberty'. 'But the liberty', he went on, 'the *only* liberty, I mean is a liberty connected with *order*'.[81] And it was this principle, 'liberty connected with *order*', that was now to become dominant in the English garden.

## ix

CAPABILITY Brown has been identified as a follower of Burke on the beautiful. Burke had laid down that its lines should be gradual and unobtrusive; and his most concrete definition of this -- the sense of being 'swiftly drawn in an easy coach on a smooth turf' -- is exactly the experience, it has been observed, one enjoys in driving through a Brownian landscape.[82] Brown's own career ran with equal smoothness until he came up against William Chambers. Chambers had studied architecture in Paris and Rome; but he lost the commission for Clive's house to Brown.[83] As Brown came from a farming family, Chambers put out a pamphlet which spoke of clowns emerging from the cabbage-patch;[84] and he went on, compounding his folly, to attack Brown on his own ground, or patch. It was all very well for Temple and Addison to assume that *sharawadgi* was absolute in China, as neither of them had been there. But Chambers had:[85] and in their gardens, he now reported, the Chinese had no aversion whatever to straight lines, finding them 'productive of grandeur'.[86] This, however it may accord with Chinese practice,[87] takes its form from Burke's sublime.[88] 'The great', Burke had written, '...loves the right line'.[89]

The connotation that 'grandeur' had for Chambers is evidently connected with his position as architect to George III, to whom his earlier *Designs of Chinese Buildings* had been dedicated.[90] He is found, then, proposing an imperial mansion which is to dominate the kingdom from the centre; and, lest the moral should somehow be missed, has a Chinese visitor declare that 'the rigours of an Emperor are less frightful to me, than the frolics of a savage mob'.[91] Sublimity, for Burke, inhered in all sources of terror;[92] and Chambers ornamented his absolutist landscape with tombs, gibbets and wretched inhabitants.[93] All of which appears to have been too much for George III: who, in his fits of derangement, displayed an inordinate fondness for the pagoda which Chambers had constructed at Kew.[94]

But Chambers' fantasia had an even more curious aftermath. The Chinese 'scenes of terror', he had written, 'are composed of gloomy woods, deep vallies inaccessible to the sun, impending barren rocks, dark caverns, and impetuous cataracts rushing down the mountains'. In their 'subterraneous vaults' were to be found the 'pale images of antient kings', and from 'dark passages, cut into rocks', was to be heard 'all the noise of war'. In the scenes of beauty which he contrasted with these were to be seen water–palaces, and 'Tartarean damsels, in loose transparent robes, that flutter in the scented air'.[95] These manifestations of terror and beauty were to reappear in a great romantic poem: in the 'caverns measureless to man', with their 'ancestral voices prophesying war', the 'dome of pleasure' shadowing the waves, and the 'damsel with a dulcimer' of *Kubla Khan*.[96]

However 'incongruous, chaotic, and variegated' the materials of the poem,[97] they have been combined, like the Roman and Gothic columns that are gathered into the great mosque of Cordoba, into a coherent vision, polarised around the opposites of sun and ice, order and chaos, energy and control, and, again, beauty and terror. These pairs in turn coalesce around the 'main facts' of the poem's landscape: 'the dome and the river'.[98] And in the deep woods and the meandering stream, hovered over by their measured architecture, we may find the lingering silhouette -- locked within the song that is the momentary apprehension of a ruined dream -- of the Roman temple in the Chinese landscape which was the English romantic garden.

## X

HUMPHRY REPTON was the owner of a small estate who found its planting, and the painting of its scenery, insufficient to occupy his time, and one sleepless night had the idea of combining both as a landscape gardener. Demand for Brown's work had increased; but as none of his sons cared to succeed him -- the first became a courtier, the second an admiral and the third a clergyman -- Repton acquired the master's plans, and followed his practice: hills, woods and water harmoniously interwoven. For this he was attacked by the new proponents of wildness.[99]

The other Brown, he who had sketched so effectively the threat of England's decline, had shown an equal sensitivity to terror in his native Lake district, finding '*Beauty*, *Horror*, and *Immensity*' amongst its quiet waters, threatening precipices and majestic peaks.[100] He was followed by a succession of 'dons, divines and dilettanti',[101] among them Gray, who there

> saw the solemn colouring of night draw on, the last gleam of sunshine fading away on the hilltops, the deep serene of the waters, and the long shadows of the mountains thrown across them, till they nearly touch'd the hithermost shore.

This description was published some few years afterwards: so that the Lakes were already a centre of pilgrimage by the time that Wordsworth came to consciousness among them,

> In presence of sublime or beautiful forms.[102]

## xi

AND so, as nature was experienced under its more rugged aspects, the demand arose for its representation as such in the garden, in accordance with what became known as the picturesque. This was a category intermediate between Burke's beautiful and sublime. 'While the outstanding qualities of the sublime', writes Christopher Hussey, 'were vastness and obscurity, and those of the beautiful smoothness and gentleness, the characteristics of the picturesque were "roughness and sudden variation joined to irregularity"'.[103] This was Addison's Variety, or Uncommon, now brought back into co-ordination with his Great and Beautiful. But whereas for Addison, and the garden which derived from him, all three were parts of a single entity, now they were assigned to separate places. Repton was to distinguish between 'garden scenery, park scenery, and forest scenery', or 'horticulture, agriculture, and uncultivated nature'.[104] Nature, in the background, was sublime; the park, in the middle distance, picturesque; and the garden, in the foreground, beautiful -- but no longer irregular. For, out of the controversy, a new and curious consensus had emerged. While Repton promoted more natural lines in the park, the proponents of the picturesque advocated terraces, balustrades and fountains, as framing the vista, and providing variety by contrast.[105] In this fashion, formality returned, as the landscape garden split into its component parts. Brown's park had submerged the garden, as it lapped against the walls of the house;[106] now the two, Repton decreed, were to be 'perfectly distinct'. And, while the park might be 'improved by imitating nature', the garden was 'a work of art': 'an artificial object', he declared, with 'no other pretence to be natural, than what it derives from the growth of the plants which adorn it'.[107]

Repton, then, in answering their attacks upon him, saw no difference between himself and the promoters of the picturesque.[108] These, Knight and Price, were Whigs and followers of Fox,[109] who, in a gesture which cost him the friendship of Burke, described the new French constitution as a 'glorious edifice of liberty'. At the same time he declared himself, as Burke had done, a defender of the English system against 'an absolute monarchy, an absolute aristocracy, or an absolute democracy'. In this he expressed the dilemma of the Whigs -- by instinct attracted by liberty in all its forms, by interest attached to the form which it took in England -- which left them in the wilderness until after Waterloo.[110] Knight found himself subject to the same difficulty. While deploring the savagery of the Terror, he hoped that it might prove the prelude to 'just order' and 'genuine liberty':[111] thereby echoing, as if in spite of himself, Burke's formula of 'liberty connected with *order*'.

Repton, for his part, was a friend of Burke's, who in turn considered his views on gardening 'comprehensive' and 'correct'.[112] As well he might: they were a translation into terms of landscape of his own ideas. For, in pursuit of his strategy of liberty with order, Burke had carried out a tactical operation of great subtlety and ingenuity. Like Frederick at Rossbach, he marched parallel to the French while attacking them perpendicularly: keeping pace with them in terms of nature, he pierced their lines in terms of art. And the two interlocked in a single pronouncement: 'art', he declared, 'is man's nature'. 'For man', he explained,

> is by nature reasonable; and he is never perfectly in his natural state, but when he is placed where reason may be best cultivated and most predominates.

'We are as much', he went on,

> ...in a state of Nature in formed manhood as in immature and helpless infancy. Men, qualified in the manner I have just described, form in Nature, as she operates in the common modification of society, the leading, guiding, and governing part. It is the soul to the body, without which the man does not exist.[113]

And so it was not to be wondered at that, when Repton commemorated Burke, it was as an embodiment of the formal garden, in his 'Lines on a Seat at the End of a Long Straight Walk':

> This walk an emblem of himself pourtrays,
> Who, scorning knave's, or fashion's crooked ways,
> The fair straight forward path of Honour trod,
> Leading, through Virtue's course, to Virtue's God.[114]

# CONCLUSION

BURKE, in the aftermath of the French revolution, compared the English monarchy to the 'proud Keep of Windsor, rising in the majesty of proportion, and girt with the double belt of kindred and coëval towers': the royal core surrounded by the twin houses of parliament, in a vision both feudal and defensive.[1] George III, with his once-unpopular notions of social subordination, now became a symbol of national unity; and in his rebuilding of Windsor, continued under his son, the central tower was doubled in height.[2]

The nineteenth-century Houses of Parliament are the perfect Burkean artefact: *sharawadgi* on the skyline, symmetry underneath.[3] 'Under the broad pressure', writes F.M.L. Thompson, 'of subversive and revolutionary ideas and events', the aristocracy, abetted by successive ministries, began to formalise itself into a hierarchy, obsession with degree a new phenomenon, and intermediate rankings such as marquess significantly expanded.[4]

The 'idea of a liberal descent', Burke had asserted,

> ...carries an imposing and majestic aspect. It has a pedigree and illustrating ancestors. It has its bearings and its ensigns armorial. It has its gallery of portraits; its monumental inscriptions; its records, evidences, and titles.[5]

Repton entered happily into the spirit of this pronouncement. He felt, we are told, a veneration for ancient families; and suggested to one of his clients that the market-house, monuments or milestones of the adjoining town might be adorned with his arms. For this he received much ridicule;[6] more effective was his advocacy, to another client, of the castle. It would, he argued, have 'infinitely more picturesque effect' than a classical building, 'by blending a chaste correctness of proportion with bold irregularity of outline, its deep recesses and projections producing broad masses of light and shadow, while its roof is enriched by turrets, battlements, corbels and lofty chimneys'.[7] So the castle came in, once more, through the garden; and, as 'bold irregularity of outline', retained the marks of its origin in *sharawadgi*.

The new century's castle was brought to dramatic life by Scott. Like Walpole, he built a castle of his own; like Walpole, replaced the sculpture gallery of the classical house with an armoury; and, like him, evoked the world of its origins in fiction. But *Ivanhoe*, to an immeasurably greater degree than *Otranto*, altered the consciousness of its age. The hammers of armourers rang out again in the London of the industrial revolution; tournaments were fought at the end of journeys by steamboat and train; baronies were called out of abeyance, and, when this failed, names were changed. One Wilkins, who had made a fortune in India, reinvented himself as de Winton, and built a castle to prove it. And in Pugin, for whom *Ivanhoe* was an epiphany, and who as a youth designed stage–sets for *Kenilworth*, the tide of sentiment for the middle ages threatened to sweep away the structure of classicism.[8]

This had initially been deepened by the rediscovery of Greece. Shelley, like Gibbon, saw eternity beyond the ruins of Rome; but his was the infinity of the Platonic idea.[9] Byron, for whom Gibbon's villa at Lausanne was a locus of pilgrimage, ended that most influential of his creations, his life, in the Hellenic cause of classical liberty.[10] Keats, in his contemplation of a Grecian urn, combined the freshness of the new discoveries with the abiding vision of Claude.[11]

The Greek revival in architecture, meanwhile, continuing the puritanism of its Palladian origins, evolved towards an ever greater spareness of form, which was to reach its most unflinching expression on behalf of Scots presbyterianism.[12] Yet its effective beginning had been in the Hellfire Club, whose founder, Dashwood, also founded the Society of Dilettanti: 'the nominal qualification' for which, said Horace Walpole, 'is having been to Italy, and the real one being drunk'. But the president of these debauches sat in a scarlet toga, while the Judas of the brotherhood, Sandwich, explored the classic lands beyond Sicily through the isles of Greece; and in so doing set the tone for the later Dilettanti expeditions, which recorded the monuments of Athens, Palmyra and Baalbek.[13] On the last of these is modelled the temple of Apollo at Stourhead: for in drama of disposition, and splendour of setting, the Grecian never lost its connection with the picturesque.[14]

And something of their origins continued to cling to the Dilettanti. Hamilton, whose lady was to acquire fame for its modern exemplification, was noted for his collection of antique erotica; while Knight, apostle of the picturesque, was also the philosopher of the sexual rituals of Italian Catholicism. These he identified as survivals of the ancient worship of the mystery of generation, to which nature was sacred: a worship still evident in the ecstatic religion of Greece, but repressed within that of Judaeo-Christianity.[15]

Small wonder, then, that Pugin should have seen in the Greek revival, with an emphasis still more uncompromising than that of Wesley against Rome, 'the abomination of desolation'. The Royal Academy he found preoccupied with 'pagan lectures, pagan designs, pagan casts and models'; and he shuddered at the results:

> I am sitting in a Grecian coffee room in the Grecian Hotel with a Grecian mahogany table close to a Grecian marble chimney piece, surmounted by a Grecian scroll pier glass, and to increase my horror the waiter has brought in breakfast on a Grecian sort of tray with a pat of butter stamped with the infernal Greek scroll. Not a pointed arch within miles.[16]

When Blake wrote: 'Grecian is Mathematic Form: Gothic is Living Form', he took Temple's insight, as elaborated by Walpole, and applied it to his own conviction of the superiority of Hebrew over Hellene.[17] And it was Blake, too, who by opposing the Jerusalem of nature to the satanism of the mills,[18] formulated the characteristic antithesis of the nineteenth century. The enemy, now, was within the gates: the machine was the new Versailles.

In Pugin, these perceptions became a programme. By recreating its churches, he wished to restore, amid the industrial desolation of his century, that medieval beauty which for him inhered in ritual Catholicism.[19] Ruskin, seizing on his principle of integrity in design, recaptured the movement for ethical Protestantism.[20] Morris, building on both, found in the arts of the middle ages at once adornment and occupation for his earthly paradise of socialism.[21]

And Morris is the representative figure of his age. With Pugin and Ruskin, he sees in medieval architecture the embodiment of an ideal society; with Tennyson and Arnold, he retells the medieval romances; and he illustrates them with Rossetti and Burne–Jones.[22] England, it is plain, no longer abides in the eternal moment of the Capitol; it is the middle ages, now, that constitute the living past. This is embodied in Morris' Red House, which his biographer describes as his 'dream dwelling', and he himself as 'very medieval', with its pointed arches, its gabled roof, its turretted well and deliberate asymmetry. Its garden, too, was medieval in inspiration: and so, wrote a contemporary visitor, was 'spaced formally into four little square gardens making a big square together'.[23]

The transformation of *sharawadgi* is now complete. It has long since been absorbed into picturesque architecture: has lost, even for Morris, that connection with nature which, between the English and the French revolutions, awed, unsettled and inspired all of Europe. Despotism itself applied to the *jardin anglais* for credentials. Catherine of Russia had one designed, complete with Chinese pavilions, outside St. Petersburg.[24] Outside Stockholm, Gustav of Sweden, in a room of windows and mirrors that multiply woodland and lake, created one of the loveliest spaces in the world.[25] And at the other end of the spectrum, the same held good, as Rousseau was buried on the Ile des Peupliers at Ermenonville.[26]

No less pervasive was the belief in what it signified. 'I am an Englishwoman', sings a character in Mozart, '...born to freedom': *zur Freiheit geboren.*[27] Not any more. English freedom went overboard at Boston, and disappeared with the

Bastille.[28] And its epitaph was written when, to celebrate the execution of the King of France, a tree of liberty was planted at Versailles.[29]

# NOTES

PREFACE

1. Butterfield, 76. Macaulay states the corollary: 'He who is deficient in the art of selection may, by showing nothing but the truth, produce all the effect of the grossest falsehood' (*Lays of Rome*, 8).
2. *Lays of Rome*, 36.
3. *Clio*, 146.
4. Eliot, *Poems & Plays*, 197.

INTRODUCTION

1. Lovejoy, *Chain of Being*, 15–16.
2. Lovejoy, *History of Ideas*, 99–135.
3. 'That the Chinese', wrote Gray, 'have this beautiful Art in high perfection, seems very probable...but it is very certain, we copied nothing from them, nor had any thing but nature for our model. it is not forty years, since the Art was born among us; and it is sure, that there was nothing in Europe like it, & as sure, we then had no information on this head from China at all'. Upon which his friend and editor Mason commented: 'I question whether this be not saying too much. Sir William Temple's account of the Chinese gardens was published some years before this period' (Gray, *Corr.*, 2: 814 & n.). Røstvig's contention that the 'first decisive step' was taken by Nourse in 1700 is equally unfounded: his proposal that part of the garden 'be dispos'd with that cunning, as to deceive us into a belief of a real Wilderness or Thicket' might be a paraphrase of Temple's account, ten years earlier, of his 'Chineses', whose 'greatest reach of Imagination, is employed in contriving Figures, where the Beauty shall be great, and strik the Eye, but without any order or disposition of parts, that shall be commonly or easily observ'd' (Røstvig, 2: 81, 72; Nourse, 319–22; Temple, *Miscellanea*, 1681–90, 2: 'Upon the Gardens of *Epicurus*', 57–8). Similarly, when Hussey put Vanbrugh forward as the 'original innovator' whose experiments in landscape were 'echoed' by Addison, he was answered by Allen, who failed to see how Vanbrugh's designs of 1718–19 could have influenced Addison in 1712 (Hussey, *Picturesque*, 128; Allen, 2: 250).
4. Temple, *Works*, 3: 229–30.
5. *Spectator*, 3: 551–3.

6. Martin, 7–8.
7. Mack, *Garden and City*, 8.

CHAPTER 1

1. Woodbridge, *Temple*, 59, 66; Longe, 33–4, 49; Cundall, 5–6.
2. Barbour, 11; Hamilton, *Gramont*, 139–40; Lely portrait, NPG.
3. Woodbridge, *Temple*, 66; Temple, *Works*, 1: 229–30.
4. Woodbridge, *Temple*, 59, 66; Lely portrait, NPG; Temple, *Early Essays*, 119, 212.
5. Pepys, 1: 421; Evelyn, 2: 67; Ashley, *Charles II*, 187, 301–2, 320; Hutton, 279–80, 335–7, 416–17, 429, 445.
6. Woodbridge, *Temple*, 66–72; Temple, *Works*, 1: 264–71.
7. Macaulay, *Essays*, 1: 197–9; *Inferno*, 3: 60.
8. Woodbridge, *Temple*, 51–2; Dineley, 37–45 & nn.; Garner, 19–20.
9. *Essays*, 1: 213.
10. Temple, *Early Essays*, xxiii–iv; *Poems*, 13. Temple's hand is attested to in a note by his biographer Courtenay; and such corrections as those on pp. 59, 72 and 75 are revisions of the text.
11. *Georgics*, 2: 495–9.
12. Curtis, *Ireland*, 253; Osborne, 27, 38, 54, 92, 223, 236, 255, 266.
13. Woodbridge, *Temple*, 54–9.
14. Ogg, *Charles II*, 309–12; Pepys, 2: 268.
15. Woodbridge, *Temple*, 81–6; Wolf, *Balance*, 31–2; Temple, *Works*, 1: 306–7, 322–3, 330–38, 436–8; Stoye, 270; Haley, *Diplomat*, 162–81.
16. *Essays*, 1: 223–4.
17. Woodbridge, *Temple*, 64–6; Temple, *Early Essays*, 11.
18. *Essays*, 1: 225.
19. Wilson, *Apprenticeship*, 41; Hill, *Reformation to Revolution*, 159; Haley, *Diplomat*, 43; DNB, s.v. Downing; Rowen, 458.
20. Boxer, 101, 217–25; Temple, *Works*, 1: 149; 3: 288.
21. Woodbridge, *Temple*, 92, 98–9, 105–6; Temple, *Works*, 2: 47–8.
22. Kenyon, *Stuarts*, 110, 116–17; Haley, *Diplomat*, 33–6; Jones, *Charles II*, 2–3, 87–92; *Country & Court*, 104–6; Wolf, *Balance*, 50–51.
23. Woodbridge, *Princely Gardens*, 197–201; Jellicoe, Goode & Lancaster, s.v. Hampton Court, St. James' Park.
24. Woodbridge, *Temple*, 107–10; Trevelyan, *Stuarts*, 316; Temple, *Works*, 2: 170–71.
25. Woodbridge, *Temple*, 59; Longe, 33–4; Evelyn, 2: 275; Temple, *Works*, 3: 235; 2: 178.
26. Woodbridge, *Temple*, 112–13, 128–31; Temple, *Works*, 1: 60.
27. Stoye, 277, 279; Wolf, *Louis XIV*, 222–3; van der Zee, 10–15, 67–9; Hall, *Galileo to Newton*, 172–3; Fuchs, 59–61; Wheelock, 9–13; Huizinga, *Civilisation*, 32, 84–5; Boxer, 8–10; Rowen, 15–20, 83–4, 88–9, 412–41, 594–7, 601, 879–82, 885, 892; Maland, 239–40.

28. Rowen, 889; van der Zee, 1–5, 40, 76–7, 91, 145; Macaulay, *History of England*, 2: 3–5.
29. van der Zee, 80–81; Ogg, *Charles II*, 379–83; Woodbridge, *Temple*, 118, 155–8.
30. Stoye, 278–82; Woodbridge, *Temple*, 172–4.
31. Woodbridge, *Temple*, 182–6; Ogg, *Charles II*, 338; Kenyon, *Popish Plot*, 48, 95–6, 111–16, 125–31.
32. Woodbridge, *Temple*, 193–4; Ogg, *Charles II*, 585; DNB, s.v. Bennet; Evelyn, 2: 116–17.
33. *Essays*, 1: 248–9.
34. Woodbridge, *Temple*, 194–203; Temple, *Works* 2: 522, 537. Charles had earlier reproached Temple with 'popular notions' (2: 434).
35. Woodbridge, *Temple*, 204; Temple, *Works*, 2: 550, 183.
36. Hussey, 'Templum Restauratum'; Woodbridge, *Temple*, 214–15, 229.
37. Woodbridge, *Temple*, 156, 163–4, 166–7, 171–2, 179–80; Temple, *Works* 2: 334, 420–21; Ogg, *Charles II*, 543–7.
38. *History of England*, 1: 180; 2: 494.
39. *Works*, 2: 551.
40. Woodbridge, *Temple*, 157–8, 176–8, 181–2, 188–9, 193; Jones, *Country and Court*, 169, 172–3, 198–9, 203–4.
41. Woodbridge, *Temple*, 94.
42. Temple, *Works*, 2: 540.
43. Temple, *Early Essays*, 23–5.
44. *Essays*, 1: 199.
45. Trevelyan, *Macaulay*, 1: 443, 455; 2: 231–3.
46. Trevelyan, *Macaulay*, 1: 109, 158–60, 428; Haley, *Shaftesbury*, 746. The essay on Temple was ostensibly a review of the biography by Courtenay, who had made a foolish attempt to claim Temple for the Tories: a claim dismissed by Woodbridge, while Levine classes Temple with the Whigs. Macaulay, however, chose not to dispute Courtenay's attribution: it gave him an opening, and he made brilliant use of it (Macaulay, *Essays* 1: 195–6; Courtenay, 2: 253–4; Woodbridge, 253; Levine, 301).
47. Acton, 208.
48. Macaulay, *Essays*, 1: 249–52, 272.
49. Ogg, *Charles II*, 365, 647.
50. Haley, *Shaftesbury*, 736.
51. *History of England*, 2: 379.
52. Millgate, 165–80. Macaulay, remarked J.M. Kemble, 'for the sake of displaying one giant, peoples all Europe with pigmies' (Firth, 244).
53. *Temple*, 245, 234, 259–61.
54. Acton put the matter more vehemently. 'He is, I am persuaded', he wrote of Macaulay, 'grossly, basely unfair. Read him therefore to find out how it comes that the most unsympathetic of critics can think him very nearly the greatest of English writers' (Douglas Jerrold, Introduction, Macaulay, *History of England*, 1:

x).
55. Woodbridge, *Temple*, 4–6; Jonson, 8: 94; 9: 33–4; Temple, *Works*, 3: 412; Symonds, 40–41, 69–70, 80, 84–5, 178–86.
56. Waller, 1: 64; Woodbridge, *Temple*, 7; Osborne, 109.
57. Woodbridge, *Temple*, 10–13; Temple, *Early Essays*, 5; Esther, 7:10.
58. Woodbridge, *Temple*, 13–15; Osborne, 282; Woolf, 3: 62–4.
59. Osborne, xii, 29, 22, 108. Dorothy would perhaps have been startled at the manner in which the prediction was fulfilled. Chicksands having passed from the Osborne family to the crown in 1936, it became an RAF base in World War II (Ward, *Chicksands*, 4).
60. Osborne, 129–30, 139–40, 155–6, 159–63, 166, 178–82, 185–94, 199–200; Temple, *Early Essays*, 7.
61. Osborne, 130; Woodbridge, *Temple*, 15–22; Temple, *Early Essays*, xvii–xix, 36, 44, 115, 210, 212.
62. Miller, '"Whig Interpretation"', 80n.
63. Smith, 'Romantic History', 5, 10, 11.
64. Temple, *Works*, 3: 470; Sidney, *Poems*, 185, 233. These poems, however, also depict the 'private' reserves of personal feeling, a mode in which they follow Petrarch (xxxv).
65. Osborne, 195; Temple, *Early Essays*, 6–7; *Works*, 3: 227–9; Woodbridge, *Temple*, 214.
66. Blomfield, 164–7; Strong, 117–19, 135, 144–6, 149–52, 192–4; Malins, *Landscaping and Literature*, 12–13, citing *Parliamentary Survey of Wimbledon*, 1649. Temple's visits to Moor Park were in 1652–4 (Osborne, 195).
67. Clifford, 18–38, 48–52, 100–101; Kuck, 23–5; Gothein, 1: 53–133; Masson, 47–9; Moynihan, 1–2; Crowe, Haywood, Jellicoe & Patterson, 16–17, 47, 170; Correcher, 137–8; Lablaude, 40; Oates, 185–6; Ziehr, 44; Villiers–Stuart, *Mughals*, 11. In the combination of evergreen and blossoming trees has been seen the 'eternal background upon which is spread the lovely but fragile rhythm of individual existence' (Villiers–Stuart, *Spanish Gardens*, 53).
68. Clifford, 61–77; Mumford, 444–5; Norberg–Schulz, *Baroque*, 48, 61; Fox, 62–9, 75–94; Thacker, *History of Gardens*, 143–9; Wolf, *Louis XIV*, 133–44, 269–71, 285–6; Woodbridge, *Princely Gardens*, 188–201; Weiss, 39–48; Mitford, *Sun King*, 63; Blunt, 337, 339.
69. Hyams, *Gardens & Gardening*, 169–192; Malins & Glin, 9–24.
70. 181.
71. However apparently modified by the artifice of the form (Chaudhuri, 1, 60–61).
72. Lazzaro, 111–12, citing Sannazaro, *Arcadia*; Malins, *Landscaping & Literature*, 1–2, citing *Paradise Lost*, 4: 241–7 and Tasso, *Gerusalemme liberata*:

So with the rude the polish'd mingled was,
That natural seem'd all, and ev'ry Part;
*Nature* would Craft in counterfeiting pass,
And imitate her Imitator, *Art* (16, 10, 1–4).

Spenser followed this passage in the *Faerie Queene*:

One would haue thought, (so cunningly, the rude,
And scorned parts were mingled with the fine,)
That nature had for wantonnesse ensude
Art, and that Art at nature did repine (2, 12, 59).

73. Sidney, *Arcadia*, 73.

74. Clifford, 123–4, 127–8; Blomfield, 167; Strong, 14–22. Bacon recommended a garden in which, as in the formal baroque layout which merged gradually into the park (Wölfflin, 150–51; Masson, 123–4), the outermost area was to be 'framed, as much as may be, to a natural wildness' (*Essays*, 141). Wotton felt that 'as Fabriques should bee *regular*, so Gardens should bee *irregular*, or at least cast into a very wilde *Regularitie*', and spoke of having seen a walk from which the plot below could be seen 'rather in a delightfull confusion, than with any plaine distinction of the pieces' (*Elements of Architecture*, 109). Evelyn expressed his 'abhorrency' of those 'formal projections' which 'smell more of paynt then of flowers and verdure', preferring 'Caves, Grotts, Mounts, and irregular ornaments of Gardens' (Hunt & Willis, 58). Such perceptions seem to have had little initial effect on practice: Evelyn continued to favour the quincunx plantation (Chambers, *Planters*, 44). And when Rea declared that a 'green Medow' was a 'more delightful object' than many of the gardens of his time; when he stated that here was to be found 'nature alone, without the aid of Art', he was speaking of lawns from which flowers had been banished (*Flora*, 1). The groundplans he offered remained relentlessly geometrical; and in both these respects he was echoed by Worlidge (*Systema Horti-Culturae*, 16–19). The continent seems to have been more amenable in this regard. Temple reports having seen layouts in which there were 'some parts wild, some exact' in France and Brabant (*Works*, 3: 218); and examples have been traced to Holland, to the circle of Wotton, who had also had been ambassador there (de Jong, 323–32). Addison, too, thought the 'artificial Rudeness' he had encountered in France and Italy 'much more charming' than the 'Neatness and Elegancy' with which he characterised the gardens of his homeland (*Spectator*, 3: 551). In France, indeed, there was a succession of 'heretical voices...within the camp of formalist orthodoxy'; but these were ignored by Louis XIV (Burke, *English Art*, 42–3).

75. *Works*, 3: 229–30.

76. The main attempts at solution were brought together by Lang and Pevsner (1949), who open with the statement of the *Oxford English Dictionary* that the word is 'of unknown origin'. 'Chinese scholars agree', the dictionary continues, 'that it cannot belong to that language' (OED, s.v. sharawaggi). This Lang and Pevsner term 'rather defeatist', and go on to cite two attempts to match the word with Chinese. Y.Z. Chang (1930), working at the request of A.O. Lovejoy (*History of Ideas*, 111n.) suggested *sa-lo-kwai-chi*, which he glossed as the 'quality of being impressive or surprising through careless or unorderly grace'. Ch'ien Chung-shu (1940), however, contended that this would mean no more than 'graceful...and...magnificent', and proposed instead *san-lan-wai-chi*, 'space tastefully

enlivened by disorder'. Neither, however, is supported by actual usage; and Lang and Pevsner, agreeing that both are unsatisfactory, devote much ingenuity to the argument that the word was Temple's own invention: which seems defeatist indeed. They dismiss the suggestion of E.V. Gatenby (1931, 1934) that *sharawadgi* derived from the Japanese *sorowaji*, 'not being regular', as not being Chinese. A number of writers, nevertheless, subsequently opted for the Japanese solution. Quennell (1968) quoted the Japan scholar Ivan Morris to the effect that, while it could not be Chinese, it might well be Japanese (181n.). Hadfield (1979), while noting that 'opinions differ', thought it 'probably not a Chinese word, but of Japanese origin' (177n.). Faber (1983) noted that it 'may apparently be Japanese, rather than Chinese' (142).

77. Hadfield, 96–7.

78. 2: 173. Half a century later, the interior of a '*Chinese* House' at Stowe would be described as '*Indian* Japan' (Charlesworth, 2: 69).

79. Jacobson, 43; Tanaka, 93.

80. *Works* 3: 230. Honour attests to the growing popularity of Asian design at this time, from Nell Gwynne's snuff–box to Queen Mary's porcelain (*Chinoiserie*, 69–70).

81. Kuck, 19–22, 49, 115–23, 127, 149–56, 168–9, 226–7.

82. Woodbridge, *Temple*, 282–4; Montanus, *Atlas Chinensis*, 570–71; Temple, *Works*, 3: 320–21. Montanus' illustration is a Chinese woodblock print; his volume also shows planted lakeshores with vistas of dramatic mountains and pavilions set at picturesque intervals (684–5); but his *Atlas Japannensis* is by comparison a disappointment. Its illustrations have clearly originated in Europe, the shogun's ('Emperor's') garden at Tokyo ('Jedo') being shown with matching avenues, parterres and a tree–lined circle (opposite page 146). If Temple saw this -- and it was 'Englished' by the same courtier of Charles II as the Chinese volume -- it would have increased his reluctance to make *sharawadgi* a specific attribute of Japan.

83. Sansom, 177–8; Boxer, 220–21; Woodbridge, *Temple*, 100. Honour (*Chinoiserie*, 145) Hadfield and Quennell (as above, n. 76) suggest Holland as Temple's immediate source. In his essay 'Upon the Cure of the Gout by Moxa', Temple speaks of a Chinese medical practice under its Japanese name (Miller, *Japanese Language*, 259). His information came from a Dutch friend, who had had it from 'several who had seen and tried it in the Indies', and from an 'ingenious little book' by a 'Dutch Minister at Batavia' or Djakarta (*Works*, 3: 238–65).

84. Kaempfer, 2: 174; Goodman, 18–23.

85. Kaempfer, 2: 174ff., 275–7; 3: 118, 191. Kaempfer cannot have been Temple's informant, as he made his journeys in 1691 and 1692, and the *sharawadgi* passage appeared in 1690 (in the first and second editions of Temple's *Miscellanea: the Second Part*: in the first, where the essays are separately paged, on pp. 57–8 of that on gardens; in the second, on pp. 131–2 of the volume). As he states, however, that the visit to the temples was a 'custom of long standing...by

degrees...turn'd almost to a law' (3: 117), it is evident that he trod in the footsteps of those who might have been.

86. Morris, 37–43.

87. Singer, 107, 111–13, 144–7; Fingarette, 61–4; Welch, 21, 45, 158–9; Capra, 91–2. Singer finds the same contrast in Chinese and Japanese verse–forms (133–5). Prince Mikasa has shown how, concurrently with the Chinese, an influence, ultimately Mesopotamian, favouring symmetry, was accepted, then rejected in Japan -- a rejection that he sees as characteristic of that country's aesthetics.

88. Kuck, 67; Welch, 159–61; Singer, 138–41, 147–8.

89. I owe these details to Madoka Kanai, of Tokyo University.

90. The modern equivalent is *sorowanai desho*, 'would not harmonise, balance or match': the Japanese subjunctive being a polite form of the indicative. Fumiko Daido, of Tama Art University, has suggested that Temple's informant conflated what he heard as *sharawaji* with *share* and *aji*, both nouns which might be employed of a garden showing an impressive degree of taste (*shareta niwa*; *aji ga aru niwa*).

91. Kaempfer, 2: 183–4, 203, 101.

92. *Works*, 3: 227, 230. Temple may, however, have overruled his own taboo and reached out for the forbidden fruit. It is suggested that an island with winding walks in the river Wey, on the outer verge of his parterres, represented an attempt at *sharawadgi* (Chambers, *Planters*, 17).

93. 1: 396–7.

94. Waley, *Way & its Power*, 188, 189.

95. Koestler, *Act of Creation*, 103–5.

96. Foreword, Neumann, *Consciousness*, xiii.

CHAPTER 2

1. *History of England*, 2: 241.

2. Ashley, *James II*, 10–12; Turner, 76–82; Ogg, *Charles II*, 250–51, 258–9, 267–8, 274, 285–8, 314, 388, 676–8.

3. Trevelyan, *Stuarts*, 411–25; Ashley, *James II*, 12–13, 236–48; van der Zee, 256–78; Israel, 2; Seeley, 2: 322.

4. Smithers, 367.

5. Swift, *Corr.*, 2: 277.

6. Dobrée, *Essays in Biography*, 203, 210–11, 257–8, 261–5. 'Victorian' and 'Victorianism' observes Jerome Hamilton Buckley, have acquired the status of Ruskin's 'masked words droning and skulking about us'. When Strachey, shortly before Dobrée, published *Eminent Victorians*, he struck, in Cyril Connolly's words, 'the note of ridicule which the whole war–weary generation wanted to hear'. World War I had undermined faith in institutions, and the unconventional, self–critical and creative aspects of the previous age -- 'the manifold dissatisfactions and rebellions of Carlyle, Dickens, Ruskin, Morris, Samuel Butler', its voyages of discovery, sending 'Layard to buried Nineveh, Livingstone to the dark heart of Africa', Burton to live out his 'unexpurgated Arabian nights' -- were written off

with them (Buckley, 2–5, 8, 11; Holroyd, 508–9, 603–5, 696, 731–2; Graves, 157–9, 208–9).
7. Macaulay, *Essays*, 2: 419–23, 439–47; Bahlman, 14–24. Pope long afterwards boasted of having 'moraliz'd his song' (*Poems*, 4: 120); and Sherburn lists among 'unwarranted twentieth-century assumptions' the notion that he 'hated moralising' (*Early Career*, 24).
8. 245–6.
9. Ehrenpreis *Swift*, 2: 289–94, 439–44.
10. Smithers, 150–2, 270; Carswell, 44, 58–9.
11. *Variety of Ways*, 88, 98.
12. *The Theatre*, 55–6.
13. 'Addison', 155–6.
14. Bloom, *Critical Heritage*, 35; *Sociable Animal*, 3. In Addison's version of the advice of father to son in Ovid -- 'Keep the mid way, the middle way is best' (*Misc. Wks.*, 1: 68) -- Dobrée professes to find autobiographical significance (*Essays in Biography*, 219–20). How far in fact it is applicable may be judged from what follows.
15. Lewis, 'Addison', 150–51, 153–4, 156. McCrea traces a further decline in Addison's reputation, now accompanied by that of Steele, due to their apparent failure to provide the ambiguities demanded by formalist criticism (117–35).
16. *Essays in Biography*, 211.
17. Smithers, v–vi.
18. 1–11.
19. Courthope, 25; Smithers, 145, 182–4, 228–9; Swift, *Prose Works*, 15: 69.
20. Smithers, 9.
22. *Tatler*, 3: 215–16 & n.
22. 32. Courthope had earlier been troubled by a sensation of 'formalism and priggishness' (26).
23. Connely, 20–21.
24. DNB, s.v. Addison, citing *Tatler* no. 252. Bond in his edition does not give this number to Steele (3: 280n.); but there is a substantially identical account of Addison in the *Egmont Diary* (Spence, 1: 62).
25. Macaulay, *Essays*, 2: 455.
26. Courthope, 22–4; Smithers, 14.
27. Birch & Lockman, 107 & n.
28. Johnson, 2: 80 & n.
29. *Essays*, 2: 456–7; Smithers, 11–13.
30. Addison, *Misc. Wks.*, 1: 42, 237–8, 242.
31. Smithers, 14–15, 43, 80–81.
32. Addison, *Letters*, 45.
33. Smithers, 80–81.
34. Ogg, *James II & William III*, 54, 56.
35. *History of England*, 2: 104, 108.
36. Jones, *Revolution*, 314–15, 317–18.

37. Filmer, 39–41; Macpherson, 244; Locke, 324, 330.
38. Johnson, 2: 85.
39. DNB, s.v. Somers, Montagu; Smithers, 27–33, 42–3.
40. Tyers, 25. In this he conflated two statements of Johnson: that the description of the 'minute republick' was the 'most amusing' part of Addison's book; and that, of many other passages in it, 'it is not a very severe censure to say that they might have been written at home' (2: 87).
41. 63.
42. Speck, 11, 103.
43. *Misc. Wks.*, 2: 71, 73, 76.
44. Bloom, '"Liberalism"', 560–62; Kenyon, *Revolution Principles*, 105–6, 123–4; Dickinson, *Liberty & Property*, 65–6; Locke, 155, 287.
45. *Letters*, 10–11. Had Addison known the truth -- that it was the king's gardener and not the king who had 'Humourd the Genius of the place' -- his preconceptions would have been still more strongly confirmed. Le Nôtre had wished to leave the gardens of Fontainebleau in harmony with the rambling house; Louis however insisted upon his enlarging the parterre and canal, and making the lines of the lake more regular (Fox, 135). Possin has seen in Addison's *Erlebnis von Fontainebleau* an *Abwendung vom Formalistischen System* (30–37). His exposition of the development of Addison's thought on landscape is a model of its kind, lucid, concise and comprehensive. If I differ from it, it is by way of addition: of the psychological factors that I believe to have influenced that development.
46. *Misc. Wks.*, 2: 83. This, too, had been anticipated while Addison was still in England. In the simple garden that Vergil glimpsed under the ramparts of Taranto, he thought, there was 'more pleasantness' than in 'all the spacious walks and water–works of *Rapin*' (*Misc. Wks.*, 2: 11, citing *Georgics*, 4: 125–46): who, in his poem on gardens, had glorified those of Louis XIV (Rapin, 147).
47. *Misc. Wks.*, 1: 55–6, 58.
48. Smithers, 69.
49. 72–3.
50. Trevelyan, *Queen Anne*, 1: 348–54, 370–76, 384.
51. Trevelyan, *Stuarts*, 461; Green, *Anne*, 26, 53, 56, 63–4, 71–3.
52. Churchill, 1: 22–38, 46–8, 51–64, 79–129, 133–59, 408–20, 757–9.
53. Gregg, 59–66.
54. Clark, *Later Stuarts*, 199; Miller, *William & Mary*, 115–19.
55. Woodbridge, *Temple*, 95.
56. Kenyon, *Stuarts*, 178.
57. Thacker, *History of Gardens*, 168–9; Jacques & van der Horst, 57; Janssens-Knorsch, 277–80.
58. van der Zee, 215.
59. Gregg, 68–109.
60. Gregg, 152–3; Green, *Anne*, 94–5; *Gardener*, 64–5, 74.
61. Gregg, 124–7; Lecky, 1: 24–33; Trevelyan, *Q. Anne*, 1: 244–5, 317–18, 341.

62. Trevelyan, *Q. Anne*, 1: 221–2, 374–98; *Stuarts*, 474; Hadfield, 155–6.
63. Trevelyan, *Q. Anne*, 1: 391, 395–7.
64. Smithers, 88–96.
65. Trevelyan, *Q. Anne*, 1: 277–80, 291–2, 330–32; 2: 12–16, 25–32, 388–90; Smithers, 99–100, 141–2; *New Enclopædia Britannica*, s.v. Addison.
66. Trevelyan, *Q. Anne*, 1: 401; 2: 57, 103–119; Churchill, 1: 883–4.
67. Wolf, *Louis XIV*, 544–6, 550–51; Trevelyan, *Q. Anne*, 2: 356–66.
68. Fox, 98, 101–2; Woodbridge, *Princely Gardens*, 220–21; Mitford, *Sun King*, 68.
69. Wolf, *Louis XIV*, 555–77; Trevelyan, *Q. Anne*, 2: 395–406; 3: 1–21, 33–5; Holmes, *Sacheverell*, 165.
70. Smithers, 13, 24–5 & n.
71. Trevelyan, *Q. Anne*, 1: 49–50, 52; 3: 47–8.
72. Holmes, *Sacheverell*, 61–75, 78–9, 89–94, 156–69, 223–5, 228–32.
73. Trevelyan, *Q. Anne*, 3: 61–74; Smithers, 184–92.
74. Trevelyan, *Q. Anne*, 3: 89–94, 247–50.
75. Holmes, *Sacheverell*, 61.
76. Trevelyan, *Q. Anne*, 3: 48.
77. Gregg, 297.
78. *Tatler*, 2: 397–401.
79. Willard Connely, 'Addison and Steele', in Dobrée, *Anne to Victoria*, 15–17; Connely, *Steele*, 45–63; Winton, *Captain Steele*, 56.
80. Connely, *Steele*, 105–8, 141–5; 'Addison and Steele', 19.
81. Winton, *Captain Steele*, 52–3, 148–9; *Sir Richard Steele*, 102–3, 202, 222–3.
82. Courthope, 89–104; Smithers, 160–64; Steele, *Corr.*, 510; Beljame, 261–2; Connely, 'Addison and Steele', 20–23; *Spectator*, 1: 5–6.
83. 4: 508.
84. Thackeray, 129.
85. Steele, *Corr.*, 511.
86. Woolf, 1: 91.
87. 278.
88. 27.
89. *Spectator*, 1: 362–3, citing Horace, *Odes*, 3, 4.
90. Jung & von Franz, 39.
91. Bettelheim, 93–4.
92. von Franz, 84–5.
93. Whitmont, 101.
94. 75–6, 102, 217n., 94n.
95. *Spectator*, 1: 362.
96. 3: 552–3.
97. Cooke, 376–81.
98. Cooke, 382. In Addison's comedy *The Drummer* (*Misc. Wks.*, 1: 423–90), the protagonist lives in a mansion 'haunted' by her missing husband: as Lady Warwick continued to live at Holland House (Smithers, 134). The characters, however, are

reversed: here it is the husband who is faithful and the suitor who is the rake.
99. Cooke, 381–2.
100. *Spectator*, 4: 596–8; 5: 1–3.
101. Cooke, 377.
102. Smithers, 234–7, 280–81.
103. Cooke, 385, 387.
104. *Spectator*, 5: 2.
105. Smithers, 283–6, 352–3.
106. Michael Strutt, head porter of Magdalen, kindly devoted a Sunday morning to helping me locate the gates: having been placed in an inaccessible corner, they had been virtually forgotten at the time of my visit. Brenda Parry–Jones, the college archivist, with equal kindness provided extensive documentation of their provenance, and their rescue by Peter Smithers.
107. Sutherland, 128.
108. Saintsbury, 180–81.
109. *Spectator*, 3: 535–6. Addison built upon the empirical philosophy of the seventeenth century (*Spectator*, 3: 536n., 547n.; Elioseff, 154–88); and to him in turn, writes Carritt, 'the succeeding critics of his century owed almost everything' (27): a view concurred in by Kallich (311).
110. *Spectator*, 3: 540–44.
111. *Classic to Romantic*, 154.
112. Shipley, s.v. romanticism.
113. 'Addison's Contribution to Criticism', 317, 324.
114. 241.
115. *Spectator*, 3: 548–53. Though Addison speaks of 'Writers' on China, even the most cursory comparison reveals Temple (*Works*, 3: 229–30) as his only necessary source.
116. 'Addison's interest in planting and gardening was aesthetic rather than practical' (Smithers, 310).
117. Smithers, 247–50, 277–8; Addison, *Letters*, 279 &n., 282.
118. Addison refers to him as 'Kinsman'; the exact relationship between them is unknown (*Letters*, 283 & n.).
119. This tale of neglect is reiterated further down. 'Your game' -- upon which Addison had prided himself the previous autumn -- 'is mostly destroy'd for want of looking after'; a state of affairs for which the captain proposed a military solution: '2 days after I came here I met a pack of Hounds in full cry...and promis'd the Huntsman to be at the Expence of a little Buck shott when he next came that way' (Addison, *Letters*, 282, 492–3).
120. Smithers, 278–312; Winton, *Sir Richard Steele*, 2. There was a summer visit to Bilton (Smithers, 282; Addison, *Letters*, 285); but that this was exceptional is indicated by Addison's later query as to whether two and a half days will be sufficient to bring him there from London (*Letters*, 495).
121. Addison, *Letters*, 495.
122. Kingsbury describes Addison's estate as follows: 'Dugdale...says of Bilton: --

"The Gardens attached to Bilton Hall are rather extensive: they continue as they were long since laid out, in straight lines, with long and thick hedges of yew. On the north side of the grounds is a long walk, still called 'Addison's Walk', once the promenade of that elegant writer. Its seclusion was deepened by rows of trees, some of which were Spanish oaks, raised by Addison himself from acorns given him by Secretary Craggs, but the unsparing axe has levelled these to the ground since the death of his daughter". (There is however a pencil note in the book after the last paragraph saying, "This is a mistake, they still exist"). This form of straight line is that to which in his earliest years he seems to have been attracted, as part of the walks of Magdalen College, Oxford, which follow this model, are also known as "Addison's Walk". Probably few people, comparatively, today read the somewhat sanctimonious, sermonising Joseph Addison...' (17).

It will be seen that the supposed preference of Addison for straight lines comes from Kingsbury, and is linked with a view of personal rigidity the sources of which we shall examine in the next chapter. It is not part of the quotation from 'Dugdale'. The original Dugdale was of course Sir William, the great antiquarian, who, as he lived from 1605 to 1686, cannot have had anything to say about Addison's plantations. The reference is to the 1817 *Warwickshire...from...Dugdale and Other Later Authorities* (154).

For her frontispiece, Kingsbury reprints an 'old pencil drawing' of a formal avenue from which pathways branch obliquely, and beyond which, in front of the Jacobean house, is a clearing of irregularly-spaced trees and shrubs. The provenance of these elements -- whether from before, during or after Addison's tenure -- in the absence of further evidence, and in view of the virtual obliteration of the site, remains uncertain.

Kingsbury's book is in the nature of a family album, the house having passed from Addison's daughter to the author's grandfather, amongst whose descendants it remained until 1898; it does not pretend to historical scholarship (Kingsbury, 7, 9–10, 14). Leatherbarrow however quotes it uncritically, from the appeal to 'Dugdale' to Addison's alleged linear addiction, and succeeds in adding confusions of his own. Edward Addison is described as the essayist's brother, which he was not (Addison, *Letters*, 283 & n.; Smithers, 3–5); and the same attitude to evidence prevails throughout. Addison purchased Bilton Hall on 27 February 1713 (Addison, *Letters*, 279n.). Leatherbarrow's taking this as 1712 enables him to place Addison's essay of 6 September 1712 (*Spectator*, 4: 188–92), describing an 'irregular and wild' garden, 'exactly six months' later, and make it a portrait of Bilton, which is now promoted, by virtue of its yew hedges, into a topiary garden (Leatherbarrow, 334–5): an unwarranted equation, as Chambers has pointed out (*Planters*, 51).

Leatherbarrow's underlying argument is that when Addison describes an irregular garden he means a regular one: his writings therefore do not 'foretell the coming of the new informal gardens' (334). This illusion is perpetrated by sleight of hand, Addison being slipped into a consideration of Shaftesbury, who in his garden called explicitly for arboreal 'Globes, and Pyramids', while outside it uttering a

celebrated apostrophe to 'things of a natural kind' (Leatherbarrow, 332, 343–4, 354–5; see below, Ch. 6, n. 33). In the latter, however, as Leatherbarrow acknowledges (353), he was not referring to garden design. And as Addison was, and as he had explicitly condemned trees which rose in 'Cones, Globes, and Pyramids' (*Spectator*, 3: 552), the analogy collapses on both counts.
I am grateful to Joanna Grindle, Clare Spruce and Sandra Barnsley of Rugby Library, Gary Archer of Leamington Library and Rob Eyre of the Warwickshire County Record Office for providing me with materials relating to Bilton, and to Jonathan Lovie for sharing his knowledge of the site with me.
123. *Spectator*, 4: 190–91.
124. Addison's kinsman writes to him that he has 'Turff'd your new Walke, and...to give you the better Idea of it I here send you its demtions (viz) -- 105 yards long, and 17 ffoot wide, and but a very easie Assent. I am now ffencing it in with a vary hansom paile, 6 foot–high, and a coping Raile upon it with a Row of Iron Spikes to secure your fruit: I make you a door out of the Garden into this Walke' (Addison, *Letters*, 491–2). It is clear from this need to describe his own walk to him that Addison left a very large discretion to his 'oporators'.
125. Walpole, *Anecdotes*, 3: 81; Hussey, *English Gardens*, 148.
126. 'Averroes' Search' (*Labyrinths*, 180–88).
127. 8–9.
128. Addison, *Letters*, 492, 494–5, 496.
129. Addison 'made little use of his country property' (Smithers, 422).
130. Smithers, 313–448.
131. Switzer transcribes *Spectator* 414 (3: 548–53) in the *Nobleman, Gentleman, and Gardener's Recreation* of 1715 (256–9), and again in the expanded version of 1718 (*Ichnographia Rustica*, 1: 338–43).
132. Hussey, *English Gardens*, 23, 32–4, 59. 'Hedge Rows, little natural Coppices, large Woods, Corn Fields, *& c.* mix'd one amongst another, are as delightful as the finest Garden' (Switzer, *Ichnographia*, 3: 46; *Spectator*, 3: 552). 'Switzer's writings attempt to give practical form to Addison's ideas' (Hunt, *Garden & Grove*, 186).
133. *English Gardens*, 32–7.
134. Walpole, *Anecdotes*, 3: 80. This might stand for a description of Addison's garden, raising the possibility of contact, direct or indirect, between them. Bridgeman had connections with the Whig Kit–Cat Club (Willis, *Bridgeman*, 134), of which Addison was a member (Smithers, 90, 410), and which indeed has been described as the earliest focus of the landscape movement (Dorothy Stroud, 'Eighteenth Century Landscape Gardening', in Singleton, 1: 37). Some such contact, certainly, would explain what followed the publication of his 'Chinese' essay. He had concluded this with a repudiation of topiary sculpture, and the comment: 'But as our great Modellers of Gardens have their Magazines of Plants to dispose of, it is very natural for them to tear up all the Beautiful Plantations of Fruit Trees, and contrive a plan that may most turn to their own Profit, in taking off their Evergreens, and the like Moveable Plants, with which their Shops are

plentifully stocked' (*Spectator*, 2: 553). Thus the essay of 25 June 1712; on 6 September, Hussey has suggested, Addison 'made amends for this nasty cut at the Brompton nurserymen with a handsome tribute to London and Wise' (*English Gardens*, 30). These, he wrote, were the 'Heroick Poets' of gardening, while his own preference was for the '*Pindarick*' mode (*Spectator*, 4: 190).
London and Wise, in their nursery at Brompton, on the site of the Victoria and Albert Museum -- which was indeed 'plentifully stocked', being estimated to contain 14,500,000 plants and to be worth £40,000 -- trained the 'leading later practitioners', amongst whom were Switzer and Bridgeman (Hussey, *English Gardens*, 23, 32, 37, 59). This being the case, one may suggest the following scenario. Addison in June 1712 publishes an essay which offends the susceptibilities of the Brompton brotherhood. One of these registers a protest, and Addison in September prints a generous disclaimer. In February 1713 he purchases Bilton, and in October and November of the same year commences planting. In November 1714, he receives word that this has failed; and in December the judgement of his 'London oporator' is being relayed to him (Addison, *Letters*, 279–82, 491–5). In 1715, Switzer quotes Addison's essay virtually entire, omitting only the offensive reflection on nurserymen, though agreeing with it in substance (*Recreation*, 256–60). All this being the case, one may speculate that one of the Brompton nurserymen was Addison's 'London oporator'.
A motive for their acceptance of the new style is suggested by the fact that Wise and Bridgeman attributed the high cost of maintaining the royal gardens to the 'Minute Forms and Compositions which were the Fashion at the time the gardens were made' (Hussey, *English Gardens*, 27). Likewise Switzer, in echoing Addison's recommendation: 'Besides as these Hedge Rows, little natural Coppices, large Woods, Corn Fields, *&c.* mix'd one amongst another, are as delightful as the finest Garden; so they are much cheaper made, and still cheaper kept' (*Ichnographia*, 3: 46).
135. *Spectator*, 3: 552. Walpole does not mention Addison in this connection. He had been stung by the French description of the landscape garden as *anglo-chinois*: 'They have detected us for having stolen our gardens from the Chinese. I shall tell them another tale' (*Corr.*, 28: 222). Tell them he did; but the tale was curiously inconclusive. Bridgeman's ancestry in Temple is betrayed by the statement that he 'disdained to make every division tally to its opposite'. Temple, however, is mentioned only to be ridiculed for having advised against imitation of the 'Chineses'; while Addison, as presumably too dangerous a witness, is not referred to at all. Instead, the 'reformation' is attributed either to Bridgeman's 'good sense', or the 'admirable paper' on the subject by Pope (Walpole, *Anecdotes*, 3: 74–83). Pope's paper, however, is a tissue of borrowings from Temple and Addison (see below, Ch. 3, n. 185).
136. Hussey, *English Gardens*, 39.
137. Robinson, 17; Hunt, *Kent*, 44.
138. Walpole, *Anecdotes*, 3: 81–2; Hussey in Jourdain, 22; Hunt, *Kent*, 45.

139. Jourdain, 25–37; Harris, *Palladian Revival*, 197–8.
140. Sir Thomas Robinson to the Earl of Carlisle 1734, cited Harris, *Palladian Revival*, 196. Harris remarks on Robinson's privileged position in relation to contemporary gardening as a result of his close friendship with Burlington, who employed Kent at Chiswick: a position enhanced by his being son-in-law to Carlisle, creator of the great landscape garden at Castle Howard (Hussey, *English Gardens*, 116–17), which Chambers sees as influenced by Addison, like Carlisle a member of the Whig Kit-Cat Club (*Planters*, 64, 130–32).
Jacques, amazingly, cites this letter of Robinson's on the 'new taste' established by Kent to refute what he describes as the 'Supposed Chineseness of the English Landscape Garden' (180). This he accomplishes by suppressing its Chinese reference. In *Georgian Gardens*, he quotes the passage more completely, but still elides the reference to the Chinese (32). Williamson in turn cites Jacques as an authority for the dismissal of Chinese influence (*Polite Landscapes*, 65, 172), and quotes the Robinson letter with the same significant omission (59). The resulting fiction is bolstered by the adoption (48–52) of Leatherbarrow's untenable hypothesis that Addison did not advocate informality in gardening (above, n. 122). Temple and Addison having been rendered irrelevant, the 'new irregular style' can be held to have originated with Kent (58–9).
Williamson evidently does not place any very great value on historical sequence. In '1715', he informs us, 'following the accession of Queen Anne, Richard Temple (later the 1st Viscount Cobham) was dismissed from his post as an army commander because of his Whig beliefs' (63). In point of fact, 1715 was the year in which Cobham was reappointed to an army command because of his Whig beliefs (*DNB*, s.v. Temple), and this followed the accession of King George. Queen Anne's accession took place in 1702, and she reigned until 1714. Given this underlying sense of the historical landscape, it is not to be expected that Addison should be placed upon it with any accuracy, Williamson classing him as he does among 'noted critics of the Walpole regime' (52). Addison died in 1719; the Walpole regime began in 1722.
141. The Italian missionary Matteo Ripa was attached to the Chinese court from 1711 to 1723, and in 1724 visited London. As one of the rare copies of his engravings of Chinese imperial gardens bears the bookplate of Kent's patron Burlington, Wittkower suggests that the latter had access to these, with their 'artful irregularity' of 'winding brooks...little islands and a great variety of trees in their natural growth' (*Palladio*, 185–6). Lang admits that they 'confirmed Temple's and Addison's views on *Sharawadgi*' ('Genesis', 26); and Jacques, in the face of this fact, concedes that Kent's layouts were perhaps 'an attempt to imitate Chinese gardens' (*Georgian Gardens*, 34).
142. Hayden, 100–103. Other examples are cited, curiously, by Leatherbarrow (336) and Jacques (*Georgian Gardens*, 43–5).
143. *Spectator*, 3: 552.
144. *Spectator*, 1: lxxxiii–vii, xcvi–c; Kimball, 209.
145. Lord Burlington, Brigadier Dormer and Sir Richard Temple subscribed to the

edition of 1712–13 (*Spectator*, 1: lxxxviii–ix & nn.).
146. Addison's vision of the Temples of Virtue, Vanity and Honour in the *Tatler* (2: 209–14, 224–9) contains 'all the features of Kent's Elysian Fields' (Robinson, 86–7).
147. Walpole, *Anecdotes*, 3: 81; *Spectator*, 3: 551–2.
148. *Spectator*, 3: 538. The remarkable peacefulness of his death is reliably attested (Smithers, 448n.).
149. The tributaries which flowed into the stream of the landscape garden have sometimes been taken for its central course. Much has been made of Kent's background in painting, and in particular scene-painting, which involved landscape (Lang, 'Genesis', 27–9; Hunt, *Kent*, 29–32; Elisabetta Cereghini, 'The Italian Origins of Rousham', in Mosser & Teyssot, 320–22). But Kent returned from Italy in 1719 (Jourdain, 36), while Addison's recommendation that an estate be turned into a garden by the incorporation of natural features was printed in 1712, and incorporated into Switzer's *Gardener's Recreation* in 1715. And Addison's proposal had been formulated, as Hunt has pointed out (*Gardens & the Picturesque*, 106–7), according to the pictorial categories of 'Prospect' and 'Landskip' (*Spectator*, 3: 552). For this see below, Ch. 6.
So also Kent's experience of Italian gardens (Masson, 198, 228; Lang, 'Genesis', 27), in the external reaches of which informal planting made a deliberate contrast with internal formality, to emphasize the creation of order out of disorder: 'which was to be feared' (MacDougall, 51–3). Addison in the same place had expressed his admiration for the element of 'artificial Rudeness' in the 'agreeable mixture of Garden and Forest' that he had encountered in Italy and France (*Spectator*, 3: 551). For him, however, the emphasis was reversed.
Likewise Chambers' derivation of the landscape garden from the 'union of ancient philosophical ideals, the sudden expansion of botany, and practical silviculture' (*Planters*, 3). Lubbock finds Addison 'directly recommending' the programme of arboriculture of which Chambers treats, and fully aware of its social and economic advantages (178, 185, citing *Spectator*, 3: 551–4; 4: 592–5). The role of 'ancient philosophical ideals', meanwhile, was far more comprehensive than the influence of the *Georgics*; and Addison was at the centre of this also (see below, Ch. 4–6).
Bound up with these is the element of timing. All of the subsidiary forces are swept into the current of the revolution of 1688, and the formulation of its ideology of liberty as a return to nature by Addison. In the shaping of the landscape garden, Müllenbrock has insisted, 'the several contributory strands fuse into a genetic pattern of...indigenous mould': a 'counter-design to the French formal garden with its absolutist aura'. Here Addison is central; and, in his writings, 'the connection between liberty in politics and liberty in landscape is established beyond any doubt' (97–9). The catalytic agency of the 'Chinese' example, meanwhile, since Addison cites it at a crucial moment, and the later landscape gardeners echo it, is no less undeniable.
150. *Spectator*, 1: lix. Switzer, quoting Addison on the garden with approval, attributes his work to Steele (*Recreation*, 65–8, 210–14, 256–9, citing *Spectator*,

3: 548–53; 4: 592–5; 5: 84–7).
151. 2: 145–8.
152. 'Addison', 153.
153. Addison, *Freeholder*, 113.

## CHAPTER 3

1. Sherburn, *Early Career*, 26, 23.
2. Stephen, *Pope*, 147–51.
3. Pope, *Corr.*, 1: xi, xviii; 4: 214, 337–8.
4. Pope, *Poems*, 1: 306–7.
5. Mack, *Pope*, 153.
6. Dennis, 1: 416–17.
7. Sherburn, *Early Career*, 88–9.
8. Dennis, 2: 370, xxvii.
9. 1: 396.
10. *Spectator*, 2: 481–6.
11. Pope, *Poems*, 1: 277–9.
12. Pope, *Works*, 2: 25–6.
13. Pope, *Poems*, 8: 25; 2: 311; 3, 1: 48.
14. Ault, 195.
15. Addison, *Misc. Wks.*, 1: 11, 14, 16, 18. The gibe about '*Sleep*' was perhaps suggested by Wycherley's assertion that Pope was not a poet of this type (*Poetical Miscellanies*, 254).
16. Ault, 107–8; Pope, *Poems*, 2: 38; Addison, *Misc. Wks.*, 1: 61.
17. Pope, *Poems*, 1: 245 & n.; Addison, *Misc. Wks.*, 2: 66.
18. *Early Career*, 156.
19. Ault, 11, 126.
20. Adler, 368.
21. Nicolson & Rousseau, 13–18; Pope, *Poems*, 1: 332, 336, 338, 341, 346–9.
22. Pope, *Poems*, 1: 387–90.
23. 1: 379–82.
24. Mack, *Collected in Himself*, 382.
25. Pope, *Poems*, 1: 331, 366, 372.
26. 1: 395, 399. The brother in Ovid is simply one of a series of trials, his disgrace being listed with the loss of a father and the birth of a daughter (*Heroides*, 15: 59–70). In Pope the father is unmentioned and the daughter subordinated to the brother, who speaks of her as an antidote to grief.
27. As is the image of an imagined throne (Pope, *Poems*, 1: 418, 399, 428, 424; Addison, *Misc. Wks.*, 1: 33, 163). Maynard Mack has examined some of these poems as they relate to autobiography; but the theme of the rival receives only passing mention, and the *Thebais* is not considered (*Collected in Himself*, 380–82).
28. 1: 383.
29. Winn, 412–16, 434–5.
30. F.B. Thornton suggests that the attack on Dennis was motivated by a desire

to take revenge on him for the anti–Catholic opinions which went with his being a Whig (58–9); and this pious motive would hold good for Addison too. But the *Essay on Criticism* would be an unfortunate place to seek support for it: for it was here that Pope condemned those who would confine faith to '*one small Sect*', and asserted that 'the *Monks* finish'd what the *Goths* begun' (*Poems*, 1: 285, 318): lines which so angered his co–religionists that he was forced to shuffle, typically, to evade their censure (Sherburn, *Early Career*, 95–6; Thornton, 59–64).
31. 1: 415–16.
32. Pope, *Works*, 1: 61n., 72n.
33. 1: ix. Pope's juvenile epic concerned a 'prince, driven from his throne' (Spence, 1: 17); the fact that his name was Alcander suggests a conflation of political and personal motives.
34. Smithers, 34–5.
35. 116–17.
36. *Poems*, 1: 451.
37. Mack, *Pope*, 129–31.
38. Sherburn, *Early Career*, 248–62.
39. Lord, 407, 422, 427.
40. Pope, *Poems*, 1: 471.
41. Aden, 65–70.
42. Pope, *Poems*, 2: 61, 66.
43. Pope, *Works*, 1: 138n., 149n.
44. Pope, *Poems*, 2: 52–4, 38.
45. Dennis, 1: 396.
46. Pope, *Works*, 2: 13; *Corr.*, 1: 121.
47. Pope, *Prose Works*, 1: xv–xviii, xxviii–xxxiii, 5.
48. 1: 415.
49. *Spectator*, 2: 482.
50. *Poems*, 2: 270–72.
51. Pope, *Corr.*, 1: 140, 154.
52. Pope, *Works*, 1: 324–6, 329.
53. Addison, *Misc. Wks.*, 1: 57; Pope, *Poems*, 1: 152–9 & nn.; J.R. Moore, '*Windsor Forest* and William III', in Mack, *Essential Articles*, 232–6.
54. Pope, *Poems*, 1: 131–4, 141, 148n., 175n.
55. Ault, 31–4. In the *Miscellaneous Poems And Translations* of 1712, pp. 321–52 are missing; in the edition of 1714, *Windsor–Forest* appears on pp. 321–44, followed by the *Ode for Musick*.
56. Mack, *Pope*, 274, 865.
57. Sherburn, *Early Career*, 148.
58. 115–17.
59. Smithers, 250–56.
60. Pope, *Corr.*, 1: 173; *Poems*, 6: 96.
61. Dennis, 2: 44.
62. Pope, *Prose Works*, 1: 155–68.

63. Johnson, 2: 102.
64. Dennis, 2: 371; Pope, *Works*, 6: 398–9n.
65. *Spectator*, 5: 25–8; DNB, s.v. Dennis.
66. *Essays*, 2: 514.
67. *Spectator*, 4: 505–11. Dennis' publisher, Lintot, was also Steele's (Dennis, 2: 371; Steele, *Plays*, 107–8); and it seems possible that Addison learned of the antecedents of the *Cato* pamphlet from this source.
68. Wilde, 360.
69. *Essays*, 2: 512–13.
70. R.E. Tickell, 38–9, 47–8.
71. Spence, 1: 68–9.
72. Sherburn's reiteration of Pope's charge is accompanied by the ritual invocation of the Victorians. 'A surprising number of persons in the eighteenth century believed this', he maintains, 'but since 1800 practically no one has done so'; and he goes on to produce his 'surprising number'. He summons eight witnesses: two of whom (Cibber and Cooke) he dismisses himself, as relying on 'gossip': i.e., the campaign of defamation set on foot by Pope; four more of whom were cronies of Pope's, two of them (Bathurst and Young) noted sycophants, the other two (Lyttelton and Harte) six years old at the time of the translations, and all cited with doubt in the original source; and another of whom ('Tickell') is Pope himself, alleging the witness of others (Sherburn, *Early Career*, 131; Warton, 2: 305–9; Boswell, 991; DNB, s.v. Lyttelton, Harte & Young; Spence, 1: 69–70). Seven of the eight, then, are ruled out of court: which leaves the surprising number of one. Yet that one would seem, at first sight, to make Sherburn's case. When Tickell omitted the anonymous *Drummer* from his edition of Addison's works, Steele reprinted it with the remark: 'I hope, nobody will be wrong'd, or think himself aggrieved, that I give this rejected Work where I do; and if a certain Gentleman is injur'd by it, I will allow I have wrong'd him, upon this Issue, that (if the reputed Translator of the first Book of *Homer* shall please to give us another Book) there shall appear another good Judge in Poetry, besides Mr. *Alexander Pope*, who shall like it' (Steele, *Corr.*, 516). The inference seems clear: Tickell's Homer was not his own; it was as much the work of Addison as the anonymous comedy. Yet there is a certain anomaly to this evidence of Steele's. 'Mr. Dean *Addison*', he writes in the same place, 'Father of this memorable Man, left behind him four Children, each of whom, for excellent Talents and singular Perfections, was as much above the ordinary World, as their Brother *Joseph* was above them' (514). This does not sound a very likely conspirator. Or was Steele also part of the plot? The context, however, suggests quite another scenario. Steele made his statement, as Sherburn admits, 'when angry' (*Early Career*, 131); and for his anger there was very good reason. The Whigs, secure in the Hanoverian triumph, had split into rival factions, leaving Addison in one and Steele in the other (Williams, *Whig Supremacy*, 164–72; Smithers, 435–40; Steele, *Theatre*, 56). Into the gap left by this estrangement stepped Tickell. To Steele, he was doubly an upstart. A recent convert to the Whigs, he was rewarded through Addison with public

office, as Steele himself had not been (Smithers, 371; Winton, *Sir Richard Steele*, 5); and to this he added more intimate offence. He had been named by Addison as the editor of his writings (Smithers, 442–4); and he used this position to imply that, as Steele observed, in their joint undertakings 'I had not sufficiently acknowledged what was due to Mr. *Addison*' (Steele, *Corr.*, 508). No more infuriating injustice could have been perpetrated: lack of generosity had never been one of Steele's faults, and this was particularly so where Addison was concerned. 'I fared', he had written of his friend's role in the *Tatler*, 'like a distressed Prince who calls in a powerful Neighbour to his Aid; I was undone by my Auxiliary; when I had once called him in, I could not subsist without Dependance on him' (*Tatler*, 1: 4); while of the *Spectator* he had asked: 'how would it hurt the reputed Author of that Paper, to own that of the most beautiful Pieces under his Title, he is barely the Publisher?' (*Spectator*, 3: 434) To have such abnegation thrown back in one's face would have enraged a man far less volatile than Steele. His reply was an angry *tu quoque*: as he had been merely the 'reputed Author' of the *Spectator*, so was Tickell merely the 'reputed Translator' of the *Iliad*. Steele's anger, in fact, was such that he charged Tickell with being no poet at all, having 'adorn'd his heavy Discourse with Prose in Rhime...upon Mr. *Addison*'s Death' (Steele, *Corr.*, 517). And on this matter we know him to have been wrong. The elegy on Addison has since been recognised as Tickell's masterpiece (Butt, 299): neither he nor Addison, stated Johnson, 'ever produced nobler lines'; nor was there 'a more sublime or more elegant funeral poem to be found in the whole compass of English literature'. And from this he drew the logical inference: a poem written by Tickell after Addison's death 'could owe none of its beauties to the assistance which might be suspected to have strengthened or embellished his earlier compositions' (2: 310).

73. Blackstone, 58n.

74. R.E. Tickell, 38–9. Tickell's avowed motive in publishing was, he stated, as an advertisement for an *Odyssey* (Tickell, *Iliad*, 'To the Reader'). This, however, did not appear; and Tickell's actual motive in publishing his *Iliad* fragment is suggested by its dedication to Addison's patron Montagu, Earl of Halifax, whom he places at the head of the 'Cause of Liberty'. In his poem on the peace with France, he had taken a Tory view of that accomplishment (R.E. Tickell, 24), for which Addison commended him to the then ministry (*Spectator*, 4: 361 & n.). Nothing, however, was done for him, and he apparently began to look to the Whigs, commencing at this time a translation of the republican Lucan (R.E. Tickell, 28–35).

75. 3: 132.

76. *Essays*, 2: 505.

77. Spence, 1: 82–3.

78. Smithers, 23–4.

79. Sherburn speaks of Tickell as Addison's 'servant' in the matter (*Early Career*, 127); for Pope, he is his 'slave' (Pope, *Corr.*, 1: 306).

80. Spence, 1: 69–70.

81. *Early Career*, 127.
82. Smithers, 302–3, 371–2, 442–4.
83. Johnson, 2: 305.
84. Above, note 72.
85. Beljame, 367–8. The affront to Tickell's loyalty will have been compounded by an assault on his self-esteem. Tickell had written a series of papers for Steele's *Guardian*, in which he praised the pastoral poems of Addison's friend Ambrose Philips (105–9, 122–4, 128–30, 135–7); to which Pope, apparently feeling his own pastorals slighted, responded with a parody (160–65). Among the circumstances adduced by Sherburn to indicate that this was justified is the fact that 'Tickell in *The Prospect of Peace* called Philips "a second Spenser"' (*Early Career*, 118–19). He omits to note that Tickell in the same place had written:

Like the young spreading laurel, Pope! thy name
Shoots up with strength, and rises into fame (Tickell, *Poetical Works*, 25).

86. Johnson, 2: 145. Addison had stated the same principle against the pedantry of Dennis (*Spectator*, 5: 26).
87. Tickell, *Iliad*, 'To the Reader'.
88. R.E. Tickell, 47–8. Pope paid him the compliment he had paid Addison, of appropriation (R.E. Tickell, 46–7; Conington, 264n., 267n., 268n., 269n.; Rosslyn) compounded with ridicule (Pope, *Prose Works*, 2: 217).
89. Steele, *Corr.*, 514.
90. Addison, *Misc. Wks.*, 1: xxiv.
91. The bearing of the lines was remarked on by Macaulay (*Essays*, 2: 512).
92. *Pope*, 58.
93. Pope, *Corr.*, 1: 183 & n., 154; 201–2 & n., 185.
94. Erskine-Hill, *Social Milieu*, 46, 71.
95. Pope, *Works*, 5: 292–3. The transcriptions are now believed to have been made by Caryll's daughter (Erskine-Hill, *Social Milieu*, 89).
96. Elwin in Pope, *Works*, 1: cxxvi.
97. Pope, *Corr.*, 1: 183–4.
98. 1: 244–5. Here Philips is accused of fomenting hostility between Addison and Pope. A genuine letter of the following year, however, not printed by Pope, shows Philips working to gather subscriptions for his *Iliad* (295–6). In Pope's version, an abusive confrontation with Addison follows (263–4), on which Stephen observes: 'had such a letter been actually sent as it now stands, Addison's good nature could scarcely have held out' (*Pope*, 56). Yet Addison's good nature was such that he franked another genuine letter of a few months afterwards, again unprinted by Pope, and on business connected with his *Iliad* (Pope, *Works*, 8: 35–6 & n.).
99. *Pope*, 18. Pope had attached himself in youth to the playwright Wycherley, who grew distrustful of his extravagant flatteries: not knowing, he said, 'whether I am more Complimented than abused' (Pope, *Corr.*, 1: 14). In the published version, however, Pope 'ascribed the adulation to Wycherley, and the rebuke of it to himself' (9–10; Pope, *Works*, 1: cxxix).

100. Maynard Mack has unwittingly demonstrated the psychological impossibility of Pope's version of the relationship. In his initial account of it, the review of the *Essay on Criticism* is described as a 'puff', after which 'friendship...seems to have matured rapidly'. It is only after this has dissolved that we are informed that Addison's review had 'constituted a wanton...affront to character'. How can a 'puff' on one page, leading to rapid friendship, turn into an 'affront' on another? How could Pope -- a man who, we are assured, 'had a streak of pugnacity not found in Addison' -- have based friendship on an affront? The answer is that this is the tale told by the bogus correspondence. Here Pope is discovered swallowing his affront, burbling about his love and esteem for Addison -- or, as Mack puts it, 'radiating a healthy combination of sense, fun, affection and good will' (*Pope*, 208, 272, 278–9, 662) -- only to explode into pugnacity years afterwards and demand to know why he has been so wantonly affronted (Pope, *Corr.*, 1: 263–4).
101. 2: 125.
102. *Corr.*, 1: 263, 306.
103. Winton, *Sir Richard Steele*, 2. He had been named secretary to the regency (Smithers, 283–96).
104. Griffith, 41; Smithers, 330.
105. R.E. Tickell, 65–8. One of the more curious aspects of Pope partisanship is its taste in company. It might have gone for its Addison to Berkeley and Steele and Swift; but it prefers to huddle with Burnet. For Sherburn, his letters are 'invaluable' (*Early Career*, 116); for Ault (105) and Mack (*Pope*, 865), they are the witness of one of Addison's 'friends'. This friend wrote: 'It has very often made me smile at the pitifull soul of the Man, when I have seen Addison caressing Pope, whom at the same Time he hates worse than Belzeebub & by whom he has been more than once lampooned' (Burnet, *Letters*, 99). Ault quotes this as evidence of the surprising fact that Addison 'did not like Pope' (105); but this is not what Burnet means. It is the dislike that he thinks natural, given the lampoons, and the 'caressing' that he cannot understand. His remark occurs in the context of Addison's commendation of Pope's *Iliad* in his *Freeholder*: an action which followed naturally on his persuading Tickell to drop the rival version. This upset Pope's scenario of a sudden revelation of Addison's villainy in the matter, and he pretended to read it as an apology. Addison, he claimed to have discovered, had paid for a printed attack on him that has never been found, upon which he sent him an accusatory letter that, as Birkbeck Hill acidly observes, he forgot to forge (Johnson, 3: 133n.). 'Open warfare of this kind', states Courthope simply, 'was not in Pope's manner' (Pope, *Works*, 5: 161); and even his adherents are embarrassed by the tale (Spence, 1: 71–2; 2: 625; Sherburn, *Early Career*, 147; Ault, 114–17; Case, 189–91; Sherburn, 'Alexander Pope', 215; Dobrée, *Pope*, 38). Addison's commendation, though occurring in a journal designed to reconcile Tory voters to Whig rule, is far removed from apology. Here he repeats his strictures on the slander of fellow-authors, and passes from Pope's Homer to Lucan as the poet of liberty (*Freeholder*, 2–4, 19–22, 214–18). What Burnet could not comprehend in all this was that one might treat an opponent with

dignity. Life for him was a scramble in which no tactic was too degraded. When Tickell was promoted he composed a satire upon him, with the notion, as he avowed, that 'rightly cutting him down might put me in his place'. And when he heard that Addison's health was failing, he wrote: 'considering to how little purpose he has lived, I think he cannot dy too soon'. Addison's littleness of purpose in living, it appears, lay in his failure to provide for Tom Burnet (*Letters*, 158, 156, 78). 'I saw then at once', wrote Wilde, 'that what is said of a man is nothing. The point is, who says it' (*Letters*, 502). This is a cardinal principle of evidence; but it is lost upon the partisans of Pope.

106. Burnet, *Letters*, 127.

107. Mack, 373–5, 570, 603, 621–2, 649–51; DNB, s.v. Mordaunt.

108. Smithers, 397; Addison, *Letters*, 358–9, 501.

109. Montagu, *Letters*, 3: 65; *Essays & Poems*, 98–9. To a satirical essay of Addison's on women, she responded with one on men -- which, characteristically, he printed (*Spectator*, 4: 515–18, 556–61). Her husband and Addison had been close friends (Smithers, 227–8).

110. Swift, *Corr.*, 5: 275, citing his printer, Faulkner, who had refused to make a dishonest profit from the Pope–Swift correspondence (Stephen, *Pope*, 150).

111. Pope, *Poems*, 2: 66.

112. *Cythereia*, 92–4. These lines are a further rebuttal of the Pope–inspired thesis of a 'fair, worthy' Tickell perverted by a villainous Addison; and Sherburn attempts to evade their implications by means of an extremely tortuous argument. This is to the effect that, since there seems to have been a 'friendly understanding' between Tickell and Pope after Addison's death, Tickell's verses were written some years earlier. How this would blunt their force it is difficult to imagine; but it is in any case contradicted by Tickell's text. 'Still ADDISON shall live' (*Cythereia*, 94) clearly implies that it was written after his death. Against this, Sherburn can only marshal two ambiguous fragments of fact. The first is Tickell's acceptance of a prefatory poem by Pope for his edition of Addison's works. This rather implies the scenario I have outlined above: of a truce between Pope on the one side, and Tickell and Addison on the other, as the result of Tickell's withdrawal of his translation: a truce broken by Pope with the publication of his verses against Addison. It is confirmed by Tickell's text:

When stipulative Terms were form'd for Peace,
And Foes agreed all Hostile Acts to cease,
Sly *Pandarus*, the Battle to renew,
Amongst the Adverse Ranks a Javelin threw:
The *Greeks* saw *Sparta*'s injur'd MONARCH bleed,
But saw not who perform'd the perjur'd Deed (*Cythereia*, 93).

This seems an obvious reference to Pope's underhand publication of his lines on Addison (below, note 166). Sherburn's second attempt at barricade lies in Tickell's 'sending to Pope his sympathy or "services" in two letters' after this time' (*Early Career*, 127 & n.). But this too suggests a very different sequence of events. The notion of a 'friendly understanding' is severely shaken by a letter of slightly earlier date. 'Let us sacrifice', Pope had written to a collaborator on the *Odyssey*, '...that animal who coming, unfortunately for himself, too near our altars, stuck in the brambles, and still sticks there'. Elwin makes the obvious identification with Tickell (Pope, *Works*, 8: 65n.), who had put forward his single book of the *Iliad* ostensibly as an advertisement for an *Odyssey*. Eight years had passed, with no sign of this translation; and the natural inference is that Pope intended to glory in the fact at the expense of his erstwhile rival. Sherburn's distress is apparent from his pathetic suggestion that, while this interpretation is borne out by other letters of the time, 'some totally unknown translator may have tried to intervene' (Pope, *Corr.*, 2: 159, 161, 164n.). The sequence that suggests itself, then, is as follows. In the same month as Pope had begun to gloat over the prospective sacrifice of Tickell, Tickell's reply to himself appeared (Pope, *Corr.*, 2: 163–4; Griffith, 108). This devastating exposure of his manoeuvres will have suggested that here was an enemy to be feared. At the same time, for Tickell, it was inadvisable to provoke Pope's vindictiveness. Two months earlier, Pope had written to an official in his government office undertaking to discontinue his translation of the *Odyssey* if Tickell would 'Faithfully promise for himself, or if his Superiors will but ingage for him, that he will do Homer this justice' (*Corr.*, 2: 158). This mention of 'Superiors' carries ominous overtones. Tickell, as a recent arrival in the camp of the Whigs, and particularly since the death of Addison, who had promoted him, and of Craggs, to whom the latter had commended him, was professionally in a vulnerable position. This Pope had the power to exploit: he had access to high influence among the Whigs, and later evidence suggests that he was willing to use it against personal enemies (Mack, *Pope*, 286–9; DNB, s.v. Boyle, Richard, third Earl of Burlington; Pope, *Poems*, 3, 2: lvii–lviii). Hence, no doubt, the 'friendly understanding' that appears subsequently in the letters cited by Sherburn (Pope, *Corr.*, 2: 223; 4: 3). That it implied any change of heart by Tickell is unlikely: he had inscribed on his monument that his 'highest honour was that of having been the friend of Addison' (Smithers, 452).

113. Halsband, *Hervey*, 89–91, 109–11.

114. Pope, *Poems*, 4: 117–20 & nn.

115. Griffin, 178–9, 182–4.

116. Rogers, 88n.

117. Hervey, *Memoirs*, 13, 140–41.

118. 102–3.

119. Pope, *Poems*, 4: 380; Halsband, *Hervey*, 111–14. The duel was halted by the seconds after blood had been drawn on both sides.

120. Pope, *Poems*, 4: 119 & n.

121. Halsband, *Montagu*, 118, 140–43. Pope speaks of their collaboration on a reply to him as a species of '*Witty Fornication*' (*Prose Works*, 2: 447). He made laboured attempts to justify his animosity towards them; but Rogers concludes that he was the aggressor (133).

122. Halsband, *Montagu*, v, 8.

123. Halsband, *Montagu*, 57–8, 62–4, 75–6, 97; Pope, *Corr.*, 1: 354, 364–5, 368,

407; 2: 82; *Poems*, 6: 225; Quennell, 171.
124. Halsband, *Montagu*, 113–14, 129–32, 140–42; Montagu, *Essays & Poems*, 37; Spence, 1: 306–7; Pope, *Poems*, 4: 13.
125. Halsband, *Montagu*, 88–9; Pope, *Prose Works*, 2: 472.
126. Griffin, 183.
127. Halsband, *Montagu*, 51–2, 71–2, 80–81, 104–5, 109–12, 114, 255.
128. Pope, *Poems*, 4: xviii–xix. The relation between history and literature has proved a troubled one for Pope's admirers. Dobrée defends the bogus correspondence as an idealised self-portrait (*Pope*, 82), Mack as a framework for the no less 'rhetorical' satire (*Collected in Himself*, 60). Behind their efforts lies some such vision as that of Collingwood, of the work of art as a 'world wholly self-contained' (cited Abrams, 48). I have no difficulty with this formulation; but I fear the defender of Pope's poetry may. For the poetry of Pope, says Erskine-Hill, is 'filled with proper names' (*Social Milieu*, 5). This is so even when on occasion it appears to be otherwise. Pope changed the name of Addison to Atticus, claims David Nichol Smith, to show that he was 'thinking of the type and not the individual' (23–4). But he added a footnote reference to sources in which Addison was named (Pope, *Poems*, 4: 111n.; 5: 32–3). The disguise, indeed, is so transparent that Erskine-Hill can state of it: 'Pope now speaks out about Addison' (*Augustan Idea*, 312). None of this is a problem for the historian, who will evaluate charges against historical personages in historical terms. The problem is a problem for the justifier of Pope's work as an autonomous world. I do not accuse these of going too far in his defence; I say that they do not go far enough. They ought, in deference to his 'poetry as poetry' (Leavis, 88–9) to abandon all hope either of reconciling it to, or divorcing it from, fact. Once this was done it would be seen, in all its tortured brilliance, for what it is: a poetry of caricature: the art of a Lautrec, in which cruelty is inherent in the sense of line. But this, apart from fleeting asides (Mack, *Pope*, 489; Tillotson, 156–7), they do not care to do; and the reason is obvious. Pope himself would have had nothing to do with this business of types, or trials in rhetoric, or idealised portraits; he mounted an elaborate campaign of deception to prove that these caricatures of his were grimly, literally true: that they were, in the words of Elwin, 'an authentic register of historical...events' (Pope, *Works*, 1: cxxvii). So that if the consequences are damaging to the poetry, it is because the poet himself has hauled it before the court of fact (Reeves, 54).
129. Smithers, 353; Halsband, *Montagu*, 58.
130. Cooke, 373–4; Courthope, 154–5. To Halsband, the letter quoted in this connection as from Lady Mary to Pope is so obviously spurious that he refuses even to print it (Montagu, *Letters*, 1: xviii, 371). Sherburn, predictably, manages to stifle his doubts (Pope, *Corr.*, 1: 421–4 & nn.).
131. Smithers, 51, 129–30.
132. Pope, *Poems*, 2: 327 & n., citing Addison: 'And those who paint 'em truest praise 'em most' (*Misc. Wks.*, 1: 170). The compulsive character of the borrowing appears in the ineptitude noticed by Johnson: 'Martial exploits may be *painted*;

perhaps *woes* may be *painted*; but they are surely not *painted* by being *well–sung*: it is not easy to paint in song or to sing in colours' (2: 129).
133. Add. Ms. 4807, f. 118v.
134. Lewis, 'Addison', 145–6; *Spectator*, 2: 3.
135. DNB, s.v. Addison.
136. *Essays*, 2: 484; Swift, *Prose Works*, 5: 235.
137. Steele, *Corr.*, 514–15.
138. Pope, *Poems*, 4: 109–11.
139. *Pope*, 210.
140. Ehrenpreis, 'Swift and the Comedy of Evil', 212. Mack is compelled to agree. Pope's pretensions to virtue, he admits, are phrased 'so immoderately, so ludicrously', that he seems parodic 'to the point of farce'. But 'alas, it is not so: he appears to be deadly serious' (*Collected in Himself*, 367).
141. *Spectator*, 1: 200–204; 2: 228, 465–6 & n.; 5: 44.
142. 2: 450.
143. *Early Career*, 124; Pope, *Poems*, 6: 99–100.
144. *Pope*, 865.
145. *Spectator*, 1: 382–4; 3: 276; 4: 580–82.
146. 2: 215–16.
147. *Tatler*, 2: 462 & n.
148. 'That Addison', Macaulay further observes, 'was not in the habit of "damning with faint praise" appears from innumerable passages in his writings, and from none more than from those in which he mentions Pope' (*Essays*, 2: 514). The rest of the charges will bear as little examination. Pope in his early assaults on Addison had shown himself perfectly 'willing to wound'; but when taxed with his doings, 'afraid to strike'. The incitement of Dennis against him showed both a 'tim'rous foe', and a friend of whom one would do well to be suspicious. The persistent attacks upon a host of lesser versifiers proved that he was in the habit of dreading those who he represented as 'fools'; while the 'Testimonials' he prefixed to the *Dunciad* proved how pleasing it was to him to be 'by Flatterers besieg'd'. In his case, indeed, the charge of sitting 'attentive to his own applause' was quite literally true: the character reference in the same place is admitted by his editor to have 'all the marks of Pope's style' (Pope, *Poems*, 4: 109–11; 5: xxv).
149. Smithers, 145, 182–3.
150. Smithers, 140.
151. Swift, *Prose Works*, 15: 52
152. Ehrenpreis considers Swift to have been at fault (*Swift*, 2: 434–9). Goldgar comments that Addison was a man 'he had never ceased to respect' (*Curse of Party*, 160).
153. Swift, *Corr.*, 2: 277.
154. Addison, *Letters*, 406.
155. Aikin, 2: 125.
156. Pope, *Poems*, 4: 109–11; 6: 96.
157. 301.

158. Spence, 1: 304.
159. *Corr.*, 1: 204.
160. *Poems*, 2: 101; 4: 5 & n.
161. 1: 417–18.
162. Sherburn, *Restoration & Eighteenth Century*, 731.
163. One of Pope's collaborators on the *Odyssey* described him as a 'Caesar in poetry', who 'will bear no equal' (Pope, *Works*, 8: 106). To Fielding, he was a Domitian (Grundy, 243), and a Nero to Cibber, who observed that the character he had given Addison 'falls still short of yours' (Cibber, 10–11).
164. 168.
165. Pope, *Poems*, 5: 32–3; Spence, 1: 73; Dennis, 2: 325.
166. Pope, *Poems*, 5: 32–3; M. Ellwood Smith; *St. James' Journal*, 29, 30, 33, 34. The first of these four articles is signed by 'Townly', the next three by 'Dorimant'. Sherburn's discovery of another article by 'Dorimant' (*St. James' Journal*, 52) is not, as he implies (*Early Career*, 272–3 & n.), an argument against the authorship of the others by Pope. It is an ironic commendation of Philips' *Distrest Mother* (as the earlier ones are of Steele's *Conscious Lovers*): a play that Pope ridiculed in the same terms elsewhere (*Poems*, 6: 137, 139). Likewise the implication that 'Townly' and 'Dorimant' are different writers: both are characters in Etheredge's *Man of Mode*; and Dorimant, as the 'Rake of Wit', was a character that Pope liked to assume (Cobb, 350). To adduce against their ridicule of Dennis (including a reappearance of his unfortunate toad) the fact that Pope at this time had 'made peace' with him is disingenuous, since Dennis records, in the source that Sherburn cites (*Critical Works*, 2: 370–72), how this truce was cynically broken. And to say, as Sherburn does, that the letters are ascribed to Pope 'simply because the lines on Addison are included' is quite untrue. Smith points out that their author is an enemy to Dennis, Addison and Steele -- whom Pope also ridiculed elsewhere (*Prose Works*, 2: 210) -- that his shiftings and subterfuges are of the same kind as an earlier feigned commendation of Philips (*Guardian*, 160–65, 640–41), and the 'imposture, falsification, and trickery' practised elsewhere in Pope's publications, that the letters lead up to the lines, and that they allowed him to print them without incurring the odium of doing so under his own name.
167. Pope, *Poems*, 6: 202–7; Ault, 110–14, 119–26.
168. 126.
169. Pope, *Prose Works*, 2: 91, 217–18, 266.
170. Maresca, 73.
171. *Poems*, 4: 111n.
172. Griffith, 269, 292.
173. *Poems*, 4: 213.
174. *Poems*, 4: 111. It is a curious feature of this line that it can be read to mean that it is Atticus who does the weeping: that it is the narrator, in reality, who is Atticus.
175. 61.
176. *Pope*, 279–80.

177. Blackstone.
178. Horne, 311–12.
179. 71.
180. Pope, *Poems*, 3, 2: 141n.
181. 105.
182. Addison's paper appeared on 25 June 1712 (*Spectator*, 3: 548), Pope's on 29 September 1713 (*Guardian*, 562). Pope lived at his parents' home in Windsor Forest until April 1716 (Sherburn, 159), of which the one detail he reveals is that its trees were planted in a straight line (*Poems*, 4: 273).
183. *Epigrams*, 3, 58.
184. *Guardian*, 562.
185. *Spectator*, 3: 549, 551. Peter Martin admits that Pope has 'almost plagiarised' Addison; that his reliance upon him is 'somewhat slavish' (7). This has long been recognised. 'The most influential early advocate of...escape from the artificial in gardening', stated Elizabeth Manwaring, 'was Addison' (124). 'Addison', agreed Osvald Sirén, 'was the first wholehearted propagandist of an entirely new style of gardening' (17); 'Pope', he added, 'hardly goes farther than his predecessor' (20). Brownell pushes Pope's 'sensibility' back to the *Pastorals* of 1709 (74–8); but Addison had expressed a preference for the simple garden of Vergil over current French elaboration in 1697 (*Misc. Wks.*, 2: 2, 10–11). Brownell next goes on to Pope on Homer (78–85), whose work he described (1715) as a 'wild Paradise' (*Poems*, 7: 3). Four years earlier, Addison had contrasted him with Vergil as a 'Wilderness...without any certain Order or Regularity' (*Spectator*, 2: 129). When Pope remarks that Homer and Vergil have each pictured a garden in which they are 'wholly unconfined, and Painting at Pleasure' (*Guardian*, 562), he conflates an observation of Addison's with one of Temple's. In the 'wide Fields of Nature', Addison had written, 'the Sight wanders up and down without Confinement' (*Spectator*, 3: 549); while to Temple, Homer's garden of Alcinous seemed 'made at the pleasure of the painter' (*Works*, 3: 209). Pope refers in his essay both to Temple and to Addison by name: to Temple for this passage, and to Addison for his 'excellent' translation from Vergil (*Guardian*, 562–3). Those disposed to charity may see this as amends for his previous ridicule; those less so may suspect an uneasy sense of larger indebtedness. Even the burlesque catalogue of topiary with which his essay ends (*Guardian*, 564–5) is, as Manwaring noted (125), worked up from Addison (*Spectator*, 3: 552).
186. 180.
187. 94.
188. The original version, Pope's editors observe, 'expressed the conception of an old-fashioned Stuart monarchy' (Pope, *Poems*, 1: 249 & n.). It is only by mistaking the revision for the original that Hussey can have Addison 'apply' Pope's thesis in his *Spectator* essay of the following year (*English Gardens*, 29).
189. Plumb, *Eighteenth Century*, 52–5; Williams, *Whig Supremacy*, 156–7; Pope, *Poems*, 4: 363.
190. Sherburn, 159; Erskine-Hill, 'Political Poet', 132; Mack, *Pope*, 289.

191. Plumb, *Political Stability*, 174–9, 185–8; *Eighteenth Century*, 60–61, 68–9.
192. *Essays*, 1: 353.
193. Brooks–Davies, vi–viii; Mack, *Garden & City*, 126–8, 134–5, 169–71.
194. Pope, *Works*, 5: 357.
195. *Corr.*, 1: 306.
196. *Prose Works*, 2: 370.
197. A.L. Altenbernd, 'On Pope's "Horticultural Romanticism"', in Mack, *Essential Articles*, 142, alluding to Pope, *Poems*, 3, 2: 148; Sambrook; Walpole, *Anecdotes of Painting*, 3: 83–4.
198. Hampshire, 221.
199. *Corr.*, 21: 417.
200. Pope, *Corr.*, 2: 296. Mack observes that the 'point of visual and emotional climax' in Pope's garden was the 'obelisk to the memory of his mother' (*Garden & City*, 28); Brooks–Davies speaks of him in this connection as 'regressive' (vii).
201. *Poems*, 4: 96. Concealment was curiously twinned with liberation in Pope's consideration of landscape. In a letter to Steele, he had placed himself among those who, having 'a natural Bent to Solitude, are like Waters which may be forc'd into Fountains, and exalted to a great Height, may make a much nobler Figure and a much louder Noise, but after all run more smoothly, equally, and plentifully, in their own natural Course upon the Ground'. This was an adaptation of Addison's contrast between Terni and Versailles; but upon it Pope has overlaid another, and a very different, psychology: that of those 'who have more to hide than to shew: As for my own Part, I am one of those of whom *Seneca* says, *Tam Umbratiles sunt, ut putent in turbido esse quicquid in luce est*. Some Men, like Pictures, are fitter for a Corner than a full Light' (*Spectator*, 3: 518). The combination may seem incomprehensible; but it becomes less so when one remembers that Addison had recently lifted Pope's secret nature out of the shadows. This was an event so traumatic that it is not surprising to find the association repeated two decades later in those 'rules' of gardening he had appropriated from his self–chosen rival. Here, again, we learn that the natural landscape is one where 'half the skill is decently to hide'; while the formal garden offers no such opportunity: 'no artful wildness to perplex the scene'. The attraction of the irregular, then, for Pope is bound up with its capacity for concealment and confusion. But what is most striking about these 'rules', as Pope has adapted them, is that the ultimate hatefulness of symmetry lies in its admission of an equal: 'Grove nods at grove, each Alley has a brother' (*Poems*, 3, 2: 142, 148–9). This line has a complex prehistory in the saga of Pope's hostilities. It is modelled on a couplet by Dennis which had been quoted by Addison (*Spectator*, 1: 201), and alluded to by Pope when he had attempted to turn Dennis' observations back upon him (*Prose Works*, 1: 15).
202. Ripley Hotch, 'The Dilemma of an Obedient Son: Pope's *Epistle to Dr. Arbuthnot*', Mack & Winn, 440; Pope, *Poems*, 4: 109–11.
203. *Corr.*, 21: 417.
204. Mack, *Garden & City*, 63–5, 287–8.
205. Spence, 1: 74.

206. *Misc. Wks.*, 1: 35, 39.
207. Smithers, 97.
208. 261.
209. 1: 93–4.
210. 281.
211. *Spectator*, 1: 44.
212. 2: 482.
213. Budgell, *Cleomenes*, 207–10.
214. Ketton–Cremer, *Walpole*, 123, 113; Low, 238–9; Gibbon, *Autobiographies*, 190.
215. Budgell, *Bee*, 1: 27.
216. *Spectator*, 1: 2, 5.
217. 4: 470–71.
218. 4: 498–500, citing Horace, *Satires*, 1, 3: 18 (altered) & *Aeneid*, 2: 471–5.
219. 4: 505–11.
220. 4: 492 & n., citing Nichols, 1788–89.
221. *Spectator*, 1: xliv; 2: 360–61.

CHAPTER 4

1. Green, *Anne*, 247; Swift, *Prose Works*, 15: 230; 16: 635, 637.
2. Ehrenpreis, *Swift*, 1: 257; Swift, *Prose Works*, 15: 230–31.
3. 16.
4. *Essays*, 2: 114.
5. 1: 264.
6. Elias finds Swift 'implicitly contemptuous' of Temple (159). As Ehrenpreis sees it, however, he 'admired Temple's character and his mind' (*Swift*, 1: 92).
7. *Essays*, 1: 265.
8. Burlingame, 157.
9. Jebb, 40–54.
10. Jebb, 38, 128, 137–8, 219–20.
11. 'Dissertation Upon Phalaris', 5.
12. Jebb, 64–5, 76–8.
13. Boyle, Preface, 199–200.
14. Vergil, *Eclogues*, 1: 53–5; Swift, *Prose Works*, 1: 151.
15. Arnold, 263.
16. Swift, *Prose Works*, 1: 109–10.
17. Temple, *Works*, 3: 235.
18. Lamb, 4: 44–7.
19. *Works*, 3: 234.
20. Woodbridge, *Temple*, 128–31, 254–60.
21. *Works*, 3: 219, 224, 229–30.
22. 3: 195.
23. *Essays*, 1: 229.

24. Temple, *Works*, 3: 195–206.
25. 203–6. Mayo finds Temple's urbanity on the subject 'insidious' (94).
26. Koyré, 98–9, 108–9, 282–3, citing the burning of Bruno, the condemnation of Copernicus and Galileo, and the apparent prevarication of Descartes. It is difficult to speak of a debate, observes Aylmer, 'when one side is disabled from free expression of its viewpoint' (46).
27. Herm, 95.
28. Jung, *Memories, Dreams, Reflections*, 181–2.
29. Willey, *Seventeenth Century*, 13–14; King, 30–37.
30. Koestler, *Sleepwalkers*, 370–72.
31. Smith, *Wotton*, 1: 5, 486; 2: 469.
32. Donne, 213–14.
33. Nicolson, '"New Astronomy"', 428–9; *Breaking of the Circle*, 119–20; Donne, 214.
34. Spink, 103, 138; Jones, *Epicurean Tradition*, 178–80.
35. Dryden, 13. While deploring his atheism, Dryden admired Lucretius' 'sublime and daring genius' (Hadzsits, 297–8). Hooker speaks of his interest in the topic as an obsession (131).
36. Muirhead, 27–30, 33.
37. Marburg, 15–16.
38. *Early Essays*, 157.
39. Woodbridge, *Temple*, 25.
40. 124, 125, 128.
41. 219, 211.
42. 124, 125.
43. 209–10.
44. *Works*, 10: 407–8.
45. Bennet, *Meetings with Jung*, 64.
46. Browne, 76–7.
47. *Books & Characters*, 39–40, 43.
48. Browne, 229.
49. DNB, s.v. Burnet; Burnet, *History of My Own Time*, 2: 70. Temple, he goes on, 'was a corrupter of all that came near him, and he delivered himself up wholly to study ease and pleasure'. This was to take 'epicure' in its grosser connotation; and Swift, when he came to annotate this passage, denied it with vehemence. 'Sir William Temple', he stated, 'was a man of virtue, to which Burnet was a stranger' (*Prose Works*, 5: 276).
50. Lucretius, *De Rerum Natura*, 1: 146–634.
51. *Inferno*, 10: 13–15.
52. Jebb, 20–22; Mayo, 192–3.
53. *Works*, 3: 200–201. Temple's religion, claimed his sister, 'was y[t] of the church of England he was borne & bred in...' She has, however, been convicted elsewhere of distortion in the interests of family respectability (Ehrenpreis, *Swift*, 2: 340–42); and she reveals the truth unwittingly in what follows: '...& thought

nobody ought to change since it must require more time and pains than ones life can furnish to make a true judgement of that wch interest & folly were commonly the motives too' (Temple, *Early Essays*, 31). This lack of enthusiasm for the state religion was noted by others, including Princess Mary (Woodbridge, *Temple*, 192), of whom Burnet was the close confidant (DNB, s.v. Burnet). Temple's sister's remark, however, that he was accustomed to resign himself to divine providence (Temple, *Early Essays*, 25) is borne out by his will (Courtenay, 2: 484). Temple in his maturity, then, might be described as a deist, agnostic towards the claim of any given theology: a position that Bentley regarded as tantamount to atheism (Jebb, 21–2).
54. *Works*, 3: 202.
55. Swift, *Prose Works*, 1: 110.
56. A point noted by Ward (*Swift*, 94) and Elias (168–9).
57. Bailey, 104.
58. *De Rerum Natura*, 4: 33–45; Traugott, 116–17.
59. *History of My Own Time*, 2: 70.
60. *Works*, 3: 334–5.
61. 3: 323–4. Temple posited a causal link between Greek and Chinese philosophy, citing the classical accounts of journeys into India (III, 436–43). Creech had made the same connection (*T. Lucretius Carus*, 'The Life'; Mayo, 10).
62. Needham, 2: 453–4; Welch, 158–9.
63. While the Confucian attitude is linked with the Stoic (Needham, 2: 63–7).
64. Waley, *Three Ways of Thought*, 45–6.
65. Capra, 95.
66. Blyth, 1: 149.
67. *Works*, 3: 230.
68. *Essays*, 1: 207.
69. *Early Essays*, 149–50. 'Independency' suggests a parallel with Temple's political thought: as Macpherson sees the atomic theory behind the individualism of Locke (243).
70. Woodbridge, *Temple*, 23.
71. *De Rerum Natura*, 1: 951–1113. A medieval adaptation (the *Roman de Thèbes*) of a classical text (the *Thebaid*) automatically turns an open landscape into an enclosed garden (Pearsall & Salter, 54–5).
72. Needham, 3: 219–21. The 'romantic aestheticism' of the Chinese landscape artists, says Waley, 'had always a fuller intensity, for no conception of a personal Divinity competed with it' (*Chinese Painting*, 137). The notion of a celestial lawgiver, on the other hand, in unified and centralised Babylon, left the west with a natural order dominated by a 'rational personal being' (Needham 2: 518, 533–43, 581). In painting, the contrast appears as the moving focus of China and the single–point perspective of Europe (Rowley, 61–3).
73. Koestler, *Sleepwalkers*, 372–3.
74. Nokes, 297.
75. Ehrenpreis also suggests that the malady had emotional overtones (*Swift*, 2:

298–300).
76. Ehrenpreis, *Swift*, 1: 106.
77. Swift, *Poems*, 59.
78. Ehrenpreis, *Swift*, 2: 342.
79. *Prose Works*, 1: 99.
80. *Poems*, 59.
81. Ehrenpreis, *Swift*, 1: 145–8.
82. Swift, *Tale*, 314, 324.
83. Swift, *Poems*, 164, 671; Ehrenpreis, *Swift*, 2: 632–3.
84. Hall, '"Inverted Hypocrite"', 39.
85. Ehrenpreis, *Swift*, 3: 69–70; Hall, '"Inverted Hypocrite"', 42–4.
86. Swift, *Tale*, 321–6; Brown, *Life Against Death*, 179–201.
87. Swift, *Prose Works*, 1: 107 & n.
88. Hunter, 130; Nicolson, *Science & Imagination*, 176, 193–7; Swift, *Poems*, 531. Ehrenpreis finds Lilliput and Brobdingnag foreshadowed in Pascal's response to infinity (*Personality*, 91, 98–9). The insight was cross-fertilised, no doubt, by Irish myth (Grennan, 188–97). Burke's nightmare vision of conspiracy as a gigantic spider (*Works*, 7: 51) is acutely noted by Kramnick as 'Swiftian' (36).
89. *Personality*, 92–8. Conversely, Elias has detected seepage from the *Tale of a Tub* into the *Battle of the Books* (186–94).
90. Johnston, 188–200; Yeats, *Plays*, 602.
91. 484.
92. Woodbridge, *Temple*, 239.
93. Alcorn, 116.
94. 1: 145–6.
95. Lawrence, 541.
96. *Works*, 3: 202.

CHAPTER 5
1. *Spectator*, 4: 529–31.
2. *Swift*, 2: 238–9.
3. Passmore, 19–22; Tuveson, 21–2, 34.
4. Burnet, *Sacred Theory*, 1: 135–6, 172.
5. Macklem, 6–8.
6. Willey, *Eighteenth Century*, 38.
7. Burnet, *Archaeologiae Philosophicae*, 280–81.
8. DNB, s.v. Burnet.
9. Smithers, 39.
10. 'Resolved great hidden truths to trace,
Each learned fable you despise;
And, pleased, enjoy the famed disgrace
To think and reason, singly wise:
Each tale reject by time allowed,
And nobly leave the erring crowd...

New heavens revealed, the silver train
The sun beneath their waves admire;
And gliding thro' th'enlightened main,
Gaze at each star's unwonted fire.
Well pleased the moon's bright orb survey,
Trembling along their azure play'
(Addison, *Misc. Wks.*, 1: 285–9; *Works*, 6: 583–5).

11. Addison, *Works*, 6: 607–12; *Misc. Wks.*, 2: 466–9.
12. Nicolson & Rousseau, 137–56.
13. Pope, *Corr.*, 1: 26.
14. 1: 185–6, 201–3.
15. Sherburn's sneer at Addison in this connection as 'that supposed model of orthodoxy' ('Pope and "The Great Shew of Nature"', 310) is an excellent example of cyclical argument: it is the followers of Pope who suppose him a 'model of orthodoxy'.
16. *Corr.*, 1: 185, 202.
17. *Pope*, 162–3.
18. Nuttall, 179–88. Nuttall demonstrates how Pope, in a panic over the attacks on his position, altered his correspondence to reflect on the 'guide, philosopher and friend' who had influenced it (Pope, *Poems*, 3, 1: 166).
19. Addison, *Misc. Wks.*, 1: 356.
20. Empson's ingenious defence of the double reading in Pope is vitiated by its failure to explore its historical dimension: except in his suggestion that its 'original antithesis' is close to 'that between art and nature' (*Seven Types of Ambiguity*, 203–5): which is of course the basis of Addison's garden aesthetic.
21. Temple, *Works*, 3: 230.
22. 306.
23. Koestler, *Sleepwalkers*, 505–6, 509–17.
24. Koyré, 178–9. It would be another century before Laplace, answering Bonaparte's question about the role of divinity in the universe, would reply that he had found no need of that hypothesis (276).
25. *Spectator*, 4: 532.
26. 417. 'Mysteries', C.S. Lewis also found, 'attract him' ('Addison', 153).
27. *Spectator*, 2: 213–14.
28. *Paradiso*, 33: 145.
29. Mitford, *Sun King*, 11.
30. Thacker, *History of Gardens*, 152–3. Louis' infinity was explicitly asserted (Weiss, 66).
31. *Letters*, 8.
32. Thacker, *History of Gardens*, 153.
33. *Spectator*, 3: 541.
34. 36.
35. *Spectator*, 3: 545–6.
36. 37. Addison resolved, says Tuveson, the aesthetic dilemma which had puzzled

Burnet by separating the Great from the Beautiful (38).
37. *Spectator*, 3: 541.
38. 37.
39. *Spectator*, 3: 540–53.
40. *Chain of Being*, 15–16.

CHAPTER 6
1. Possin, 97–108.
2. Addison, *Misc. Wks.*, 2: 122, 168.
3. 'Subjects', 213, 223.
4. Röthlisberger, *Paintings* 1: 6; Koestler, *Sleepwalkers*, 497–8.
5. Röthlisberger, *Paintings* 1: 41, 167; Fox, 163.
6. West, 89–92; Frank, 47, 102–6.
7. McKay, 'Virgilian Landscape', 148.
8. Blunt, 301.
9. *quam magnus Orion,*
*cum pedes incedit medii per maxima Nerei*
*stagna viam scindens, umero supereminet undas,*
*aut summis referens annosam montibus ornum*
*ingrediturque solo et caput inter nubila condit*
(*Aeneid*, 10: 763–7).
10. *Spectator*, 3: 540–4. Manwaring observes that Addison 'paints a Claudian landscape' from Albano (11).
11. *Misc. Wks.*, 2: 168–9.
12. *Corr.*, 13: 231. 'As in my journey from *Rome* to *Naples* I had *Horace* for my guide, so I had the pleasure of seeing my voyage, from *Naples* to *Rome*, described by *Virgil*' (Addison, *Misc. Wks.*, 2: 128).
13. Trilling, 46.
14. Lecky, 4: 84–5; 5: 72n.; *Aeneid*, 4: 340–44.
15. Boswell, 325.
16. *Spectator*, 3: 549, citing Horace *Epistles*, 2, 2: 77 & Vergil, *Georgics*, 2: 467–70.
17. Pope's claim, then, to have discovered the irregular layout in 'the Taste of the Ancients in their Gardens' (*Guardian*, 562), was, like so much else of his in this connection, a distorted appropriation from Addison. His statement was repeated, however, by Robert Castell, in his claim that the classical garden contained 'a close Imitation of Nature' (116). His text was Pliny, but the meaning he extracted from him was as forced and unnatural as Pope's earlier attempt upon Martial. The strongest statement he was able to find was Pliny's observation that from his garden 'you have the View of a Meadow not less beautiful by Nature, than these the fore-mentioned Works of Art': *Pratum inde non minus Natura, quam superiora illa, Arte visendum* (83). This might seem an anticipation of Addison's remark that 'there is generally in Nature something more Grand and August, than what we meet with in the Curiosities of Art' (*Spectator*, 3: 551); but in fact it is its

opposite. Pliny's contention is that nature sometimes comes up to the level of art; and it is clear that his gardens are overwhelmingly formal. There is a clearing set symmetrically with small plane–trees (*medium in Spatium brevioribus utrinque Platanis adornatur*): which gives, he feels, the effect that 'a sudden Imitation of the Country seems accidentally introduced' (*subita velut illati Ruris Imitatio*). If so, it is only, as in Temple's remembered Moor Park, in terms of its context. Here 'the Box describes a thousand different Forms; sometimes in Letters which tell the Name of the Master, sometimes that of the Artificer: in some Places they grow like Cones, and in other Globular' (89). It would be difficult to find a more apt illustration of the artifice that Addison ridiculed (*Spectator*, 3: 552); and indeed his champion is forced to concede that Pliny's trees were 'cut into unwarrantable Forms'. The true source of Castell's natural garden is unwittingly revealed in his language. The Romans, he claims, went through three phases, the first being simple and natural, a 'rough Manner'. Growing dissatisfied with this, they turned to a 'Manner of laying out the Ground and Plantations of Gardens by the Rule and Line'. This is a clear echo of Addison: 'the Inhabitants of that Country laugh at the Plantations of our *Europeans*, which are laid out by the Rule and Line' (*Spectator*, 3: 552). And the supposed third manner of the Romans, a combination of the former two, is simply a transcription of Temple, consisting of a 'close Imitation of Nature; where, tho' the Parts are disposed with the greatest Art, the Irregularity is still preserved; so that their Manner may not improperly be said to be an artful Confusion, where there is no Appearance of that Skill which is made use of'. Castell, indeed, admits that his hypothetical Roman style is reconstructed from 'the Accounts we have of the present Manner of Designing in *China*' (116–17). Masson has since argued that the sacred landscape, the sanctuary in the wild, was suggested in Roman gardens (33–6); but the Pope–Castell 'Taste of the Ancients' is a backward projection of Temple and Addison.

18. Voitle, 5–7.

19. Shaftesbury, *Second Characters*, xvii, 21–3.

20. *Spectator*, 1: 268. On Gothic as irregular, see chapter 7.

21. Potter, 116.

22. *Palladio & English Palladianism*, 178, 183. The contrast is heightened by the baroque aesthetic of movement and incompletion (Wölfflin, 58–63; Maravall, 218–19).

23. Fink, 157.

24. Ackerman, 19, 54–65, 160–62, 165–7; Wittkower, *Architectural Principles*, 70–72, 126–42.

25. Ackerman, 75–8, 128–9, 143–4, 156–8.

26. Lees–Milne, 113; Summerson, *Architecture in Britain*, 318. Elsewhere Summerson observes that this had been preceded by the patronage of a 'wide and and important circle of Whigs', of whom Montagu was one ('Classical Country House', 549); while Addison's other patron, Somers, helped supervise Burlington's education (Harris, 36–7).

27. Lees–Milne, 115–16, 122–5, 127–8, 139–40, 149–53. A great deal of labour

has been expended upon the thesis that, in the words of Reuben Brower, Pope and Burlington were 'fellow workers in the latest phase of the Renaissance' (283). Some, indeed, would imply that Pope's achievement as a poet is contingent upon his embodying this role. 'Pope', writes Howard Erskine–Hill, 'pays honour to the paradox at the heart of the concept of the Renaissance, in active reverence for the past': it was necessary for him 'to be able to admire' (*Social Milieu*, 321, 325–6). For Maynard Mack, this is the motive out of which sprang an ambitious aim: 'the goal of enlarging and enriching the national culture by causing to be poured into it the great works of antiquity' (*Garden & City*, 39). More than a public programme, however, this was a personal quest. Pope, says Tillotson, is 'half a Roman poet': his Roman predecessors 'help him in his search for what may be accounted beautiful and for the substance of the good life'; they 'deepen his mood and strengthen his sense of what is worthy' (11). And among these figures, it is asserted, two stand supreme. In his rural retirement, states Mack, he created a larger historical personality by identifying himself with Horace; and he quotes Brower to the effect that his career is 'progressively an *Imitatio Horati*' (*Garden & City*, 233–4, citing Brower, 165). But his 'profoundest kinship', urges Tillotson, 'is with Virgil' (11): a claim with which Mack implicitly concurs. 'Always in Pope', he writes, 'the thing that is being lost, or lost and recovered, or lost and recovered and lost again, is a vision of the civilised community, the City' (*Garden & City*, 4–5); and the connection is made explicit on a later page: the throne, 'usurped, or...occupied by shadows' awaits in vain a monarch 'who will fulfil in Britain the vision of law and government' of the sixth *Aeneid* (234–5). All this, as exegesis, is unexceptionable: it is the manner in which Pope represented himself. But the connoisseur of his psychology will have seen how it was bound to end. These poets, he now discovered -- these exemplars, these household gods -- these poets lacked integrity. Vergil had, it seems, in advance of the fact, been on the wrong side of the current quarrel between the king's minister and the parliamentary opposition. Pope accordingly discovered that to the republican Cato, the Roman poet had 'pay'd one honest line'. In private, he made it clear that it was Vergil's *only* 'honest line'; and, he added, he had begun to have doubts even of that (*Poems*, 4: 320; Spence, 1: 229–30). Pope was at the end of his monumental *Imitations of Horace* when he made this discovery. But Horace, too, it seems, was not above suspicion. In an epitaph he composed for himself disdaining burial in Westminster Abbey, he bade its 'HEROES, and KINGS' to keep their distance from one who 'never flatter'd Folks like you...' He affected, remarks Elwin, a 'disdain of royalty'; but was 'ready enough to flatter it when he had his own ends to serve'. In a reign that seemed to favour his native Toryism, he had compared the corpulent and prolific Queen Anne to the goddess Diana (Pope, *Works*, 1: 331). But by some strange dodge of the brain, this was not flattery of royalty. Nor was it flattery of heroes when he asserted that his military friend Peterborough had 'conquer'd *Spain*' (*Poems*, 4: 19), when in fact he had lost it (Trevelyan, *Q. Anne*, 2: 146–59). It was no doubt, then, with a glowing sense of moral exaltation that, in declining to enter the national pantheon, Pope declared: 'Let Horace blush, and Virgil too' (*Poems*, 6: 376). And it was with a certain unwitting genius that his literary executor placed what Stephen calls this 'stupid inscription' over his grave in Twickenham church (*Pope*, 209). Pope has a different, though in its own fashion no less appropriate, monument at Stourhead, the great masterpiece of the English classical garden. Here his grotto is imitated, as a representation of the Vergilian underworld (Woodbridge, *Landscape & Antiquity*, 2, 34–6). But it was ultimately impossible for Pope to enter into the feelings with which Dante had cried out to the Roman poet: *O degli altri poeti onore e lume* (*Inferno*, 1: 82), and made him his guide through the circles of hell. For Pope, the classical poets were necessarily transformed into versions of the inevitable rival; and he accused Vergil, as he had accused Addison, of what was true of himself: that he was 'very sparing in his commendations of other poets' (Spence, 1: 230–31). Being what he was, Pope could not resist the temptation to subvert that which alone could give his own work value. It was not possible, however, to vex so majestic a spirit. He had come through a deeper and more desolate darkness, invulnerable, bearing a golden bough.

28. *Misc. Wks.*, 2: 50.

29. Introduction, Jourdain, 16.

30. 61–2.

31. 68, 71. Moore traces what has been described as the 'pre–Romantic streak' in Pope (Nuttall, 192) to the influence of Shaftesbury (Moore, 84), as does Robertson, who suggests that his doctrines were filtered through Bolingbroke, but unacknowledged by the latter because of 'Shaftesbury's unanswerable indictment of his career in the *Characteristics*' (Introduction, Shaftesbury, *Characteristics*, 1: xxv–vi & n.; 2: 261–2 & n.). Once Pope was himself suspected of heterodoxy, he attempted a characteristic denial by 'attacking the heterodoxies of others' (89), amongst whom he explicitly repudiated Shaftesbury (Pope, *Poems*, 5: 389–90 & nn.): whose writings, he claimed, had 'done more harm to revealed religion in England than all the works of infidelity put together'. It is in this context that Robertson -- and not Leslie Stephen, as Sherburn states (*Early Career*, 23) -- describes Pope as 'the most untruthful man of his age' (Shaftesbury, *Characteristics*, 1: xxvii).

32. Moore, 73.

33. *Characteristics*, 2: 123. The passage that follows is sometimes cited in histories of the landscape garden: ''Tis true, said I, Theocles, I own it. Your genius, the genius of the place, and the Great Genius have at last prevailed. I shall no longer resist the passion growing in me for things of a natural kind, where neither art nor the conceit or caprice of man has spoiled the genuine order by breaking in upon that primitive state. Even the rude rocks, the mossy caverns, the irregular unwrought grottos and broken falls of water, with all the horrid graces of the wilderness itself, as representing Nature more, will be the more engaging, and appear with a magnificence beyond the formal mockery of princely gardens...However, said I, all those who are deep in this romantic way are looked upon, you know, as a people either plainly out of their wits, or overrun with

melancholy and enthusiasm' (125). Hussey suggests that this apostrophe, printed in 1709, was the source of Addison's reform of gardens in 1712 (*English Gardens & Landscapes*, 28–9). While it may indeed have reinforced Addison's thought, it cannot have initiated it: he had written of the 'Genius of the place' at Fontainebleau in 1699 (*Letters*, 11), and his contrast between the magnificence of nature at Terni and its princely mockery at Versailles was published in 1705 (*Misc. Wks.*, 2: 83).
34. *Second Characters*, 120. For Shaftesbury and his school, writes Stephen, 'Nature...was the new temple' (*English Thought*, 2: 14).
35. *History of England*, 1: 61–2.
36. *Second Characters*, 120, 126.
37. Hill, *Century of Revolution*, 219; Williamson, *Contexts*, 218–19; Tucker, 14, 93–4.
38. 89, 105. Weber adduces Buddhist and Cistercian puritanism as transformative forces in art (*India*, 237).
39. *Paradise Lost*, 4: 237–43; Walpole *Anecdotes*, 3: 72–4.
40. Walpole, *Anecdotes*, 3: 73nn.; *Faerie Queene*, 2, 12: 58–9; Tasso, 16, 8–10, where the 'crooked Paths' of the maze are also anticipated.
41. Donne, 215.
42. Panichas, 41–5; DeWitt, 16–17; Haynes, 100. Westfall sees in the preoccupation with the quincunx of Sir Thomas Browne a preference for Plato over Epicurus (147).
43. *Studies in Words*, 251, citing 'Il Penseroso', 69–70.
44. Hill, *Milton*, 53–4.
45. *Studies in Words*, 250–51, 254–5.
46. Jebb, 181–2, 188–9.
47. Bentley, *Milton*, 1: 579–87; 4: 268–85.
48. *Pastoral*, 163.
49. Bentley, *Milton*, 4: 268–75.
50. *Pastoral*, 173, 177.
51. Bentley, *Milton*, 4: 705–8.
52. *Pastoral*, 169, 190–91.
53. *Paradise Lost*, 2: 636–42.
54. *Pastoral*, 171.
55. 678, 712.
56. 2: 14.
57. Hill, *Milton*, 173–6.
58. Phillips, 200.
59. 3: 355.
60. *Characteristics*, 1: 91–2.
61. 3: 356.
62. *Tatler*, 2: 398–9.
63. *Paradise Lost*, 1: 446–57.
64. *Spectator*, 3: 87.

65. Temple, *Select Letters*, 213–16.
66. Killeshin was a site of great importance in early times (O'Donovan, 2: 81). A nineteenth–century clerical scholar gave a saint Diarmaid as its founder; but confessed that nothing was known of him, and that the name was a common one among the abbots of the place (Comerford, 3: 241, 243). Somewhat later, another pair of clerical scholars doubted the existence of this first Diarmaid, equating him with one of the later figures (O'Hanlon & O'Leary, 1: 259); and it is a detail preserved by Comerford which offers the vital clue to the identity of this strangely divided and anonymous figure: a local tradition that the church was built to commemorate a 'prince who met his death in this place whilst engaged in hunting' (Comerford, 3: 245–6). The Celtic god Diarmaid, lover of Gráinne, goddess of nature, met his death in this fashion (Mac Cana, 111–15, 120), in a precise parallel to the myth of Tammuz–Adonis (Frazer, 426–31).
67. Temple, *Works*, 3: 535–6; *Poems*, 69–79.
68. Jung & Kerényi, 26–7.
69. Weber, *Judaism*, 187–93.
70. *Song of Songs*, 145–53.
71. James, 65; Jung, *Animus & Anima*, 66–7; Mac Cana, 131; Stephen, *English Thought*, 1: 215–16 & n.; Knight, *Priapus*, 13–23; Moss & Cappannari, 64–5.
72. Ogg, *Charles II*, 1.
73. Draper, 89, no doubt influenced by Psalm 19; Jung, *Works*, 14: 515.
74. *Paradise Lost*, 4: 219–22.

## CHAPTER 7

1. Walpole, *Corr.*, 13: 206.
2. Plumb, *Walpole*, 1: 368; 2: 81–7; Williams, *Whig Supremacy*, 180–81.
3. Lang, *Handel*, 133, 142, 483–4; Hatton, 265. It is scarcely coincidence that what has been called Handel's 'musical image of a tree' -- *Ombra mai fù* (Bronson, 20) -- should have been composed in Georgian England.
4. Plumb, *Walpole*, 1: 201–3; *Georges*, 41–3; Hatton, 49–64, 132–6, 172.
5. Hatton, 90n., 130–32, 170–71, 290–91, 370.
6. Trench, 18, 39–40, 173–4; Plumb, *Georges*, 69, 72; *Walpole*, 2: 157.
7. Trench, 10, 40, 156, 200–202; Plumb, *Georges*, 44–5, 69–71; *Walpole*, 2: 157–62.
8. Trench, 40–41; Walpole, *Corr.*, 23: 313 & n.
9. Trench, 75–7; Hatton, 197–214.
10. Plumb, *Walpole*, 2: 162–6.
11. Plumb, *Walpole*, 1: 286; 2: 164–6; Trench, 200.
12. Plumb, *Walpole*, 2: 167–76; *Georges*, 68–9; Trench, 132–6.
13. Plumb, *Walpole*, 2: 80–81, 91–102; Owen, 38–9.
14. Plumb, *Walpole*, 2: 101; Coxe, 1: 758–9.
15. George I said that Walpole could turn stones into gold; while to George II, as to his subjects, the prime minister was the Great Man (Trench, 133, 175; Plumb,

*Walpole*, 2: 80–81).
16. Plumb, *Georges*, 41; Trench, 110–13.
17. Plumb, *Walpole*, 2: 249; Hussey, *Early Georgian*, 76.
18. Ketton-Cremer, *Gray*, 37–8; *Walpole*, 56–9; Walpole, *Corr.*, 13: 199–200.
19. Walpole, *Corr.*, 13: 208–9, 217; Gray, *Corr.*, 1: 166–7.
20. Walpole, *Corr.*, 13: 222–4; 21: 31.
21. Ketton-Cremer, *Walpole*, 32–6, 68–9; *Gray*, 25, 38–42; Walpole, *Corr.*, 13: 192; Gray, *Corr.*, 1: 170.
22. Ketton-Cremer, *Walpole*, 59, 64–6, 68–76; Walpole, *Corr.*, 13: 200–201; 28: 68; Gray, *Corr.*, 1: 172.
23. Williams, *Whig Supremacy*, 181–2; Plumb, *Walpole*, 2: 249–50, 280–81, 330–33; Robinson, 31–4.
24. Robinson, 70. Cobham had been ennobled by George I and sent to the Emperor to announce his accession (34).
25. Hussey, *English Gardens*, 94, 106–9.
26. Robinson, 86–7; *Tatler*, 2: 224–5. Horace declared himself to have 'no patience at building and planting a satire' (Walpole, *Corr.*, 35: 76 & n.).
27. Robinson, 90–91.
28. Plumb, *Walpole*, 2: 238, 281; *Georges*, 90–92; Willcox, 57–63.
29. Young, *Fred*, 130, 167; Marshall, 162–4; Trench, 187; Hervey, 234–5; Robinson, 95; Mack, *Pope*, 755–7. Perhaps the most ingenious transition in the *Golden Treasury* is that from Gray's ode on a drowned cat, through Philips' on a female infant, to the martial strains of 'Rule, Britannia' (nos. 120–22). Since the infant was a Pulteney, and the cat Horace Walpole's -- with Gray's feline 'a favourite has no friend!' so applicable to his father -- all three are united by the theme of opposition to the Great Man.
30. Young, *Fred*, 145–6; Williams, *Whig Supremacy*, 209–10; Walpole, *Corr.*, 17: 170–71; 13: 11n.
31. Walpole, *Corr.*, 17: 243, 299, 318; Owen, 87; Young, 161–2.
32. Williams, *Whig Supremacy*, 238; Owen, 115–17; Pope, *Poems*, 4: 330–37; Mack, *Pope*, 802–4; Dickinson, *Bolingbroke*, 272–5; Gibbon, *Autobiographies*, 30.
33. Walpole, *Corr.*, 1: 225–6 & n., 240–41; 2: 1; 11: 97 & n.; 17: 245–6; 29: 39n.; 35: 142 & n.; Ketton-Cremer, *Walpole*, 26–9, 44–5. Walpole's *Mysterious Mother* is a drama of oedipal incest (Ketton-Cremer, *Walpole*, 251–4); and Halsband suggests that his dislike of Lady Mary Wortley Montagu derived from her association with his mother's rival. He portrayed her in the terms made current by Pope, in particular of the syphilis which in a more sober mood he admitted to be smallpox (Halsband, *Montagu*, 118–19, 200–201, 203–4, 218 & n.).
34. Walpole, *Corr.*, 17: 248; Ketton-Cremer, *Walpole*, 84–9; Coxe, 1: 762.
35. Walpole, *Corr.*, 35: 186.
36. 20: 119.
37. Haecker, 118; Psalm 78 (Vulgate).
38. Henderson, 179–80; Lovejoy, *Ideas*, 136–7.
39. Clark, *Gothic Revival*, 11–27; Clapham; Colvin; Summerson, *Architecture in*

*Britain*, 172–4, 219, 253–4, 313–14; McCarthy, *Gothic*, 66.
40. McCarthy, *Gothic*, 5–9, 27; Summerson, *Architecture in Britain*, 395–401; Walpole, *Corr.*, 20: 127. Later Walpole saw Fingal's Cave as proof that 'Nature loves Gothic architecture' (*Corr.*, 1: 329).
41. Henderson, 180; Lovejoy, *Ideas*, 153.
42. Henderson, 180; Lewis, *Walpole*, 101.
43. Panofsky, 7, 28–35, 44–51, 58.
44. Henderson, 49–70.
45. Panofsky, 11–14.
46. Henderson, 104–23.
47. *Ideas*, 165.
48. *Architecture in Britain*, 403.
49. *Anecdotes of Painting*, 1: 119.
50. Ketton-Cremer, *Walpole*, 137.
51. *Corr.*, 19: 414, 486 & n.; 37: 269.
52. Walpole, *Otranto*, 16–17.
53. *Corr.*, 1: 88.
54. Ketton-Cremer, *Walpole*, 193–4.
55. Lewis, 'Genesis', 88–90.
56. *Otranto*, 5–6.
57. *Corr.*, 23: 350.
58. 1: 88.
59. *Ars Poetica*, 7–9.
60. *Otranto*, xii–xiii, citing epigraph to the second edition.
61. *Otranto*, 32–3.
62. *Otranto*, x, citing *Corr.*, 3: 260: *j'ai laissé courir mon imagination; les visions et les passions m'échauffaient. Je l'ai fait en dépit des règles, des critiques, et des philosophes...*
63. *Otranto*, 7–8.
64. Walpole, *Corr.*, 29: 256.
65. Tucker, 29, citing Henry Wharton, *Enthusiasm of the Church of Rome* (1688).
66. Lovejoy, *Ideas*, 138, citing Evelyn, *Account of Architects and Architecture* (1697).
67. Henderson, 183–4, citing Bacon, *Advancement of Learning* (1605).
68. *Corr.*, 13: 168–70 & n.
69. Lewis, *Walpole*, 107; Walpole, *Corr.*, 20: 372; *Anecdotes of Painting*, 1: 117–19.
70. Walpole, *Corr.*, 22: 136. Kenneth Clark observes that the action was prophetic, Strawberry Hill having afterwards been converted into a Catholic college (*Gothic Revival*, 63 & n.).
71. Walpole, *Corr.*, 10: 71; 20: 372; 37: 270 & n.; Ketton-Cremer, *Walpole*, 110–12.
72. Pope, *Poems*, 2: 310, 312.
73. 115, 123. In the nominalist dissolution of the universal into an infinity of

particulars, Panofsky sees prefigured the dissolution of the medieval universe (12–16).
74. *Otranto*, 108.
75. Ketton–Cremer, *Walpole*, 145–6; Gray, *Corr.*, 1: 326–7, 341.
76. Ketton–Cremer, *Gray*, 49–51, 65–6; Gray, *Corr.*, 1: 209.
77. Ketton–Cremer, *Gray*, 66–8; Gray, *Poems*, 75.
78. Ketton–Cremer, *Gray*, 75, 95–6, 265; Gray, *Corr.*, 1: 326.
79. Ketton–Cremer, *Gray*, 44–51.
80. Kathleen Mahaffey, 'Timon's Villa: Walpole's Houghton', in Mack & Winn, 315–51; Mack, *Garden & City*, 117–20, 131–2, 139–41, 272–8; Goldgar, *Walpole*, 81–2, 199.
81. Gray, *Elegy*, 74. Perhaps the most striking instance of Gray's alienation is the work in which a Welsh protagonist with whom he explicitly identified -- 'I felt myself the Bard' -- upholds the reign of poetry against the 'vice and infamous pleasure', 'tyranny and oppression' of the rulers of England (Ketton–Cremer, *Gray*, 132–6; Gray, *Poems*, 177–200).
82. Ketton–Cremer, *Gray*, 101–2.
83. Gray, *Poems*, 130n.
84. Starr, 9; Ketton–Cremer, *Gray*, 99, 110.
85. Ketton–Cremer, *Gray*, 72–5, 89–90, 102, 107–110; Gray, *Corr.*, 1: 226; Walpole, *Corr.*, 9: 76.
86. *Elegy*, 70–71.
87. *De Rerum Natura*, 3: 894–6.
88. Gray, *Poems*, 130n. A similar absence of religious consolation has been noted elsewhere (Ketton–Cremer, *Gray*, 193; Gray, *Poems*, 210).
89. Gray, *Corr.*, 1: 172.
90. Moore, 183–5, 195, 210–16; *Spectator*, 3: 454; Montagu, *Letters*, 2: 119.
91. Williams, *Whig Supremacy*, 248–57; O'Callaghan, 350–67; Trench, 230; *DNB*, s.v. William Augustus, Duke of Cumberland; Gray, *Corr.*, 1: 166, 235; W.M. Newman, 'When Curfew Tolled the Knell', in Starr 18; Gray, *Elegy*, 74.
92. Plumb, *Walpole*, 2: 326–7.
93. Ketton–Cremer, *Walpole*, 98.
94. Walpole, *Corr.*, 9: 24.
95. Brown, *Estimate*, 18–20, 27–35, 38, 91, 112–115.
96. Walpole, *Corr.*, 9: 219–21; 14: 159.
97. *Essays*, 1: 392.
98. Brown, *Estimate*, 136, 141–4, 201.
99. Williams, *Pitt*, 1: 30, 63, 190–94; Walpole, *Memoirs George III*, 3: 30.
100. Williams, *Pitt*, 1: 40–41, 65–77, 191.
101. Williams, *Pitt*, 1: 4–26, 72–4; Plumb, *Eighteenth Century*, 71–2.
102. Williams, *Pitt*, 1: 100–116, 123–4, 129–30, 141–6; Trench, 217–23.
103. Walpole, *Corr.*, 19: 229.
104. Williams, *Pitt*, 1: 147–55; Plumb, *Walpole*, 1: 203–9; Brown, *Pitt* 79–80.
105. Williams, *Pitt*, 1: 163–8.

106. Norberg-Schulz, *Late Baroque*, 175–7; Wangermann, 14–15, 29–30; Crankshaw, 9–10.
107. Crankshaw, 3–5, 11–13, 135–9; Norberg-Schulz, *Late Baroque*, 14–16; Jellicoe, Goode & Lancaster, s.v. Schönbrunn.
108. Carsten, 1–9; Marriott & Robertson, 45–6, 52–9, 69; Koch, 21, 25.
109. Marriott & Robertson, 84, 92–3, 97–9; Koch, 68.
110. Frey, 92–4.
111. Cronin, *Catherine*, 17.
112. Young, *Frederick*, 16–17.
113. Cronin, *Catherine*, 18–19.
114. Young, *Frederick*, 19–21, 25–32; Simon, 99–100.
115. Young, *Frederick*, 33–43, 70–3; Hubatsch, 12–13; Simon, 109–22.
116. Mitford, *Frederick*, 155; Young, *Frederick*, 17, 52–60, 70, 75–8; Hubatsch, 35–40; Koch, 101; Simon, 143–4, 171.
117. Simon, 115–19; Marriott & Robertson, 117–21; Gooch, 5–9, 13.
118. Gooch, 14, 23, 26, 126, 147; McKay & Scott, 164–6; Koch, 112–14; Marriott & Robertson, 123–4; Crankshaw, 208; Duffy, 74; Young, *Frederick*, 411.
119. Acton, 274–5; Crankshaw, 205–17, 231–7; Willcox, 67.
120. Gooch, 40–42; Koch, 126; Brown, *Pitt*, 161; Willcox, 77.
121. Macaulay, *Essays*, 2: 175.
122. Williams, *Pitt*, 1: 350; Koch, 127–8.
123. Young, *Frederick*, 347; Gooch, 103–5; Mitford, *Frederick*, 291.
124. Williams, *Pitt*, 1: 250–51, 329–31, 374–6; Flexner, 3–36; Tunstall, 192–9; Walpole, *Corr.*, 21: 131.
125. Gascoigne, 31–3, 47–8, 68–70, 97–9, 109–18, 131–4, 149–54, 181–2; 224–46; Shearer, 312–13; Crowe, Haywood, Jellicoe & Patterson, 167–73.
126. Davies, 545, 552; Macaulay, *Essays*, 1: 488.
127. Davies, 557; Woodruff, 64, 70, 74; Shearer, 57; Lawford, 24; Edwardes, 27; *Murray*, 115; Mookerjee, 62–3.
128. Edwardes, 19, 29–32, 39–60; Garrett, 108–10.
129. Edwardes, 76–8; Lawford, 33; Garrett, 17, 23, 36, 38, 42–3, 45–6, 54–5, 62–88.
130. Edwardes, 122–58; Garrett, 147.
131. Williams, *Pitt*, 1: 341–3, 349, 365–7, 372–4, 395–7; 2: 8–13, 24; Grinnell-Milne, 57–8, 66–8, 159, 207–57, 269–70, 279–81.
132. Gray, *Elegy*, 71, 83–8.
133. *Corr.*, 21: 518.
134. Walpole, *Corr.*, 21: 311; Ketton-Cremer, *Walpole*, 143–5, 177–9; *Otranto*, 108.
135. Mellor, 15–16, 87–91; Tacitus, *Germania*, 7: 1; 11: 1, 2.
136. Kliger, 7–13, 112–13, 118–19, 194–6; Temple, *Works*, 3: 366–7, 407.
137. Hill, *Puritanism*, 65.
138. Pocock, 64, 87–8 & n., 108–116, 123, 184–6, 196–211, 227–31.
139. Kliger, 28, 203; Robinson, 98–103.

140. *Corr.*, 21: 433.
141. *Germania*, 9: 2.
142. 2: 407.
143. 20.
144. *Corr.*, 10: 22.

CHAPTER 8
1. Woodbridge, *Landscape*, 2–3, 33–6, 58; *Aeneid*, 6: 126, 258.
2. Gibbon, *Autobiographies*, 57–8.
3. Low, 23–4; *Autobiographies*, 43.
4. *Autobiographies*, 48.
5. de Beer, 6; Low, 32; *Autobiographies*, 59.
6. *Autobiographies*, 63, 74–6, 83–6; Low, 40–42.
7. Low, 98, 44–7, 50–53; *Autobiographies*, 137; Gibbon, *Letters*, 1: 3.
8. Low, 5, 57, 73; Craddock, *Young Gibbon*, 110–15, 327–9.
9. Craddock, *Young Gibbon*, 86, 114, 123–4, 132, 329; *Autobiographies*, 155–8.
10. Craddock, *Young Gibbon*, 131–2; Low, 85; *Letters*, 1: 106.
11. *Autobiographies*, 239; Low, 89; *Letters*, 1: 122.
12. DNB, s.v. Pitt; Gibbon, *Journal 1763*, 20–22; Low, 59, 94–5, 99–100, 106–25.
13. Craddock, *Young Gibbon*, 170–76; Low, 144–6; Gibbon, *Letters*, 1: 135, 144, 152, 160–61; *Journal à Lausanne*, 51.
14. Low, 164–7; Gibbon, *Journal à Lausanne*, 217, 222, 238.
15. *Autobiographies*, 302.
16. Low, 176–83; Gibbon, *Journey to Rome*, 213, 235.
17. Freud, *Works*, 21: 69–70. For the painter Thomas Jones, steeped through Wilson in Claude, every scene about Rome 'seemed anticipated in some dream' (Herrmann, 53, 66–7).
18. *Autobiographies*, 302.
19. *Decline & Fall*, 7: 132.
20. Low, 191–3 & n.; *Letters*, 1: 201 & n.; Craddock, *Young Gibbon*, 227–8; *Autobiographies*, 271.
21. Low, 97–9, 205–7; *Autobiographies*, 249–50, 285.
22. Low, 212–13, 233, 236–9; Merrifield, 46; *Letters*, 2: 32, 61, 56.
23. Marshall, 316–17; Watson, 2–7; Brooke, 75, 85–6, 104, 116–17, 120–23.
24. Brooke, 129–31; Tillyard, 111–21.
25. Brooke, 143–6, 148–9.
26. Brooke, 136–7; Williams, *Pitt*, 2: 35–57, 84–6, 97–8, 101, 105–14.
27. Williams, *Pitt*, 2: 114–18.
28. Williams, *Pitt*, 2: 118–23; Walpole, *Corr.*, 21: 541; Tunstall, 310–11.
29. Williams, *Pitt*, 2: 139–48, 179–85, 190–202, 206; Plumb, *Eighteenth Century*, 126–7; Christie, 89–90.
30. Williams, *Pitt*, 2: 208–14, 227–9, 234; Walpole, *George III*, 2: 273.
31. Young, *Frederick*, 112, 173–4, 187; McKay & Scott, 176, 186, 195, 225–7;

Koch, 129–32; Duffy, 188; Cronin, *Catherine*, 19–20, 67, 113, 125, 133–58; Crankshaw, 281–6; Walpole, *Corr.*, 24: 55.

32. *Corr.*, 23: 562.
33. Williams, *Pitt*, 2: 234–40; Watson, 127.
34. Williams, *Pitt*, 2: 303.
35. *Corr.*, 41: 334–5.
36. 29: 98.
37. Gibbon, *Misc. Wks.*, 5: 571.
38. *Decline & Fall*, 3: 467.
39. *Letters*, 1: 193; *Decline & Fall*, 4: 191–2; 6: 437–8.
40. Low, 320–21.
41. Dawson, xi.
42. *Decline & Fall*, 4: 147.
43. Curtis, 'Paradise Lost' 84.
44. *Decline & Fall*, 4: 160.
45. *Decline & Fall*, 1: 6; Swain, 128–9.
46. *Decline & Fall*, 3: 357.
47. 7: 325.
48. *Portraits in Miniature*, 159–60.
49. 7.
50. Macaulay, *Ruins*, 9–35, 165–92.
51. Ogden, 53; Deborah Howard, 'Claude and English Art', in Kitson, *Art of Claude Lorrain*, 9–10; Manwaring, 95–107; Dyer, 224.
52. Clarke & Penny, 40–41; Röthlisberger, 'Subjects' 218.
53. Pace, 737.
54. Keats, 320–26, 514–21, 523–41, 650–55; Jack, 127–30, 219–21; Kitson, *Liber Veritatis*, 153–4; Langdon, 133–6; Harold Bloom, 'The *Ode to Psyche* and the *Ode on Melancholy*', in Bate, *Keats*, 93–8; Neumann, *Amor & Psyche*, 9–11, 79–84.
55. Clark, *Landscape into Art*, 65; Röthlisberger, *Paintings*, 1: 35; 'Subjects', 221–2; Kitson, '"Altieri Claudes"', 312–15; McKay, 'Virgilian Landscape into Art', 147–8; *Aeneid*, 1: 459–62. *Lacrimae rerum* has an almost exact Japanese equivalent in *mono-no-aware*. *Aware* is rooted in the interjectional 'ah!'; while *mono* is both 'palpable matter and formless space', permeated by an as yet undifferentiated spirit (Morris, 208; Hisamatsu, 13–16; Ueda, 199–204; Tange & Kawagoe, 20–23); as *res*, in its relation to *reri*, 'thing' to 'think' (Knight, *Roman Vergil*, 240–41), recalls the ancient *participation mystique*. Vergil's poignant juxtaposition of vanished past and vivid present may also be found in Buson:

*Shiraume ya sumi kanbashiki korokan* (Blyth, 2: 300–301):

White plum-blossoms;
in the Korokan, the aroma
of ink.

The Korokan was a Chinese Office which had disappeared centuries before; and its distance from the immediacy of early spring is heightened by the contrasts: the flower, with its sweetness, white, and the ink, with its astringency, black: the latter, like Vergil's Trojans, carrying within itself the entire tradition of an antique culture.

56. *Decline & Fall*, 1: 39, 56–7, 194; 2: 44; 3: 207–8, 414–15; 4: 405.

57. 5: 170. Hoxie speaks of the invasion of life by style, in the Byzantine emperor's standing motionless, hour after hour, in the flat planes of his robes (282–3).

58. He goes on to excoriate an artifact in the imperial palace: 'a golden tree, with its leaves and branches, which sheltered a multitude of birds, warbling their artificial notes' (*Decline & Fall*, 6: 75–7). Yeats was to glorify it for precisely this reason: that it was out of time, an 'artifice of eternity' (*Poems*, 217–18).

59. *Decline & Fall*, 1: 2, 213.

60. *Corr.*, 15: 331; 34: 79; 42: 221.

61. Manwaring, 137; Hunt, *Kent*, 41–2, 79–88.

62. Clark, *Gothic*, 47–50; Macaulay, *Ruins*, 22–33. Switzer had advocated Roman ruins in the garden to suggest the 'Instability of all Sublunary Affairs' (*Ichnographia Rustica*, 1: 198).

63. Bailyn, 19, 22, 41–4, 94.

64. Gage, 76.

65. Walpole, *Corr.*, 29: 115; *Decline & Fall*, 3: 480.

66. Macaulay, *Ruins*, 29–30; Robinson, 90.

67. Bailyn, 51.

68. Macaulay, *Ruins*, 36. A triumphal arch in Yorkshire was inscribed to 'Liberty in North America' (Pevsner, 178).

69. *Corr.*, 29: 135.

70. Wills, 133–7.

71. Summerson, *Architecture in Britain*, 546–9; Richard, 45–6.

72. *Eclogues*, 4: 36.

73. *Corr.*, 24: 103.

74. 29: 136.

75. *Decline & Fall*, 1: 56, 78–9.

76. Jordan, 216 n.; Fielding, 545, 597 & n.

77. Malins, *Landscaping & Literature*, 43–4.

78. Stroud, *Brown*, 49–55, 186–8; Hussey, *English Gardens*, 47.

79. *Corr.*, 29: 286.

80. Stroud, *Brown*, 121–4, 133, 135–6, 142–4.

81. Stroud, *Brown*, 129–30; Downes, 72–3; Fleming & Gore, 118; Whistler, 126.

82. Stroud, *Brown*, 236; Hussey, *Gardens*, 52; Jellicoe, Goode & Lancaster, s.v. Prior Park; Watkin, 69–70; Summerson, *Architecture in Britain*, 325.

83. Fielding, 58–9.

84. Cross, 1: 17; 2: 164–5.

85. Manwaring, 204–5.

86. Browne, 170.

87. Wesley, 6: 128, 257.

88. Gibbon, *Letters*, 2: 260; Craddock, *Luminous Historian*, 118–20; Carnochan,

111.
89. *Anecdotes*, 3: 84.
90. Ashe, 111–18, 126–31, 143–4, 171–2.
91. Ashe, 102, 141, 150–64; Gibbon, *Journal to 1763*, 145; Postgate, 30–38, 45–84; Pope, *Poems*, 3: 11; Hamilton, *Infamous Essay*, 213; Christie, 75–7; Plumb, *Eighteenth Century*, 122–3.
92. Rudé, *Wilkes*, 191; Bakhtin, 6–8, 13n., 288; Ashe, 9–24, 118, 127, 171–2; Manwaring, 178.
93. 39.
94. Young, *Gibbon*, 96–8.
95. *Decline & Fall*, 4: 57, 248; 5: 339.
96. Young, *Gibbon*, 146–7.
97. *Decline & Fall*, 5: 123–4.
98. Walpole, *Corr.*, 33: 313.
99. Swain, 43; Young, *Gibbon*, 133–4; Gibbon, *Letters*, 2: 162–3.
100. Low, 258–60; *Decline & Fall*, 2: 216–17.
101. Low, 299; *Decline & Fall*, 2: 185; *Autobiographies*, 329.
102. *Decline & Fall*, 6: 333n.
103. 4: 66.
104. *Autobiographies*, 333.
105. 341.

CHAPTER 9
1. *Letters*, 3: 276, 291–2.
2. Rudé, 'French Revolution', 657.
3. *The Times*, 10, 16 January 1788.
4. Christie, 158; Hibbert, 30–32, 36–41.
5. Gay, 34–65; Walpole, *Corr.*, 41: 153.
6. Thacker, 'Voltaire & Rousseau', 1601–3.
7. Kimball, 209–10; Adams, 111; Neumeyer, 193; Thacker, 'Voltaire and Rousseau', 1607; John N. Pappas, Foreword, Aricò, vii; Willis, 'Rousseau, Stowe and *Le Jardin anglais*', 1792–6; Rousseau, 2: 87–103.
8. Bréhier, 157–70.
9. Doyle, 94.
10. Daniel Mornet, 'The Intellectual Origins of the French Revolution', in Church, 113–14.
11. Hibbert, 40–44.
12. Herold, 5–9, 21.
13. When Suzanne was relinquished by her English lover, Jean–Jacques was asked by an intermediary to employ his eloquence on her behalf. At first he agreed to speak to Gibbon, but later changed his mind. 'I should like to diguise my feelings, but I could not. I should like to be of use, and I feel that I shall spoil everything'. The feeling was well founded. 'I would rather', he wrote to her intercessor, 'that he should leave her poor and free in your midst, than to take her away to be

unhappy and rich in England'. The English did not understand freedom; they were all of them rich; and there was also the question of character: 'Who does not realise her value is not worthy of her, but he who has known it and can break off is a man to despise'. Gibbon, when he saw this startling epistle in print years afterwards, was judicious and restrained. 'That extraordinary man', he wrote, 'whom I admire and pity, should have been less precipitate in condemning the moral character...of a stranger'. And he gave his opinion of Jean-Jacques by indirection, acknowledging the futility of appealing from his 'judgement, or taste, or caprice': equating the three in a masterly diminuendo (Low, 137–43; Gibbon, *Autobiographies*, 298n.).
14. Herold, 23, 28.
15. Huizinga, *Making of a Saint*, 164–8, 262.
16. Herold, 10, 29–31, 33.
17. 36, 38–9.
18. 22, 24–8, 40–41.
19. Herold, 27–8, 40–43.
20. Herold, 71; Rudé, 'French Revolution', 657.
21. Herold, 74–5; Brodie, 241.
22. Herold, 75–8; Hibbert, 50.
23. Herold, 78–80.
24. 80–81.
25. Herold, 81–4; Brodie, 241.
26. Herold, 84–6.
27. Brown, *French Revolution*, 29–31; Magnus, 187.
28. 'Guillaume Penn pouvait se vanter d'avoir apporté sur la terre l'âge d'or dont on parle tant, et qui n'a vraisemblablement existé qu'en Pennsylvanie' (Voltaire, 19).
29. Ehrenpreis, *Swift*, 3: 915–18; Burke, *Sublime & Beautiful*, xv–xviii.
30. Monk, 18–21, 44–5, 207; Dennis, 2: xciv–v, 380–81.
31. Smithers, 73–4; Addison, *Misc. Wks.*, 2: 202.
32. Thorpe, 'Two Augustans', 478.
33. *Spectator*, 3: 535–82.
34. *Sublime & Beautiful*, xvi, lxxv, 31, 54, 64, 101.
35. O'Brien, 3–14; Cobban, 101–7.
36. Burke, *Works*, 2: 73.
37. Magnus, 167–71.
38. Laski, 149.
39. Burke, *Reflections*, 164–70.
40. Hibbert, 148–50; Cronin, *Napoleon*, 73.
41. Eliot, *Prose*, 38.
42. Burke, *Reflections*, 170; *Works*, 4: 109–10; Cobban, 109; Williams, *Ancien Régime*, 252; Ogg, *Ancien Régime*, 60–61.
43. *Reflections*, 346; Lock, 19–20.
44. Lock, 2–4; Burke, *Works*, 1: 491–3.

45. *Works*, 4: 93–5. His claim is borne out by the facts. Burke had praised Louis XVI, as a would-be reformer, a decade before the French revolution (Lock, 46). His most memorable defence of aristocracy came before that revolution (Burke, *Corr.*, 2: 377–8), his most memorable attack upon it after (*Works*, 5: 171–229). And it is notorious that his impassioned campaign for the rights of the peoples of India was carried on long after events in France had driven what little support there was for it from the minds of others (O'Brien, 503–4). On the general issue, Burke had already, as a student, appealed to ancestral wisdom (Cone, 1: 9 & n.), or, as he now put it, 'nature, which is wisdom without reflection, and above it' (*Reflections*, 119).
46. Bailyn, 67.
47. *Reflections*, 121–2, 129, 133–4.
48. Magnus, 218; Bailyn, 273–4, 288–91.
49. Doyle, 94; Williams, *Ancien Régime*, 240.
50. Burke, *Works*, 4: 107.
51. *Reflections*, 285–6, 314–15, 342, 344.
52. 339, 341.
53. Gérard Gengembre, cited in O'Brien, lxxiii.
54. *Reflections*, 171–2.
55. Hibbert, 187; Woodbridge, *Princely Gardens*, 242–4.
56. Cronin, *Napoleon*, 359–60.
57. *Reflections*, 104, 121, 152, 172, 267, 281.
58. *Sublime & Beautiful*, 82.
59. Baigent, Leigh & Lincoln, 70–77.
60. *Poems*, 231.
61. 25 January 1793.
62. Gibbon, *Letters*, 3: 161.
63. Brown, *French Revolution*, 43, 49, 168; Jack 67.
64. *Letters*, 3: 184, 229, 318.
65. *Walpole*, 305.
66. *Corr.*, 42: 303.
67. *Reflections*, 169–70.
68. *Corr.*, 34: 98; *Aeneid*, 1: 405.
69. *Corr.*, 12: 48.
70. 34: 177.
71. Brown, *French Revolution*, 31–2, 89.
72. Lock, 158.
73. Leonard Woolf, 'Tom Paine', in Dobrée, *Anne to Victoria*, 504–9; Paine, *Common Sense*, 81.
74. Paine, *Rights of Man*, 178, 180.
75. Woolf, 'Tom Paine', 511–12.
76. *English Thought*, 2: 212.
77. *Rights of Man*, 47, 166.
78. Ogg, *James II & William III*, 54–7; Goodwin, 100.

79. Commager & Morris, 317; Lefebvre, 209, 221; Paine, *Rights of Man*, 113, 166.
80. Bailyn, 246; Hibbert, 282
81. *Works*, 4: 97.
82. Hussey, *Picturesque*, 137; Introduction, Stroud, *Brown*, 31.
83. Harris & Crook, 5–7; Stroud, *Brown*, 143.
84. Stroud, *Brown*, 37–8, 165; Chambers, *Dissertation*, 106.
85. Harris & Crook, 4–5.
86. Chambers, *Dissertation*, 17.
87. Bald, 303.
88. Thacker, *History of Gardens*, 216–17; Wiebenson, 41.
89. *Sublime & Beautiful*, 124.
90. Summerson, *Architecture in Britain*, 423–4; Harris, 8–9.
91. Bald, 314–17; Chambers, *Dissertation*, 134, 141.
92. *Sublime & Beautiful*, 57.
93. Chambers, *Dissertation*, 130–34. Horace Walpole was only too happy to indicate ironic agreement (Sirén, 81; Chase, 190–97); he was less happy, however, with the appellation, which Chambers helped to propagate, of the *jardin anglo-chinois* (Wiebenson, 41–2; Harris & Crook, 161). See above, ch. 2, n. 135.
94. Harris & Crook, 37–8; Honour, *Chinoiserie*, 186.
95. Chambers, *Dissertation*, 40–45. Chambers' three categories of Pleasing, Terrible and Surprising echo Addison's Beautiful, Great and Uncommon. As however the Terrible merges into the Surprising, one is left with Burke's Beautiful and Sublime (Chambers, *Dissertation*, 39; Wiebenson, 40; Harris & Crook, 156–7; Thacker, *History of Gardens*, 216–17).
96. Coleridge, 297–8.
97. Lowes, 4.
98. MCMillan, 91–2; House, 118; Peckham, 113, 302. Shaffer sees the number five as enhancing the paradisiacal order here (103–9), as it had for Sir Thomas Browne.
99. Stroud, *Repton*, 21–2, 27–35, 82–3; *Brown*, 144, 204–5.
100. This description occurs in a letter to Lord Lyttelton, nephew of Lord Cobham of Stowe and himself creator of the notable garden at Hagley (Eddy, 78–82; Jellicoe, Goode & Lancaster, s.v. Hagley Hall).
101. Bicknell, xi–xii.
102. Ketton-Cremer, *Gray*, 241–4; Wordsworth, Jaye & Woof 146–50; Monk, 230–31; Wordsworth, *Poetical Works*, 585. When Wordsworth spoke of the garden he had helped lay out, following Addison, at Coleorton, as embodying 'art in nature lost' (Anderson, 210–11; *Poetical Works*, 122), he reverted to Temple's *sharawadgi*. Carritt traces his aesthetic of imagination, too, to Addison (26–7), and Moore his religion of nature to Shaftesbury (89).
103. Hussey, *Picturesque*, 13–14; Price, *Picturesque*, 1: 34–45, 76–86.
104. *Landscape Gardening*, 329.
105. Fleming & Gore, 160; Stroud, *Repton*, 35; Hussey, *Picturesque*, 173–84.
106. Thacker, *History of Gardens*, 211; Hussey, *Picturesque*, 142.

107. *Landscape Gardening*, 329, 430.
108. 353.
109. Clarke & Penny, 10–12.
110. Magnus, 213–20; Brown, *Revolution*, 38–40, 101, 197–8.
111. Knight, *Landscape*, 72–3.
112. Stroud, *Repton*, 91.
113. Burke, *Works*, 4: 176.
114. Repton, *Odd Whims*, 2: 156.

CONCLUSION

1. Burke, *Works*, 5: 210; Fussell, 208.
2. Pares, 194–5; Girouard, 23–8.
3. Clark, *Gothic*, 120–21.
4. Thompson, 8–14.
5. *Reflections*, 121. In contrast to Addison, who had seen the untrimmed tree as a counterpart to liberty, Burke, who knew the oak as sacred to the Druids, because, he surmised, of its 'greatness', 'shade', 'stability and duration' (*Works*, 7: 183), found all these qualities in a land ruled by aristocracy (*Corr.*, 2: 377–8): an image taken as characteristic by Yeats (*Poems*, 268).
6. He was attacked by Knight, lampooned by Peacock and satirised by Jane Austen (Stroud, *Repton*, 79, 83–4; Malins, *Landscaping & Literature*, 126–38).
7. Hussey, *Late Georgian*, 60–61. Here, in the citation of 'picturesque', is a further instance of Repton's synthesis with his critics. The facade of Knight's earlier castle at Downton is described by Hussey as 'effectively asymmetrical', thus placing it in the tradition of Walpole, while its interior is 'wholly classical', the combination in keeping with the vision he derived from Claude (Hussey, *Mid Georgian*, 152; Clarke & Penny, 40–41). Mavis Batey sees the same influence in his landscape; and when Repton admired its 'art clandestine and conceal'd design' (Batey, 124–6), he, like Wordsworth (above, ch. 9, n. 102), invoked *sharawadgi*.
8. Girouard, 40–41, 50–53, 90–110, 205–6, 295; Wilson, *Scott*, 147–8.
9. Shelley, 442–4; Holmes, *Shelley*, 429–38; Bornstein, 69–94; Ross Woodman, '*Adonais*', in Reiman & Powers, 659–75.
10. Holmes, *Shelley*, 337; Marchand, 75–80, 244–5, 463–4.
11. Crook, 39; Jack, 217–221.
12. Crook, 21–3, 70–71, 80–89, 146–52.
13. 6–19.
14. Woodbridge, *Stourhead*, 58; Crook, 91–107.
15. Crook, 10–11; Peter Funnell, 'The Symbolical Language of Antiquity', in Clarke & Penny, 50–64; Knight, *Priapus*, 26–31, 204–5.
16. Crook, 134–5.
17. Blake, *Writings*, 3: 361–2; Frye, 148–9.
18. *Poems*, 488–9.
19. Clark, *Gothic*, 125–6, 138–40, 144–8.
20. Clark, *Gothic*, 139–41, 149, 193, 195–7, 201–2, 206.

21. Clark, *Gothic*, 141, 202; MacCarthy, *Morris*, 69–75, 84–5, 155, 161, 168–9, 476–80, 589–99.
22. Girouard, 178–96.
23. MacCarthy, *Morris*, 154–5, 161–2, 164–5; Baker, 41–4.
24. Craig, 109–12; Jellicoe, Goode & Lancaster, s.v. Tsarskoye Selo; Shvidkovsky, 97–106, 167–83.
25. di Niscemi, 30–35.
26. Thacker, *History of Gardens*, 205–7.
27. Brophy, 215; *Die Entführung aus dem Serail*, Act 2.
28. A process confirmed in the French revolutionary festivals, where liberty was hymned at Notre-Dame, and nature celebrated in the form of a mountain at the Tuileries (Kennedy, 343–5). And the French revolution, like the American, eclipsed any English claim on the republicanism of antiquity (Richard, 67–72, 232–3; Wills, 111–15, 227–8; Honour, *Neo-classicism*, 171; Parker, 139–45).
29. Lablaude, 165.

# SOURCES

Abrams, M.H. 'From Addison to Kant: Modern Aesthetics and the Exemplary Art'. In *Studies in Eighteenth-Century British Art and Aesthetics*, ed. Ralph Cohen, 16–48. Berkeley & Los Angeles, 1985.

Ackerman, James S. *Palladio*. Harmondsworth, 1966.

Acton, John Lord. *Lectures on Modern History*. London & Glasgow, 1960.

Adams, William Howard. *The French Garden, 1500–1800*. London, 1979.

Addison, Joseph. *The Freeholder*. Ed. James Leheny. Oxford, 1979.

------. *Letters*. Ed. Walter Graham. Oxford, 1941.

------. *Miscellaneous Works*. Ed. A.C. Guthkelch. 2 vols. London, 1914.

------. *Works*. Ed. Henry G. Bohn. 6 vols. London, 1901–12.

Aden, John M. *Pope's Once and Future Kings*. Knoxville, 1978.

Adler, Alfred. *Individual Psychology*. Ed. Heinz L. & Rowena R. Ansbacher. New York, 1964.

Aikin, Lucy. *The Life of Joseph Addison*. 2 vols. London, 1843.

Alcorn, John. *The Nature Novel from Hardy to Lawrence*. New York, 1977.

Allen, B. Sprague. *Tides in English Taste (1619–1800): A Background for the Study of Literature*. 2 vols. 1937. Reprint. New York, 1969.

Anderson, Anne. 'Wordsworth and the Gardens of Coleorton Hall'. *Garden History*, 22 (1994): 206–17.

Aricò, Santo L. *Rousseau's Art of Persuasion in 'La Nouvelle Héloïse'*. Lanham, New York & London, 1994.

Arnold, Matthew. *Prose and Poetry*. Ed. Archibald L. Bouton. New York, Chicago & Boston, 1927.

Ashe, Geoffrey. *Do What You Will: A History of Anti-Morality*. London & New York, 1974.

Ashley, Maurice. *Charles II: The Man and the Statesman*. St Albans, 1973.

------. *James II*. London, 1977.

Ault, Norman. *New Light on Pope*. 1949. Reprint. Hamden, 1967.

Aylmer, G. E.: 'Unbelief in Seventeenth-Century England'. In *Puritans and Revolutionaries*, ed. Donald Pennington & Keith Thomas, 22–46. Oxford, 1978.

Bacon, Francis. *Essays*. London, 1972.

Bahlman, Dudley. *The Moral Revolution of 1688*. Hamden, Conn., 1968.

Baigent, Michael, Richard Leigh & Henry Lincoln. *The Holy Blood and the Holy Grail*. London, 1983.

Bailey, Cyril. *The Greek Atomists and Epicurus*. Oxford, 1928.

Bailyn, Bernard. *The Ideological Origins of the American Revolution*. Cambridge, Mass., 1982.

Baker, Derek W. *The Flowers of William Morris*. London, 1996.

Bakhtin, Mikhail. *Rabelais and his World*. Transl. Hélène Iswolsky. Cambridge, Mass. & London, 1968.

Bald, R.C. 'Sir William Chambers and the Chinese Garden'. *Journal of the History of Ideas*, 11 (1950): 287–320.

Barbour, Violet. *Henry Bennet, Earl of Arlington*. Washington & London, 1914.

Bate, Walter Jackson. *From Classic to Romantic: Premises of Taste in Eighteenth-Century England*. Cambridge, Mass., 1946.

------ (Ed.). *Keats: A Collection of Critical Essays*. Englewood Cliffs, 1964.

Batey, Mavis. 'The Picturesque: An Overview'. *Garden History*, 22 (1994): 121–32.

de Beer, Sir Gavin. *Gibbon and His World*. London, 1968.

Beljame, Alexandre. *Men of Letters and the English Public in the Eighteenth Century*. Transl. E.O. Lorimer. Ed. Bonamy Dobrée. London, 1948.

Bennet, E.A. *Meetings with Jung*. Zürich, 1985.

Bennett, Joan. *Sir Thomas Browne*. Cambridge, 1962.

Bentley, Richard. 'Dissertation Upon Phalaris, Etc.'. In Wotton, William, *Reflections Upon Ancient and Modern Learning*. 2nd ed. London, 1697.

------. *Milton's Paradise Lost*, London 1732.

Bettelheim, Bruno. *The Uses of Enchantment: The Meaning and Importance of Fairy Tales*. New York, 1977.

Bicknell, Peter. *Beauty, Horror and Immensity: Picturesque Landscape in Britain, 1750–1850*. Cambridge, 1981.

Birch, T. & J. Lockman. *The life of J. Addison, extracted from...the General Dictionary*. London, 1733.

Blackstone, Sir William. 'Account of the Quarrel between Pope and Addison'. *Biographia Britannica*. 5 vols. London 1778–93. 1: 56–8n.

Blake, William. *Poems*. Ed. W. H. Stevenson & David V. Erdman. London, 1971.

------. *Writings*. Ed. Geoffrey Keynes. 3 vols. London, 1925.

Blomfield, Reginald. *The Formal Garden in England*. 1901. Reprint. New York, 1972.

Bloom, Edward A. & Lillian D. *Addison and Steele: The Critical Heritage*. London, Boston & Henley, 1980.

------. *Joseph Addison's Sociable Animal: In the Market Place, on the Hustings, in the Pulpit*. Providence, R.I., 1971.

------. 'Joseph Addison and Eighteenth-Century "Liberalism"'. *Journal of the*

*History of Ideas*, 12 (1951): 560–83.
Blunt, Anthony. *Art and Architecture in France, 1500–1700*. Harmondsworth, 1982.
Blyth, R.H. *Haiku* 4 vols. Tokyo, 1949–52.
Bond, Harold L. *The Literary Art of Edward Gibbon*. Oxford, 1960.
Borges, Jorge Luis. *Labyrinths: Selected Stories & Other Writings*. Ed. Donald A. Yates & James E. Irby. Harmondsworth, 1970.
Bornstein, George. *Yeats and Shelley*. Chicago & London, 1970.
Boswell, James. *Life of Johnson*. Ed. R.W. Chapman & J.D. Fleeman. London, 1970.
Boxer, C.R. *The Dutch Seaborne Empire, 1600–1800*. Harmondsworth, 1973.
Boyle, Charles. *Dr. Bentley's Dissertations on the Epistles of Phalaris, and the Fables of Aesop, Examin'd*. London, 1698.
Bréhier, Émile. *The Eighteenth Century*. Transl. Wade Baskin. Chicago & London, 1967.
Brodie, Fawn M. *Thomas Jefferson: An Intimate History*. New York, 1974.
Bronson, B.H. 'When Was Neoclassicism?' In *Studies in Criticism and Aesthetics, 1660–1800*, ed. Howard Anderson & John S. Shea, 13–35. Minneapolis, 1967.
Brooke, John. *King George III*, St. Albans, 1974.
Brooks-Davies, Douglas. *Pope's* Dunciad *and the Queen of Night: A Study in Emotional Jacobitism*. Manchester, 1985.
Brophy, Brigid. *Mozart the Dramatist: A New View of Mozart, his Operas and his Age*. New York, 1964.
Brower, Reuben A. *Alexander Pope: The Poetry of Allusion*. Oxford, 1968.
Brown, John. *An Estimate of the Manners and Principles of the Times*. London, 1757.
Brown, Norman O. *Life Against Death: The Psychoanalytic Meaning of History*. New York, 1959.
Brown, Peter Douglas. *William Pitt, Earl of Chatham: The Great Commoner*. London, 1978.
Brown, Philip Anthony. *The French Revolution in English History*. London, 1965.
Browne, Sir Thomas. *Religio Medici and Other Writings*. London & New York, 1906.
Brownell, Morris R. *Alexander Pope and the Arts of Georgian England*. Oxford, 1978.
Buckley, Jerome Hamilton. *The Victorian Temper: A Study in Literary Culture*. London, 1952.
Budgell, Eustace. *The Bee, or Universal Weekly Pamphlet*. 9 vols. London, 1733–35.
------. *A Letter to Cleomenes King of Sparta*. London, 1731.
Burke, Edmund. *Correspondence*. Ed. Thomas W. Copeland et al. 10 vols. Cambridge & Chicago, 1958–78.
------. *A Philosophical Enquiry into the Origin of Our Ideas of the Sublime and*

*Beautiful*. Ed. J.T. Boulton. Notre Dame and London, 1968.

------. *Reflections on the Revolution in France*. Ed. Conor Cruise O'Brien. Harmondsworth, 1986.

------. *Works*. 12 vols. London, 1899.

Burke, Joseph. *English Art, 1714–1800*. Oxford, 1976.

Burlingame, Anne Elizabeth. *The Battle of the Books in its Historical Setting*. 1920. Reprint. New York, 1969.

Burnet, Gilbert. *The History of My Own Time*. Ed. Osmund Airy. 3 vols. Oxford, 1897.

Burnet, Thomas. *Archaeologiae Philosophicae: sive, Doctrina Antiqua de Rerum Originibus*. London, 1692.

------. *The Sacred Theory of the Earth*. 2 vols. London, 1759.

Burnet, Thomas. *Letters to George Duckett, 1712–22*. Ed. David Nichol Smith. Oxford, 1914.

Burton, Robert. *The Anatomy of Melancholy*. 3 vols. London, 1932.

Butt, John. 'Notes for a Bibliography of Thomas Tickell'. *Bodleian Quarterly Record*, 5 (1928): 299–302.

Butterfield, Herbert. *The Whig Interpretation of History*. Harmondsworth, 1973.

Capra, Fritjof. *The Tao of Physics*. New York, 1984.

Carnochan, W.B. *Gibbon's Solitude: The Inward World of the Historian*. Stanford, 1987.

Carritt, E.F. 'Addison, Kant and Wordsworth'. *Essays & Studies*, 22 (1937): 26–36.

Carsten, F.L. *The Origins of Prussia*. Oxford, 1954.

Carswell, John. *The Old Cause: Three Biographical Studies in Whiggism*. London, 1954.

Case, Arthur E. 'Pope, Addison, and the "Atticus" Lines'. *Modern Philology* 33 (1935): 187–93.

Castell, Robert. *The Villas of the Ancients Illustrated*. London, 1728.

Chambers, Douglas. *The Planters of the English Landscape Garden: Botany, Trees & the Georgics*. New Haven & London, 1993.

Chambers, William. *A Dissertation on Oriental Gardening*. London, 1773.

Chang, Y.Z. 'A Note on Sharawadgi' *Modern Language Notes*, 45 (1930): 221–4.

Charlesworth, Michael, ed. *The English Garden: Literary Sources and Documents*. 3 vol. Mountfield, 1993.

Chase, Isabel Wakelin Urban. *Horace Walpole: Gardenist*. Princeton, 1943.

Chaudhuri, Sukanta. *Renaissance Pastoral and its English Developments*. Oxford, 1989.

Chesterton, G.K. *Twelve Types*. London, 1902.

Ch'ien Chung-shu. 'China in the English Literature of the Seventeenth Century'. *Quarterly Bulletin of Chinese Bibliography*, English ed., n.s., 1 (1940): 351–84.

Christie, Ian R. *Wars and Revolutions: Britain 1760–1815*. London, 1982.

Church, William F., ed. *The Influence of the Enlightenment on the French Revolution*. Lexington, Toronto & London, 1974.

Churchill, Winston S. *Marlborough: His Life and Times*. 2 vols. London, 1947.
Cibber, Colley. *A Letter from Mr. Cibber, to Mr. Pope*. London, 1742.
Clapham, Sir Alfred. 'The Survival of Gothic in Seventeenth-Century England'. *Archaeological Journal*, 106 (1952): Supplement, 4-9.
Clark, Sir George. *The Later Stuarts, 1660-1714*. Oxford, 1961.
Clark, Kenneth. *The Gothic Revival*. London, 1970.
------. *Landscape into Art*. London, 1949.
Clarke, Michael & Nicholas Penny, ed. *The Arrogant Connoisseur: Richard Payne Knight, 1751-1824*. Manchester, 1982.
Clifford, Derek. *A History of Garden Design*. London, 1962.
Cobb, Margaret Eulalie. 'Pope's Lines on Atticus'. *Modern Language Notes*, 36 (1921): 348-52.
Cobban, Alfred. *Edmund Burke and the Revolt against the Eighteenth Century*. 1929. Reprint. New York, 1978.
Coleridge, Samuel Taylor. *Poems*. Ed. Ernest Hartley Coleridge. London, 1931.
Colvin, H.M. 'Gothic Survival and Gothick Revival'. *Architectural Review*, 103 (1948): 91-8.
Comerford, Michael. *Collections relating to the Dioceses of Kildare and Leighlin*. 3 vols. Dublin & London, 1886.
Commager, Henry Steele & Richard B. Morris. *The Spirit of 'Seventy-Six: The Story of the American Revolution as Told by Participants*. New York, 1983.
Cone, Carl B. *Burke and the Nature of Politics*. 2 vols. Lexington, Kentucky, 1957-64.
Conington, John. 'Pope's Ms. Notes on Tickell's "Homer"'. *Frazer's Magazine*, 62 (1860): 260-73.
Connely, Willard. *Sir Richard Steele*. London, 1937.
Cooke, Arthur L. 'Addison's Aristocratic Wife'. *PMLA*, 72 (1957): 373-89.
Correcher, Consuelo M. *The Gardens of Spain*. Transl. Wayne H. Finke. New York, 1993.
Courtenay, Thomas Peregrine. *Memoirs of the Life, Works and Correspondence of Sir William Temple, Bart.* 2 vols. London, 1836.
Courthope, W.J. *Addison*. 1889. Reprint. New York, 1968.
Coxe, William. *Memoirs of the Life and Administration of Sir Robert Walpole, Earl of Orford*. 3 vols. London, 1798.
Craddock, Patricia B. *Young Edward Gibbon: Gentleman of Letters*. Baltimore & London, 1982.
------. *Edward Gibbon: Luminous Historian*. Baltimore & London, 1989.
Craig, Maurice. 'The Palace of Tsarskoe Selo'. *Country Life*, 73 (1966): 108-12.
Crankshaw, Edward. *Maria Theresa*. London, 1983.
Creech, Thomas. *T. Lucretius Carus the Epicurean Philosopher, His Six Books* De Natura Rerum *Done into English Verse*. Oxford, 1682.
Cronin, Vincent. *Catherine: Empress of all the Russias*. London, 1978.
------. *Napoleon*. Harmondsworth, 1982.
Crook, J. Mordaunt. *The Greek Revival: Neo-Classical Attitudes in British*

*Architecture, 1760–1870*. London, 1972.
Cross, Wilbur L. *The History of Henry Fielding*. 3 vols. New York, 1963.
Crowe, Sylvia, Sheila Haywood, Susan Jellicoe & Gordon Patterson. *The Gardens of Mughul India: a History and a Guide*. London, 1972.
Cundall, H.M. *Bygone Richmond*. London, 1925.
Curtis, Edmund. *A History of Ireland*. London, 1961.
Curtis, Lewis P. 'Gibbon's Paradise Lost'. In *The Age of Johnson: Essays Presented to Chauncey Brewster Tinker*, ed. Frederick W. Hilles, 73–90. New York, 1978.
*Cythereia: or, New Poems upon Love and Intrigue*, London, 1723.
Davies, C.C. 'Rivalries in India'. In *The Old Regime, 1713–63*, ed. J.O. Lindsay, 541–65. Cambridge, 1957.
Dawson, Christopher. Introduction to *Decline and Fall*, by Edward Gibbon. London & New York, 1966–74.
Dennis, John. *Critical Works*. Ed. E.N. Hooker. 2 vols. Baltimore, 1939–43.
DeWitt, Norman Wentworth. *Epicurus and his Philosophy*. Minneapolis, 1954.
Dickinson, H.T. *Bolingbroke*. London, 1970.
------. *Liberty and Property: Political Ideology in Eighteenth-Century Britain*. London, 1979.
Dineley, Thomas. *Observations in a Voyage through the Kingdom of Ireland...in the Year 1681*. Dublin, 1870.
Dobrée, Bonamy. *Alexander Pope*. London, 1963.
------. *Essays in Biography, 1680–1726*. London, 1925.
------. *From Anne to Victoria*. London, Toronto, Melbourne & Sydney, 1937.
------. *Variety of Ways: Discussions on Six Authors*. Oxford, 1932.
Donne, John. *Poetical Works*. Ed. Sir Herbert Grierson. London, 1933.
Downes, Kerry. *Vanbrugh*. London, 1977.
Doyle, William. *Origins of the French Revolution*. Oxford, 1980.
Draper, John W. *The Funeral Elegy and the Rise of English Romanticism*. 1929. Reprint. New York, 1967.
Dryden, John. *Poems and Fables*. Ed. James Kinsley. London, 1962.
Duffy, Christopher. *Frederick the Great: A Military Life*. London, Melbourne & Henley, 1985.
Dunn, William P. *Sir Thomas Browne: A Study in Religious Philosophy*. Menasha, 1926.
Dyer, John. *Poems*. In *Works of the English Poets*, ed. Alexander Chalmers, 13: 223–53. London, 1810.
Eddy, Donald D. 'John Brown: "The Columbus of Keswick"'. *Modern Philology*, 73 (1976), Supplement, 74–8.
Edwardes, Michael. *The Battle of Plassey and the Conquest of Bengal*. New York 1963.
Ehrenpreis, Irvin: *The Personality of Jonathan Swift*. London, 1958.
------. 'Swift and the Comedy of Evil'. In *Jonathan Swift: A Critical Anthology*, ed. Denis Donoghue, 207–14. Harmondsworth, 1971.

------. *Swift: The Man, his Works, and the Age*. 3 vols. London, 1962–83.
Elias, A.C., Jr. *Swift at Moor Park: Problems in Biography and Criticism*. Philadelphia, 1982.
Elioseff, Lee Andrew. *The Cultural Milieu of Addison's Literary Criticism*. Austin, 1963.
Eliot, T.S. *Complete Poems and Plays*. London & Boston, 1969.
------. *Selected Prose*. Ed. Frank Kermode. London, 1975.
Empson, William. *Seven Types of Ambiguity*. London, 1953.
------. *Some Versions of Pastoral*. New York, 1974.
Erskine-Hill, Howard. 'Alexander Pope: The Political Poet in His Time'. *Eighteenth-Century Studies*, 15 (1981–2): 123–48.
------. *The Augustan Idea in English Literature*. London, 1983.
------. *The Social Milieu of Alexander Pope*. New Haven & London, 1975.
Evelyn, John. *Diary*. 2 vols. London, 1952.
Faber, Richard. *The Brave Courtier: Sir William Temple*. London, 1983.
Fielding, Henry. *The History of Tom Jones*. Ed. R.P.C. Mutter. Harmondsworth, 1985.
Filmer, Sir Robert. *Patriarcha and Other Political Works*. Ed. Peter Laslett. Oxford, 1949.
Fingarette, Herbert. *Confucius: The Secular as Sacred*. New York, Hagerstown, San Francisco & London, 1972.
Fink, Zera S. *The Classical Republicans: An Essay in the Recovery of a Pattern of Thought in Seventeenth Century England*. Evanston, 1945.
Firth, Sir Charles. *A Commentary on Macaulay's History of England*. London, 1938.
Fleming, Laurence and Alan Gore. *The English Garden*. London, 1979.
Flexner, James Thomas. *Washington: The Indispensable Man*. New York, 1984.
Fox, Helen M. *André le Nôtre: Garden Architect to Kings*. London, 1963.
Frank, Tenney. *Vergil: A Biography*. Oxford, 1922.
Franz, Marie-Louise von. *Problems of the Feminine in Fairytales*. Dallas, 1988.
Frazer, Sir James George. *The Golden Bough: A Study in Magic and Religion*. London, 1957.
Freud, Sigmund. *Complete Psychological Works*. Ed. James Strachey et al. 24 vols. London, 1953–74.
Frey, Linda & Marsha. *Frederick I: The Man and his Times*. New York, 1984.
Frye, Northrop. *Fearful Symmetry: A Study of William Blake*. Princeton, 1947.
Fuchs, R.H. *Dutch Painting*. London, 1978.
Fussell, Paul. *The Rhetorical World of Augustan Humanism: Ethics & Imagery from Swift to Burke*. Oxford, 1965.
Gage, John. 'Turner and Stourhead: The Making of a Classicist?' *Art Quarterly*, 37 (1974): 59–87.
Garrett, Richard. *Robert Clive*. London, 1976.
Garner, William. *Carlow: Architectural Heritage*. Dublin, 1980.
Gascoigne, Bamber. *The Great Moghuls*. London, 1971.

Gatenby, E.V. 'The Influence of Japanese on English'. *Studies in English Literature*, Tokyo, 11 (Oct. 1931): 508–20.

------. 'Sharawadgi'. *Times Literary Supplement*, 1672 (15 Feb. 1934): 108.

Gay, Peter. *Voltaire's Politics: The Poet as Realist*. New Haven & London, 1988.

Gibbon, Edward. *Autobiographies*. Ed. John Murray. London, 1896.

------. *The Decline and Fall of the Roman Empire*. Ed. J.B. Bury. 7 vols. London, 1909–13.

------. *Journal à Lausanne: 17 Août 1763–19 Avril 1764*. Ed. Georges Bonnard. Lausanne, 1945.

------. *Journal to January 28th, 1763*. Ed. D.M. Low. London, 1929.

------. *Journey from Geneva to Rome: Journal from 20 April to 2 October 1764*. Ed. Georges A. Bonnard. Edinburgh, 1961.

------. *Letters*. Ed. J.E. Norton. 3 vols. London, 1956.

------. *Miscellaneous Works*. 5 vols. London, 1814.

Girouard, Mark. *The Return to Camelot: Chivalry and the English Gentleman*. New Haven & London, 1981.

Goldgar, Bertrand A. *The Curse of Party: Swift's Relations with Addison and Steele*. Lincoln, Nebraska, 1961.

------. *Walpole and the Wits: The Relation of Politics to Literature, 1722–1742*. Lincoln, Nebraska & London, 1976.

Goldstein, Laurence. *Ruins and Empire: The Evolution of a Theme in Augustan and Romantic Literature*. Pittsburgh, 1977.

Gooch, G.P. *Frederick the Great: The Ruler, the Writer, the Man*. London, 1947.

Goodman, Grant K. *Japan: The Dutch Experience*. London & Dover, N.H., 1986.

Goodwin, Albert. *The Friends of Liberty: The English Democratic Movement in the Age of the French Revolution*. London, 1979.

Gothein, Marie-Luise. *A History of Garden Art*. Transl. Laura Archer-Hind. Ed. Walter P. Wright. 2 vols. New York, 1979.

Graves, Robert. *Goodbye to All That*. Harmondsworth, 1960.

Gray, Thomas. *Correspondence*. Ed. Paget Toynbee & Leonard Whibley. 3 vols. Oxford, 1935.

------. *An Elegy Written in a Country Church yard*. Ed. Francis Griffin Stokes. Oxford, 1929.

------, William Collins & Oliver Goldsmith. *Poems*. Ed. Roger Lonsdale. London & New York, 1976.

Green, David. *Gardener to Queen Anne: Henry Wise (1653–1738) and the Formal Garden*. London, 1956.

------. *Queen Anne*. London, 1970.

Gregg, Edward. *Queen Anne*. London, Boston, Melbourne & Henley, 1984.

Grennan, Margaret R. 'Lilliput and Leprecan: Gulliver and the Irish Tradition'. *ELH*, 12 (1945): 188–202.

Griffin, Dustin H. *Alexander Pope: The Poet in the Poems*. Princeton, 1978.

Griffith, Reginald Harvey. *Alexander Pope: A Bibliography*. 1922–27. Reprint. New York, 1975.

Grinnell-Milne, Duncan. *Mad, Is He? The Character and Achievement of James Wolfe*. London, 1963.
Grundy, Isobel M. 'New Verse by Henry Fielding'. *PMLA*, 87 (1972): 213-45.
*Guardian, The*. Ed. John Calhoun Stephens. Lexington, 1982.
Hadfield, Miles. *A History of British Gardening*. London, 1979.
Hadzsits, G.D. *Lucretius and His Influence*. New York, 1935.
Haecker, Theodor. *Virgil, Father of the West*. London, 1934.
Haley, K.H.D. *An English Diplomat in the Low Countries: Sir William Temple and John De Witt, 1665-1672*. Oxford, 1986.
------. *The First Earl of Shaftesbury*. Oxford, 1968.
Hall, A. Rupert. *From Galileo to Newton, 1630-1720*. London & Glasgow, 1970.
Hall, Basil. '"An Inverted Hypocrite": Swift the Churchman'. In *The World of Jonathan Swift*, ed. Brian Vickers, 38-68. Oxford, 1968.
Halsband, Robert. *The Life of Lady Mary Wortley Montagu*. Oxford, 1956.
------. *Lord Hervey: Eighteenth-Century Courtier*. Oxford, 1973.
Hamilton, Adrian. *The Infamous Essay on Woman*. London, 1972.
Hamilton, Anthony. *Memoirs of the Comte de Gramont*. Transl. Peter Quennell. London, 1930.
Hampshire, G. 'Johnson, Elizabeth Carter and Pope's Garden'. *Notes & Queries*, n.s., 19 (1972): 221-2.
Harris, John. *The Palladian Revival: Lord Burlington, his Villa and Garden at Chiswick*. New Haven & London, 1994.
Harris, John & Eileen, and J. Mordaunt Crook. *Sir William Chambers: Knight of the Polar Star*. London, 1970.
Hatton, Ragnhild. *George I, Elector and King*. London, 1978.
Hayden, Peter. *Biddulph Grange, Staffordshire: A Victorian Garden Rediscovered*. London, 1989.
Haynes, Denys. *Greek Art and the Idea of Freedom*. London, 1981.
Henderson, George. *Gothic*. Harmondsworth, 1967.
Herm, Gerhard. *The Celts: The People who Came out of the Darkness*. London, 1976.
Herold, J. Christopher. *Mistress to an Age: A Life of Madame de Staël*. London, 1959.
Herrmann, Luke. *British Landscape Painting of the Eighteenth Century*. London, 1973.
Hervey, John Lord. *Memoirs*. Ed. Romney Sedgwick. London, 1952.
Hibbert, Christopher. *The French Revolution*. Harmondsworth, 1982.
Hill, Christopher. *The Century of Revolution, 1603-1714*. London, 1969.
------. *Milton and the English Revolution*. London, 1979.
------. *Puritanism and Revolution: Studies in Interpretation of the English Revolution of the 17th Century*. London, 1962.
------. *Reformation to Industrial Revolution*. Harmondsworth, 1969.
Hisamatsu Sen-ichi. *The Vocabulary of Japanese Literary Aesthetics*. Tokyo, 1963.

Hobbes, Thomas. *Leviathan*. Ed. C.B. Macpherson. Harmondsworth, 1968.
Holroyd, Michael. *Lytton Strachey: A Biography*. Harmondsworth, 1971.
Holmes, Geoffrey. *The Trial of Doctor Sacheverell*. London, 1973.
Holmes, Richard. *Shelley: The Pursuit*. Harmondsworth, 1987.
Honour, Hugh. *Chinoiserie*. London, 1961.
------. *Neo-Classicism*. Harmondsworth, 1977.
Hooker, Edward N. 'Dryden and the Atoms of Epicurus'. In *Dryden: A Collection of Critical Essays*, ed. Bernard N. Schilling, 125–35. Englewood Cliffs 1963.
Horne, Colin J. 'The Biter Bit: Johnson's Strictures on Pope'. *Review of English Studies*, n.s., 27 (1976): 310–13.
House, Humphry. *Coleridge*. London, 1953.
Hoxie, Albert. 'Mutations in Art'. In *The Transformation of the Roman World: Gibbon's Problem after Two Centuries*, ed. Lynn White, Jr., 266–90. Berkeley, Los Angeles & London, 1973.
Hubatsch, Walther. *Frederick the Great: Absolutism and Administration*. London, 1975.
Huizinga, J.H. *Dutch Civilisation in the Seventeenth Century and Other Essays*. Transl. Arnold J. Pomerans. New York & Evanston, 1969.
Huizinga, J.H. *The Making of a Saint: The Tragi-comedy of Jean-Jacques Rousseau*. London, 1976.
Hunt, John Dixon. *Garden & Grove: The Italian Renaissance Garden in the English Imagination, 1600–1750*. Princeton, 1986.
------. *Gardens & the Picturesque: Studies in the History of Landscape Architecture*. Cambridge, Mass. & London, 1992.
------. *William Kent: Landscape Garden Designer*. London, 1987.
------ & Peter Willis. *The Genius of the Place: The English Landscape Garden 1620–1820*. London, 1975.
Hunter, Michael. *Science and Society in Restoration England*. Cambridge, 1981.
Hussey, Christopher. *English Country Houses: Early Georgian, 1715–1760*; *Mid Georgian, 1760–1800*; *Late Georgian, 1800–1840*. 1955. Reprint. Woodbridge, Suffolk, 1986.
------. *English Gardens and Landscapes 1700–1750*. London, 1967.
------. *The Picturesque*. 1927. Reprint. London, 1967.
------. 'Templum Restauratum: Sir William Temple's House and Garden at Moor Park, Farnham, Reconstructed'. *Country Life*, 106 (25 Nov. 1949): 1578–81.
Hutton, Ronald. *Charles II, King of England, Scotland and Ireland*. Oxford, 1991.
Hyams, Edward. *The English Garden*. London, 1966.
------. *A History of Gardens and Gardening*. New York & Washington, 1971.
Israel, Jonathan I., ed. *The Anglo-Dutch Moment: Essays on the Glorious Revolution and its World Impact*. Cambridge, 1991.
Jack, Ian. *Keats and the Mirror of Art*. Oxford, 1967.
Jacobson, Dawn. *Chinoiserie*. London, 1993.
Jacques, David. *Georgian Gardens: The Reign of Nature*. London, 1990.

------. 'On the Supposed Chineseness of the English Landscape Garden'. *Garden History*, 18 (1990): 180–91.

------ & Arend Jan van der Horst. *The Gardens of William and Mary*. London, 1988.

James, E.O. *The Tree of Life: An Archaeological Study*. Leiden, 1966.

Janssens–Knorsch, Uta. 'From Het Loo to Hampton Court: William and Mary's Dutch Gardens and their Influence on English Gardening'. In *Fabrics and Fabrications: the Myth and Making of William and Mary*, ed. Paul Hoftijzer & C.C. Barfoot, 277–96. Amsterdam & Atlanta, 1990.

Jebb, R.C. *Bentley*. London & New York, 1889.

Jellicoe, Sir Geoffrey & Susan, Patrick Goode & Michael Lancaster, ed. *The Oxford Companion to Gardens*. Oxford & New York, 1991.

Johnson, Samuel. *Lives of the English Poets*. Ed. George Birkbeck Hill. 3 vols. 1905. Reprint. Hildesheim, 1968.

Johnston, Denis. *In Search of Swift*. Dublin, 1959.

Jones, Howard. *The Epicurean Tradition*. London & New York, 1989.

Jones, J.R. *Charles II: Royal Politician*. London, 1987.

------. *Country and Court: England, 1658–1714*. London, 1980.

------. *The Revolution of 1688 in England*. London, 1972.

de Jong, Erik. 'Virgilian Paradise: A Dutch Garden near Moscow in the Early 18th Century'. *Journal of Garden History*, 1 (1981): 305–44.

Jonson, Ben. *Works*. Ed. C.H. Herford, Percy & Evelyn Simpson. 11 vols. Oxford, 1925–52.

Jordan, David P. *Gibbon and his Roman Empire*. Urbana, Chicago & London, 1971.

Jourdain, Margaret. *The Work of William Kent*. London, 1948.

Jung, C.G. *Collected Works*. 20 vols. London & Henley, 1953–79.

------. *Memories, Dreams, Reflections*. Glasgow, 1977.

------ & C. Kerényi. *Introduction to a Science of Mythology: The Myth of the Divine Child and the Mysteries of Eleusis*. Transl. R.F.C. Hull. London, 1951.

Jung, Emma. *Animus and Anima*. Dallas, 1981.

------ & Marie–Louise von Franz. *The Grail Legend*. Transl. Andrea Dykes. Boston & London, 1986.

Kaempfer, Engelbert. *The History of Japan*. Transl. J.G. Scheuchzer. 3 vols. 1906. Reprint. New York, 1971.

Kallich, Martin. 'The Association of Ideas and Critical Theory: Hobbes, Locke, and Addison'. *ELH*, 12 (1945): 290–315.

Keats, John. *Poems*. Ed. Miriam Allott. London, 1975.

Kennedy, Emmet. *A Cultural History of the French Revolution*. New Haven & London, 1989.

Kenyon, J.P. *The Popish Plot*. Harmondsworth, 1974.

------. *Revolution Principles: The Politics of Party, 1689–1720*. Cambridge, 1977.

------. *The Stuarts: A Study in English Kingship*. Glasgow, 1966.

Ketton-Cremer, R.W. *Horace Walpole: A Biography*. London, 1964.
------. *Thomas Gray: A Biography*. Cambridge, 1955.
Kimball, Fiske. *The Creation of the Rococo Decorative Style*. New York, 1980.
King, Henry C. *The History of the Telescope*. London, 1955.
Kingsbury, D.G. *Bilton Hall: Its History & Literary Associations*. London, 1957.
Kitson, Michael. 'The "Altieri Claudes" and Virgil'. *Burlington Magazine*, 102 (1960): 312–18.
------. *The Art of Claude Lorrain*. London, 1969.
------. *Claude Lorrain: Liber Veritatis*. London, 1978.
Kliger, Samuel. *The Goths in England: A Study in Seventeenth and Eighteenth Century Thought*. New York, 1972.
Knight, Richard Payne. *A Discourse on the Worship of Priapus and its Connection with the Mystic Theology of the Ancients*; *Sexual Symbolism: A History of Phallic Worship*. Ed. Ashley Montagu. New York, 1957.
------. *The Landscape: A Didactic Poem*. London, 1794.
Knight, W.F. Jackson. *Roman Vergil*. Harmondsworth, 1966.
Koch, H.W. *A History of Prussia*. London & New York, 1978.
Koestler, Arthur. *The Act of Creation*. London, 1970.
------. *The Sleepwalkers: A History of Man's Changing Vision of the Universe*. Harmondsworth, 1968.
Koyré, Alexandre. *From the Closed World to the Infinite Universe*. Baltimore & London, 1968.
Kramnick, Isaac. *The Rage of Edmund Burke: Portrait of an Ambivalent Conservative*. New York, 1977.
Kuck, Loraine. *The World of the Japanese Garden*. New York & Tokyo, 1968.
Lablaude, Pierre-André. *The Gardens of Versailles*. London, 1995.
Lamb, Charles. *Life, Letters and Writings*. Ed. Percy Fitzgerald. 6 vols. London, 1875.
Lang, Paul Henry. *George Frideric Handel*. London, 1967.
Lang, Susan. 'The Genesis of the English Landscape Garden'. In *The Picturesque Garden and its Influence outside the British Isles*, ed. Nikolaus Pevsner, 1–29. Washington, 1974.
------ & Nikolaus Pevsner. 'Sir William Temple and Sharawadgi'. *Architectural Review*, 106 (1949): 391–2.
Langdon, Helen. *Claude Lorrain*. Oxford, 1989.
Laski, Harold J. *Political Thought in England: Locke to Bentham*. London 1949.
Lawford, James P. *Clive: Proconsul of India*. London, 1976.
Lawrence, D.H. *Phoenix II*. Ed. Warren Roberts & Harry T. Moore. London, 1968.
Lazzaro, Claudia. *The Italian Renaissance Garden*. New Haven & London, 1990.
Leatherbarrow, David. 'Character, Geometry & Perspective: The Third Earl of Shaftesbury's Principles of Garden Design'. *Journal of Garden History*, 4 (1984): 332–58.
Leavis, F.R. *The Common Pursuit*. London, 1953.

Lecky, William Edward Hartpole. *A History of England in the Eighteenth Century*. 8 vols. London, 1890–91.
Lees–Milne, James. *Earls of Creation: Five Great Patrons of Eighteenth–Century Art*. London, 1962.
Lefebvre, Georges. *The Coming of the French Revolution*. Transl. R.R. Palmer. Princeton, 1967.
Levine, Joseph M. *The Battle of the Books: History and Literature in the Augustan Age*. Ithaca & London, 1994.
Lewis, C.S. 'Addison'. In *Eighteenth–Century English Literature: Modern Essays in Criticism*, ed. James L. Clifford, 144–57. Oxford, 1959.
------. *Studies in Words*. Cambridge, 1967.
Lewis, Wilmarth Sheldon. 'The Genesis of Strawberry Hill'. *Metropolitan Museum Studies*, 5 (1934–6): 57–92.
------. *Horace Walpole*. New York, 1961.
Lock, F.P. *Burke's Reflections on the Revolution in France*. London, 1985.
Locke, John. *Two Treatises of Government*. Ed. Peter Laslett. Cambridge, 1960.
Longe, Julia. *Martha Lady Giffard*. London, 1911.
Lord, George de F. 'The *Odyssey* and the Western World'. *Sewanee Review*, 62 (1954): 406–27.
Lovejoy, Arthur O. *Essays in the History of Ideas*. Baltimore, 1948.
------. *The Great Chain of Being: A Study of the History of an Idea*. Cambridge, Mass., 1974.
Low, D.M. *Edward Gibbon, 1737–1794*. London, 1937.
Lowes, John Livingston. *The Road to Xanadu: A Study in the Ways of the Imagination*. London, 1978.
Lubbock, Jules. *The Tyranny of Taste: The Politics of Architecture & Design in Britain 1550–1960*. New Haven & London, 1995.
Macaulay, Rose. *Pleasure of Ruins*. London, 1953.
Macaulay, Thomas Babington Lord. *Critical and Historical Essays*. Ed. A. J. Grieve. 2 vols. London, 1907.
------. *History of England*. 4 vols. London, 1967–72.
------. *Lays of Ancient Rome & Miscellaneous Essays and Poems*. London & New York, 1968.
Mac Cana, Proinsias. *Celtic Mythology*. London, 1970.
MacCarthy, Fiona. *William Morris: A Life for Our Time*. London, 1996.
McCarthy, Michael. *The Origins of the Gothic Revival*. New Haven & London, 1987.
McCrea, Brian. *Addison and Steele are Dead: The English Department, its Canon, and the Professionalisation of Literary Criticism*. Newark, London & Toronto, 1990.
MacDougall, Elisabeth. '*Ars Hortulorum*: Sixteenth Century Garden Iconogaphy & Literary Theory in Italy'. In *The Italian Garden*, ed. David R. Coffin, 37–59. Washington, 1972.
Mack, Maynard. *Alexander Pope: A Life*. New Haven & London, 1985.

------. *Collected in Himself: Essays Critical, Biographical and Bibliographical on Pope and Some of His Contemporaries*, Newark, London & Toronto 1982.

------, ed. *Essential Articles for the Study of Alexander Pope*. 1964. Reprint. London, n.d.

------. *The Garden and the City: Retirement and Politics in the Later Poetry of Pope*. Toronto, Buffalo & London, 1969.

------ & James A. Winn, ed. *Pope: Recent Essays*. Hamden, 1980.

McKay, A.G. 'Virgilian Landscape into Art: Poussin, Claude and Turner'. In *Virgil*, ed. D.R. Dudley, 139–60. London, 1969.

McKay, Derek & H. M. Scott. *The Rise of the Great Powers, 1648–1815*. London & New York, 1983.

Macklem, Michael. *The Anatomy of the World: Relations between Natural and Moral Law from Donne to Pope*. Minneapolis, 1958.

MCMillan, Peter. 'A Miracle of Rare Device: "Kubla Khan" and Its Interpretations'. *Kyorin University Review*, 4 (1992): 76–92.

Macpherson, C.B. *The Political Theory of Possessive Individualism: Hobbes to Locke*. London, Oxford & New York, 1964.

Magnus, Sir Philip. *Edmund Burke: A Life*. London, 1939.

Maland, David. *Europe in the Seventeenth Century*. London & Basingstoke, 1983.

Malins, Edward. *English Landscaping and Literature, 1660–1840*. London, 1966.

------ & the Knight of Glin. *Lost Demesnes: Irish Landscape Gardening, 1660–1845*. London, 1976.

Manwaring, Elizabeth Wheeler. *Italian Landscape in Eighteenth Century England: A Study Chiefly of the Influence of Claude Lorrain and Salvator Rosa on English Taste 1700–1800*. London, 1965.

Maravall, José Antonio. *Culture of the Baroque: Analysis of a Historical Structure*. Transl. Terry Cochran. Manchester, 1986.

Marburg, Clara. *Sir William Temple: A Seventeenth Century 'Libertin'*. New Haven, 1932.

Marchand, Leslie A. *Byron: A Portrait*. London, 1971.

Maresca, Thomas E. *Pope's Horatian Poems*. Columbus, 1966.

Marriott, Sir J.A.R. & Sir Charles Grant Robertson. *The Evolution of Prussia: The Making of an Empire*. Oxford, 1946.

Marshall, Dorothy. *Eighteenth Century England*. London, 1974.

Martin, Peter. *Pursuing Innocent Pleasures: The Gardening World of Alexander Pope*. Hamden, Conn., 1984.

Masson, Georgina. *Italian Gardens*. London, 1966.

Mayo, Thomas Franklin. *Epicurus in England (1650–1725)*. Dallas, 1934.

Mellor, Ronald. *Tacitus*. New York & London, 1994.

Merrifield, Ralph. *Roman London*. London, 1969.

Mikasa, Prince Takahito. 'Symmetry and Dissymetry: A Comparative Cultural Study of Japanese and non-Japanese Cultures'. *Transactions of the Asiatic Society of Japan*, 4th ser., 10 (1995): 199–202.

Miller, Henry Knight. 'The "Whig Interpretation" of Literary History'. *Eighteenth-Century Studies*, 6 (1972–3): 60–84.
Miller, John. *The Life and Times of William and Mary*. London, 1974.
Miller, Roy Andrew. *The Japanese Language*. Chicago & London, 1967.
Millgate, Jane. *Macaulay*. London & Boston, 1973.
Milton, John. *Poetical Works*. Ed. H.C. Beeching & W. Skeat. London, 1938.
*Miscellaneous Poems And Translations: By Several Hands*. London, 1712.
------. *The Second Edition*. London, 1714.
Mitford, Nancy. *Frederick the Great*. Harmondsworth, 1973.
------. *The Sun King: Louis XIV at Versailles*. London, 1976.
Monk, Samuel H. *The Sublime: A Study of Critical Theories in XVIII-Century England*. Ann Arbor, 1960.
Montagu, Lady Mary Wortley. *Essays and Poems and Simplicity, a Comedy*. Ed. Robert Halsband & Isobel Grundy. Oxford, 1977.
------. *Complete Letters*. Ed. Robert Halsband. 3 vols. Oxford, 1965–7.
Montanus, Arnoldus. *Atlas Chinensis*. Englished by John Ogilby. London, 1671.
------. *Atlas Japannensis*. Englished by John Ogilby. London, 1670.
Montesquieu, Charles Louis Secondat, Baron de la Brède et de. *Oeuvres Complètes*. Ed. Roger Caillois. 2 vols. Paris, 1949–51.
Mookerjee, Ajit. *Kali: The Feminine Force*. London, 1988.
Moore, Cecil A. *Backgrounds of English Literature, 1700–1760*. Minneapolis, 1953.
Morris, Ivan. *The World of the Shining Prince: Court Life in Ancient Japan*. Harmondsworth, 1969.
Moss, Leonard W. & Stephen C. Cappannari. 'In Quest of the Black Virgin: She Is Black Because She Is Black'. In *Mother Worship: Theme and Variations*, ed. James J. Preston, 53–74. Chapel Hill, 1982.
Mosser, Monique & Georges Teyssot, ed. *The History of Garden Design: The Western Tradition from the Renaissance to the Present Day*. London, 1991.
Moynihan, Elizabeth B. *Paradise as a Garden: In Persia and Mughal India*. London, 1980.
Muirhead, John H. *The Platonic Tradition in Anglo-Saxon Philosophy: Studies in the History of Idealism in England and America*. London & New York, 1931.
Müllenbrock, Heinz-Joachim. 'The "Englishness " of the English Landscape Garden and the Genetic Role of Literature: A Reassessment'. *Journal of Garden History*, 8 (1988): 97–103.
Mumford, Lewis. *The City in History*. Harmondsworth, 1966.
*Murray's Handbook for Travellers in India and Pakistan, Burma and Ceylon*, London, 1949.
Murry, John Middleton. *Jonathan Swift: A Critical Biography*. New York, 1955.
Needham, Joseph. *Science and Civilisation in China*: 1, Introductory Orientations; 2, History of Scientific Thought; 3, Mathematics and the Sciences of the Heavens and the Earth. Cambridge, 1954–9.

Neumann, Erich. *Amor and Psyche: The Psychic Development of the Feminine*. Transl. Ralph Manheim. Princeton 1971.
------. *The Origins and History of Consciousness*. Transl. R.F.C. Hull. Princeton 1970.
Neumeyer, Eva Maria. 'The Landscape Garden as a Symbol in Rousseau, Goethe and Flaubert'. *Journal of the History of Ideas*, 8 (1947): 187–217.
Nicolson, Marjorie. *The Breaking of the Circle: Studies in the Effect of the 'New Science' upon Seventeenth-Century Poetry*. New York & London, 1962.
------. 'The "New Astronomy" and English Literary Imagination'. *Studies in Philology*, 30 (1935): 428–62.
------. *Science and Imagination*. Ithaca, 1956.
Nicolson, Marjorie & G.S. Rousseau. *This Long Disease, My Life: Alexander Pope and the Sciences*. Princeton, 1968.
Niscemi, Maita di et al. *Manor Houses and Castles of Sweden: A Journey through Five Centuries*. New York, 1988.
Nokes, David. *Jonathan Swift: A Hypocrite Reversed*. Oxford, 1987.
Norberg-Schulz, Christian. *Baroque Architecture*. London, 1986.
------. *Late Baroque and Rococo Architecture*. London, 1986.
Nourse, Timothy. *Campania Foelix, or, A Discourse of the Benefits and Improvements of Husbandry*. London, 1700.
Nuttall, A.N. *Pope's 'Essay on Man'*. London, 1984.
Oates, Joan. *Babylon*. London, 1986.
O'Brien, Conor Cruise. *The Great Melody: A Thematic Biography of Edmund Burke*. Chicago & London, 1992.
O'Callaghan, John Cornelius. *History of the Irish Brigades in the Service of France*. Glasgow, 1870.
O'Donovan, John. *Letters containing Information relative to the Antiquities of the Queen's County*. Typescript. 2 vols. National Library of Ireland, Dublin, 1926.
Ogden, H.V.S. & M.S. *English Taste in Landscape in the Seventeenth Century*. Ann Arbor, 1955.
Ogg, David. *England in the Reign of Charles II*. Oxford, 1967.
------. *England in the Reigns of James II and William III*. Oxford, 1969.
------. *Europe of the Ancien Régime, 1715–1783*. Glasgow, 1965.
O'Hanlon, John & Edward O'Leary. *History of the Queen's County*. 2 vols. Dublin, 1907–14.
Osborne, Dorothy. *Letters to William Temple*. Ed. G.C. Moore Smith. Oxford, 1928.
Owen, John B. *The Rise of the Pelhams*. New York & London, 1971.
Pace, Claire. 'Claude the Enchanted: Interpretations of Claude in England in the Earlier Nineteenth Century'. *Burlington Magazine*, 111 (1969): 733–40.
Paine, Thomas. *Common Sense*. Ed. Isaac Kramnick. Harmondsworth, 1986.
------. *Rights of Man*. Ed. Henry Collins. Harmondsworth, 1969.
Panichas, George A. *Epicurus*. New York, 1967.
Panofsky, Erwin. *Gothic Architecture and Scholasticism*. New York, 1974.

Pares, Richard. *King George III and the Politicians*. London, Oxford & New York, 1967.
Parker, Harold T. *The Cult of Antiquity and the French Revolutionaries: A Study in the Development of the Revolutionary Spirit*. Chicago, 1937.
Passmore, J.A. *Ralph Cudworth: An Interpretation*. 1951. Reprint. Bristol, 1990.
Pearsall, Derek & Elizabeth Salter. *Landscapes and Seasons of the Medieval World*. London, 1973.
Peckham, Morse. *Beyond the Tragic Vision: The Quest for Identity in the Nineteenth Century*. New York, 1962.
Pepys, Samuel. *Diary*. 2 vols. London, 1906.
Pevsner, Nikolaus. *The Englishness of English Art*. Harmondsworth, 1964.
Phillips, John. *The Reformation of Images: Destruction of Art in England, 1535–1660*. Berkeley, Los Angeles & London, 1973.
Plumb, J.H. *England in the Eighteenth Century*. Harmondsworth, 1973.
------. *The First Four Georges*. London & Glasgow, 1966.
------. *The Growth of Political Stability in England, 1675–1725*. Harmondsworth, 1973.
------. *Sir Robert Walpole*. 2 vols. London, 1972.
Pocock, J.G.A. *The Ancient Constitution and the Feudal Law: A Study of English Historical Thought in the Seventeenth Century*. New York, 1967.
*Poetical Miscellanies: The Sixth Part*. London, 1709.
Pope, Alexander. Add. Ms. 4807. British Library.
------. *Correspondence*. Ed. George Sherburn. 5 vols. Oxford, 1956.
------. *Poems*. 10 vols. London, New Haven & New York, 1953–82.
------. *Prose Works*. Ed. Norman Ault & Rosemary Cowler. 2 vols. Oxford, 1936–86.
------. *Works*. Ed. Whitwell Elwin & W.J. Courthope. 10 vols. London, 1871–89.
Possin, Hans-Joachim. *Natur und Landschaft bei Addison*. Tübingen, 1965.
Postgate, Raymond. *'That Devil Wilkes'*. London, 1956.
Potter, Simeon. *Our Language*. Harmondsworth, 1966.
Price, Martin. *To the Palace of Wisdom: Studies in Order and Energy from Dryden to Blake*. New York, 1965.
Price, Uvedale. *Essays on the Picturesque*. 2 vols. London, 1794–8.
Quennell, Peter. *Alexander Pope: The Education of Genius, 1688–1728*. New York, 1968.
Rapin, René. *Of Gardens*. Transl. James Gardiner. London, 1728.
Rea, John. *Flora: seu, de Florum Cultura*. London, 1665.
Reed, Michael. *The Georgian Triumph, 1700–1830*. London, Boston, Melbourne & Henley, 1983.
Reeves, James. *The Reputation and Writings of Alexander Pope*. London & New York, 1976.
Reiman, Donald H. & Sharon B. Powers, ed. *Shelley's Poetry and Prose*. New

York & London, 1977.

Repton, Humphry. *Landscape Gardening and Landscape Architecture*. Ed. J.C. Loudon. London, 1840.

------. *Odd Whims, and Miscellanies*. 2 vols. London, 1804.

Richard, Carl J. *The Founders and the Classics: Greece, Rome, and the American Enlightenment*. Cambridge, Mass. & London, 1994.

Robertson, J.G. *Studies in the Genesis of Romantic Theory in the Eighteenth Century*. Cambridge, 1923.

Robinson, John Martin. *Temples of Delight: Stowe Landscape Gardens*. London, 1990.

Rogers, Robert W. *The Major Satires of Alexander Pope*. Urbana, 1955.

Rosslyn, Felicity. 'Pope and Tickell'. *Notes & Queries*, n.s, 24 (1977): 236–7.

Røstvig, Maren–Sofie. *The Happy Man: Studies in the Metamorphosis of a Classical Ideal*. 2 vols. Oslo & Oxford, 1958–62.

Röthlisberger, Marcel. *Claude Lorrain: The Paintings*. 2 vols. London, 1961.

------. *Claude Lorrain: The Drawings*. 2 vols. London, 1968.

------. 'The Subjects of Claude Lorrain's Paintings'. *Gazette des Beaux–Arts*, 55 (1960): 209 –24.

Rousseau, Jean–Jacques. *La Nouvelle Héloïse*. 2 vols. Paris, 1993.

Rowen, Herbert H. *John de Witt, Grand Pensionary of Holland, 1625–1672*. Princeton, 1978.

Rowley, George. *Principles of Chinese Painting*. Princeton, 1959.

Rudé, George. 'The Outbreak of the French Revolution'. In *The American and French Revolutions, 1763–93*, ed. A Goodwin, 653–79. Cambridge, 1965.

------. *Wilkes and Liberty: A Social Study*. London, 1983.

Ruskin, John. *The Stones of Venice*. Ed. J.G. Links. New York, 1985.

*St. James' Journal*, 29, 30, 33, 34, 52 (London, 15 & 22 Nov., 8 & 15 Dec. 1722; 20 Apr. 1723).

Saintsbury, George. *A History of English Criticism*. Edinburgh & London, 1911.

Sambrook, A.J. 'The Shape and Size of Pope's Garden'. *Eighteenth–Century Studies*, 5 (1971–2): 450–55.

Sansom, G.B. *The Western World and Japan*. New York, 1973.

Seeley, Sir J.R. *The Growth of British Policy: An Historical Essay*. 2 vols. Cambridge, 1895.

Shaffer, E.S. *'Kubla Khan' and* The Fall of Jerusalem*: The Mythological School in Biblical Criticism and Secular Literature, 1770–1880*. Cambridge, 1980.

Shaftesbury, Anthony Lord. *Characteristics of Men, Manners, Opinions, Times, etc.* 2 vols. 1900. Reprint. Gloucester, Mass., 1963.

------. *Second Characters, or The Language of Forms*. Ed. Benjamin Rand. 1914. Reprint. New York, 1969.

Shearer, Alastair. *The Traveller's Key to Northern India: A Guide to the Sacred Places of Northern India*. New York, 1983.

Shelley, Percy Bysshe. *Poetical Works*. Ed. Thomas Hutchinson & G.M. Matthews. London, 1971.

Sherburn, George. 'Alexander Pope'. *Philological Quarterly*, 21 (1942): 215–16.
------. *The Early Career of Alexander Pope*. New York, 1963.
------. 'Pope and "The Great Shew of Nature"'. In R.F. Jones et al., *The Seventeenth Century*, 306–15. Stanford, 1951.
------. *The Restoration and Eighteenth Century, 1660–1789*. New York, 1948.
Shipley, Joseph T., ed. *Dictionary of World Literary Terms*. London, 1970.
Shvidkovsky, Dimitri. *The Empress & the Architect: British Architecture and Gardens at the Court of Catherine the Great*. New Haven & London, 1996.
Sidney, Sir Philip. *The Countess of Pembroke's Arcadia*. Ed. Maurice Evans. Harmondsworth, 1977.
------. *Poems*. Ed. William A. Ringler, Jr. Oxford, 1962.
Simon, Edith. *The Making of Frederick the Great*. London, 1963.
Singer, Kurt. *Mirror, Sword and Jewel: The Geometry of Japanese Life*. Tokyo, New York & San Francisco, 1981.
Singleton, William A., ed. *Studies in Architectural History*. 2 vols. London & York, 1954–6.
Sirén, Osvald. *China and the Gardens of Europe of the Eighteenth Century*. New York, 1950.
Smith, D. Nichol. *Some Observations on Eighteenth Century Poetry*. Oxford, 1937.
Smith, Logan Pearsall. *The Life and Letters of Sir Henry Wotton*. 2 vols. Oxford, 1907.
------. 'The Romantic History of Four Words'. *S.P.E. Tract 17*. Oxford, 1924.
Smith, M. Ellwood. 'Four Hitherto Unidentified Letters by Alexander Pope'. *PMLA*, 29 (1914), 236–55.
Smithers, Peter. *The Life of Joseph Addison*. Oxford, 1954.
*Song of Songs*. Transl. Marvin H. Pope. Garden City, N.Y., 1977.
Speck, W.A. *Reluctant Revolutionaries: Englishmen and the Revolution of 1688*. Oxford, 1988.
*Spectator, The*. Ed. Donald F. Bond. 5 vols. Oxford, 1965.
Spence, Joseph. *Observations, Anecdotes, and Characters of Books and Men*. Ed. James M. Osborn. 2 vols. Oxford, 1966.
Spenser, Edmund. *The Faerie Queene*. Ed. A.C. Hamilton. London & New York, 1980.
Spink, J.S. *French Free-Thought from Gassendi to Voltaire*. London, 1960.
Starr, Herbert W., ed. *Twentieth Century Interpretations of Gray's Elegy*. Englewood Cliffs, 1968.
Steele, Richard. *Correspondence*. Ed. Rae Blanchard. Oxford, 1941.
------. *Plays*. Ed. Shirley Strum Kenny. Oxford, 1971.
------. *The Theatre*. Ed. John Loftis. Oxford, 1962.
Stephen, Leslie. *Alexander Pope*. London, 1914.
------. *History of English Thought in the Eighteenth Century*. 2 vols. New York & London, 1962.
Stoye, John. *Europe Unfolding, 1648–1688*. London, 1969.

Strachey, Lytton. *Books and Characters: French and English*. London, 1922.
------. *Portraits in Miniature & Other Essays*. London, 1931.
Strong, Roy. *The Renaissance Garden in England*. London, 1979.
Stroud, Dorothy. *Capability Brown*. London, 1975.
------. *Humphry Repton*. London, 1962.
Summerson, John. *Architecture in Britain, 1530–1830*. Harmondsworth, 1970.
------. 'The Classical Country House in 18th–Century England'. *Journal of the Royal Society of Arts*, 107 (1959): 539–87.
Sutherland, James. 'The Last Years of Joseph Addison'. In *Background for Queen Anne*, 127–44. London, 1939.
Swain, Joseph Ward. *Edward Gibbon the Historian*. London & New York, 1966.
Swift, Jonathan. *Correspondence*. Ed. Harold Williams. 5 vols. Oxford, 1963–5.
------. *Complete Poems*. Ed. Pat Rogers. Harmondsworth, 1983.
------. *Prose Works*. Ed. Herbert Davis et al. 16 vols. Oxford, 1939–74.
------. *A Tale of a Tub, & c.*. Ed. A.C. Guthkelch & D. Nichol Smith. Oxford, 1973.
Switzer, Stephen. *The Nobleman, Gentleman, and Gardener's Recreation*. London, 1715.
------. *Ichnographia Rustica*. 3 vols. London, 1718.
Symonds, J.A. *Sir Philip Sidney*. 1889. Reprint. New York, 1968.
Tanaka Ichimatsu. *Japanese Ink Painting: Shubun to Sesshu*. Transl. Bruce Darling. New York & Tokyo, 1974.
Tange Kenzo & Noboru Kawagoe. *Ise: Prototype of Japanese Architecture*. Cambridge, Mass., 1965.
Tasso, Torquato. *Jerusalem Delivered: or Godfrey of Bulloign*. Transl. Edward Fairfax. London, 1749.
*Tatler, The*. Ed. Donald F. Bond. 3 vols. Oxford, 1987.
Temple, Sir William. *Early Essays and Romances*. Ed. G.C. Moore Smith. Oxford 1930.
-------. *Miscellanea*, Parts I & II. London, 1681, 1690.
-------. *Miscellanea*, Part II. 2nd ed. London, 1690.
-------. *Poems*. Privately printed, n.d. (unique copy, British Library).
-------. *Select Letters*. London, 1701.
-------. *Works*. 4 vols. London, 1757.
Thacker, Christopher. *The History of Gardens*. London, 1979.
------. 'Voltaire and Rousseau: Eighteenth–Century Gardeners'. *Studies on Voltaire and the Eighteenth Century*, 90 (1972): 1595–1614.
Thackeray, W.M. *The English Humourists; Charity and Humour; The Four Georges*. London, 1912.
Thompson, F.M.L. *English Landed Society in the Nineteenth Century*. London & Toronto, 1971.
Thornton, Francis Beauchesne. *Alexander Pope: Catholic Poet*. New York, 1952.
Thorpe, Clarence DeWitt. 'Addison's Contribution to Criticism'. In R.F. Jones et al., *The Seventeenth Century*, 316–29. Stanford, 1951.

------. 'Two Augustans Cross the Alps: Dennis and Addison on Mountain Scenery'. *Studies in Philology*, 32 (1935): 463–82.

Tickell, Richard Eustace. *Thomas Tickell and the Eighteenth-Century Poets*. London, 1931.

Tickell, Thomas. *The First Book of Homer's Iliad*. London, 1715.

------. *Poetical Works*. London, 1796.

Tillotson, Geoffrey. *On the Poetry of Pope*. Oxford, 1938.

Tillyard, Stella. *Aristocrats: Caroline, Emily, Louisa. and Sarah Lennox, 1740–1832*. New York, 1994.

Traugott, John. '*A Tale of a Tub*'. In *Focus: Swift*, ed. C.J. Rawson, 76–120. London 1971.

Trench, Charles Chevenix. *George II*. London, 1973.

Trevelyan, G.M. *Clio, A Muse & Other Essays*. London, New York & Toronto, 1949.

------. *England under Queen Anne*. 3 vols. London, 1934–6.

------. *England under the Stuarts*. London, 1965.

Trevelyan, Sir George Otto. *The Life and Letters of Lord Macaulay*. 2 vols. Oxford, 1978.

Trilling, Lionel. *Freud and the Crisis of Our Culture*. Boston, 1955.

Tucker, Susie I. *Enthusiasm: A Study in Semantic Change*. Cambridge, 1972.

Tunstall, Brian. *William Pitt, Earl of Chatham*. London, 1938.

Turner, F.C.: *James II*, London, 1948.

Tuveson, Ernest. 'Space, Deity and the "Natural Sublime"'. *Modern Language Quarterly*, 12 (1951): 20–38.

Tyers, T. *An Historical Essay on Mr. Addison*. London, 1783.

Ueda Makoto. *Literary and Art Theories in Japan*. Ann Arbor, 1991.

Villiers-Stuart, C.M. *Gardens of the Great Mughals*. London, 1913.

------. *Spanish Gardens*. London, 1929.

Voitle, Robert. *The Third Earl of Shaftesbury*. Baton Rouge & London, 1984.

Voltaire, François Marie Arouet de. *Lettres philosophiques; ou, Lettres anglaises*. Ed. Raymond Naves. Paris, 1964.

Waley, Arthur. *An Introduction to the Study of Chinese Painting*. 1923. Reprint. New York, 1974.

------. *Three Ways of Thought in Ancient China*. Garden City, N.Y., 1956.

------. *The Way and its Power: A Study of the Tao Tê Ching and its Place in Chinese Thought*. New York, 1958.

Waller, Edmund. *Poems*. Ed. E. Thorn Drury. 2 vols. London, 1905.

Walpole, Horace. *Anecdotes of Painting in England, with Some Account of the Principal Artists*. Addns. by James Dallaway. Rev. Ralph N. Wornum. 3 vols. London, 1888.

------. *The Castle of Otranto: A Gothic Story*. Ed. W.S. Lewis. London, Oxford, New York, 1969.

------. *Correspondence*. Ed. W.S. Lewis et al. London, Oxford & New Haven, 1937–83.

------. *Memoirs of the Reign of King George III*. 4 vols. London & New York, 1894.

------. *The Mysterious Mother*. In *The Modern British Drama*, 2: 549–70. London, 1811.

Wangermann, Ernst. *The Austrian Achievement, 1700–1800*. New York, 1973.

Ward, David. *Jonathan Swift: An Introductory Essay*. London, 1973.

Ward, Roger W. *A Brief History of Chicksands Priory*. Chicksands, 1984.

Warton, Joseph. *Essay on the Genius and Writings of Pope*. 2 vols. London, 1772–82.

*Warwickshire:...a Concise Topographical Description...from the Elaborate Work of Sir William Dugdale and Other Later Authorities*. Coventry, 1817.

Watkin, David. *The English Vision: The Picturesque in Architecture, Landscape and Garden Design*. London, 1982.

Watson, J. Steven. *The Reign of George III, 1760–1815*. Oxford, 1960.

Weber, Max. *Ancient Judaism*. Transl. Hans H. Gerth & Don Martindale. New York & London, 1967.

------. *The Religion of India: The Sociology of Hinduism and Buddhism*. Transl. Hans H. Gerth & Don Martindale. New York & London, 1967.

Weiss, Allen S. *Mirrors of Infinity: The French Formal Garden and 17th–Century Metaphysics*. New York, 1995.

Welch, Holmes. *Taoism: The Parting of the Way*. Boston, 1966.

Wesley, John. *Journal*. Ed. Nehemiah Curnock. 8 vols. London, 1938.

West, David. *The Imagery and Poetry of Lucretius*. Edinburgh, 1969.

Westfall, Richard S. *Science and Religion in Seventeenth–Century England*. Ann Arbor, 1973.

Wheelock, Arthur K., Jr. *Vermeer and the Art of Painting*. New Haven & London, 1995.

Whistler, Laurence. *Sir John Vanbrugh, Architect and Dramatist, 1664–1726*. 1938. Reprint. Millwood, 1978.

White, T.H. *The Age of Scandal*. Harmondsworth, 1962.

Whitmont, Edward C. *The Symbolic Quest: Basic Concepts of Analytical Psychology*. Princeton, 1978.

Wiebenson, Dora. *The Picturesque Garden in France*. Princeton, 1978.

Wilde, Oscar. *Letters*. Ed. Rupert Hart–Davis. London, 1962.

Willcox, William B. *The Age of Aristocracy, 1688–1830*. Lexington, Mass., 1971.

Willey, Basil. *The Eighteenth–Century Background: Studies on the Idea of Nature in the Thought of the Period*. Harmondsworth, 1972.

------. *The Seventeenth–Century Background: Studies in the Thought of the Age in Relation to Poetry and Religion*. London & Henley, 1979.

Williams, Basil. *The Life of William Pitt, Earl of Chatham*. 2 vols. London, 1913.

------. *The Whig Supremacy, 1714–1760*. Rev. C.H. Stuart. Oxford, 1974.

Williams, E.N. *The Ancien Régime in Europe: Government and Society in the*

*Major States, 1648–1789*. Harmondsworth, 1992.
Williamson, George. *Seventeenth Century Contexts*. London, 1960.
Williamson, Tom. *Polite Landscapes: Gardens & Society in Eighteenth-Century England*. Baltimore, 1995.
Willis, Peter. *Charles Bridgeman and the English Landscape Garden*. London, 1977.
------. 'Rousseau, Stowe and *Le Jardin anglais*: Speculations on Visual Sources for *La Nouvelle Héloïse*'. *Studies on Voltaire and the Eighteenth Century*, 90 (1972); 1791–8.
Wills, Garry. *George Washington and the Enlightenment*. London, 1985.
Wilson, A.N. *A Life of Sir Walter Scott, the Laird of Abbotsford*. London, 1996.
Wilson, Charles. *England's Apprenticeship, 1603–1763*. London, 1971.
Winn, James Anderson. *John Dryden and His World*. New Haven & London, 1987.
Winton, Calhoun. *Captain Steele: The Early Career of Richard Steele*. Baltimore, 1964.
------. *Sir Richard Steele, M.P.: The Later Career*. Baltimore, 1970.
Wittkower, Rudolf. *Architectural Principles in the Age of Humanism*. London, 1973.
------. *Palladio and English Palladianism*. London, 1974.
Wolf, John B. *Louis XIV*. London, 1968.
------. *Toward a European Balance of Power, 1620–1715*. Chicago, 1970.
Wölfflin, Heinrich. *Renaissance and Baroque*. Transl. Kathrin Simon. London, 1984.
Woodbridge, Homer E. *Sir William Temple: The Man and his Work*. New York & London, 1940.
Woodbridge, Kenneth. *Landscape and Antiquity: Aspects of English Culture at Stourhead, 1718 to 1838*. Oxford, 1970.
------. *Princely Gardens: The Origins and Development of the French Formal Style*. London, 1986.
Woodruff, Philip. *The Men Who Ruled India: The Founders*. London, 1976.
Woolf, Virginia. *Collected Essays*. 4 vols. London, 1966–7.
Wordsworth, Jonathan, Michael C. Jaye & Robert Woof. *William Wordsworth and the Age of English Romanticism*. New Brunswick & London, 1987.
Wordsworth, William. *Poetical Works*. Ed. Thomas Hutchinson & Ernest de Selincourt. London, 1950.
Worlidge, John. *Systema Horti-Culturae, Or The Art of Gardening*. London, 1677.
Wotton, Henry. *The Elements of Architecture*. 1624. Reprint. Amsterdam & New York 1970.
Yeats, W.B. *Collected Plays*. London, 1952.
------. *Collected Poems*. London, 1950.
Young, Sir George. *Poor Fred: The People's Prince*. London, 1937.
Young, G.M. *Gibbon*. London, 1932.

Young, Norwood. *The Life of Frederick the Great*. London, 1919.
van der Zee, Henri & Barbara. *William and Mary*. London, 1973.
Ziehr, Wilhelm. *The Ancient World: From Ur to Mecca*. London, 1982.

# INDEX